AND DON'T
f&%k IT UP

"¡Amo este libro! It's dripping with cuchi, uniqueness, nerve, and talent!"
—Charo

"Everything you wanted to know (and more) about the twisted minds behind the best mothertucking show on earth."
—Simon Doonan, author of *Drag: The Complete Story*

"The queens of *Drag Race* spill the tea on what it took to turn this queer little show into a global phenomenon."
—Loni Love

"Finally, the *Drag Race* book that sets the record straight. I mean queer."
—Alec Mapa

"Everyone who works in my stores spends all day talking about *Drag Race*. Now they can spend all day talking about *And Don't F&%k It Up*. I can't wait!"
—Jonathan Adler

"If you want to know how drag changed the world, and might just save it, read this book."
—Ronan Farrow, *New York Times* bestselling author of *Catch and Kill*

"For fans of the show, the book's juicy specifics from cast and crew will provide a wealth of new background about their favorite unforgettable moments, as well as details about things left on the cutting-room floor."
—Daily Beast

"Journalist Fernandez's fabulous debut serves the tea on *RuPaul's Drag Race*...The behind-the-scenes stories feel as if readers are eavesdropping on the show's "werkroom," but this oral history really shines in its willingness to tackle weightier issues, as when RuPaul opines on the importance of queer representation and when performer Asia O'Hara reflects on dealing with racism from the show's fandom. Hilarious and affecting, it's an uproarious celebration of what has become a television institution." —*Publishers Weekly*, starred review

"The heart of [*And Don't F&%k It Up*] lies in the candid, witty commentary of show producers, queens, judges, and RuPaul himself, as each shares memorable moments from the first ten seasons...A commemorative celebration and a must-have for fans."
—*Kirkus Reviews*

"[A]n immensely entertaining look at how a little TV show shot in a basement studio went from a cult favorite to a taste-making cultural juggernaut and global success...Loaded with heartbreaking and hilarious first-person confessions, this book's a winner, baby!"
—*Library Journal*, starred review

"Few stones go unturned, and readers will find here the origins of the most iconic lines ("Go back to Party City where you belong!") to the truth about how the queens really felt about each other...The audience for the show has grown, and with all the earlier seasons available on streaming, this will be an essential addition to any pop-culture collection." —*Booklist*

AND DON'T
f&%k IT UP

AN ORAL HISTORY OF

(THE FIRST TEN YEARS)

MARIA ELENA FERNANDEZ

GRAND
CENTRAL

New York   Boston

Grand Central Publishing
Hachette Book Group
1290 Avenue of the Americas, New York, NY 10104
grandcentralpublishing.com
@grandcentralpub

Originally published in hardcover and ebook in June 2023
First trade paperback edition: June 2024

Grand Central Publishing is a division of Hachette Book Group, Inc. The Grand Central Publishing name and logo is a registered trademark of Hachette Book Group, Inc.

The publisher is not responsible for websites (or their content) that are not owned by the publisher.

Grand Central Publishing books may be purchased in bulk for business, educational, or promotional use. For information, please contact your local bookseller or the Hachette Book Group Special Markets Department at special.markets@hbgusa.com.

Photos © World of Wonder Productions, Inc.

Print book interior design by Amy Quinn

Library of Congress Cataloging-in-Publication Data

Names: Fernandez, Maria Elena, author.
Title: And don't f&%k it up : an oral history of RuPaul's drag race (the
    first ten years) / Maria Elena Fernandez.
Other titles: And don't fuck it up
Description: First edition. | New York : Grand Central Publishing, 2023.
Identifiers: LCCN 2022061481 | ISBN 9781538717660 (hardcover) | ISBN
    9781538717677 (ebook)
Subjects: LCSH: RuPaul's drag race (Television program : 2009-) | RuPaul,
    1960- | Talent shows (Television programs)—United States—History and
    criticism. | Drag queens—United States—Interviews. | Television
    personalities—United States—Interviews.
Classification: LCC PN1992.77.R87 F47 2023 | DDC
    791.45/72—dc23/eng/20230210
LC record available at https://lccn.loc.gov/2022061481

ISBNs: 9781538717653 (trade paperback), 9781538717677 (ebook)

Printed in the United States of America

LSC-C

Printing 1, 2024

For the man in the skirt, with my eternal love.

Preface

THE ORIGIN STORY

RUPAUL'S DRAG RACE NEVER SET OUT TO WIN OVER CONVENTIONAL America, climb the ladder of mainstream pop-culture success, or conquer the world. Its first season was classic counterculture, developed and filmed while President G. W. Bush was in office but launched at a time when Obama fever was at a national high. Fourteen years and about a couple hundred drag queen contestants later, everything from its language and style has seeped into the culture, cementing its place in herstory, one tuck at a time. From the halls of Congress to Wall Street, from schoolyards to universities, from big cities to small towns across the world, who doesn't throw shade or serve tea? *Drag Race* has become a worldwide phenomenon. It has become its own economy. With twenty-six Emmy wins, it is TV's most awarded reality competition show, has spawned several spin-off series, and is blossoming internationally with eighteen shows across the globe and half a dozen more in the works. It also led to the creation of RuPaul's DragCon, catapulting many of the contestants to international stardom.

Drag Race was conceived as a classic reality competition show that derived from and playfully mocked other popular shows in the genre. It was part *America's Next Top Model*, part *Project Runway*, but made by your coolest arty friends. And as a show about personal evolution, where people representing every corner of the gender spectrum put their drag personas through unimaginable tests, the show surprised everyone with its uncanny ability to connect. It was *fun*. Through the process of queens "reading" each other, or writing musicals, or sewing intricate garments, the success of *Drag Race* has lived in how expertly it weaves entertainment, comedy, and emotional truth to tell the story of personal transformation. Nowhere else on the TV dial do reality show contestants have to sew their own costumes, beat their faces, do their hair, tuck their you-know-whats, write songs or scripts, choreograph routines, and prepare a lip-sync routine in less than a day.

At its core, *Drag Race* was built on RuPaul's guiding principle: "We're all born naked and the rest is drag." This is the story of the first decade of a phenomenon that became a franchise and evolved into an empire, changing many hearts along the way.

RUPAUL: Our show exemplifies the movement of a bigger consciousness arising. Drag is part of that. It's having fun and understanding who you really are. I think the audience relates to that without even knowing specifically that that's the thing. Watching a drag queen who was bullied as a kid becoming a star on her own terms is a rush for a lot of people because they, too, have longed for something but didn't know what.

EXECUTIVE PRODUCER TOM CAMPBELL: Drag queens have always been on the front lines of the big social changes in society and especially in the LGBTQ society, whether it's Stonewall, the AIDS crisis, marriage equality. But drag queens are outsiders. They're underdogs. But instead of buying into society's bullshit, they've turned their insecurities and pain into something visual and powerful. Like butterflies, they stick out in a crowd, and their beauty cannot be denied. Their vulnerability and ferocity is an amazing combination, and it attracts all kinds of people.

EXECUTIVE PRODUCER AND CO-FOUNDER OF WORLD OF WONDER FENTON BAILEY: Drag is a part of music, it's a part of theater, it's a part of performance, it's a part of film and TV. But drag has something else, which is this whole idea that Ru talks about, which is about not taking things too seriously and having that humor about things because life is hard and it's frustrating and people are unkind and cruel. So the ability to turn around a negative situation into a positive or into something funny is a unique thing of drag.

EXECUTIVE PRODUCER AND CO-FOUNDER OF WORLD OF WONDER RANDY BARBATO: I loved everything about drag because I loved the glamour of it. Everything was larger than life. I loved the ingenuity, the creativeness. Everyone was scrambling to make a buck and making something out of nothing. The inventiveness often took my breath away. I just loved all the creative genius and I loved how engaged the art form was with the world around it. So much of drag then and now is this commentary on the world we live in.

MICHELLE VISAGE: Drag is saying F-you to society, drag is becoming somebody else wholeheartedly. Drag is performing, drag is making us laugh, drag is dancing, singing, acting. It's all of the above.

RUPAUL: In male-dominated culture, using femininity as a palette is akin to treason. So when I was growing up—and even when I first started doing drag—there was a lot that I had to work through on a personal level to be able to do it. And things would come up in my psyche—and I would go, where did that come from? And I would retrace my steps and realize it came from my conditioning.

MISS FAME: A good drag queen will make you feel like you've lost every word in your mouth, that you have nothing to say. You're just baffled by the beauty, baffled by the integrity of the work.

ALEXIS MATEO: People always say that watching a drag show is so much fun, but drag is liberating. Drag is liberating for me as a performer and it's liberating for whoever is watching me perform in drag because you realize that you don't have to be what people expect you to be. You can just be whoever you wanna be and you just have to be happy with who you are.

THORGY THOR: It was only later in college or late high school where I started to get into the form of drag, like how cool it is to just transform yourself because it's entertainment, it's *Look at me and wooo.* It's also artistic and you get to become anything you want to. It was always inside of me. Drag was a nice medium to let out all of my energy and crazy ideas.

RAJA: I miss the rawness of what drag used to be. I miss no selfies, no videos. I was bad, I did a lot of fucking bad things. And I have zero regrets. There was no one there to record it, there was no receipt or anything. So it was a wonderful time to really explore drag, especially being as beautiful as I was in my twenties, fuck, I miss being her. I had a really, really, really good time.

BENDELACREME: Regardless of whether you want to be a drag queen or not, what draws people to drag is that idea of self-invention. It's the idea of making your own rules. It's the idea of creating the life you want with whatever you've been given. And I think that it is that sharing of stories. And it's not just straight people understanding the queer community. It's people in the queer community understanding each other.

TOM CAMPBELL: There is a great line that Ru says that makes me tear up: "The most powerful thing you can do is to become the image of your own imagination." That's really what drag queens do. They bring humor and they don't take themselves too seriously. Drag queens went from being on the outskirts and pointed at and made fun of in the gay culture to being the savior.

JINKX MONSOON: Drag comes out of wanting to love yourself. Drag comes out of finding things about yourself to celebrate. And one thing I think we all share is we go to drag to experience that self-love, to get that attention, to get that validation, and to feel glamorous and fantastic and fabulous because we all have an experience in our life that made us feel the exact opposite way. Every drag queen I know has had darkness in their life.

SASHA VELOUR: I feel like if people aren't prepared to hear about the real lives and experiences and emotions of queer people, then they don't get to enjoy the lip syncing and the costumes. They're so connected. My lip syncing is connected to the emotions that I feel because my experiences with images of my own body or grieving and thinking about my connection to my mom after her death—all of that comes into putting on an outfit, surprisingly, or putting on a show. And so I feel like you can't have the one without the other with drag.

FENTON BAILEY: By the time they come to *Drag Race*, they have already been through so much.

NINA FLOWERS: Before *RuPaul's Drag Race*, doing drag was like eww, you do drag? That was the kiss of death. People didn't want anything to do with you. You were a freak. You were one of those cross-dressers—what are you, confused? Are you a man or a woman?

JUJUBEE: Queer art is very important, especially being a queer Asian man of color, left-handed, abandonment issues, an alcoholic, an addict. But I'm here, I've survived, and drag did that for me. Drag saved my freaking life.

REBECCA GLASSCOCK: Drag gave me the confidence to stay alive. Before I started doing drag, I was suicidal and I was at a bad place in my life because people tell you enough times that you're going to go to hell, and that you are going to get AIDS and die, and some people actually wish this on you and you start to believe it. And then that really messes with your head and your inner being.

JINKX MONSOON: There was a time when drag was not easy, was not glamorous, was not a way to get famous. It wasn't celebrated. It was stigmatized. To be a drag queen got you labeled as something, even within the LGBTQ community, as something negative. Activists told me that being a drag queen was holding our community back. I was told by women in my community that, because I was a drag queen, I was inherently misogynist when they weren't considering the fact that maybe I was on my own gender journey and that drag was a way to discover my own truth.

ADORE DELANO: They used to make fun of me in high school because I was in full-on makeup and they called me RuPaul. They used to always call me RuPaul as an insult growing up. Down the hallways they'd be like, "RuPaul!" And I'm like, shut up. I told Ru that on the show and he was like, ha ha ha. Now if they call you RuPaul, you're a boss. Isn't that wild?

RuPaul's mother always knew it, though. A psychic had told her when she was pregnant that her child was a boy and he was going to be famous. By the time production company World of Wonder conjured up a reality television competition featuring drag queens, RuPaul had served as Queen of Manhattan, Supermodel of the World, a pop-music hitmaker, a cult movie actor, a talk-show host, a radio deejay, and an author. By all show business standards, he was a star, as his mother had predicted when he was a boy. By drag queen standards, he was a superhero. Or a superheroine. With RuPaul, you could always choose your own adventure.

At the time, RuPaul had been lying low for a decade, and it was hard for him to picture what the next big thing could be. Enter World of Wonder's new head of development, Tom Campbell, who had been entranced by the Queen of Drag since he first laid eyes on her during the 1993 March on Washington for Lesbian, Gay, and Bi Equal Rights and Liberation. It was now 2006 and Campbell was determined to find a new glittery project for RuPaul. Reality competition shows, like *Survivor*, *Project Runway*, and *America's Next Top Model*, were hot in the early aughts, and the world's most famous drag queen seemed a perfect fit for the genre. Problem was, RuPaul wasn't having it. Until one day when Campbell pitched a competition show with a drag race motif and RuPaul was persuaded to gamble on the trust and friendship he had shared with World of Wonder co-founders Fenton Bailey and Randy Barbato for two decades.

The rest is herstory.

FENTON BAILEY: When Randy and I were forming as the Fabulous Pop Tarts in Atlanta, one day Dick Richards of Funtone Records, the local independent label, was taking us around. I remember this figure in these thigh-high wader boots and a jockstrap and football shoulder pads with these tattered bin liners hanging off, wheat-pasting posters of himself. They said: RUPAUL IS EVERYTHING. He wasn't waiting around for someone to discover him. That is my first memory of meeting RuPaul, but Randy and I sometimes argue about this.

RUPAUL: When I got into drag the first time, it was always punk rock. It was what boys were not supposed to do. It had more to do with pushing boundaries, not gender identity. So we were doing gender-fuck drag—smeared lipstick, combat boots. This was the Reagan '80s. It was a social commentary. I'm not gonna fit into your blah-blah.

RANDY BARBATO: My recollection of first meeting Ru was him walking down the street in Times Square in '86 in a pair of wader boots, football shoulder pads, shredded fabric. I feel like he had a jockstrap on and a dress, maybe. It was this insane, gender-fuck, punk-rock drag. Fenton and I had a band and we used to spend time making music and deejaying. Dick Richards was there at the New Music Seminar and another artist on his record label was RuPaul, who had his record "Sex Freak" that he was promoting.

RUPAUL: The New Music Seminar was an annual event in New York City where unsigned bands would go and meet with record company executives and indie labels to network and schmooze all the people who were doing what we were doing.

RANDY BARBATO: It took place every year at the Marriott Marquis in Times Square, which had just been built. It was so fabulous. It meant going uptown. It was a really glamorous kind of schmooze fest.

RUPAUL: We were all devotees of the Warhol experience, as many of the people in the Village were at the time. We were from the church of Warhol. I grew up reading *Interview* magazine and thinking my path will be to go to New York, become a Warhol superstar, create a persona, and then move to Hollywood. I think everyone felt and thought that, so Randy, Fenton, and I came together on that.

RANDY BARBATO: We were huge fans of the drag scene. We were never drag queens, but so many of our friends were drag queens and virtually all of our extracurricular activity was spent watching drag queens and fanning out to drag queens. We knew Lady Bunny and Sister Dimension and Taboo. The hothouse for drag in those days in the East Village was the Pyramid Club. Fenton and I lived a couple blocks from the Pyramid Club, and many drag queens lived in our building. Our band, the Fabulous Pop Tarts, performed in those same circles.

FENTON BAILEY: In the East Village in the '80s, there was this huge drag movement and it was unlike drag from other generations. Drag had been very Hollywood-focused and very much a soigné take on glamour, whereas this super drag was like everything and the kitchen sink. It was like taking all of pop culture and putting it into a blender. It wasn't necessarily particularly feminine or necessarily even glamorous. It was taking on all of pop culture and turning it into a look, a look that on the one hand celebrated pop culture and on the other hand made fun of its ridiculousness. Up until then, drag queens and trans personalities had an aura of melancholy around them. Andy Warhol did a series about it. But what punk gave drag was this fuck-you energy. You could break out of the shadows of that melancholy. Divine was an example of a super drag personality. She was really more punk than your traditional drag queen, an assault on the senses.

CARSON KRESSLEY: I moved to New York City in my twenties and there was a lot of drag going on in the early '90s. It was the Wigstock era. There was a club on the Lower East Side called the Pyramid Club that had a famous queen that I loved called Miss Understood. Of course I was a fan and was aware of Ru. He had his daytime talk show and it was quite a golden era of drag in New York City.

RANDY BARBATO: Drag queens provoked thought and they entertained on a level that I felt like I was in some secret club. On the one hand, it felt foreign in terms of the world I came from. On the other hand, it felt so familiar. It's like, oh my god, this is a language I understand. We're all in this club. And even in those days, I really felt like this is a world that the rest of the world needs to see.

FENTON BAILEY: Funnily enough, the Ru we met and talked to is very much the same Ru of today, that sort of soft-spoken, very gentle, really super quick-witted. Oftentimes when you remember meeting someone, you end up having a very different perspective on them, especially after thirty years. But Ru is actually the same. I suppose the look has changed but he was always this incredibly gentle and wise person.

RANDY BARBATO: I fell in love with him the moment I met him. I was obsessed. He was such a star. And there was an instant camaraderie. There was a shared fearlessness. We were out hustling doing our thing. We all had stars in our eyes. We all went and worked the rotating bar at the Marriott Marquis, which was a lot of fun. There were lots of people from the East Village scene there.

RUPAUL: When I met Randy, he looked at me with eyes that saw the position I'm in today. It was startling because I could see that he could see what I saw. I had had glimpses of that with other people, but he saw what I have become. My mother told me when I was a kid that I would be famous and a star, but to have that confirmation from another human being was amazing.

RANDY BARBATO: We first produced his album *Starrbooty*. Well, really it was Fenton and I and Ru, because Ru produces everything. And none of us really knew what we were doing. We were just all figuring it out. Ru had very specific ideas of what that album should be and even the cover. So much of what we know about Ru today, things he says, the kind of totality and the spirituality, the person was fully formed and fully baked back then. He was young and yet he was so wise already.

FENTON BAILEY: Randy and I met at New York University film school in '82 on the first day of school. It was a pretty instant meeting of the minds. We became friends right away and we were working on each other's projects. Then we became boyfriends. At the time that we started working with RuPaul, Randy and I still both had day jobs. I was working as a videotape editor in an investment bank in Wall Street and he was working on Madison Avenue at an advertising agency. We were realizing that our days as pop stars were probably numbered and we saw an opportunity to get into public access television in 1991.

RANDY BARBATO: We were complete failures as pop stars, but it allowed us to make music and meet all these people. And our intention all along had been to make money as pop stars so we could become film directors, so we just took our DIY aesthetic to the next level and sold our first TV series to the UK, Channel 4. It was called *Manhattan Cable* and it was inspired by Manhattan Cable's public access, which was pre-YouTube, pre–social media. It was real people making crazy, insane TV, from Robin Byrd to Mrs. Mouth to Ed Wallowitch and all these people that we loved. We licensed clips from them, repackaged it, and then hired our friends to host it and to be roving reporters. It gave us the opportunity to give RuPaul TV time.

FENTON BAILEY: Ru did a number of woman-on-the-street roving reports for us from the streets of Manhattan. One I especially remember is from the Meat Market. Before its gentrification, it was pretty gay and had nightwalkers and streetwalkers. Ru did a bit for us walking the streets as a lady of the night in Manhattan and it was really good.

RANDY BARBATO: Ru would take everything so seriously. Ru would take any job; put a camera in front of him, and he would deliver as if it was prime-time broadcast television because he spoke all of that language so fluently. Ru was that alien who says he learned everything he knows from TV.

RUPAUL: I told myself I'm done with my Black hooker *Soul Train* dancer look. I'm gonna give these bitches glamazon! My friend Larry Tee, who was a deejay, called me up and said he noticed I was doing a supermodel look and he wanted me to hear the lyrics to a song he wrote.

RANDY BARBATO: Then Ru just came to us one day and said, "Would you guys manage me?" And we're like, well, we don't really do that. I was nervous about it because I just always thought he was in a different league. It was not something you could phone in. I knew it was a turning point.

FENTON BAILEY: RuPaul told us that he had recorded a demo with Eric Kupper and it was this song called "Supermodel (You Better Work)," which he wrote with Larry Tee and Jimmy Harry. We were just starting World of Wonder and he said he wanted us to get him a record deal. Maybe he came to us 'cause we had a fax machine and we had desks and computers. It was a loft on Varick Street, right by the Holland Tunnel. The front part of the loft was the office and we lived in the back, where there was a bedroom and bathroom and stuff. It looked like it was a real company.

RANDY BARBATO: Fenton and I had a conversation and one of us said, if we can manage RuPaul and have a pop hit, we would never have to do anything again in our lives. We will have made such a contribution to culture.

FENTON BAILEY: We sent the demo out to every record label and pretty much every label said no. But finally one day Monica Lynch from Tommy Boy Records called up, and we thought it's gotta be a prank because we just couldn't imagine Ru as a drag queen on this hip-hop label. But Monica totally got it, totally embraced it, and she ran with it. Tommy Boy then said we have a few dollars to make a video and we just figured we could make that money go the furthest if we direct and produce it as well ourselves. So we did. We did the "Supermodel" video.

RANDY BARBATO: And he did have a pop hit!

FENTON BAILEY: "Supermodel" was a great success and it was a wonderful, breakout hit for RuPaul. I think what wasn't so great about it was that people didn't get to see him as this sensitive person. They got the joke and the novelty and the humor of "Supermodel" and that almost precluded them from seeing Ru as a sensitive, insightful person. His ability to connect with people and to see what's going on with them and to call them out on it and to encourage them is an incredible talent.

TOM CAMPBELL: There was a queer march on Washington in '93 and it was a big deal because of HIV. There still wasn't a treatment for HIV that worked and it was this big moment. I went with a group of friends from LA on a plane full of gay men and lesbians, all going to the march. It filled my soul and filled my spirit. We marched by the White House and we landed on the Mall. There were a million people there. And on the stage, at the end of the Mall, were all these entertainers and speakers, from all walks of life. Jesse Jackson spoke. Cybill Shepherd spoke. All well intentioned. But it became clear to me that there wasn't a genuine leader of the gay movement. And then the announcer said, "Ladies and gentlemen, the supermodel of the world, RuPaul." RuPaul, a ten-foot-tall blond glamazon wearing a Wonder Woman outfit, takes the stage and starts to sing "Supermodel." Every man, woman, and child stopped what they were doing and turned to watch. After Ru finished the song he cracked a few lines. "We're coming back. And we're gonna paint the White House pink!" The crowd went wild. At that moment, a thought blazed across my mind: *A drag queen will lead us.*

CO-EXECUTIVE PRODUCER THAIRIN SMOTHERS: He was a real gay superhero. [I was] an eighteen-year-old from the Midwest coming out of the closet; he was the popular gay celebrity that was breaking into mainstream, kind of how Madonna did in her time. But Ru was the gay god, the gay pop icon, busting in with "Supermodel." I was fascinated by him. The way I look at him on the runway today in drag is the same way I looked at him back then as an eighteen-year-old. It's hypnotic. You cannot take your eyes off of it.

BENDELACREME: I came out at thirteen and I knew I was queer and I knew there were gay people in the world but I didn't know where or what they were like or whether there would be a place for me there. I remember when "Supermodel" came out and just being mesmerized. I didn't understand what RuPaul was. I loved the song and danced around to it everywhere. But I didn't get what Ru was. I knew there was something about her and I feel like I understood that there was gender complexity but I don't think I understood drag queen exactly. There was this MTV red carpet where she was speaking. I think they asked Ru what's the most sensual fruit and she said an apple. Just the way she said it, what she looked like when she said it, everything about it, stuck with me.

I didn't understand why but I knew that there was something about this creature out in the world that was connected to who I was very deeply.

SHEA COULEÉ: I will never forget seeing RuPaul for the first time. I was only four years old. We were still living in Indiana. We had a split-level house and our basement was the family room area and it looked out upon all these woods. It was beautiful, always such gorgeous natural light down there. My older sister was babysitting me and she put on VH1 and she played the "Supermodel of the World" video by RuPaul. I remember seeing that gorgeous, luxe, black-and-white music video and just sitting with my legs crossed, back fully straight, like I was in preschool when you all gather around. My sister is one of the people that always nurtured my creative side and my feminine side and she knew she was planting a seed. I feel like it was one of my first instances of representation without even knowing how important that was because I just saw myself in RuPaul and I had no idea what a drag queen was. But I saw something of myself in that, even at such a young age.

ADORE DELANO: I knew Ru from *The Brady Bunch Movie* and *But I'm a Cheerleader*. I knew how iconic he was because of Nirvana and that famous picture growing up, just him being a pop-culture icon and my mom telling me about him and stuff. I was hella young but I remember my brother telling me about his show on VH1.

PANDORA BOXX: When RuPaul came onto the scene, things changed in the drag world. It became more popular, which helped us when we were doing our shows. RuPaul came out with her song "Supermodel" and everybody knew who she was and then movies like *The Adventures of Priscilla, Queen of the Desert,* and *To Wong Foo* came out, and it was just like people knew what drag was or knew that it was more than what they had seen before of it.

GINGER MINJ: RuPaul was it for me. I had Divine and then I had RuPaul. Unfortunately, Divine had passed away, so the one shining beacon of light and hope that all of us queer little kids had was RuPaul. In Orlando, there used to be a strip that was called Rainbow City. It was just little storefronts with rainbow flags and they sold all sorts of little gay things inside. And they had the RuPaul doll, which I am sure I still have somewhere, and a giant framed picture of RuPaul in the red "Supermodel." I wanted that picture so bad but they wanted $1,000 for it. Years later, after it had changed hands a couple of times, I finally got that poster. I won it in a raffle. It meant so much to me for so long. And then when I started taking drag kids under my wing, it passed its way down to them. It's still out there in the world, inspiring people, still making people want to be fabulous.

BENDELACREME: Ru was a segue to finding things like the *Wigstock* movie and figuring out who Lady Bunny was. When I went to Walnut Hill, I would take the train into Boston by myself on the weekends and I would go to the one seedy gay bookstore that I knew of in Boston. I would search for anything that contained drag queens. I researched everything about drag but it was definitely that first exposure to Ru that was the first bread crumb on that path.

SHANNEL: When I was very young and I would be drawing portraits, I would listen to RuPaul's CDs…Yeah, like "House of Love" and all of that sort of stuff because it was all around that same time with "Supermodel," the '92, '93, '94, that whole era. It was very influential for me at a very, very young age.

NINA FLOWERS: When Ru released "Supermodel" and it became super popular, I was like, oh my god. I was already a makeup artist, and I was already playing with makeup but when this bitch came on with the music video and everything and everywhere, doing fashion shows, doing runway, being on the music awards and everywhere I mean it was like wow, I want to be like her when I grow up. Big inspiration.

FENTON BAILEY: And then there was his MAC Cosmetics Viva Glam deal and Ru ended up being the first male supermodel. And then there was a book deal with Hyperion for his autobiography *Lettin It All Hang Out*. And then there was his talk show on VH1, *The RuPaul Show*.

JUJUBEE: The first time I saw RuPaul was in *To Wong Foo, Thanks for Everything! Julie Newmar*. And I was terrified because I didn't know how to react, I didn't know how to feel. And I was like, wow, he's so beautiful. But why is he dressed up like this? And I always questioned that. And I was like, is this the kind of person that I also am? Is this also what I want to do? And I was afraid. And it stuck for a while and was my world of wonder, if you want to put it that way.

ALYSSA EDWARDS: RuPaul is the first drag queen I ever saw. It was on *To Wong Foo, Thanks for Everything! Julie Newmar*. I was allowed to watch that because Patrick Swayze was a dancer and I was so inspired by him. And I was so confused. I remember asking my granny what is this? She said those are drag queens. She might have said cross-dressers.

BOB THE DRAG QUEEN: I thought *To Wong Foo* was a great movie and I loved the notion of dressing up and I was so intrigued by RuPaul in the movie. I remember thinking these queens—Patrick Swayze, John Leguizamo, and Wesley Snipes—look good, but who's that bitch in the beginning in the Confederate flag? Who is that bitch? I remember thinking to myself that she should have been in the whole fucking movie. This is the one I want to see. But I didn't think about doing drag then because I didn't have any representation of what drag is for a living. *To Wong Foo* doesn't tell you what that is. They're not even making money in *To Wong Foo*. They're just driving around.

LAGANJA ESTRANJA: Because I had a gay sister, I was exposed to *But I'm a Cheerleader, The Adventures of Priscilla, Queen of the Desert*, all of his cameo roles that he had made. I really respected him and I still do to this day. I think he is a trailblazer and he represents what a true queen is and that is someone who doesn't stop until they get what they want. I just felt like to be able to be in this presence was an extreme gift from the universe. I just wanted his approval and still do to this day. I just wanted him to love me and to see the light that I had inside of me.

VIOLET CHACHKI: I discovered RuPaul when I was in eighth grade. I thought he was a cross-dresser or something. I remember walking down the school hallway singing "Supermodel" with my friend and getting really weird looks from teachers. I definitely was nervous meeting her but I like to think of her back in Atlanta, running around with football pads on. I can see myself in that RuPaul. I can see myself in the RuPaul backstage at the Versace show getting pushed aside to take pictures of Naomi Campbell. Those are the moments in RuPaul's early career that I like to think about that I can really relate to.

RONAN FARROW: When you go back to those clips from the early '90s of Ru on Geraldo's show, getting in the little sound bites and moments in a panel context, just being such a canny self-brander and promoter and having this extraordinary confidence, this is someone who just believed they were a star and sold it hard and through an incredible amount of hard work and a refusal to compromise. It is an incredible example of someone not leaving their community behind, or the things that make them marginalized behind, but instead not only bringing it along but harnessing that for power. Ru's impact on the culture can't be overstated. It's only going to grow and grow. I can't think of anyone else like RuPaul. As someone who grew up seeing RuPaul on talk shows and stuff interact in an era where there really weren't many other mainstream examples that were accessible to a lot of us of drag. It's definitely a legacy and it's that memory that meant that when I started to encounter Ru in the world as an adult, it was always a bit of a thrill.

RUPAUL: It wasn't about the fun of drag anymore. I realized I was representing a community that had no voice.

FENTON BAILEY: When we were working with Ru on his first book, we learned that Ru, growing up, had some real hardships. It took real smarts and dedication to know that what people responded to in him, the tall, leggy, blond supermodel, I mean there was no road map for that. Celebrity drag queens up to that point were people like Milton Berle, which is a completely different thing. There is an ocean between those two entities.

RANDY BARBATO: There was a duality there that was intense. Ru knew how to walk into and own a room. It was just instinctual. On the one hand, he understood the language, not only of television, but of stardom and celebrity. He knew it like a science. On the other hand, he was incredibly introverted and quiet and grounded and spiritual.

Ever since I've known Ru, I could have real and meaningful conversations about anything. He understood that celebrity was a construct and that it was not a transformational journey that he was on. His expectation was to fulfill and share something larger. I always think there was this spiritual awareness that was super evolved and that differentiated him from everyone around him. He was always kind of a loner, not because he was a snob, but he was always in it for a different reason. He was on a different journey.

RUPAUL: I took a few years away from the business because I wanted to reevaluate what I was doing, what I wanted to do, where I wanted to go. I moved out to Los Angeles and got to know my nieces and nephews and had barbecues and stopped dieting for a while, which is wild. I also stopped drinking. I was just turning forty. I had done it my whole life since I was ten years old.

I wasn't even sure if I was going to go back to singing and dancing and prancing around onstage. I was prepared to not do that.

That was during the Bush era and I thought, ya know, I need to step away from the canvas. I worked, I paid my bills, I didn't go without, but I didn't work in the ambitious style I had been.

RAJA: In the early 2000s, RuPaul was going through a section of his life where he had gone sober and everything had halted. He had such a huge popularity and trajectory and then, all of a sudden, it stopped for a bit. He moved to LA and he would come to the clubs. There wasn't that much drag like there is now so he went to every show, made friends with all the queens, usually hung out just in the deejay booth. He would always cheer really loudly and stay in his little box in the deejay booth and watch all of us perform. I would see RuPaul at different clubs all the time. It was like him wanting to connect with drag while not doing drag. He even performed with us at Peanuts one night and Ru became acquaintances with all of us.

RAVEN: I met Ru for the first time years before the show. I was with my boyfriend and we'd gone to the *Dreamgirls* show at Micky's and then went to see another show at Peanuts, the club I went to in drag for the first time. We saw Raja standing out in front of the club talking to this tall, thin guy in one of those big corduroy jackets. Raja was someone that I looked at for paving the way for newer queens to come out. So I said hello to Raja and Raja said, "This is my friend, Ru." I looked up and I went, "Oh my gosh, you're RuPaul." I remember him taking me and turning me to the light so it could hit my face and he goes, "Did you do your makeup yourself?" And he went, "Wow." And then we went inside to see the girls and he got whisked into the deejay booth and I didn't see him again until *Drag Race*.

MORGAN MCMICHAELS: I had met her before *Drag Race*. Delta Work had a show in Pasadena at a club called Encounter and Ru had visited. I'd also seen Ru at Peanuts, Club 7969. She was always there on Mondays and Fridays. And she'd show up to *Dreamgirls Revue*. When she came to Delta Work's show, the spotlight guy did not show up and Ru sat behind the spotlight and spotted the girls for the whole show. I know that room was tiny and it must have been about two thousand degrees, so that meant a lot. Even to this day, I am so nervous around her. I've met Gaga and Rihanna and tons of stars and I'm never that way around any of them, but I am so nervous around Ru. And she has only ever been nice.

RAJA: There was a time when he actually was giving things away out of his closet and throwing shit out. And I have some Ru-me-downs. I still have some of it. I treasure them. I have his original robe that he wore in the "Supermodel" video. I own that.

FENTON BAILEY: There was no question the very first time we saw Ru, oh my god, he is a huge star. It was really just this question of waiting for the world to catch up. I think his intuition about pop culture was so smart and ahead of its time and prescient. After "Supermodel," the culture thought it was a novelty hit and that was another barrier for Ru to break through that would take time. I think he needed to have that time out before people would look again and say oh hang on, there's more here than we thought there was. I think it's more about other people than about Ru.

RANDY BARBATO: He was saying, "Everybody say love," thirty-something years ago. He was saying, "If you can't love yourself, how are you going to love somebody else?" He was fully realized and he was completely self-aware. He was packaging it a little differently but we saw that and it has just taken three decades for everybody else to see it in a way. It was hard for a lot of people to get beyond the wig and the heels. It has really taken a long time for people to not only be in awe of the visual spectacle but appreciate the wisdom and the ideas that come from him.

MISS FAME: I saw RuPaul perform at our Gay Pride in San Louis Obispo County before *Drag Race*. She was dressed as a cowgirl and she came out and did a song. I think it was 2006. I was standing there with a giant pompadour with my little Mexican grandmother. I had a geisha parasol. I had butterflies down the tail of my mohawk. I had a flannel that was fitted like nobody's business and these size 0 Abercrombie & Fitch woman's jeans. And RuPaul pointed at me during the performance and I felt so seen. I started feeding my feminine side even more. I had determination. I couldn't resist. I got RuPaul's books and I was reading them and studying them, just reflecting on the career. I was completely obsessed.

FENTON BAILEY: We started World of Wonder in New York and we moved to LA in 1992. When we were still in New York, we had talked about doing a competition show to find the top drag queen from every different state across the US. So it was an idea that was percolating underneath for a long time.

RUPAUL: Around the mid-2000s, Randy asked me if I was serious about coming back to the business and I said yes. He said I should do another *Starrbooty* movie and I thought that was a great idea, so we did it. It hit the film festival circuit in 2007.

TOM CAMPBELL: I started at World of Wonder in July of 2006. At that time, it seemed that anybody who had been famous in the '90s was getting their own reality show. And here's this megastar, RuPaul, that they have such a good relationship with, so I said we should do something with RuPaul.

FENTON BAILEY: We told Tom we have tried. At the time, drag queens had been in shows but there was no drag-queen-focused show. It just seemed that there never would be. But Tom really did persist.

TOM CAMPBELL: They were like, "You talk to him." They're like family and RuPaul was still active but he was taking a bit of a break. I went to Ru one-on-one. He can be very intimidating in the best way, but we get along great. And he said, "I'll do anything but a competition elimination show." I said, ohh, okay.

RUPAUL: I stayed away from reality television for years because I didn't want to do anything mean-spirited. Most of the reality television that was making noise at that time didn't feel positive.

TOM CAMPBELL: So Ru and I came up with a kind of *Strangers with Candy* funny thing with Ru resurrecting the drag queen—the monster comes back to life. When we pitched it to Randy and Fenton, we all laughed. I thought we'd really scored. And Ru goes, "You know what we really need to do? A competition reality show." I don't know why but he'd changed his mind.

RUPAUL: Things were changing. The Obama movement was happening and I could feel the winds of change in my bones. It was time. I knew if we did this show, it would have to be with a reverence and a love for these creative, courageous souls who do drag. I knew I would be safe with Randy and Fenton. I knew they would look out for me and I knew that I could really be myself with them because whatever concerns I have they would also share because they are my family. They are my tribe. But it was also Tom. He came up with the format with the racing motif. I knew he understood my voice and that he could write for my voice and that he's really smart and really funny.

TOM CAMPBELL: And with a small group of people, we brainstormed. I said, we'll call it *RuPaul's Drag Race*. And then it's like, what will they do? Well, they'll do something every week that Ru had to do. And so we just started riffing. A lot of the language came up in that meeting. "Gentlemen, start your engines." All that kind of stuff.

RANDY BARBATO: We didn't do a pilot. We were figuring it out.

ENTERTAINMENT WEEKLY SENIOR WRITER JOEY NOLFI: The format is essential to all of this because the element of reality here signifies to the audience watching at home that these are real people. These are people who do this. The only reason they are on the show is because they do this in real life and it is rooted in reality. We're showing real artists and that extends to Ru. We know that there are producers and there are things behind the scenes happening, but Ru is not a character. Ru is not someone who dresses up and is playing necessarily a character. I know a lot of people think that drag queens are characters but I don't see them that way. I see Ru as an artist. I see these queens as artists. And I think it was so essential to the rise of this show and the boundaries that it crossed and the bridges that it built. You are seeing a heightened version of it on a reality TV competition. We know it's fantastical in some elements. It's funny, it's campy, but those are all the things that drag is, too. If you're flipping through the TV and you come across *Drag Race*, and you see these wigs and colors and these people interacting, it feels like a glimpse into a hidden treasure of this subculture that not many people knew about.

BEBE ZAHARA BENET: I always tell people BeBe is a color of who I am. There are some people who would say I created this character or this alter ego but that is not the case for me. I like to describe BeBe as my twin sister. I think a lot of people maybe actually use the idea of alter egos because there is something about themselves they are not comfortable with. Maybe it's because they really want to hide under another identity. There are things about ourselves that we choose to celebrate and there are things about ourselves that we feel like it's a taboo and we shove it under the rug because we don't want people to know, because we are ashamed of it. I feel like BeBe is a part of me, it's a color of who I am, and I bring so much light to her. So she is part of me.

RUPAUL: In drag, I've taken on those roles my whole life. I've had to manage myself, write my songs, because our culture—even show-business culture—isn't designed for drag queens. We've all had to be that for ourselves or have a drag mother who teaches us how to be that. Drag is really a sampling of everything in our culture. That's why people have made comparisons of our show with other shows. The truth is that drag takes little bits and pieces from everything. That's the nature of drag. Drag has always reminded our culture not to take itself so seriously. We make fun of everything. That's why drag belongs up there with all the important elements of our culture. It deserves to be up where it belongs.

TOM CAMPBELL: RuPaul has a talent and a skill and a charisma that he figured out how to package and share with the world. He also talks about wanting to do things that make him happy. *Drag Race* makes him happy, and helping other queens makes him happy. But none of that came easily. And showbiz can be very unkind to anybody at any point.

SHOWRUNNER (SEASONS 1–4) CHRIS MCKIM: For four years, I shared a cubicle with Ru. Pretty fabulous, right? We would all sit around. It would be Ru, Randy, Fenton, Tom, and Mathu Andersen. We all had a very similar language and sensibility and we'd talk about when a queen is eliminated, how do we get rid of them? Bees or a trapdoor or whatever it might be. We'd sit around talking about challenges and coming up with the creative language. I remember the day Ru came into the office and said Mathu had suggested, "Shantay, you stay" and "Sashay away."

RANDY BARBATO: When you think of drag queens, you think of lip syncs. Early on in the development of it, I do remember having that conversation of like, wait, there's no lip syncing in this. And then I think Tom came up with oh my god, lip sync for your life. That first season the language was evolving live. It felt like we had cracked the DNA of the show.

TOM CAMPBELL: We were trying to come up with the criteria and I said that whatever it is, it should spell something, like boobs, 'cause I'm classy. Chris McKim came back with creativity, uniqueness, nerve, and talent. I said creativity and talent are the same thing. He came back with charisma, uniqueness, nerve, and talent. Cunt! I'm sold! A huge, tacky pun—that's what we love.

FENTON BAILEY: The charisma, uniqueness, nerve, and talent mantra works so perfectly because that is what we cast for. We don't cast based on that idea that you've got to have one of this or one of that. It's actually this undefinable it factor. It's that certain something, it's that magic. Diversity is almost in the DNA of what drag is to begin with. And then you go internationally and you see that every country has a drag tradition and a drag culture. It's different, but it's absolutely recognizably drag.

RUPAUL: For the challenges, we needn't look further than what I've had to do in my own career: writing books, or working with a rock band singing a song. For rock 'n' roll, you don't have to have a great voice. My voice is whatever. I know how to inject my all into it. That's why every human alive should find the drag queen in them. Everybody has powers that they can bring up. Years ago, I had to learn how to inject my drag persona into my daily life so that I could access that power when I needed it. I had put them in two separate compartments. The truth is, it all comes from the same source and I can access that at any time. Of course, it helps, depending on what I'm wearing. But the truth is you have the force with you at all times.

RANDY BARBATO: We pitched it to eight to twelve networks. I think there was a lot of enthusiasm for it, but no one dared do it because it was drag queens. It didn't feel like you could do that on TV. It still felt like too out there, ohhh, here comes World of Wonder with some craaaazy whackadoodle thing, like, that's never gonna get made.

TOM CAMPBELL: We went to all the hot cable channels at the time thinking this is something special. And they were all really lovely people and were like oh my gosh, we love you guys, we love Ru, it's such a great idea, laugh, laugh, laugh. But...ad sales. We really can't do this kind of thing.

FENTON BAILEY: I remember being in one pitch meeting, one name-less network with one nameless executive, and halfway through the pitch meeting he just burst out laughing. And we thought, oh this is great, it's going well, he's enjoying the idea and the show. And then he said, "Yeah, ya know, the reason I'm laughing is because we would never, ever, ever consider making a show like this."

RANDY BARBATO: Brian Graden was running MTV and Logo and he green-lit *Drag Race* in March of 2008. He really was the one who saw the opportunity. We were super excited. It seemed unbeliev-able that we were actually going to be making a show for TV with drag queens. It also was a little bit scary because we had literally no money to make it. But we were in a unique opportunity because Logo was so small it couldn't really afford to fully finance it, so it gave us an opportunity to partially finance it but retain ownership. RuPaul was a big name for Logo, and it was a big swing for them. But it was a bigger gamble for us because it was and still has been more of a financial investment than what we do with most of our shows, which are usually fully licensed from a network and we get some back end. We really wanted to make the show, we really believed in Ru, and we are always trying to own everything. Finally, there was an opportunity to do that with something that excited us more than anything on our slate, ever.

SHANNEL: I never even heard of Logo before.

RONAN FARROW: The idea of a Logo reality show about drag queens was, of course, anything but a sure thing. When it starts out, there is something that is compelling in a different way about those early seasons—the Vaseline blur filter and the low production values, and so forth. But also, more significantly, the kind of queen that was on the show and the set of expectations that they had. They were all joining something that was at the time less elevated and less of a sure thing. There is a kind of scrappiness and unpredictability, and a little bit less of an infiltration of reality TV tropes in the early seasons, which are uniquely compelling in a way that probably can't be replicated now.

TOM CAMPBELL: The first draft of the script was due to the network, Logo, and I think we ran out of time and Daniel Rogge, a producer on the first season, had written the line for Ru: "Good luck and don't fuck it up." I read it and I thought ohhh we can't say *fuck* on television. I'm like, just send it in, they'll give us notes and we'll figure it out. And the only note they gave was make sure you bleep the word *fuck*.

CHRIS MCKIM: We were in the thick of the Obama/McCain election and we thought if McCain gets in, nobody is going to watch this show. It was interesting because Ru went away at the beginning of the Bush years and came back out that March or April before Obama was elected.

JOEY NOLFI: We were on the brink of really transitioning from the pop culture and the celebrity era of glamour and beauty to very odd-ball obsession. It was right as Lady Gaga and Nicki Minaj, Kesha, many of these pop stars that were influencing culture on a bigger scale were leaning into more renegade forms of beauty, ushering in the era of the weirdo. And that tapped into something that all audiences I think needed at the time. Lady Gaga, in particular, I think ushered in a new era for queer culture, dance music. There was a cultural shift in beauty standards, which I think dovetailed really nicely with *Drag Race*, sort of giving rise to the outsider on television. It was almost like a destined space for the drag industry to carve out its niche in the mainstream, because society wanted to break free from rigid standards in favor of the alternative.

CHAD MICHAELS: The majority of us were like, ha ha ha, okay, RuPaul sounds great, but this sounds like a fucking booby trap. So many of us had just been the joke for so long. No matter how much we put into our work, in many circles, we were still just the clown. I think a lot of us looked at it like this could be sabotage. This could just be an opportunity for some people to put us on TV and make us look stupid. Most of us said no.

BEBE ZAHARA BENET: Every time I saw drag on television, everybody was laughing at the drag artists. And I was like, these are such talented people, why are we laughing at them? Or if you talked about drag with people, it always felt like this thing that people would laugh at. I laugh at myself aaallll the time. But it's the idea of you laughing with me that's different. That's why when I was first approached about doing the show, I had reservations.

TOM CAMPBELL: *Drag Race* was introduced in the way that all great gay things are, as part of the subculture, from underneath, bubbling up, whether it's disco or whatever. We were this thing people found.

FENTON BAILEY: I do think Ru has said every time he bats his eyelash it's a political act, which is funny and also seriously true because I think the message of *Drag Race* is about people not kowtowing to some idea of what is normal, not editing themselves to fit in with some kind of notion of what people should be but instead people finding out who they are and bringing that out. And I think that that's fundamentally a very political message. It's about self-expression rather than conformity. So I think the show is inherently political without necessarily being Democrat or Republican. Political in a larger sense, probably in the more important sense.

VICTORIA "PORKCHOP" PARKER: Barack Obama had just been sworn in as president, the nation was going through a huge cultural change, and it was a good time for the show to premiere because it went along with everything else that was happening in society. It caused everyone to look into an arena that they had always heard about, that they thought was taboo. Well, here it was, right in front of them on their television screen.

MERLE GINSBERG: RuPaul is a unique talent that deserved to be known by everyone. And it's not even the drag. It's the personality. It's the mind, it's the humor, it's the insight, it's the humanity. RuPaul is a philosopher of life and RuPaul could have a show and just sit there and talk. He's magnetic.

RUPAUL: The show's mission statement was to celebrate the art of drag, and drag has more significant meaning and power than just what it seems like on the surface. That's why [with] all of our challenges, even sometimes as hokey as they may seem on paper, once you add drag queens and the duality of someone in drag doing it, it takes on a mystical, deeper meaning.

MERLE GINSBERG: We laughed our asses off. I started having friends of mine who designed clothes make me more and more fabulous outfits. I wore giant hair. I really got into the spirit of it. And I wanted to change my look for every show. I would tell friends I'm in this thing, it's gonna be fabulous. But even my gay friends would tell me that gay people were embarrassed by drag and were not going to watch this and I shouldn't embarrass myself. I didn't care. We had a fabulous time. We laughed all summer.

RANDY BARBATO: Ru is a walking sampling machine. Ru has some weird ear that he can go "Nina Bo'nina Brown bada da bah." He hears something and he just starts repeating it.

FENTON BAILEY: "Camarooooon!"

TOM CAMPBELL: Newark, LaGuardia, Kennedy! It just makes him happy, it gives him something to do. The Nina Bo'nina Brown he just could not get over.

RUPAUL: I have always collected sayings. My mother collected sayings. She'd write them down. One that I've had for thirtysomething years is "She'd already done had herses." I heard that at Crystal's, the White Castle of the South in Atlanta. We were there after the club and this girl walks up to the counter to grab one of the bags that had been prepared for someone behind the counter and she said, "Uh-uh, nah, nah, she'd already done had herses."

FENTON BAILEY: Ru locks onto the viral moments in everything. Before YouTube, before TikTok, before all these platforms, you had Ru and other queens all locking onto these little gems in pop culture and recognizing them and identifying them and amplifying them, turning the volume up. Ru will not thank me for remembering this but Ru would do lip syncs as part of his performance to Champale commercials. They had these very iconic ads and Ru would do brilliant lip syncs to Champale commercials.

MERLE GINSBERG: I have only lived in New York and LA, I have always been around drag queens, performers, makeup artists. I never thought of these people as being brave. That wasn't something that occurred to me. But Ru would start talking about that, about how brave it is, because these people were judged and made fun of and picked on and in so many ways they were just celebrating one of the great parts of life, which is just dressing up and being outrageous. And Ru would always say we are all wearing drag, which is true. I learned a lot from them. I learned a lot about makeup, hair, and I learned about accepting yourself for who you are.

FENTON BAILEY: To be a drag queen is not to be a wallflower or to be worried about fitting in or being seen to be normal. To be a drag queen is to have the courage and commitment to strike out on your own and do your own thing in spite of what people may say. There is a lot of stick-with-it-ness and courage and initiative and all sorts of qualities that are required.

CARSON KRESSLEY: When they are putting on their makeup, I feel like it's the moment in *La Cage aux Folles* when the drag queen is singing the song "I Am What I Am." *I've been through all of this but I have finally found myself and I am proud of who I am and damn it, I'm not going back in the closet.* Those are those moments we see on the show where you hear the backstory of the trials and tribulations some of these queens have had to go through. It doesn't change how we're going to judge them but, my goodness, as people it makes us respect them so much. I don't know if I could have pushed through and persevered like that, and it makes us respect and love them even more. And that's not to say that they're all underdogs because that sounds like they're not superstars, which they are. But everybody on the show has had an underdog moment where it didn't look like life was gonna pan out for them and they managed to persevere and be on the show and be successful and be celebrated, and that is just so inspiring for me and I think for so many people watching.

RUPAUL: All of us are in drag in some form or fashion so once you are able to step into that werkroom, it's really breaking things down to who you are underneath all of the paint and powder—not just the drag queens but every human alive. So when I'm able to discover a person's blockage, I'm actually always really talking to myself. I see myself in them. I see myself, really, on their audition reel, so once they're in the werkroom, I am able to identify myself in them and understand the self-doubt. I understand that I have worked on that myself so I'm able to speak frankly with them about that.

TOM CAMPBELL: It's not always Oprah's Master Class. It's in the context of this crazy show, but it's powerful. We didn't know how much that was baked into the show but that has been the spirit of the show that has come. We've put all the elements together. That's what rises above it and that's what I think makes it ultimately special. There's a lot of love in it.

RUPAUL: It is an integral part of my personality but I didn't realize it would become such a big component of the different sides of the show. Duality exists throughout the show, not only the showmanship of the performance of drag but also the heart. I don't think any of us anticipated that aspect of the show.

CARSON KRESSLEY: *Drag Race* has heart and, yes, it's funny and, yes, we have amazing queens but we have the secret sauce that is RuPaul Andre Charles. He brings something to the production that is ethereal and spiritual and I am unable to put my finger on it. But it's a grace and a wisdom that helps the contestants, of course, every week but it also guides all of us on the cast and crew.

RONAN FARROW: Even though Ru is in some ways so stylized and such a performer, I think there is always an authenticity that underpins his presence on-screen. And it's curious, in a way, because he keeps his cards quite close. He is not a part of the Zoomer culture of confessional, oversharing, naked vulnerability. It's very intellectualized and it is in some ways at an emotional remove, but it's also utterly Ru all the time.

ASIA O'HARA: When Ru comes into the werkroom and she talks to us, it's like, oh my god, this is RuPaul. But when the cameras were down for a reset, I would watch her body language and just feel her energy and that was another thing that made me feel at ease. I liked being in the room with Ru. I like the way that she makes me feel. It's a feeling of vulnerability but also admiration because since my father's passing, it had been a long time since I had been in the presence of a professional Black male that I really admired and respected. And it was the first time ever in my life where I was in front of a Black gay male that I really admired and looked up to. Meeting Ru just makes me feel like I can do anything, and the only thing standing in my way is me.

JOEY NOLFI: Drag queens in pop culture in the '90s and early 2000s were the butt of the joke and these little side characters in sitcoms and movies that the audience is meant to laugh at. But seeing Ru walk through those werkroom doors in a suit just as Ru, the host version of Ru, it's amazing how simple a change in clothing changes how you see him. A lot of people don't know his name is actually RuPaul and Ru in the werkroom adds a whole other layer to his pop-culture persona and to him as a person. And later in the show, when you see Ru in the wigs and the gowns and the makeup, this is RuPaul the artist.

JUJUBEE: When I was in high school, my friend Tee, her name's Chameleon. She's my drag sister. We emailed Ru through her website and we asked Ru how do we cover our eyebrows? We didn't expect a reply at all. And she replied. We got an email back and she taught us. She said there's two products. There's the wax stick that Kryolan Cosmetics sells and you can rub it on your eyebrows and then powder it and flatten it out and then put foundation over it. And she's like, if you can't find that, darling, you could use Ivory soap. Just use the soap and just rub it on and then the thickness of that soap would seal it down. And it worked. We did it. We were these high school students who wanted to experiment with drag and we did it. And I don't think I actually ever mentioned that to Ru in the werkroom, but yeah. That was pretty special. Ru's been in my life for more than he thinks.

RAVEN: I have always had a certain level of respect for RuPaul knowing that he was doing it when it was not popular. He was doing it when people were still spitting on drag queens and ridiculing drag queens. The straight and gay communities would oust you and push you aside for being a drag queen, and he was still doing it whether you liked it or hated it.

MORGAN MCMICHAELS: Back in the '90s, RuPaul kicked down one door being the first superstar drag queen. We had Divine and it was a very niche corner that Divine had conquered. The same with Sylvester, a disco artist, also very amazing. But even though it was the time of grunge, and there was a big political backlash against LGBTQ people, RuPaul really kicked down that door. So, when I saw the promo for Season 1 of *RuPaul's Drag Race*, I was like, she's fuckin' done it again! She kicked down another door.

SASHA VELOUR: *Drag Race* came on right after I had read RuPaul's first two books and I was watching John Waters movies. That started to paint a picture of drag in a way that I hadn't experienced it before— the deeper connections to community, to queer identity, and the kind of radical quality of drag that, maybe as a kid, I wasn't picking up on. I had seen *To Wong Foo, Thanks for Everything! Julie Newmar* as a little kid. RuPaul is an absolute goddess, even in her crazy Confederate flag dress. And the thing about that movie is that it got me excited about putting on dresses but I didn't understand the life or the beliefs of what drag was. So it put the fantasy in my head and kept this question burning until I did a little bit more digging.

RONAN FARROW: The way that it uplifts and empowers people who otherwise are often coming from pretty marginalized backgrounds, places where they don't have a form of expression and empowerment, it's just a wonderful, positive thing to be exposed to.

My little nieces, who are in their early teens, watch it religiously. I think it is such a wholesome thing for young people to watch on the most fundamental level, even though of course it has that ribald humor and the rough-around-the-edges vaudevillian quality that drag has. None of that really matters in comparison to the fundamental values of the show, which are so much about lifting people up.

JOEY NOLFI: The unspoken through-line of this show is that you know when you turn it on, you are with the family. It's a cast of queer people. It felt so interesting and exciting and kinetic and electric that it was just naturally populated by members of the community.

RUPAUL: The thing I'm the most proud of is inspiring people to love drag and invite drag back into their lives. For so many years, drag clubs closed down. Kids had to do shows with no lighting, no stage, while people are eating. It had become really bad. Especially in gay culture, it had become very enthralled with straight acting. Or men who were feminine were ostracized from gay culture. And to a certain degree, that's always been the case, but more so in the decade before the show premiered.

MERLE GINSBERG: Maybe drag wasn't a big deal then and the gay community was looking down on it, but the minute they saw this, it completely changed. Drag is bigger than ever.

CHAD MICHAELS: After we saw the show, I was like, this is cool. I get where they're going with it. I'd like to be a part of this.

MORGAN MCMICHAELS: Drag in some areas was so very well received, but on the flip side of the coin, straight people would laugh at drag and they would want to be entertained by drag but they wouldn't really be allies for our rights. Being able to talk about that on international television—because people were finding ways to watch it around the world—that's what drag queens have been doing from the beginning. We have always fought for LGBTQ rights.

RONAN FARROW: Part of what worked there was RuPaul's absolute commitment to what he wanted to do in the world, and then time and persistence. Someone who has, in this futuristic way, had a vision of mainstream drag as an elevated form and just chipped away at the public until they came around to it—that's a pretty amazing thing, and a lesson.

JOEY NOLFI: When the show premiered, a lot of people outside of the queer community still didn't think or accept that someone like Ru could have a position of power in the entertainment industry as a mogul. RuPaul was still a niche artist beloved by a community and peripherally known to the mainstream for his success with the VH1 talk show and his music, which definitely built bridges and made a name for himself. But I think the success of *Drag Race* then opened doors to legitimize Ru and maybe drag artists in general as entities and celebrities with respectable might in the industry. It wasn't until Ru was on *Drag Race* and the show dovetailing with that rise of the oddball in mainstream culture, that really catapulted Ru to a new level that legitimized drag for a lot of people on the mainstream stage, and in Hollywood, as a viable, successful career that someone could aspire to outside of a nightclub or a bar or just being the one in literally three billion. It really was a stepping-stone for not just Ru and his career but for an entire industry.

RUPAUL: We finished filming the first season a few days before the Republican convention. It was a long weekend and I was using a friend's pool in Beverly Hills that overlooks all of Los Angeles. I was by myself and I remember being in the water on that hot day thinking from this moment on, my life will be very different. And it absolutely has been since that day. I knew it would define the third act of my career. I know in most people's eyes it's the second act. But before I got famous, I lingered in the Village for ten years—before Grandma and Grandpa knew who RuPaul was.

Chapter 1

THE PILOT SEASON

IN AUGUST 2008, NINE DRAG QUEENS FROM ACROSS THE NATION SA-shayed into a teeny soundstage in Burbank, California, armed with very little information. They had signed up for drag competition helmed by their idol RuPaul, but what did that involve? Two of the queens, Shannel and BeBe Zahara Benet, had worked together in Las Vegas. Another, Victoria "Porkchop" Parker, was the breakout star of the documentary *Pageant*, released earlier that year. Puerto Rican native Nina Flowers, known for her punk aesthetic and tattoos, had lived in the US less than a year. Wig-averse Ongina, on leave from the Los Angeles retail store she managed, arrived with an arsenal of tiny hats. Tammie Brown, who defies descriptors to this day, winked her way into drag herstory. Rebecca Glasscock, a novice with a gorgeous face and penchant for pissing people off, made the cut, too. A self-declared bitch with a proclivity for nudity, Akashia relished being the resident troublemaker. Dancer Jade, with the good looks and sweet disposition, would deliver the show's shadiest zinger, calling Rebecca "the fakest bitch I've ever known." These girls didn't know it then but they were pioneers, and they were flawless, hunty.

Behind the scenes, RuPaul's regal glamour was a contrast with the dark, cramped soundstage that production could afford. A well-intended decision to soften harsh lighting resulted in the show's famous blurry appearance, arguably its most lasting quality. Reality TV fans probably recognized judge Santino Rice from *Project Runway* but were meeting judge Merle Ginsberg, a fashion and culture writer, for the first time. The reunion show, with its many confrontations and the first Miss Congeniality, remains the most entertaining and enlightening reunion episode of the hit series. Years later, when the first cycle re-aired as "The Lost Season," producer Randy Barbato noted, "It was lost because we buried it, but the joke's on us because it's a classic season with so many gems."

The nationwide search for the cast took months. Hundreds of drag artists competed online for the slot won by Nina Flowers. Others were discovered by casting scouts at clubs or word-of-mouth. If the contestants had anything in common, it was their admiration of RuPaul, which sparked their interest in trying out for the show and willingness to be the most vulnerable contestants to date. For producers, only one thing had mattered as they picked their first group of queens.

RANDY BARBATO: *Diversity* wasn't used in the way it's used now, but that was always understood. Even back then, it was also about having all different kinds of drag—pageant drag, glam drag, fashion drag. Everyone has their own perception of who they are and how they want to represent themselves. I feel that at *Drag Race* we take representing people and who they are very seriously. That's what the whole show is about; it's about celebrating these people.

CHRIS MCKIM: In terms of the story and the types of content we wanted from the queens, for me it was *The Adventures of Priscilla, Queen of the Desert* and *Paris Is Burning*. The performances and stuff is all great but it's all about the conversation and the specificity of the language. I had everybody that worked on the show—queen wranglers, production assistants, everyone—watch *Paris Is Burning* so that they heard and loved the spirit of the world that we really wanted to capture.

SHOWRUNNER MANDY SALANGSANG: We do a nationwide outreach via a casting team and, ultimately, with Ru and the producers, we whittle down all the submissions to a smaller group of say twenty-five or so who then will go into the casting process, which is multi-tiered. There's a lot of levels of creative approval from the executive producers to network consideration, and Viacom obviously weighs in on the vetted group. And then the queens go through a series of background checks and psych evaluations, which is standard procedures for reality competition shows. Ultimately, we narrow it down to whatever cast size we need; it depends on the number of episodes we're doing.

JOEY NOLFI: There is such a considered and deliberate and intentional way of casting this show that is not just oh that drag queen is pretty, let's put her on the show. That drag queen won this pageant, let's put her on the show with her. There is a science and study and a deliberate quality of choosing the queens and pairing them the way they do because of that magic that can only be brought out by people who complement your personality and who understand what you're going through and maybe have similar or vastly different life experiences as you do all under the umbrella of the queer community.

BENDELACREME: I think one of the best things about *Drag Race* is how racially diverse it is and how culturally diverse it is. White queens—like, coming from Seattle, an ultra-white place—have a very limited understanding of other parts of the queer community. When we get to see queens from all these other demographics explaining their experiences, explaining what they are passionate about, that bridging of worlds happens not just with straight people seeing us but with us getting to see the wide range of experiences within the queer community and how they all tie together and what bonds us all. All of that is revealed through that vulnerability and that humanity that is the best part of the reality television format, for me. At its best, it is getting to see these people do what they love, shine within that field, and share their hearts.

BEBE ZAHARA BENET: A friend mentioned there was this thing online and people submitted pictures and got votes for this thing. I was like, oh no, because I was not sure what this [was]. From what I had seen prior to that, people just seemed like they were always laughing at drag entertainers instead of laughing with them. So I said no. Later, the producers actually came into the city and they were scouting entertainers. They connected with me and asked me if I would audition and send a tape. But I didn't follow up. The third time, I was performing "Circle of Life" and RuPaul was in the audience. She sure looked good! When I was done performing, Chi Chi LaRue came to my dressing room and said, hey, you know about this blah-blah-blah that RuPaul is doing? RuPaul is actually here in the audience. So I met RuPaul, who is a big inspiration of mine, and that's what really sealed the deal for me because someone that I look up to, someone who I respect, somebody who I aspire to be, is part of this situation, which means it can only be good, right? He must be trying to do something that is elevating the community, elevating the art form, and creating opportunity. So that's when I finally decided to do my tape and submit it to be chosen.

VICTORIA "PORKCHOP" PARKER: In 2008, I had done a documentary called *Pageant* and I traveled all over the world with it to film festivals. Some friends of mine who were promoters of the Miss Gay America prelims in DC called me and asked if I'd heard about this new reality show that RuPaul is doing. I said no. So they told me RuPaul was hosting a reality show called "RuPaul's Next Drag Superstar" or something like that and that it was going to start casting soon and they thought that I should try to get on the show. I called up the director of *Pageant* and asked if they could get me a number for the producers. I talked to someone at World of Wonder and they knew who I was. At that point, they were doing an online competition for people to be voted onto the show. But he told me not to pay that any mind because they were only selecting one person from that. He told me how to apply online. I filled out an application and sent a video. I filmed myself at the bar that I worked at backstage, in the dressing room, pointing out who I was and what I had done. I was just being myself. I got approved to the next round.

NINA FLOWERS: A friend of mine found out about *RuPaul's Drag Race*.

There was a voting competition online. And there were thousands of queens there from all over the country. I did my profile and I remember calling my friends in Puerto Rico and telling everybody, "Listen, bitches, I am in this competition, guys, go and vote." It lasted two months. We would have to perform to certain songs that were allowed and we'd have to do the videos and then post the videos and then people would vote and the other contestants' followers would throw hate at you. It was very elaborate. The entire competition they kept eliminating and eliminating and they did it until there was like ten or fifteen of us and then it was down to five. It was a really long journey. I ended up winning the online voting and that's how I got my spot.

REBECCA GLASSCOCK: I had already been performing full-time in Fort Lauderdale and some random guy had approached me through my MySpace email and told me I should audition for this new drag show. So I did it and then someone contacted me and asked me to send a better video because I had sent the most Mickey Mouse video. It was very amateur, shot on the worst camera ever. So I did a better tape and they must have seen something they liked and I was picked.

ONGINA: After I did the in-studio interview, I got a card signed by Ru. It said: "Thank you for being the fierce queen that you are. I have no idea how we are going to pick the candidates for a show because the response has been overwhelming and the queens are all amazing. I just wanted to take a moment to thank you personally." And it's RuPaul's real signature. It's not a stamp. I could probably sell this, maybe. I feel like I'm still on a Season 1 budget so I can at least get $100 for this.

TAMMIE BROWN: I did the online audition but nothing really came of that. Though Nina Flowers told me later, "Don't forget you were number twenty." Then one night I was performing at the Here Lounge, which I did regularly in West Hollywood. Candy Ass was there scouting and he told me I should come in and audition. I nailed the audition but they were like, "Oh, we're on the fence. Some of the producers like you; some of them don't." And I got really upset. I was like, "Oh really? This is my dream, my goals, and you're telling me what? I studied RuPaul's book, don't give me a bunch of bullshit!" I knew drag. And then they were like, "That! This is what we need." I got cast right after that.

TOM CAMPBELL: She is odd, and that's what I love. We kept seeing her as this classic, '40s glamour girl and Tammie's like, nope, I'm Tina Turner. And we learned that she is both. She is all those things. I fought for her from the beginning.

RUPAUL: The network was like, um, really, Ru? I didn't necessarily have to fight but I had to insist that she be a part of it because the ensemble is so important in this and she represents an aesthetic in drag that is very important to the ensemble, especially as we are reintroducing drag to the American public.

REBECCA GLASSCOCK: When I first met Tammie, I thought, she's weird. She's staring and it's awkward and she keeps winking and it's creepy.

TAMMIE BROWN: If I wanna be nice, I wink or say hi. I've always been nice. I'm one of the people that can walk into the room and they're gonna say my life is on fire, I light up the room. I came to the show thinking I was gonna be on RuPaul's Best Friend Race—not a competition or a game show.

VICTORIA "PORKCHOP" PARKER: I remember at one point I did notice Tammie was winking and I looked over at Rebecca to see what her reaction was and she was just kind of like, *What's that one doing?*

REBECCA GLASSCOCK: I was really young and I didn't get it at first. Now, as an adult, I'd give it right back. I'd blow her a kiss.

CO-EXECUTIVE PRODUCER JOHN POLLY: I loved Tammie because she's bonkers. Bonkers! A little scary and completely delightful.

JOEY NOLFI: You can't describe Tammie Brown with words. It's just a feeling, it's a vibe.

PANDORA BOXX: When I saw Tammie, I was like, whaaaat is happening? But I love her because she's like a cartoon character come to life. Just her facial expressions and the way she does her makeup.

NINA FLOWERS: I have so much respect for Tammie and I'm gonna tell you why. Tammie is an original. There is no one like Tammie Brown. She has an exceptional aesthetic and she doesn't think about what anybody else thinks about her.

REBECCA GLASSCOCK: The format of the show initially was going to be the drag queen and their sidekick. Each girl was going to have their BFF sidekick. When I did my audition, I did it with my BFF. But then they decided they were not going to use the BFFs.

SHANNEL: The original premise was that you and your fashion designer were going on this show together competing against other teams. So my costume designer, who has been a gown designer for thirty years, Coco Vega, and I decided that we were going to team up together and go on the show and compete against the other teams.

VICTORIA "PORKCHOP" PARKER: The sidekick had to audition as well. Mine was Troy Ford. They wanted us to come in with a sidekick who was gonna help us do whatever we could not do. In my case, that was sewing, as everyone in the world has seen. The producers knew everything about us, all the good, the bad, and the ugly, and they also knew what all of us could not do. And they knew I could not sew.

SHANNEL: It wasn't until literally right before filming that they decided that the designer was out, that the queen was competing by herself. I was shocked because I felt I was going on this show knowing someone else and we're going to be able to do it together. In fact, had I known that, I don't know that I would have gone through with it. But I was so involved at that point. I was so invested, all this video submission, everything had been sent in, so I felt like I was locked into it.

TOM CAMPBELL: We shoot an episode in two days. At first, we thought there's no way they can take stuff from a dumpster and make a beautiful dress out of it. They're going to need help and they should bring a designated helper.

CHRIS MCKIM: We scrapped it because the idea of starting off with eighteen people in that room is just outrageous.

Even after they signed their contracts, the queens did not know details about the show's format or what the competition entailed. They were excited to go to Hollywood to meet their idol. What they didn't realize was that Hollywood was really the San Fernando Valley and their next month would be spent at a budget hotel having fast food for dinner.

EXECUTIVE PRODUCER MICHELE "MEESH" MILLS: Before we start filming, I go through all the research they give us from the queens. I go through their audition tapes, the casting document with highlights, and then I make my own opinions about what I think is interesting about them or who they are or whatever. Then I do a pre-interview, which is usually one to three hours, and get to know them. From that, I make assessments about stories that they might have that would be interesting to tell, who is probably going to be really good at speaking and good at interviews, those kinds of things. And we stick with the queens all the way through to the end of the show.

MANDY SALANGSANG: They are also in touch with a supervising producer from the creative team at that point, who will call to see if they have any questions about the cast welcome letter with the wardrobe looks that they are required to bring.

ONGINA: They called and asked me a few questions. I think they were just trying to figure out if I wasn't fully crazy. I had stepped out of my job because nobody was supposed to know. So I told them I had to go back and that's when they said, "Wait, before you go, we want you to know we have chosen you to be on *RuPaul's Drag Race*." I started jumping up and down and screaming in the middle of the crossroad. There were honks! I went back into the store giddy. I was twenty-six, and I was careless and free. I was living life. I was on a better path, I'd moved to Los Angeles and things were going amazingly in my life. And this added icing on the cake.

BEBE ZAHARA BENET: There was no blueprint, there was nothing. So they just said, "Pack four boxes of whatever you can bring." I was more curious than nervous because I didn't know what it was. It was such a whirlwind, so fast.

NINA FLOWERS: I was traveling to Panama for the first time with my husband to go meet his family and I got the call for the show two days before my trip to Panama. Filming was beginning the day after my return from Panama. They gave us certain categories, so I had two days to put all my shit together before we went to Panama. They did a really good job at keeping us in suspense. For example, for the challenge that was inspired in Oprah, they just said bring an office reality look.

SHANNEL: I was very successful in my career in Vegas and there had never been anything like this. I thought, I really have nothing to lose and if I'm being asked to be a part of this show, then obviously somebody thinks I'm good enough to compete. They gave us a list that said pack ten of your best outfits and go. We had nothing to go off of. It was very challenging for me to get everything packed into those suitcases.

CHRIS MCKIM: The beginning of every season is like a new school year. Tom, Randy, and I went to the hotel to meet the queens. What was exciting about Season 1 is no one knew what the show was. It was such a scene—these young men surrounded by their suitcases and some of them making costumes in the hotel room. They'd only been there twenty hours and there was a glue gun or some soldering iron in the corner and all their suitcases.

ONGINA: All I knew is that it was a reality TV show. I felt like maybe it would be "Amazing Race Drag Race." But it wasn't.

SHANNEL: In my head, I thought maybe I'm gonna be driving race cars in drag. I literally had no concept of what this show was going to be.

REBECCA GLASSCOCK: When I heard the name *Drag Race*, initially I thought it was gonna be like *Wipeout* in drag. I'm a big reality TV show fan. At that time, I was very young so I had a lot of spare time to watch a lot of reality TV and I used to watch a lot of *Wipeout*. I'm pretty athletic so I thought this was right up my alley because I'll just put two little braids and a bandanna and shorts and sneakers and I'll be flying through that obstacle course.

ONGINA: We stayed at the very prestigious Ramada Inn.

SHANNEL: The hotel was nothing to speak of. When you get there, you're basically quarantined. You can't leave your room, you've got to slip a note under the door if you've got to go out or need something. I remember one of the production assistants came in and they gave me some paperwork to look over and then they opened up my luggage and went through everything to make sure you don't have a phone or a computer or things of that nature. And I remember just feeling really nervous and extremely alone. I felt like I was stranded on a deserted island and I was at the mercy of everybody around me. It was exciting but it was also nerve-racking because I literally had nothing to go by at all.

VICTORIA "PORKCHOP" PARKER: I believe we arrived on a Saturday and that evening the producers of the show came to all of our hotel rooms and met us individually and explained a little bit about the show. On Sunday, we did some interviews as boys and then we got picked up individually at the hotel in drag already at 5:30 a.m. and were taken to the studio. They wanted it to be a surprise who was in the cast. They told us to wear something that you don't plan on ever using again.

TOM CAMPBELL: We were in a little studio that in hindsight feels like it might have been an industrial garage. It was in Burbank and it was called Redemption Stages, which was telling.

RUPAUL: It was literally, what the fuck is this?

FENTON BAILEY: There was a modest stage for the runway. I remember everyone being in this corridor and there wasn't really a control room. There was a makeshift table with some bits of equipment on it and everybody just had to be really quiet because the queens were on the other side in a corridor, waiting. And it was just very by-the-seat-of-the-pants.

RUPAUL: When it's hot in LA, it's ten degrees hotter in Burbank. It was a very hot, tiny studio. We did the best we could with the budget we had.

CHRIS MCKIM: It looked like a shoebox for sure. It was basically two halves of a big square house, almost like an airline hangar. And it was broken into two soundstages. We only rented one soundstage because that's all the money we had. And we had the werkroom and the main stage, the runway, on that one soundstage. As long as nobody rented the other side, we were allowed to use it. We never could have done the show without it because that's where we ended up doing all the challenges. But there was no lighting and it was a shoebox.

RANDY BARBATO: Everything was cramped. There was a little lobby. Every morning, when the girls would come in, we would be sprawled out, looking at production notes for that day or whatever, BeBe would walk by, "Good morning, gentlemen." She'd always acknowledge us. She was so charming. To me, she represented an old-school drag. She had a pageantry. She was young then, but I loved ultimately that she won just because it felt like a nod to traditional drag to me.

TOM CAMPBELL: The queens would be dropped off in the morning and they would walk through our hallway where we were writing and so we'd cover the script as they came through and they'd flirt.

"Good morning, gentlemen. How are you?" We were right in it with each other.

CHRIS MCKIM: The control room was so tiny and we were all wedged in there and we were very close to the stage. And so when we were shooting the eliminations and something outrageous would happen on the main stage, we would all react very loudly. And Ru would be like with his little fan, "We can hear you, motherfuckers."

RANDY BARBATO: There'd be times where we'd howl with laughter and they could hear us in the werkroom.

FENTON BAILEY: We hadn't figured out all the lockdown procedures of the very strict, military way it's run now.

TOM CAMPBELL: The control room was a door away from the stage in a small area. If we laughed, the queens would hear it. When there was crying, we had to quiet our sobs. We didn't quite get the lighting figured out until about episode 3. So there was a lot of bright lights and dark shadows. And the kiss and cry room! It's such a big part of any of these competition shows. While judges are deliberating, "Well, so-and-so did a terrible job this week" and you cut to that queen in the kiss and cry room.

RANDY BARBATO: There was also a ladies' room that sometimes we would go and have our meetings—our secret sashay, shantay meetings. Those became our "meeting in the ladies' room."

CHRIS MCKIM: It was basically a little post-lip-sync huddle to just assess what happened onstage after the lip sync for your life.

TOM CAMPBELL: There is a script for setting up challenges. Ru reads it and adds his personal touches. I'm lucky that we share a twisted sense of humor. I'm often in his ear so I live in his head.

JOHN POLLY: We write it, we read it through with Ru at some point or Tom goes over the script with Ru, and then when we're filming, he's reading it through Ru's ear and Ru is on the floor. It's amazing. I don't know how Ru does it. The ability to speak three words ahead of what is being told to you in your ear, I don't know how that works. It freaks me out or it just impresses me to no end.

RUPAUL: One time, Alaska was walking down the runway and she had to make some outfit out of trash and she made it out of a plastic trash bag. She looked gorgeous and she was sauntering. She had this big trash bag with her and it looked like a dog poop bag. And Tom said to me, "She must have the biggest dog in the world."

TOM CAMPBELL: After a season is over, I don't talk to Ru for months because I'm afraid he's just gonna be like "Stop talking!"

JOHN POLLY: For the runway, typically the writers will go spy on the girls through the two-way mirror and see what they are looking like, so far. And ideally we try to get there...close to the moment they're ready to see their finished look. We'll see what the time is—they're all mermaids or it's feathers or "Think Pink." What is she going off with that? You riff on puns that you see. It's like is she Big Bird? Is she Tweety Bird? Is she the Goose that Laid the Golden Egg? And then we'll put a list on the computer in Google Docs and the runway begins and we have a list of things that we've come up with already. But then I swear to god, you'll see a queen who wasn't wearing that cape when I saw her in the werkroom five minutes ago. Or what you thought was an orange dress looks purple on the stage under the lights. So you have to deal with all the new things.

SHOWRUNNER STEVEN CORFE: Everyone was on top of each other. That was a hard season to book judges.

We were reaching out to people, "Hi, we've got this unknown drag queen competition show on Logo, a tiny little LGBT network on basic cable, will you come and spend twelve hours on our set for not very much money?" It wasn't even a proper television studio. It was a photography studio. It wasn't fully soundproof and it literally only had one celebrity dressing room between two judges. So Alicia Magana, who still books talent on the show, and I had to do this whole juggling game. *I think Tori Spelling is still in her underwear right now so don't knock on the door. Oh, but Bob Mackie needs to go inside and get dressed. He is needed in ten minutes.* It was like an English farce, just juggling celebrities between this one changing room. It was so janky, I'm not going to lie.

RANDY BARBATO: Right outside the control room, there was a couch in a hallway and the queens would come out there. I became obsessed with just watching them. I remember distinctly saying, "You guys, this is a TV show. They are just sitting there with their corsets out." That was the birth of *Untucked*.

TOM CAMPBELL: While the judges were deliberating, we're all paying attention to their monitors. Randy, on the other hand, was just pressed up against the one monitor focusing on the queens waiting in the hallway. I remember Randy watching and saying, "*This* is the show." It was just the queens, kicking back and talking real smack. We did it as a digital show called *Under the Hood* the first season and then it became *Untucked*. So many of the iconic moments and iconic phrases and things that people associate with the show happened in *Untucked*. I came up with "If you're not watching *Untucked*, you're only getting half the story." It's a promo line and it's a mantra that I carry with me, thank you very much.

STEVEN CORFE: We all found in the control room we were listening in to what the queens were talking about. It looked very lively and animated and, I'm not going to lie, more interesting than deliberation. I very distinctly remember Randy saying this is where the show's at and then once we were in post-production, Randy assigned me to post-produce the very first season of *Untucked*, which was called *RuPaul's Drag Race: Under the Hood*. I got a pile of VHS tapes on my desk. Nothing had been produced in that room. I don't even think the audio was running. It was just whatever the cameras managed to pick up on the camera microphones, and Randy said, "Here, make a show of this." It had little Barbie doll animations at the beginning of it, which was just me down in the basement at World of Wonder playing with RuPaul Barbie dolls. Fun times.

RANDY BARBATO: Frankly, I could have sat in that broom closet of a control room and watched the monitor and just had fun. From Shannel to Tammie, what more do you need? I felt like I was back at the Pyramid Club.

Without any insight into the process, the queens wondered why they were being individually sequestered in offices around the set. Soon they'd be walking into the werkroom for the first time.

CHRIS MCKIM: It's exciting the first day to run around the building because they're all put in different rooms and we're trying to see what they're wearing to determine what order we're going to put them in for the entrances. We start off with a sheet with the queen casting faces on it, which the whole crew has. Over the course of the season, we cross queens off.

BEBE ZAHARA BENET: You couldn't talk to anybody. There were no cell phones, there was nothing, nothing, nothing.

SHANNEL: I was the first person ever to walk on set, which is pretty cool because nobody else can say that. I remember thinking how crazy and surreal it was that I was literally the first image of walking into *RuPaul's Drag Race* werkroom. And then I saw the sewing machines and I freaked out because I'm not a seamstress. Where's my costume designer? I saw all of the mirrors with the bulbs and I thought, I hope I don't have to sit at one of those stations because I like to paint with my own light-up mirror where I'm really close to it.

NINA FLOWERS: I was a nervous wreck because you get into the studio and they put you in this tiny room where you have to sit and

wait. And I had no idea what was happening. I didn't know if someone was coming into the room with cameras or what. And then finally someone from the production walks me out. They said to hold
there a couple of feet away from the door. There were no cameras
around me but I could see the doors and the lighting and everything.
And then they gave me the direction, "Nina, go through the doors,
you're going to walk into the room and the minute you step in, you
are already working. You are on set. You are on the show. From that
point on forward everything is being recorded." I was super nervous,
but in my mind I said, fuck it, I'm just going to walk in and just be
Nina Flowers. I was very spontaneous. I didn't rehearse or practice
what I was gonna say.

SHANNEL: As everybody started entering the room and you start
looking at the other queens, I felt very polished and I felt very confident because, aside from a couple of the queens, I didn't feel like I
have a lot of competition here. Simply based on aesthetics. I felt very
confident in who I was and what I brought. If this is a beauty pageant,
I'm good.

NINA FLOWERS: At first, I thought the room was totally empty but
then I saw Shannel. I saw her buck-naked and looking bored and I was
like, holy shit, this is about to get real. I was stunned by her beauty and
actually a little intimidated also because her presence is very glamorous and very out there. But she seemed really nice. She was very cool,
and as nervous as I was. And so then the girls start coming in and the
only thing I remember was I was always very loud, as I am. That's part
of who I am and part of my personality. I just remember embracing
every girl, as they were walking in, as sisters. Shade is not in my blood.
I know reading is fundamental but that's not really one of my greatest
assets. I always try to make people feel comfortable around me. I don't
want people to feel threatened by me. And sometimes I have to work a
little harder for that because my look is very out there.

ONGINA: I remember getting onto set and walking in and Rebecca,
Nina, and Shannel were already there. I was wearing Proenza Schouler

shoes, my Prada French bag, a custom corset that I spray-painted, some leggings from my friend who owned a leggings company, and my blouse was from Esprit. And I had a headpiece. *Oh god, Ongina, 2008!* But anyway, I walked in and I was like, who are these ladies? I asked, "Are you guys hosts?" They were so fabulous, and I thought that they were the hosts of the show and I was the first queen to walk in and they were going to welcome me. But they were competitors and I was like, what am I doing here? Like, look at Shannel, okay. Look at Nina, and then I turned and I see Rebecca and I'm a haggard mess. And then we had to line up and Ru appears and I can't really describe all the emotions. It was happening. It was real.

VICTORIA "PORKCHOP" PARKER: Ongina was, out of all of us, the most original and the most unusual of us all because she was something that no one had ever seen before in a serious manner. I would never have imagined passing someone like Ongina on the show but I learned through watching the show and getting to know her and the other queens who have been on it that you have to appreciate every type of impersonation. Every type of drag queen deserves to be recognized. She certainly has represented herself well, and I learned that you can't underestimate anyone because of their inexperience.

BEBE ZAHARA BENET: When I walked in the door, I remember going straight to the girls. I was so curious about which other people were going to be with me and what their stories were all about. The only person I knew was Shannel. We had worked together at her show in Vegas. Everybody else was brand-new to me. I was very excited. I was like, okay, this is real now. I still did not know what the show was in details, but I was excited seeing people because we had been stuck in a room.

NINA FLOWERS: That bitch! BeBe came in with her glam. Immediately as I saw her walking in the room I said, okay, we have some competition. When I saw Shannel and I saw BeBe, I immediately thought these are the bitches to beat. But I also knew right away we would be sisters.

REBECCA GLASSCOCK: When you're in drag, at least, for me, you're thinking about so much stuff that I was not thinking about the cameras; I was not thinking about anybody else. Eighty percent of the time, I'm in my own little bubble, I'm in my own little world, which can come off as standoffish or stuck-up or whatever, but it's because I'm in my little happy place and I'm doing my own thing. I really didn't think much about the cameras or anything because I was thinking more like oh my feet hurt, I want to take off this girdle, which is really tight, and my contacts are scratching my eyes.

SHANNEL: Nina was the only one I thought looked absolutely head-to-toe put together. She is beautiful, she's polished, her makeup is amazing, her wardrobe, she had a great personality, just great energy. And I was really drawn to her. In my head, I immediately thought this is going to be my competition. Ongina walked in as a bald queen and was just this tiny person. I was shocked. Her makeup wasn't very good and she admits it. I helped her a lot with her makeup on the show. Jade I thought was pretty but I could see her beard shadow coming through and she had really light makeup. Tammie, I just remember thinking wow, this is an oddball, this is a real character and really kooky and really out there. Rebecca looked like a bitch from the get-go to me. I was surprised BeBe was there. She had probably done my show at least three or four times. I knew Porkchop from the pageant scene. I had always heard and knew that she was a really strong competitor in the world of pageants. So when I saw her I thought oh, she's going to be someone not to play with because when it comes to interviews and things of that nature, she is really on point. She's a really strong pageant queen competitor. So Porkchop and Nina were the two that I really felt were the girls that will really try to come for me.

VICTORIA "PORKCHOP" PARKER: I had met Shannel previously. And I knew who Nina Flowers was because she had competed at Miss Continental one year. When I saw Tammie Brown, I remember I thought wow, because I'd never seen a queen look like that before. I learned real quick what you see is what you get from Tammie. I just remember looking around the room and, besides Shannel and Nina, thinking there were a lot of young kids. On the online polls, there were very experienced queens who had been in the industry for years, but a lot of these people had not been doing drag for very long so I felt pretty confident to begin with.

NINA FLOWERS: I ended up selecting that particular jumpsuit because of the color print. It is made out of flowers. And the yellow and the orange, I knew right away that walking into that scene, those colors were going to pop out, and I was like okay, this is what I'm going to wear.

ALEXIS MATEO: When I was fifteen years old, I illegally entered a bar in Puerto Rico, and Nina was the first drag queen I saw perform in person. Oh my god that thing is little, but she got a lot of power, baby! So it was interesting to see her on the show. And of course, she was the Puerto Rican one so I was going to be rooting for her the whole way.

SHANNEL: They said that it needed to be something that could possibly be ruined because you might be getting wet. So it was the one thing in my wardrobe that if I have to throw this away, I'll throw it away. Plus, it showed a lot of body so I thought, well, let's just be scandalous right off the bat. I would wear it in my shows in Vegas and every time I wore it, people always loved it. So I thought, well, when it airs on TV all of the people that come to see my shows at least will be able to see me wearing something that they've seen me wear in the bars there.

RANDY BARBATO: I remember gagging over Shannel. Everything about her, just the way she would tell a story, oh my god, she is the embodiment of drag. She is very 360 about her drag. She never comes out of it. She was such a great character. I just remember being fascinated by her, like in the werkroom and the way she would look in the mirror and stuff.

ONGINA: At the time, I didn't really know how to cleverly market some of the things that I was saying. Like *hieeee!* was very much something that I said, but I didn't market it the same way Alaska marketed it. I don't know why I never created headpieces or headbands. I feel maybe there would have been a market for that. So even though I was the first one to say *hieeeee*, I wasn't smart enough to make it marketable. So here I am just receiving checks from Alaska, which is good with me. It's fine.

TOM CAMPBELL: I knew drag queens but I wasn't an aficionado of drag and I thought Ongina brought such a fresh approach to it. *Drag Race* has really made people step their pussies up in terms of fashion. But the OG queens had very little idea what they were getting into and we were all part of the creation of the show and we're forever grateful to them for what they brought.

Is something wrong with my eyes? Why is the show so blurry?

CHRIS MCKIM: We were editing the first episode. We were trying different things and one of the times we sent a cut-through for a runway walk, it had this glam-y filter on. And we got a note from Randy that said that should be on the whole thing. What you gotta know about that filter is that there was degradation between the high-res for broadcast and the online version, which looked fine in the post room. It's jokey but you can see it. By the time it got through your television, beamed through the airwaves to your TV screen or your computer screen or whatever bar you were at that was projecting it, it looked so awful that it was just a catastrophe. It's a little much.

ONGINA: Season 1 for me was definitely exciting and grand. I know a lot of people are like, low budget, Vaseline filter. Well, you know what, fuck all of you because you wouldn't have Season 13, 14, 15, or however long this is going to run for, without my season. I hate it when people say Season 1 is not even real. It was real and I was in it and it was fabulous so shut the fuck up.

JOHN POLLY: You look back and you're like, whoa, this looks so homemade. But what is amazing is it's all there. All those elements that are in the first season are in Season 10 or in Season 12. Even if some of the catchphrases weren't there yet, the tone of it was all there, waiting to be discovered.

CHRIS MCKIM: Now I think it's funny. It probably looks decadent now that it's not 2009 anymore.

ONGINA: I didn't know what high budget was at the time, I just knew that I was there at a TV show and it was fabulous. I do remember on set a man walking around with a belt with cellophane filters, like square cellophanes, and I remember we would have a camera break and all of a sudden he would be walking to the cameras and changing some of the filters. I feel like that was part of the Vaseline filter, which is crazy to me because the softness of those filters made it all look really great. I'm thankful for it, but I hate that it never gets the recognition or praise that it deserves because without the pilot season, you wouldn't have seasons after.

MERLE GINSBERG: We look like we were in heaven; there was so much Vaseline on the lens. I remember all of those types of comments. When we were shooting, I hadn't done a lot of TV, but I could tell that the lighting was not that great. RuPaul almost put a stocking over the lens. He wanted them to soften it up. And we were grateful for that. We wanted to look as good as possible. But when it actually aired, my sister and my mother watched it with me, and they were like, "It looks really weird, you can't see very clearly." But, in a way, I thought it was part of the show's charm. We're not trying to do realism here. We are in a fantasyland.

LATRICE ROYALE: Can I tell you, I just found out the funniest thing: I just found out those lights they used for Season 1 are the very same lights that they use in the basement at World of Wonder for all other filming. It works wonderful in that basement but for the whole set? That's what y'all had? No wonder y'all looked like that! Whoa!

DIDA RITZ: That Vaseline filter is i-con-ic. That's what makes Season 1. After Season 2 the whole situation was fixed, bitch. That filter made Season 1.

GINGER MINJ: The first season really opened my eyes to the fact that there can be so many different styles of drag. It blew my mind because I had never even thought about that before. I loved how raw it was. I loved the fact that it was so hazy and misty and you could barely see RuPaul through all the fog. It was Instagram filters before Instagram was a thing.

RUPAUL: I wanted to make sure that there were no rough edges, especially when it came to drag queens.

JOEY NOLFI: One of my favorite elements of all of *RuPaul's Drag Race* is that damn Season 1 filter. It is so iconic. It is so legendary. Everybody still has a good laugh about it. Of course, looking back you understand this is a show that Ru and everybody was betting on, so you want to look your best. With the rise of HDTV, of course, you're going to put a filter like that on the show.

BEBE ZAHARA BENET: That filter created the buzz of Season 1. That filter needed to happen because they are still talking about that filter. It did what it had to do. Okay?

Finally, it was time to find out what kind of race this was. The show may have kicked off as a celebration of drag at heart, but the first mini challenge in drag herstory—a car wash photo shoot—soaked many wigs and ruined outfits. (But hey, thanks for the muscular hunks!) It didn't get much better for the first maxi challenge, which involved dumpster diving for thrift store materials to make their outfits for their first runway walk.

NINA FLOWERS: I did experience photo shoots in the past but none like that, I'll tell you that. Nothing with water and all that craziness.

RUPAUL: The two Pit Crew members were so fucking sexy. They were standing outside before we were about to go hose the girls down on the cars. They had those short-shorts on and we were watching them cross the street from a glass door. The shots were so tight you could literally tell what religion they were. Oh my god.

VICTORIA "PORKCHOP" PARKER: I believe I was the third one to go outside, and I thought if my big body climbs on top of that $50,000 car I'm going to put a dent in it and somebody's gonna wanna kill me. So I just thought, well, I can forget about getting on the car. The guys that were doing the shoot with us were all really good looking. And they got my attention. Looking back on it, I probably shouldn't have been so taken by them but at that point I think there was just so much going on that I wasn't able to focus on what I needed to be focused on, which was that camera.

MANDY SALANSANG: We begin creative brainstorms for challenges about two months before we start shooting. Then, when the queens are there, the challenge team helps them prep to make sure they understand the challenge, if they need any kind of storyboard or prep materials, or to legally vet name options for a product. And then hot on our heels is the story producer, who will say okay, ladies, now that you understand the challenge, once the cameras are back up we're gonna get Team X around this table and you start by assigning the roles. And then Team Y, you're gonna go over here by this table and you'll start by assigning the roles as well. They'll just be driving the reality content as they are prepping for challenges and as they are interacting in the werkroom.

RUPAUL: The show was based on my experiences as the Queen of

Drag and so all of the challenges would be based on things that I've already done, whether it's radio or movies or being a promoter or a producer, making my own costumes and planning a tour. Every aspect that I'd already accomplished as the world's most famous drag queen would be incorporated into the show.

BEBE ZAHARA BENET: I decided I was not going to give too much and just be a lady going to lunch. So my outfit was very simple and elegant. I should have worn a better wig if I knew we were gonna do all that. I was like, water? Oh my god, they disrespected the dream, honey. But I had to sell the fantasy the best way I could. That wig was murdered, honey. I don't even know what happened to that wig after I did that. She went to the trench, honey. But she was inexpensive so I was like, okay, I can part with her.

MANDY SALANGSANG: There's a team of talent handlers who work with our stage management team to wrangle the queens and provide for their needs. They are the ones on set who are making sure that there's water with straws and fans, and who have nail glue standing by to glue on their nails and assist them in their day-to-day drag needs. They're also there to help with movement and that everyone remains on ice, or stays quiet, until the cameras are rolling.

VICTORIA "PORKCHOP" PARKER: I realized very quickly it's not my fault that they don't have anything in my size. I'm not gonna complain about it because it's not gonna do any good. I'm gonna face it and I'm gonna deal with it because that's the type of person on that show they're looking for—someone who can face a challenge and complete it to the best of their ability without complaining. When RuPaul walked around the room, I felt pretty confident because some of the criticisms she gave to Rebecca and to Akashia were much harsher than what she said to me. She kind of giggled at my outfit and said you look like Bette Midler on the beach. And so I felt okay.

BEBE ZAHARA BENET: The wig with the wood chips! I've always called my drag global drag and a lot of times people want to say it's very African, but I represent myself very globally. I felt for the first runway it would be interesting to create a look that set my foundation, which is me coming from that African continent and really showing what kind of beauty that looks like.

SHANNEL: The runway looks very long but it's actually really not. And you put on a pair of heels and you do shows in bars and it's second nature. But for some reason, when you're there and you know that it's a TV thing, that runway is the scariest thing in the world. It's slippery, it's got lights everywhere, you've got camerapeople staring at you and it's very nerve-racking. You want to be able to convey that you're strong in who you are, in what you represent, you want to feel beautiful, you want to look amazing, and you really want to impress the judges. When you put all four of those dynamics together, it's even scarier. And not having anything to base the show off of, you're walking into it blindly.

VICTORIA "PORKCHOP" PARKER: The thing that you don't realize watching it on television is that it's a cold room. When you're walking the runway, there's not any music, there's not any people clapping, there's not any comments being read about you in the background. It's just you, the judges, and the silent room of cameras and about twenty people standing around who are on the crew. You have to be able to sell it and do what you do on your own because there is no one there to encourage you with applause or screams or any type of enhancement to make your performance better.

RANDY BARBATO: Santino was a mutual friend of mine and Ru's and he had competitive reality television experience. He felt like part of the tribe and he just seemed like a different choice. Merle was someone we've known for a very long time as well. We had a series a long time ago called *The Hollywood Fashion Machine* on AMC and she was a regular pundit on it. So we knew she knew how to speak television pretty fluently and precisely and she has a really credible career in fashion commentary.

FENTON BAILEY: For some reason, I have a clear memory of standing with Santino in the corridor of the studio because there was a life-size cutout of Dirk Bogarde and it looked just like Santino. I took a picture of Santino with this life-size cutout.

MERLE GINSBERG: On the first day Santino Rice and I were on set, Tom told us what the runway theme was and he'd show us pictures or video of what else they done prior, how they had put their thrift outfits together, and he said they'd bring them in one by one and we would give an opinion when it's our turn. He said we could be as outrageous or as critical or as nice as you want, but to remember that people are watching so make it interesting. Well, Santino and I just went for it. I could tell his thing was he wanted to be critical and bossy and haughty so I thought I'm not doing that, that isn't me. I wanted to be like their aunt—sweet and nice, a little sarcastic and funny, but very encouraging. We got into a rhythm. Ru, Santino, and the guest judge would all speak before I did. While they were talking, I was writing little scripts in my head.

CARSON KRESSLEY: On those main stage days, Ru goes through quite a bit of hair and makeup, no shade, but it's a process, so we don't have to start super early even though he does. As judges, we don't know what has been going on behind the scenes. We are not watching dailies or getting updates about who had a beef with whom. Then we take our seats and Ru does his runway walk and sets up the episode. And then usually we have a break and we'll do some promos while Ru is perhaps changing from his runway look into perhaps maybe a comfortable shoe.

JOHN POLLY: The queens walk twice on the runway for every runway. The first time is to music so the queens can just walk and get their zhuzh on, get the vibe, hit their stride and work it to the music. The second time is without music and that's when the judges can make their comments, their catcalls and stuff.

CARSON KRESSLEY: We're writing down our notes what we think is gonna be funny. And then when they do the second pass without music, we get to call out our catcalls and our puns and our reads and hopefully they're good.

JOHN POLLY: Sometimes the looks are just so fierce and fabulous and elegant and edgy and fashionable that we don't even have a campy, kooky thing to say about them. We do come up with lines for Ru so Tom has things to offer Ru and Ru will also have his own things to say. If Ru likes what Tom says in his ear, he'll repeat it. But occasionally, Ru will look into the camera and be like nope, not sayin' that, which cracks us up. If he does say it, we're like, yessss he said it!

CARSON KRESSLEY: Sometimes it's tense and the queens are freaking out and it's a very overwhelming experience and that energy kind of pervades the room. These queens have to do a lot and sometimes they either get in their heads or they get in a fight with other queens or they get down on themselves. It can be very intense and it can sometimes be stressful and heavy, because it's a lot.

VICTORIA "PORKCHOP" PARKER: The guest judge Bob Mackie had this very strange look on his face about me. And I wanted so bad to be able to go backstage and put on one of my beautiful gowns and a beautiful piece of hair and come back out looking like a pageant queen who is what he is used to working with. And I just felt like a frog sitting on top of a rock waiting for a princess to come along and find me in that green outfit while Bob Mackie is standing there, looking at me with his nose crunched up going, "What is that one doing?"

ONGINA: I remember looking at Porkchop's outfit, coming from a fashion background, and just saying, what a mess, it's gotta go. When she came into the werkroom and she talked about her experience having done drag for 110 years, I expected a lot more from her. And then when I saw the way that she delivered that lip sync in that dress, I fully was on board for her to be the first one to go because I honestly thought that that was a poorly made garment.

VICTORIA "PORKCHOP" PARKER: I knew standing and listening to the critiques that I had not made a good outfit but I also knew that I had a big personality and hopefully I could turn that personality on enough to where it would outshine the awful outfit that I had made. And, unfortunately, that didn't work that day. But looking back on it now, Akashia basically took a black dress off the rack and cut a square in the front of it and put a couple of ninety-nine-cent items on and that was her outfit. I, at least, cut some things up and made a memorable outfit that I later threw away in the trash can. Which I wished I hadn't.

CHRIS MCKIM: It was very long and very painful and very stressful. It was the first time that this is all going down in the very cramped control room. It was just a hard day.

RUPAUL: The first thing I had to really overcome was the heartache of eliminating the girls. I do discuss it with the judges and their opinions do matter but, because I am the Queen of Drag, it has to come down to my decision. I wasn't really prepared for the emotional roller coaster that I would experience eliminating girls. But then after Season 1, I realized that even the first girl who is eliminated becomes a star so it doesn't bother me as much anymore.

In advance of arriving in Los Angeles, the queens were given a song list to learn, so they all knew that at some point they would be lip syncing—they just didn't know their lives would depend on it. The first battle featured Porkchop and Akashia performing RuPaul's hit "Supermodel (You Better Work)."

TOM CAMPBELL: Before *Drag Race*, we had a reality show on VH1 called *¡Viva Hollywood!* And Maria Conchita Alonso and Carlos Ponce were the judges. We were looking for the next telenovela star. There'd be acting challenges and slapping challenges and kissing challenges. Every week, we'd narrow it down to the bottom two and they'd have to tape a very short but highly dramatic telenovela death scene with two different endings.

RANDY BARBATO: Who does this?

TOM CAMPBELL: We had rented this McMansion in the Valley that was supposedly where a lot of porn was shot. Each episode, the bottom two contestants would be whisked away to perform a telenovela death scene there. For the very first one, two women got into a fist-fight and rolled down a flight of stairs. Lying faceup at the bottom of the stairs, both appeared to be dead. We'd play this scene back for the contestants to watch in front of the judges. Then boom, one actress would open her eyes, gasp for air, and escape with her life. Then the camera would zoom in on the dead actress's face as the woman playing her is crying in real life because she's no longer in the competition. And Maria Conchita Alonso would say, "I'm sorry, my dear, but *están muertos*. You must leave Casa de los Locos." So we thought how do we top that? We knew the queens were going to do challenges and they have to lip sync because that's what drag queens do. But then we thought, they don't just lip sync. They lip sync for their lives!

NINA FLOWERS: After the first day, they told us what the song was for the lip sync and instructed us to learn the words and rehearse. But there weren't really specifics about how it would go down. We found out onstage how the game was going to be played.

VICTORIA "PORKCHOP" PARKER: Right before we were put in the bottom two, they pulled us off and were interviewing us in separate sides of the room. I didn't want to talk about other people because I didn't know where this show was going to go and I had a huge career outside of the show. But I could hear what Akashia was saying. She said, "Porkchop looked a mess! Porkchop looked like a football field!" She was giving the camera sound bites.

TAMMIE BROWN: I really liked Porkchop. We got along really well and it was fun talking with her. She had that whole pageant essence about her that I respected.

VICTORIA "PORKCHOP" PARKER: All of our feet were killing us because we had been onstage all day. And by the time we got to do the lip sync, my feet were hurting so bad. I just wanted to get it over with. When it started, I felt pretty confident because once again Akashia was young and I thought to myself the one thing I'm sure I can do better than her is perform. Well, she held her own and I slipped. There was at least one slippery spot and I, of course, found it with my size 12 feet.

CHRIS MCKIM: We did the lip sync and we're trying to talk to Ru through his earpiece about who he thinks should be eliminated. But it wasn't working. So I ran out and I'm standing on the edge trying to talk to him and asked him to just come back where we were.

VICTORIA "PORKCHOP" PARKER: Ru stopped production and said, "Turn the cameras off, I don't know what to do. I'm gonna have to go talk to the producers." And she got up from the table.

CHRIS MCKIM: Ru comes to the back in full drag. And there's a little room between the control room and the main stage. It was really like a telephone booth. That was about as big as it was. It was just a buffer for sound. So, Ru comes in there towering in the heels. I just always remember this giant Ru in the wig and everything, towering over us in this cramped little room, and we're discussing who everyone thinks has to sashay away for the first time. That's when Porkchop went home.

NINA FLOWERS: I knew Vicky for a very long time because Vicky is very famous and had a big name in the pageantry system. She is a queen that has won a lot of titles. So for me, it was very sad because I never really thought that she would end up landing in the bottom two because she is a fierce competitor. Unfortunately, that first challenge was about making your own stuff and she doesn't sew, so it was to her disadvantage. It was a reality check for me also after coming in so confident because Ru very quickly slapped me in the face, even though I won the first challenge. She said, "You better give me the flower."

GINGER MINJ: I was in the pageant scene. I had been doing Miss Continental Plus, which is a national pageant for plus-size entertainers for a couple of years. And Victoria "Porkchop" Parker is a former Miss Continental Plus. So when she was announced as a contestant on the first season I know this show is going to be great. Porkchop is funny, she's fun, she's great at drag. I said if any of these girls are like her it's going to be a great dynamic. I turned on the show and, of course, she was the first one that got eliminated.

MERLE GINSBERG: Porkchop was, from minute one, the comic relief. But unfortunately, drag is about glamour and comedy is a big element but when you see all these glamorous, fabulous queens...

VICTORIA "PORKCHOP" PARKER: That evening, when I unpacked and they walked me to the van, one of the producers said, "We really like you and we didn't expect you go to home first. But I'm gonna promise you if this show goes anywhere we're gonna remember you and you will always have a place on this show." Well, I thought this show was going to be on for one season and that's it. But all this time later, they continue to bring me back and pay. I can't be mad.

FENTON BAILEY: BeBe is genius and amazing but funny enough, paradoxically, the person I think about the most from *Drag Race* Season 1 is Porkchop. It just shows that the moral of the story is there are no losers on *RuPaul's Drag Race*. It was Porkchop's destiny and role to be the first queen eliminated. And it was the perfect alignment of the opportunity and the queen.

VICTORIA "PORKCHOP" PARKER: I had been cast on the very first drag reality show. With every success, there was a failure. But, at that point, I didn't know my failure was going to be turned into a *Drag Race* Lifetime Achievement Award.

TOM CAMPBELL: I remember driving away after the first show on that second day having this out-of-body experience. I was thinking, that will never cut together.

CHRIS MCKIM: Ru didn't watch cuts until we locked them. So when he first saw the first episodes, one of the exciting things that he said was that it was the first time he had really seen himself in that way and that was so exciting. He had seen performance video, he had done *Starrbooty* where he's acting in drag, but he'd never really seen Ru in drag. He'd never seen his personality, himself, RuPaul the person, in the getup. You always want to surprise Ru.

In the second episode, destiny was not on Tammie Brown's side when she wound up on Akashia's team to perform Destiny's Child's "Independent Women" with BeBe and Jade. Her outfit was as ill fitted as the song choice for the quirky, film-star-inspired queen, and she ended up on the bottom with Akashia lip syncing to Michelle Williams's "We Break the Dawn."

BEBE ZAHARA BENET: Tammie had some issues with how Akashia was leading the group. I could see Tammie being a little bit uncomfortable about what we had to do. I don't know if we were as coordinated as we wanted to be. During the performance, I had no idea her top was falling down. I was too busy trying to catch that move and remember the choreography.

TAMMIE BROWN: I just pretended that I was Janet Jackson and I was at the Super Bowl. I was a fish out of water, perhaps. The sound thing is dripping down your back, slipping down, and wearing a stupid wig that is just not my style. It wasn't my living end.

SHANNEL: Previous to the lip sync, I think we had all been outside, maybe smoking a cigarette or something, and I remember feeling like

Tammie had been talking about the fact that she just didn't care and she didn't like the song. I remember her saying, "I don't care. If I go home, I go home."

BEBE ZAHARA BENET: It makes more sense now because when I look at Tammie I don't know if she is that kind of individual that thrives in a group setting. She is so specific in what she does and how she presents herself and I think it was probably a challenge being in a group.

TAMMIE BROWN: There was all this pressure of learning the girl group number, of making all those costumes. It's not a cakewalk and it's not a beautiful thing. I was done. I didn't want to do that song. It's not my kind of music. I didn't care. I'd already been a seasoned entertainer.

ONGINA: It was really sad to see her give up and just stop trying. And I didn't realize until after watching the episode that she said she wasn't going to do it anyway if she was on the bottom two, which is really sad. I feel like this was really outside of her element. She gave really good television, though.

MERLE GINSBERG: I remember her falling apart and kind of falling flat on her face. We knew she was really trying and she had a good shtick...She was trying to be Bette Davis. This whole eye rolling and 1950s googly-eyed. There was something kind of weird, classic old Hollywood about it that was a lot of fun.

TOM CAMPBELL: In the first season, I wanted the queen with the eyebrows, I want Tammie Brown. I will never forget that face for as long as I live. And I fought for her. So when she threw her lip sync, it was a sad moment. But it was memorable.

JOEY NOLFI: She beats to her own drummer. You cannot tell Tammie Brown what to do. I think that Tammie Brown and *Drag Race* were not a match for each other. I'm glad that it brought Tammie into my life but I don't know that Tammie Brown is cut out for someone else's reality TV show. She needs "The Tammie Brown Show." That's what she needs.

CHRIS MCKIM: Tammie is a queen among queens. I can't remember if it's in the show or not, but Ru told her to go back to her planet as part of the sashay away. In the most loving way.

The third week of *RuPaul's Drag Race* gifted the world an epic lip sync to Whitney Houston's "Greatest Love of All." It also gave viewers the Greatest Headdress Controversy of All in a lip-sync battle royale between Shannel and Akashia.

SHANNEL: I didn't feel overly comfortable in the Oprah challenge so it didn't surprise me that I was in the bottom, which is why I knew that the outfit I chose to wear on the runway had to be amazing and over the top and I felt like that was going to be my saving grace. The goal was to wear something that nobody would ever forget. Back then nobody had breastplates, and I had one. And I had that Medusa outfit.

NINA FLOWERS: Obviously, she didn't do as well as she could in the Oprah challenge, but then she came out with this freaking outfit made out of serpents, that Medusa costume. That shit was amazing. That was a true Vegas showgirl. We were all in awe when that bitch started putting herself together in the werkroom.

SHANNEL: I knew that they needed to see humility and I knew that I had to essentially prove myself to them, so in the middle of the song I jumped up and let the headdress come off. It had already been on for hours and I was sweating and I was uncomfortable and I thought what better way to shed myself and show how humble I can be in this expensive outfit than to just let everything go. It weighed about ten pounds and I had so much sweat dripping down my stomach. I jumped up and the Velcro loosened itself and it just came off. And it was the best feeling in the world because it was hurting my back 'cause it was so heavy.

TOM CAMPBELL: At the time, you could not convince me that that was a stunt. I thought it just happened and it changed my life.

NINA FLOWERS: Ohhh hellll no, honey. That's a lie. That shit fell off because she jumped and, whoops, it fell out. That's the truth. We all know, honey! We all know, that wasn't meant purposefully.

BEBE ZAHARA BENET: You have to take her at her word because I don't know if it's an accident or not.

CHRIS MCKIM: If it was an accident and she saved it or if it's a stunt, god bless her. I think it's gold either way.

ONGINA: No, bitch, you jumped and it came off! And then you became vulnerable because then, yes, she took it off—the whole thing. She took it off, she performed her heart out. I think that part was where we saw Shannel being vulnerable. Like, *I don't give a shit, this lip sync is mine, I'm going to do it after my headpiece came off.* But if we're discussing specifically if the headpiece falling off from the start was planned, I don't believe that one bit.

NINA FLOWERS: It's not how you fall; it's how you pick yourself up. And she did amazingly. But I think that in her head, Shannel is a perfectionist. The only thing I see her lacking is vulnerability.

CHRIS MCKIM: If that's something that she worked out, I think she is an even bigger star than I thought she was.

TOM CAMPBELL: That was a thousand years ago and my chest is full of feelings right now.

REBECCA GLASSCOCK: There are some people that want to be in control of everything that they do and say and there are people incapable of saying I made a mistake. She went with the flow, which is also kinda cool and genius when you own it.

SHANNEL: I didn't tell the judges I did it on purpose because that would have been way too planned. I can't change the way anybody feels. Only I know the truth because I was in the situation and it was my decision.

One of the season's most indelible images is Ongina's tearful acceptance speech when she learned she was following in RuPaul's footsteps and becoming the face of MAC's Viva Glam public charity campaign for AIDS/HIV. During the challenge, the queens wrote a commercial for their own Viva Glam campaign and had ten minutes to perform it. When Ongina was declared the winner, she revealed she was living with HIV, a poignant moment that gave the series unexpected depth.

ONGINA: I was really excited, not only because it was something that really hit close to home, but it was a challenge where I could really be myself. Nobody knew on set, with the exception of two main producers because I had to write in my application what medications I was taking. I told them I didn't want anyone to know. But this was a chance for me to show I live my life being HIV-positive. And knowing that MAC Viva Glam donates their proceeds to helping with the fight against HIV/AIDS, it all connected to me very personally.

REBECCA GLASSCOCK: For me, that was a hard challenge because I was dealing with a friend of mine who was HIV-positive but was not taking care of himself and was drinking and drugging himself to death. And there was a very legitimate worry in my mind and in my heart that this person was gonna go out with a bang in their own terms and they weren't going to let the HIV take them out. They were going to drink and party their way out. I was going through that at that moment and doing the challenge, that really triggered that for me, it really hit home for me. So I walked off set.

BEBE ZAHARA BENET: Everybody was very open prior to this episode but we did not really know who Rebecca was because she excluded herself from those downtime moments when we could just be together. So when all of a sudden, there was this emotional part and she walked off, it was hard to believe it was real then. I wish I had known her more in that moment.

ONGINA: I felt some panic wondering how am I going to do this commercial without letting anybody know that I'm experiencing this exact thing in my life? I didn't want everybody to know. My parents didn't know yet. So I went with the route of celebrating life because that is what happened in 2006 when I finally decided, enough with the bullshit, enough with beating myself down, it's time to celebrate my life. I wanted to bring that into the commercial and I wanted it to be lighthearted. I wanted it to have the message of being free of complications or sickness or sometimes depression. I wanted it to really have the essence of life being celebrated. Balloons, party, celebration. It was all in my notes.

BEBE ZAHARA BENET: Prior to the show, my extended family did not even know what I did for work. So if I ever came out in terms of my artistry and presenting it to the world, it had to be in the best light and it had to be on the best platform. So when I came to *Drag Race* that was really where my focus was—showing the beauty of diversity because I don't feel like in the past I saw that representation. It's not sufficient to be an artist and say look at how beautiful I am. What are you doing with the platform? What are you doing to move humanity forward? I felt this was a special moment to shed light about culture, about my country and some of the hardships that it's facing. Here in America, you have all these resources when it comes to HIV, but at home that didn't exist. I remember saying, "I can do this, we can do this, can you do this?"

ONGINA: She really took it to an emotional place, surrounded by people in Africa that are impacted by HIV and AIDS. I thought that it was such a beautiful message. And so when we were on the judging panel, I really thought she was going to win. But I wasn't sad or anything. I was really proud of my message. And then I won, and it was so crazy because all of these emotions, from my toes to my hair particles, took over me. I was so incredibly proud of what I had done, especially being HIV-positive. All the emotion organically pushed out these words to say why I was so happy and why I was crying happy tears onstage for winning this specific challenge that is so personal to me. And I finally came out with the status onstage because I just was overwhelmed with emotion.

CHRIS MCKIM: It was very emotional. It wasn't the shock. It was just the emotion and the rawness.

NINA FLOWERS: By then, we had already bonded with each other. But this was something that came out of nowhere and it was a surprise to everybody. It was very inspiring how she had the courage to put that out there in the world, something so personal. But at the same time, the challenge was so close to her heart because of what it meant. That in itself was very inspiring. Everybody on that set, even the camera-people, were bursting into tears.

SHANNEL: It was a beautiful moment. I think we were all shocked. And it showed a lot of vulnerability. It was the first true, heartfelt moment on the show and it showed who everybody was as a person and as a character. She had always appeared so bubbly and so talkative and vibrant and all these things. And then to break down and shed all of that, it was a beautiful thing.

REBECCA GLASSCOCK: We had no idea she was HIV-positive. It was a shock to everybody onstage. It was a shock to Ru. In fact, it was a shock to her. Ongina wasn't planning on dropping that bomb. It felt like she had a spiritual awakening. And I am so happy that I was able to be there. It changed my perspective. I was all boo-hoo my friend is gonna die and all this other stuff and here's this chick saying no, I'm gonna live and I'm gonna do drag and be happy.

RANDY BARBATO: That was so intense. Everybody was crying, and it was so embarrassing in a way. You're in a room with people crying in the dark and no one is talking and no one is looking at each other.

ONGINA: And then fast-forward to that evening, I remember two of the main producers coming to my hotel room and they're like, we're so proud of you, and asked if that's not something I want to expose. I had signed a waiver obviously that they can film and use whatever they want but it was a courtesy conversation to make sure I felt good about it. That made me feel really good because I knew they were going to use it for good. I'm so happy that I did because it lifted this weight off of my shoulders and then it also helped me tell my mom.

NINA FLOWERS: We have seen in every single season those personal experiences that we all have had and are super important to bringing to light because those are the moments that help other people feel inspired or move forward or conquer their fears if they are going through a really hard moment. That's inspiring. And I think it definitely has become an important aspect of *RuPaul's Drag Race*.

MERLE GINSBERG: I'm sure it seemed when people were watching that we knew that was coming. No one knew. We did not know. I started crying. It was really moving. That's the thing about the show. It's hilarious, it's camp, and it goes to the heart of who RuPaul is, but there is a lot of heart, a lot of emotion and acceptance and people learning about accepting people who are different from who they are. That was always at the bottom of everything.

JOHN POLLY: I remember her hard-crying because it was so guttural and so real to her. The way she was crying was not planned. There was something freeing that was happening to her and something a little scary and powerful. She was going somewhere she didn't expect to go. It was really powerful to watch. It took the show somewhere else besides just a campy competition.

FENTON BAILEY: Unlike Ru, who is very in touch with his past and his feelings, people like myself tend to bury all that stuff—the trauma, the bullying, all that stuff. In some respects, drag is a great way to avoid that. The whole point of drag is you are masking the pain so I never anticipated that these kinds of revelations would be such a key part of the show. To be able to access that is something Ru does superlatively well.

BEBE ZAHARA BENET: That was when we really got to feel something that was very human. And it wasn't just about Ongina. The whole challenge felt very connected to humanity. When you see it at home, you can identify with us as human beings and not just these characters. We have stories that are very similar to your story, so you can relate to us as people.

One week Ongina soared with her balloons for Viva Glam, the next she sashayed away. TV fans had not seen BeBe Zahara Benet lip sync for her life yet, but by the end of Britney Spears's "Stronger," her wig was off, she was on one knee onstage, and she had established herself as a real contender for the crown.

BEBE ZAHARA BENET: When I was doing "Stronger" with Ongina, my wig was about to come off and I was like, oh you are not about to get me so I took it off. I was the first person to take off their wig on the show. You are getting in my way, you gotta go. I was in my zone. I was doing my own thing. I didn't even know Ongina was there.

ONGINA: During that lip sync for your life, I gave really awful looks toward BeBe. I think I froze. I like to put energy into creating a visual performance for the words of the song and I didn't feel stronger. I got so nervous and I performed in one spot because of my shoes. BeBe outperformed me and I was happy for her. We were close during the competition. That's why I hugged her. After we performed, Ru had to leave set for like thirty minutes. We were just standing there looking at each other like, what's happening? I think at one point I sat down onstage and waited.

CHRIS MCKIM: Although Ru says, "I've conferred with my lawyer, my gardener, my housekeepers," we were the housekeepers and the janitors that Ru conferred with. We all went into the back room or into Ru's dressing room, which looked like a drag closet from one of the audition tapes because it was so tiny. Ru likes to decorate but there was no furniture to rearrange or anywhere to put it. And we went in there to evaluate the performance.

NINA FLOWERS: When Ongi went home, that was very sad. Ongi was the light of the cast. She would always bring happiness into the room. At first, I remember when people from the production would come to the hotel to pick us up at the Ramada in Burbank, she would always sit in the front and just be reading a book and very quiet. It wasn't until episode 3 when Akashia went home that she started loosening up and actually coming into herself. But I personally always identified with her.

SHANNEL: Elimination day was always sad because we were all tense. When you're in that moment and you've been filming for so many hours and you're tired and you're mentally exhausted, it all becomes overwhelming. And then feelings that you don't even realize you have just come out of you. You spend so much time with these people, good or bad, and you're competing yet you start developing actual friendships with these people and you look at it as a sisterhood. So you don't want to see anybody go, but you know eventually everyone does.

BEBE ZAHARA BENET: It was very hard for me finally when she had to go because I loved her. We had connected. That was a little sad moment for me because I wished she could have stayed.

VALENTINA: When I was a senior, *Drag Race* was on already. My dance instructor, Mr. Kenny Long, was watching it. During class one day, I was feeling myself and my teacher was saying, "Go, Ongina, go!" And I was over here thinking what do you mean, go, Ongina, go? That sounds like vagina, why are you calling me that? And then he began to tell us that there is this new show called *RuPaul's Drag Race*, and that it is a fabulous show about drag queens and this and that. There were a lot of queer students at my performing arts school in Hollywood so I checked out an episode to see what this Ongina situation was about. It caught my eye.

ONGINA: I still believe till this day that it was the right decision. I don't think I was going to be America's Next Drag Superstar. I probably would have made it top three but I don't know if I would be the chosen one.

CHRIS MCKIM: This might have been around the time Ru stopped saying "moose cock." In Season 1, the grand prize was basically a gift basket of love. For a great deal of the shooting, we didn't know what the prize was. Logo was working on the prize package. And so while we were filming, Ru says, "The grand prize," right? But for the longest time we didn't know what it was so instead of saying the amount, Ru would say "Moose cock."

TOM CAMPBELL: Moose cock! That was all Ru. What was that joke?

CHRIS MCKIM: Ru came into our little cubby one day and said he heard a great joke. There are these two hillbillies sitting on a porch and they're playing twenty questions and the one guy asks, "Is it bigger than a bread box?" Yes. "Can I stick it in my mouth?" No. "Is it moose cock?" Ru told this joke and his head exploded. He looked like Violet Beauregarde when she turns into the blueberry. When Ru laughs on the fourth floor, you hear it through the whole building. And he couldn't breathe for the longest time. Moose cock became the substitute for telling the queens what the prize was.

It only took three more episodes for another Shantroversy to surface. When RuPaul polled the queens about who should go home that week, Shannel chose herself. In her mind, that meant she quit. In RuPaul's, it was time for her to lip sync for her life again. This time, she performed "Shackles (Praise You)" against her nemesis Rebecca Glasscock.

SHANNEL: I had already made the decision. I was frustrated, I was tired, and I was irritated. I felt like nothing I'm gonna do is gonna be good enough and there is no reason for me to be here anymore. I knew, without a shadow of a doubt, that I was going to go home. I did not want to be there anymore at all. I remember my mouth dried up from nerves and anxiety and it was hard to talk, but I felt like I had made up my mind and it was what I wanted to do and I really did not care what anybody else thought.

RANDY BARBATO: Shannel is complicated. I was crushed but not surprised. That is her genius. To this day we are avid fans. Did you see the YouTube footage of Shannel's house decorated for Christmas? It makes me love her. She is a flawless queen.

BEBE ZAHARA BENET: It was a surprise because it was a different side of her I had not seen. I had always known her to be somebody grandiose and somebody of self-confidence, and very aware of their presentation. When she said she wanted to go because she wasn't acknowledged or celebrated as she would have loved to be, I didn't know that was such an issue. They told Rebecca she was beautiful. They didn't tell me that. But I was okay. I know better. I am serrrrrving. I just had that inner confidence in me where I did not need that validation.

NINA FLOWERS: It was one shocker after another and very sad when she said she didn't want to be here anymore. Shannel had already given up. I can understand why. The thing is that television, specifically reality TV, works in a very interesting way. She came in really put together with all her years of experience and her Vegas background and all the amazing costumes, probably the best costumes in the entire cast. She couldn't handle criticism well. She would always defend herself or try to justify anything that happened to her. We do take a lot and the pressure got to her. Shannel would have easily been top three of that season.

SHANNEL: I felt like nothing was working. Everything that I do and everything I know how to do, they were shutting it down. People that have done drag for a fraction of the time that I've done drag are winning challenges over me, so what's the point? I don't want to be made a fool. I could be making more money at home doing my shows. I want to sleep in my own bed. When I'm done, I'm just done.

NINA FLOWERS: I really believe that Ru had high hopes for Shannel. Ru knew the quality of entertainer that Shannel was. It's just that Shannel needed to be reminded constantly and that's not how it works. Even though she said she wanted to go home, Ru was like "No, mama, it doesn't work that way. You have to lip sync." I think a big part of it was that Ru still wanted to have Shannel turn it around.

BEBE ZAHARA BENET: I can see younger artists coming in and not knowing how to deal with judges' critiques. But someone who has been in the business for such a long time, has owned their show and been part of the scene, I feel like would have more backbone and strength to say, okay, well that's your opinion and it's what it is. At the end of the day, she was still there. Ru didn't send her away. That means you are meant to still be there. If she had stuck it out, I think she would have made it to top three.

VICTORIA "PORKCHOP" PARKER: I love Shannel but I think Shannel is the type of person who would quit the show before she lost the show.

SHANNEL: I literally don't even remember lip syncing with Rebecca. I guess I blocked it out. I remember feeling very embarrassed when I watched it because I felt like a failure that I was leaving. And I have never watched it ever again.

REBECCA GLASSCOCK: Since the beginning, I knew that Shannel was going to give me a run for my money. She was going to be tough competition. She was there to slay. She was there to win. But I was there to win, too, and I don't give up easy. For me, the performance was the easy part because that song was right up my alley because I'm a very spiritual person and I'm very connected to God and the song is about God and faith. And when I was doing the song, I was living it, I was breathing it, and I was performing it as if I was performing it inside of a church.

BEBE ZAHARA BENET: I thought Shannel was doing a great job lip syncing "Shackles" until she pulled up her dress and shook her ass to a gospel song. I just felt like that was a part that was not needed. But I don't think that that had anything to do with the decision that RuPaul made. That was just me watching the lip sync. She was doing so great and then all the sudden she pulls it up and twerks. Noooo, don't!

And just like that, *Drag Race* had its first top three. Merle and Santino broke the news to BeBe, Nina, and Rebecca that for their final challenge they would need to do a group dance, record a verse for RuPaul's "Cover Girl (Put the Bass in Your Walk)" with rapper Cazwell, and film a solo for Ru's video.

BEBE ZAHARA BENET: I was feeling great. We were almost done. Prior to *Drag Race*, I was already in the studio working on music. I don't think that people know that music is such a huge part of who I am. I grew up writing and conducting the choir and singing. So when we had that opportunity to perform and do the music video, I was like yesssss! The whole thing was sick.

MANDY SALANGSANG: Then comes time for the sit-down with Ru and it's a good sit-down. It's twenty-five to thirty minutes. It means a lot and it's a milestone in the competition, of course, to have reached that point. There is so much gleaned from that. It is an opportunity for them to really connect and be seen. Of course, that's been happening throughout the competition but reaching that point, that milestone, means a lot to them and it means a lot to RuPaul.

REBECCA GLASSCOCK: Having the one-on-one lunch date with Ru was memorable and amazing and we got to find out how she stays so thin. It's because she is on the Tic Tac diet!

BEBE ZAHARA BENET: It was very minty. That was the one time in the whole adventure that we had the opportunity to really sit and have a conversation. It didn't feel like there were cameras around. It was just having a conversation with somebody that you look up to or somebody that inspires you. It was very special.

REBECCA GLASSCOCK: The finale was a blur. It was a lot. I didn't know what it was like to be in a music video. I didn't know what it was like to write music. I didn't know what it was like to sing in a professional studio. So I was way out of my league with everything that was happening. I just put my best foot forward and I winged it and I did the best that I could.

NINA FLOWERS: Oh man, it was awesome. I enjoyed that so much. It was great because we were wearing the mechanic jumpsuits but our aesthetics were really shining. Rebecca gave us the teenage girl. BeBe gave us her African heritage. She brought that international flavor with the big hair. I brought my ponytail and my punk aesthetic. I thought it was perfect. The choreography thing went so well for BeBe and me. Rebecca struggled a little bit on that one. And she was having issues. That last episode didn't work in her favor.

BEBE ZAHARA BENET: I remember Rebecca got eliminated and Nina and I hugged each other and we just whispered, "Let's give them a show." And that's why when you watch that lip sync, even today, you will see us performing with each other as opposed to against each other because it was such a sisterhood. There was so much respect. And if Nina was pronounced the winner, I would have been just completely 100 percent happy for her. I had so much love for Nina, so we were just performing and letting RuPaul decide whatever that was.

REBECCA GLASSCOCK: People ask me whether I thought I should have been the winner. My response has always been the person who won was the one that was supposed to be the winner. I also am extremely grateful that I didn't win because I was extremely young and when you win a show like that, the fame and everything that happens afterward, I don't think that's what I needed in my life at that moment. BeBe is number one and she deserved it.

CHRIS MCKIM: When you think about people in bars watching these shows and getting excited or watching at home and cheering, we watch that thing live on six cameras at once. So all of the lip syncs are very exciting. The energy is always very high.

RANDY BARBATO: Much of what goes on surprises us. None of us would be stupid enough to predict where it's going to end. I would have thought Shannel was going to win it.

VICTORIA "PORKCHOP" PARKER: Nina had more wins and was the challenge favorite going into that final lip sync. I just think it came down to who RuPaul decided she wanted to represent the title the first season. I think that Nina would have been a better choice because Nina was more of an out-of-the-ordinary queen at that point. Both of them were phenomenal performers and both of them were very creative people. Nina was most people's favorite. That's who most people thought should win.

TOM CAMPBELL: I think either one of them could have won. They were just both hitting their stride. I love them both deeply.

BOB THE DRAG QUEEN: I was inspired by BeBe Zahara Benet, who seemed to embody everything that I was ever told was a detriment to me—being Black, being queer, being loud, being rambunctious. And she was being told on TV that all these things were actually great.

They were actually lovely things, and they could help you win $25,000 and the adoration of your peers. I was instantly hooked and I was like, well, I think I would like to be a part of a community that does that.

NINA FLOWERS: I think BeBe beat me because of her gown. She was very glamorous. Her lip sync was also awesome. She threw herself on the floor and did her little thing, which showed that just because she was in an evening gown didn't mean she didn't work for it. I was doing cartwheels on one side, so she knew she had to bring it. So she went on the floor, and I was like okay, she got it. When you're lip syncing in front of the judges and you see that your opponent is stealing most of the looks and they are paying more attention to what she is doing than what you're doing, you have to come to terms with it's not your time. I felt that but I was totally okay with it because she is a ferocious competitor. And we created such a great bond and I was happy for her. I knew she deserved it as much as I did.

BEBE ZAHARA BENET: I think I screamed a little bit instead of crying when I was pronounced the winner because that's when it actually made sense. That's when it dawned on me—I won the show, an African won the show, a Black person won. There was just so much in that whole situation. A global girl won the show.

So naturally, the global queen collapsed. And Nina's sisterly love took over as she kept coaxing her to rise: "*Loca*, get up!"

CHRIS MCKIM: It was probably a little tense because we probably had to get out of that building before they were going to charge us more.

MERLE GINSBERG: She came from, as Ru would say, Cameroooooon. And apparently it's a strict place. It's not a place where they would appreciate the persona. So we were very emotional for her because we knew that she came from a place where nobody does drag and she had to completely take a huge chance doing it.

BEBE ZAHARA BENET: Where I come from, your parents send you to America because they want you to come to school and make a better life for yourself and be able to really enrich your life. And a lot of times when it comes to African families, it's about getting all these degrees. But when it comes to the arts, they don't get the same respect. So being in that moment where I came on a television show and my hard work paid off. And I thought about another little boy that can see it back at home and say if BeBe can do it, then I can do it. Whatever I want to be I can do it, because look at BeBe making it to the next level. It was like graduating with honors.

Months after the show ended production, RuPaul, the judges, and nine queens gathered for what turned out to be the season's most explosive episode. "Re-united!" brought out the worst in almost everyone who attended and featured hostile words between Rebecca and Jade, Rebecca and Shannel, RuPaul and Tammie Brown, and Shannel and Santino Rice.

SHANNEL: It was a dark room with very little lighting and a lot of tension.

MERLE GINSBERG: I was a bit nervous because your job is to sit there and critique them and then suddenly they are critiquing you and you don't know it's coming. It's like whoa I should've been a bit nicer. But I wasn't that worried because I was fair and nice. I was never brutal. I think Santino might have been worried.

NINA FLOWERS: It was super uncomfortable. Being on a reality show and not understanding the dynamics of reality TV and how it works, it was challenging. It is hard to accept the harsh critiques. But the show was over and we filmed that reunion so many months after. You would think that people had gotten over those feelings.

BEBE ZAHARA BENET: I didn't know how much grievances existed. I know each person had certain feelings about stuff, but I did not know it was to that extent.

TAMMIE BROWN: I said the number one line of all time: "I don't see you out there walking children in nature and taking care of old ladies." But they edited it and took out the old ladies. I was volunteering here in Los Angeles once a month with one of my friends at this organization where you walk inner-city kids from the concrete jungle in nature. And I've had my boyfriends, my straight friends, ask me why I'm always hanging out with all old ladies. I like to engage and I listen and I'm not an ageist and I like being around older people because you learn so much more. That's why I said that, but people are not quite listening the right way.

FENTON BAILEY: You must put that in the book. You must reclaim "and helping old ladies."

JOHN POLLY: I don't think I would've ever seen the uncut version. But that sounds right. She might have thrown in some orcas, too.

JOEY NOLFI: That's my favorite *Drag Race* quote of all time. I don't see you walking children in nature, which Ru later did on the poster for *AJ and the Queen*, literally walked a child in nature.

VICTORIA "PORKCHOP" PARKER: When she said that to RuPaul, I remember looking at her like, what the hell did you say? It took me years to figure out exactly what she said. It really makes you think, wow, what type of nut is this who can come up with that off the top of their head?

ONGINA: I can explain because Tammie and I had a two-woman show called "Tammie Brown's Walking Ongina in Nature." It's basically a roller-coaster ride in Tammie's brain. Nature is Tammie's brain and children is just us walking all around in it. And we are just part of this journey in her little brain and you just have to accept it. I have been enjoying the walk in nature with Tammie for a few years now. And everyone should just sit down, buckle up, and enjoy it just as much as I have because, honey, let me tell you, I wouldn't change Tammie one bit.

REBECCA GLASSCOCK: I would walk in nature with Tammie except I'm not super fond of kids and I don't like snakes, bears, wolves, or mountain lions, or anything that can crawl or jump and attack me and harm me in any way. So while she's walking children in nature, I'll wait for her by the pool and I'll work on my tan.

MERLE GINSBERG: That was hilarious! I felt bad for Tammie. If I was in Tammie's shoes, I would've felt pretty bad. But Tammie had to understand the rules of the game. And Tammie probably won lot of contests in her natural habitat but she was up against the best in the world so she found herself surprised that she wasn't top dog.

TAMMIE BROWN: Ru got all enraged. And I was like, oh, please, they're not gonna show this 'cause she's all everybody say love, ya know? So to start cussing at us, you're not supposed to cuss on TV. That's gonna get bleeped out. So I said, "Excuse your mouth." And I trail-blazed with that. I'm always getting now compliments on that.

SHANNEL: I think that it's a natural inclination to want to know what people think of you. I know I'm a Cancer so as a Cancer I am naturally a very emotionally based person. And I'm a caretaker. I know that the way in which people feel about me and toward me is very important to me because I don't like confrontation. I'm a people pleaser. I think taking words of wisdom from Ru is a wonderful and a great thing but it doesn't necessarily mean that for Tammie it was the end-all, be-all.

MERLE GINSBERG: I understand the philosophy of being support-ive of our community but hello, we're on reality TV, it's supposed to be funny. It's supposed to be a little shocking. There is supposed to be drama and you just know that. You can't really hold back.

NINA FLOWERS: It was really uncomfortable, watching Tammie

Brown and Ru because I felt at some point that Tammie really got on Ru's nerves. I don't know Ru that well but you could tell by her facial expressions that she was angry and that she was uncomfortable.

RANDY BARBATO: Tammie didn't get what she needed from Ru. And I think at the end of the day what Ru says is what it's all about: This show is not here to make any of them full. We are not here to fix any of them. We are here to provide a platform and an opportunity and support and visibility and celebrate their artistry.

RUPAUL: Drag starts from the inside out—the way you carry yourself and the confidence that you have and how you hold your body. These kids who were teased when they were little had to learn how to nurture the hero inside. In fact, in that reunion show I had to reiterate that you've already won: The fact that you've understood that you can change your life and the way people see you—that is a spell you can cast at any moment. All these kids know that, whether they can articulate or not. They know they hold the power—and that's the secret of a drag queen.

SHANNEL: Ru's goal obviously is to always be able to mentor and to try to teach lessons and to impart wisdom on a situation, but that doesn't mean that everybody is going to take that wisdom. It doesn't mean that his teachings are correct. It is simply the way in which he has guided his life and the ways in which he has learned.

NINA FLOWERS: What people think of me is none of my business. Those are really wise words. I wish someone would have told me that when I was young and starting out. That really resonated with me.

BEBE ZAHARA BENET: Sometimes as artists we forget who we are. A lot of times we are seeking validation when we don't need that validation. You can be inspired but you don't need that validation.

RUPAUL: Because of what happened in that reunion episode, someone transcribed that speech when I went off on Tammie and I thought, *Oh my gosh, this is great! This is a song!* And that song turned into "Responsitrannity" and it ended up being the theme song to *All Stars*. When you listen to that song, you'll hear all the lyrics are lifted from that—"it's your responsibility to remember who you are. We are all stars."

VICTORIA "PORKCHOP" PARKER: It felt like RuPaul was really getting sick of hearing these queens complain about the opportunity they had been given because they were complaining about such minuscule things. They were thinking very small-mindedly about the comments and the critiques and impressions. So I think that's what RuPaul was trying to get into their heads: "Look at this opportunity you've been given, it doesn't matter what was said to you, it matters how you deal with it now because there's the arena, go work it."

RUPAUL: When I went off in the reunion show, I wasn't talking to those girls. I was talking to me. I need to remind myself on a daily basis of what I'm working with and not to be distracted by what the newspapers or TV or media or my next-door neighbor has to say about how to approach life. The truth is we are all co-creators with whatever force created this world so we have to remember that. That speech I gave the girls, I need to hear all the time because I forget.

JOEY NOLFI: Season 1 feels the most organic because they are doing it the only way they knew how. There was no standard in terms of pure work experience for Ru but also there is no other show like this for queer people. That clash between Ru and Tammie is significant because that's how this family talks to each other in the wild, per se. They lay it all out. They get their feelings out. You fight with your family and then you're good and Tammie is back for *All Stars*.

RANDY BARBATO: I think so much of what *Drag Race* became you could see in those moments. I think we underestimated, even back then in Season 1, the connection people would have with the show and how that would translate not only to its popularity but to its impact on the queens. We know it has a positive impact often on their career and on their celebrity but the intensity of that fan connection clearly can be not positive for them.

CARSON KRESSLEY: When it came out, it was immediately a hit within the LGBTQ community and, in Season 1 and 2, friends were already having viewing parties at their house and you would go to their house and see the show since not everyone had Logo.

BEBE ZAHARA BENET: I always tell people that I am so happy I did Season 1. It was very raw. You can hate it, you can like it, but it showed the blueprint of what it needed to be. It had heart and it had fun, regardless of the quality of production. That representation was exactly what it was, how we experienced it there. The stories we told were our stories. And whether you like us or you love us or you hate who we are, it was authentic.

NINA FLOWERS: No matter what people say about Season 1, mama, Season 1 is Season 1! Hello! The one that started it all, okay? I don't care what they say about the filter or about the prizes, or the low budget, whatever, Mami, we had to start somewhere and we were the ones who set the trend.

Chapter 2
SEASON 2

W HEN *RUPAUL'S DRAG RACE* RETURNED TO LOGO FOR ITS SECOND cycle, everything about the show was supersized. Production had moved to an expansive, colorful space in Culver City with two soundstages and a bigger werkroom that featured a two-way mirror for optimal viewing as the queens transformed for challenges. The judges' table gained star power week to week as Hollywood stars, such as Kathy Griffin and Debbie Reynolds, joined RuPaul, Santino, and Merle in front of the runway. And, *halleloo*, there were more queens.

Close friends Raven and Morgan McMichaels, already popular in Los Angeles drag circles, were ecstatic to compete together. Veteran New York drag artist Pandora Boxx was the series' first legit comedy queen. Mystique Summers dropped jaws with her splits and gagged viewers when she yelled, "Bitch, I'm from Chicago!" at Morgan McMichaels during the very first *Untucked* fight. There was also Southern diva Nicole Paige Brooks, sweet Puerto Rican queen Jessica Wild, and ballerina Sahara Davenport, who dazzled en pointe during her lip syncs. (Sahara died from heart failure in 2012.) Drag newbies Jujubee and Shangela charmed viewers with their wit and bottomless energy; Sonique stunned with her athleticism and beauty. Tatianna became the season's tart-tongued pretty face, and self-proclaimed "America's sweetheart" Tyra Sanchez took home the crown.

It was also a season of firsts: Pandora Boxx broke ground with the show's first entrance catchphrase, "Hey, fake ladies!" Shangela kicked off the tradition of writing goodbye messages on the mirror with red lipstick. Sonique revealed she is a trans woman in the reunion episode. And Snatch Game and the Reading Challenge became institutions.

CHRIS MCKIM: It was glorious. Season 2: Ru and Improved.

RUPAUL: It's funny when you see something on TV or when you're able to stand back and look at it, you're able to see what rhythm is emerging. Once we got to see the first season, that rhythm that it is now became quite clear. The first season felt like a pilot and then in the second season we understood what the show really was and what we wanted it to be.

TOM CAMPBELL: We were so happy to be back. We had a little bit more money. It was physically and visually a very different show, but I do think that the heart of it remained very much the same.

RANDY BARBATO: My personal obsession was upping the production value. But what a cast of stars! So many of our big ones were on Season 2.

MERLE GINSBERG: We shot in the summer and I couldn't wait to spend the summer again with these people. I just loved them all and I had so much fun with them. We moved to Culver City in a much better studio and with better food. Everything was better.

RUPAUL: In Season 1, we really had to reintroduce drag to the world because the world had become held hostage by our love of fear and hysteria. When fear and hysteria happens in a culture, gender issues have to take a back seat. So we did a cross section of what the collective consciousness knows about drag. All of the girls in the first season represented a distinct faction of drag. In Season 2, we were able to mix it up a little bit more and go younger and go a little edgier.

JOEY NOLFI: We were seeing the show come into its own a little bit more in terms of realizing they can really build a self-sustaining economy with these stars that they're producing. You see the introduction of something like Snatch Game, comedy challenges, more acting challenges, and a longer season. The show is realizing that the gem here, in addition to Ru, are these stars going out in the world. You're seeing the show complementing itself by tailoring the challenges to what the queens will need to do outside the show to have a successful career and carry on the name of the franchise. It was a really, really smart idea to lean into that because then I think you see it even more in Season 3 and especially then in 4 and 5, I think the show had finally found its groove of molding these queens to be successful outside the show. That's something you don't see a lot of reality shows doing.

RAVEN: When I walked in and I saw the werkroom and the main stage, I said, oh, they got the money now. I was glad I made it on this season and not Season 1. I make fun of Ru because when you watch Season 1 and you see him walk in to go meet the queens, he is so taken aback by them and he's looking for his mark on the floor. And he stands on it and he puts one foot and then the other and is just staring at them like [gasp] wow, you're here. So even from little things like that, this show has come so far.

PANDORA BOXX: After waiting like six hours in a tiny closet with only a chair and nothing else in it, all white walls, I went in and I was like, oh shit, a budget!

JUJUBEE: I was skipping in, like *ooooo!* I felt like I was living in sin because anything good is sinful. The first person I saw was Raven. I was like, god, this bitch is so pretty and this energy is so strong. I thought Nicole Paige Brooks was a skinny bitch with big hair and very Southern debutante. And then Shangela! Shangela was as green as me. That was exciting for me and scary as fuck.

RAVEN: It was really strange to walk into this room where you have been at the top of the drag food chain and there are other people who are that person in another city or state. It was very much leave your ego at the door; everyone is equal here.

PANDORA BOXX: To my surprise, everyone was a woman when I walked onto the set. I was like, what is happening, you guys? Everybody's in black and I'm in a pink tutu, and I'm just like, oh god, I'm the clown. Everyone literally looked like they were a woman. It was all a very similar style of drag. There was no Nina Flowers, or an Ongina or a Tammie Brown. It was all hello, we are all female impersonators. I knew comedy was going to be my way in the show but I didn't realize that I was going to be the only camp. If you listen to the music when I walk out, it's clown music.

RAVEN: Morgan and I started around the same time and we were close. I had an idea he was going to be there because we both worked together frequently, and we were going to be gone for a while at the same time. I told people I was going to film an independent movie in Florida. But people knew. In the drag community and a little sub-part of the gay community, everyone knew what was going on and everyone knew that when you see drag queens disappearing for a certain amount of time during the summer, we know where they're going.

MORGAN MCMICHAELS: Walking into the werkroom was sensory overload. It was just so colorful. The minute I walked through the door into the werkroom, all I heard was "Morgan, Morgan, Morgan!" It was so good to see Raven because I felt like I had a buddy. I felt like I had someone that was going to be there for me. And we got to experience it together, which was really something that furthered our bond. She scooped me off my feet. As feminine as she is, she is quite strong.

PANDORA BOXX: The first person that talked to me when I walked in was Shangela. And I was like, why doesn't she have any makeup on her face? She asked me if I knew how to sew, and I said yes, and she said, "You're my new friend." Okay! But actually, I really loved her. I got along with her really well so I was sad that she was gone first because she was the first person I bonded with.

TATIANNA: They walk you to set from the holding room and it's like a room built inside of a huge studio. So just being on the outside of it was like, oh this is weird. And then I walked in and I was very nervous and it seemed like there was a lot of people already inside. I looked around the room and there were some girls that I recognized from doing the online race stuff—Jujubee and Jessica Wild. That was cool.

PANDORA BOXX: I didn't really like a lot of the queens at first. I was like, oh god, this is going to be really hard because they're all really fucking annoying. Morgan and Raven were friends and they're from LA so they were very, oh we're LA. Everybody was a heightened version of themselves. Nicole Paige Brooks was just like, you know, I'm from Atlanta and I'm this and I'm that. And Tyra's first thing was, "How long are they going to make us stand here? My feet hurt." Girl, you literally just walked on the set and you've been sitting in a room. So, immediately, I thought the toughest part was going to be dealing with these people. I am not a drag queen who goes into drag queen mode and starts tongue popping and using drag queen lingo so I thought this was going to be tough.

RUPAUL: The first girls had no idea what they were getting into. They understood reality TV, but they had no idea what our show would do or the impact it would have. So by Season 2, they knew what they were in for.

SHANNEL: They had so much more money! It wasn't blurry and the stage, the set, was so much better. They had a firmer grasp and understanding of what the show was going to be at this point.

MORGAN MCMICHAELS: It was good there was more money, but I prayed for the Vaseline filter every day. If they had kept it for Season 2, I might have looked a little more human.

PANDORA BOXX: I had been looking forward to the filter 'cause it was going to make me look really young.

RAVEN: When I watched Season 1, I thought, how did they film this? Was it on an iPhone and they just uploaded it? But then I got there and I wanted that filter. Of course I did.

JOEY NOLFI: The queens expect to have this nice glow and then it's like, no, HD realness.

The challenges on *RuPaul's Drag Race* borrow from other reality and game shows and are built around RuPaul's experience as a drag queen. Since female and celebrity impersonation are staples of the art form, the producers strove to create a contest that incorporated comedic send-ups. The result was Snatch Game, a send-up of the popular '70s show *Match Game*, in which panelists tried to match answers given by celebrity panelists to fill-in-the-blank questions that were often formed as humorous double entendres. The drag version, which features drag queens impersonating celebrities, followed in the footsteps of the original to become an instant phenomenon.

TOM CAMPBELL: We shoot episodes in two days so we were trying to think of ways to put people to the test. *Match Game*, which we all grew up watching, seemed right.

CARSON KRESSLEY: I watched all the 1970s game shows. And when you were home sick from school it was *The Price Is Right* and *Joker's Wild* and *The Dating Game* and *Match Game*. And almost all of those shows have been honored on *Drag Race* in some sort of homage.

TOM CAMPBELL: *Snatch* rhymes with *match* and that's all we need—something a little nasty, a little silly, a little nonsensical. It was meant to be a one-off challenge but you get so much entertainment out of it because of the highest highs and the lowest lows. It's a great mash-up of the different generations. Someone might do Mae West and Little Edie or some crazy YouTube character. It helps us look at how celebrity has changed over the years.

MICHELE "MEESH" MILLS: In earlier days of drag, celebrity impersonation was more important. For some people, it was a way that you could get away with doing drag when it was more taboo. I think there is a lot of impersonation now but more in the aspect of let me dress up like Beyoncé while I sing to Beyoncé or lip sync to Beyoncé, not actually doing an impersonation. It still exists out there, but it is definitely far less. I know there's disagreement about whether Snatch Game should still be in, but I love it. Yes, we need to evolve with the stuff the kids are doing but part of drag is passing down the traditions to the new queens and making them at least aware of them even if they don't go out and do it in their career.

SHANNEL: In that show [*Dreamgirls* at Micky's in LA], you really had to be a character illusionist. It wasn't just about putting on makeup and a dress and going out and performing. You had to actually be impersonating celebrities.

CHRIS MCKIM: Standards and Practices wanted us to bleep the word *snatch*. I don't recall what they said exactly but they said we needed to change it because it was a reference to a woman's body part or something. I wrote an email that the challenge was like the rest of the show—where we are taking snatches or different elements of different competition shows and appropriating them. And rather than call it the Appropriation Game, it's just snappier to call it Snatch Game. Well, it was some good spin because we got to keep it and it became an institution. I was very proud of that.

NINA FLOWERS: I started out gender bender and it was very controversial. The previous artists, the ones that came before me in Puerto Rico, were all about impersonating. You had to look like either Madonna, Diana Ross, Cher, all the big icons. And I came in from the middle of nowhere doing the crazy makeup and the big hair, the mohawks and all the punk songs that nobody knew.

JOHN POLLY: Snatch Game is a strange thing because when they're shooting it, it can take a while. The queens are in a room on set with two guests, and it's a quiet room. It's a big set. There's crew standing around but it's pretty quiet. When you see it on the show, there's a laugh track, but in person there's a lot more empty spaces between the jokes. So it is tough. I would fail miserably on Snatch Game. I don't think I could do it. And the queens that get it just figure out how to live in that character and be ready. It's not about knowing factoids, although you need to know the character well. You need to come up with your version of the persona.

JUJUBEE: I didn't even understand what Snatch Game was, mama. I had no idea. I was like, let's choose somebody that you kind of look like and I chose Kimora Lee Simmons because I thought that the challenge itself was a look-alike challenge or an impersonation challenge. I now realize that it's actually a comedy challenge, and not just comedy but a comedy challenge that makes RuPaul laugh.

CARSON KRESSLEY: It's very difficult, so it really separates the queens from the *queens*. And it's nostalgic, which I don't know if the younger audience even knows. It's just very, very funny. And...the reason why *Match Game* actually worked was that you get these one-word answers that when they are jumbled out of context they become hilarious. So all of that combined with drag impersonation and Ru hosting it and the comedy of errors that can happen with the words, you get a great show.

JOHN POLLY: Ru does the most heavy lifting on Snatch Game just in the performance in and of itself. Ru is on full-on hosting mode. We write the questions. The idea when you're writing a Snatch Game question is the answer should be an obvious dumb answer that may never air but it helps you figure out what it is. There are basically four Snatch Game questions: Carson or Ross is so gay or Michelle is such a whore or did you hear about the new version of *Superman*? Or the new version of *Wizard of Oz*? It doesn't matter what the question is. It's all about the persona the queen is playing and how they respond.

RAVEN: We were told to bring celebrity impersonations. I brought

Cher and I brought Paris Hilton. Cher, I would do every once in a while and I only enjoyed doing it because I loved wearing the long hair and really carving my face out and making myself look so different. I absolutely loved Paris Hilton's album. And I have performed so many of those numbers. At the time, she was still pretty popular. I watched *Match Game* growing up so I thought it was a play on that. So I told myself, don't do Cher. Do something where you can just be safe, act like just a ditzy blonde and get through this because you had to lip sync two times already.

MORGAN MCMICHAELS: I'm from the UK so I never watched *Match Game*. But the same game show over there was called *Blankety Blank*. I'm a Pink impersonator but I only impersonate the movements and the lip sync. I had never done a live impersonation so I knew I was fucked. That's all that kept running through my mind. I didn't even think to be clever because I was just too much in my mind about picking the wrong character.

JUJUBEE: It was nerve-racking. I hate to admit this, but I looked around and I was like, okay, some of these bitches are a lot better than you, but you're not the worst. Sonique, I am so sorry but your Lady Gaga was not the tea and I love you so much. But also nobody knew who Lady Gaga was, either. About two weeks later, she was winning Grammys.

JOHN POLLY: I love Jessica Wild doing RuPaul, which was a train wreck but thoroughly entertaining.

TATIANNA: We didn't get warned about Snatch Game. So I was panicking, and because it's impersonation I thought I should probably look like the person. But all of the people that I thought I looked like, there wasn't anything funny about them. But you can make things funny as long as you know a lot about the person. I'm a die-hard Britney fan so I decided to do Britney. I made that crop top, crisscross-y thing out of hot glue and some fabric that was lying around. I did bring a fedora hat just to have an accessory and I had these little gloves. I borrowed a wig from Morgan, and I just went off of memory to do my makeup. I know that her eyes are big and kind of downturned. I tried to paint my eyes like she had it in the "Slave 4 U" video, 'cause there were a lot of close-ups there.

PANDORA BOXX: I had done that sketch comedy show, the *Gay Means Happy* show, and I created a sketch called Carol Channing Rambles because she was on the Tony Awards presenting with LL Cool J and I thought, what an odd combination of people presenting together, Carol Channing and LL Cool J. And then somehow he gets her to start dancing and she's just talking and I would literally watch a show called Carol Channing Rambles and she just sits there and talks about anything. But I didn't bring anything Carol Channing because I didn't think I was going to do her on the show. The PAs had seen the Carol skits and they thought I should do Carol. So I had to make an outfit and get some hair. I took the hair from my promo look, which had black in it. And I cut the black out and I teased up Carol's hair and it was good. She is a total persona with a great voice—that old style of Broadway character that there aren't too many of them now.

TATIANNA: I remember being stressed out about it. I had the mannerisms and I had the cigarette, I had the chewing gum, and the accent. I didn't really know how I pulled that one out of my ass, either. I had watched a lot of Britney interviews, though, because I was a fan and so I knew some of her mannerisms. They were all finding it funny, so I knew I was on a good path. In no way, shape, or form did I think I was going to win. I thought it was going to go to Pandora Boxx 'cause Pandora Boxx was hilarious. Pandora Boxx made me break character a couple of times.

PANDORA BOXX: In the moment, I realized that I shouldn't answer the questions even remotely close to what they are. I just thought of the most random things and it worked. I made Ru laugh. RuPaul laughing was everything to me. I'm next to one of my drag idols and I'm cracking his shit up. But I didn't win this one, either!

MERLE GINSBERG: Pandora Boxx was hilarious. And I remember she would come out every show and do something fabulously funny and Santino would give her a hard time. And I'd be like she's not trying to be beautiful. She's trying to be hilarious and she is.

JINKX MONSOON: In Season 1, I was adamantly against the show. I was becoming very hoity-toity about my drag. I was becoming a little stuck-up, and it caused me to be a little closed-minded about any drag that didn't seem like it was high art to me. But then I saw the Snatch Game episode in Season 2 and I did a complete 180. It changed my mind about everything I was preaching at the time. How could I be trying to fight for drag to be taken seriously if I dismiss a portion of the drag community, any portion of it? If I am going to fight for drag to be taken seriously as an art form, it has to be for all different types of drag. Watching Pandora Boxx playing Carol Channing was profound for me. Snatch Game is different types of drag queens portraying all these different types of celebrities and one of the celebrities was a celebrity I would have loved to impersonate. Everyone applauded her for it and I realized this show is for all types of drag queens and I need to be for all types of drag queens as well.

TATIANNA: They said I won and I was like what the fuuuuck? That was the first time ever in life that I cried from something happy, which really fucks with your mind. That had never happened to me before.

TOM CAMPBELL: Pandora Boxx's Carol Channing is still iconic and she lost to Tatianna as Britney, which was brilliant. You don't expect Tatianna to be funny and when she is, when she just embodies Britney, it's like oh my god. That's the thing with this show—even if you don't win a challenge, you can still do something iconic.

CARSON KRESSLEY: I'm very simpatico with Ru's sensibility and Tom Campbell's sensibility. When they are doing things that harken us back to the day of *The Sonny & Cher Show* or *The Carol Burnett Show* or they're doing the Snatch Game and they have an old-fashioned microphone on a stick, I love all those same things. Seventies television, gay pop icons—all of those things made the show very attractive to me, because I have that same sensibility. Young people that watch the show don't know that the history behind some of those challenges and segments are all very rooted in LGBTQ culture.

By the time the fifth episode rolled around, the pressure was starting to get to everyone. For their main challenge, the queens were given wedding gowns to alter and were instructed to shoot wedding portraits posing as both the bride and the groom. Minutes into the challenge, America's Sweetheart turned into a chaos queen, pushing the dress cart in front of the table of accessories and fabrics so that the other queens couldn't reach them. This set the stage for the epic confrontation between the rest of the cast and Miss Thing, as Jujubee called Tyra in front of the judges.

TATIANNA: There was a table of accessories and stuff behind it, so Tyra ran there and pushed the cart of dresses in front of it so people couldn't get to what they needed. I was already at a disadvantage because I was the furthest from the dresses and stuff. So by the time I got there, I thought, I'm not gonna be sitting here elbowing chicks. But I got frustrated because everything I went to touch was getting snatched. I was annoyed with the whole situation, so I pushed the shit out of that cart on top of everybody. No one knew who did it and I didn't admit to it.

RAVEN: That night, we went out to eat. Tyra had ordered her burger—she just wanted meat on a bun. When they brought it out to her, it had lettuce, tomato, and pickle. Before he could put the plate down on the table, she goes, hold on, pulls the bun off, takes all the innards of the burger out, puts it in his hand, and says, "What am I supposed to do with this?" We were all looking at her like, why would you do that to anyone? That was when I think people were like okay, we're sick of the immaturity.

The next day, after the queens completed their photo shoots as grooms, they returned to the werkroom to continue working on their bridal gowns. With earphones in, Tyra twirled around the room, terribly singing "Halo" while the other cast members attempted to work on their dresses. The more the other queens asked her to stop, the more Tyra performed. When filming wrapped that evening, producers gave the queens permission to stay in the werkroom to finish their work.

JUJUBEE: I believe that in that moment she was trying to twist our panties, and she did it. She's a pageant queen, and I think she very gracefully manipulated the situation to make it fall on us. She's a smart girl, so she ruffled our feathers and sang "Halo" poorly. It was the same thing over and over and a lot of screeching and dancing. Watching it back now, it was pretty hilarious. But it worked because we held on to that anger.

TATIANNA: Cameras were down; the big scaffolding lighting was down, we're in the werkroom, and Tyra's just being obnoxious. I said, "Hey girl, can you knock it off? You're being a dick." And we had some words across the room and she came over and got in my face and production ran in to separate us. I remember one of them running in with a camcorder in case something happened so it would be on tape. She was in my face. She was doing the chest-bump shit right here. It was going to go down that road if someone didn't break it up.

JUJUBEE: I never told her to be quiet, I don't think. But Tatianna had enough. Time wasn't on our side, either, so Tatianna asked her to be quiet. And then they got into each other's faces, and that's when a producer stepped in. And little old me was like, "Can you guys please stop? We have to love each other." I was very emotional, always emotional. I just wanted the family to be strong. I just wanted us to stay together.

RAVEN: There was never a time where I felt I can't stand being around this person. But during the wedding challenge, Tyra was being obnoxious. She wanted to do things the way she wanted to do them and she didn't want to have to be bothered with sewing or creating something or working hard on something. She just wanted to make it seem easy on her.

MORGAN MCMICHAELS: Tatianna was very vocal at the confessionals but I don't think she was as vocal to everyone's face the way I was. And I think that tells me about your character. I understand that I am very polarizing. It's the Scottish in me, and we're very blunt and brash and in your face. You know where you stand with me and that's exactly what it is. I called her a pussy because she wouldn't tell us what she really thought. I did not have a great relationship with Tatianna on the show, but she is one of my closest friends now.

TATIANNA: Obviously, the production knew what had happened the night before and so they were like, we have to address it. On the main stage, Ru was like, "What are we not seeing, Tatianna?"

PANDORA BOXX: Tyra was very extra. The days are long and she'd been singing at the top of her lungs really badly for hours. She was doing it to annoy us. We were all just tired of it. And because she was always just getting praised onstage for everything—everything she did was amazing—we were just like, fuck, it's really irritating that these judges don't get to see this behind-the-scenes stuff of her really just being terrible. We felt like she was being rewarded for this. And so I think that's where it had come to a point that we have to say something.

JUJUBEE: I broke onstage: "Girl, I know I'm gorgeous. You don't need to tell me anything, Miss Thing. Just get yourself some manners, so you won't look so damn stupid." I didn't have a lick of makeup on and there I was talking about I'm pretty! I suppose that that was the mom in me that came out because that's how I was with my sister. I said that not because I wanted to hurt her feelings, but because I wanted her to see how she was acting toward this family that we were forced into. I'll admit, it was my ego and it really wasn't my place to say it.

RAVEN: I was so tired and my feet hurt and I told Tyra and Tatianna they were both acting like a couple of bitches. But I was also getting really keen on how TV worked and I knew that with all these bitches getting mad at one person, that person is going to win the challenge. What kind of a juicy story is that? It's television. But there was no one I really despised or that I was like I'm glad they're gone or I hope they leave. But I was thirty. When we filmed that, I had just turned thirty years old and they were twenty-one years old. So there was almost a ten-year generation gap between us. So for me, it was like watching a couple of whiny kids. It was like, shut up.

PANDORA BOXX: We spoke up about it but I think that because no one saw it, the producers didn't know what to do with it. Tyra just denied it. At that point, I was pretty sure she was going to win the whole thing. They just really loved her. They loved everything she was doing. I think it should matter what happens behind the scenes with a performer, but I guess it really didn't. It was more about what she was doing onstage.

TOM CAMPBELL: Tyra was a tremendous talent and blew us away and surprised us. She was this young, beautiful queen who also seemed to have access to legendary Southern drag tricks, and that's what saved her. That's a lot of what the judges saw. We don't put up with bad behavior but we try to give everybody permission to have some bad moments. We hadn't seen in such detail a drag queen who was a father. It was a breakthrough thing for the audience to hear and see. It's not why we do this, but it's one of the gifts of *Drag Race*—seeing that other dimension to this person.

Next it was Jujubee's turn to reveal a vulnerable side that still makes her cry from shame. After her father died of cancer when she was fifteen and her mentally ill mother abandoned the family, Jujubee turned to alcohol and drugs to numb her pain. Years later, her addiction almost derailed her shot on *Drag Race* during a challenge she was expected to triumph in. The queens were asked to create a rocker chick outfit and perform live vocals to a rock-and-roll cover to RuPaul's "La-dyBoy." As the only queen who could actually sing, everyone, including Jujubee, believed her moment had arrived. Although it seemed on the episode that Jujubee had choked, something else had stopped Ju-jubee from delivering.

TATIANNA: That was a fear of mine—to have to sing in front of peo-ple. There was a point where I was about to say just send me home, I'll just take myself out now before I have to do this shit. I really was very, very uncomfortable. And I was very scared and very nervous and I did not want to do it at all.

PANDORA BOXX: I had won the mini challenge so I was feeling good. Then they said we were going to be singing live and I went, oh shit.

TATIANNA: We got a lot of alcohol that day, which really helped break the ice. Just about all of us were thinking we need liquor while we're getting ready today. We need to loosen up. And they kept 'em coming, which was a poor choice on their part.

MERLE GINSBERG: The sponsor was Absolut Vodka. And there was the Interior Illusions Lounge, which was so hilarious, and that was based on the fact that the furniture came from the store Inte-rior Illusions. They put cameras in there and we could see what they were doing.

PANDORA BOXX: I had set my drink down somewhere 'cause I only had a little bit of it because I wanted enough to calm my nerves. I was afraid that I would forget the words if I had too much, so I only had a little bit. But then when I went back, it was gone and I went, well, I know I didn't drink all of that. I was surprised.

JUJUBEE: We asked for a little bit of liquid confidence because singing in front of a group of judges on a stage like that was very terrifying for all of us. When I drink, one's too many and a thousand's never enough. And that's how I react to any kind of drugs or alcohol or even sometimes relationships. I was trying to curb the drinking but I told myself, Juju, you're probably going to go first so just get all of these drinks in you now.

MERLE GINSBERG: Jujubee came out onstage and was clearly drunk. She didn't throw up onstage but she ran off the stage and it was very clear she was gonna throw up. It looked like she's not taking this seriously. Juju had a great spirit, was hilarious and charming and bubbly, and just had good energy.

TATIANNA: Well, we were all drrrruuunk. I know that I was. I was at least three or four drinks in when I hit that stage. But Juju was the last in the lineup, so Juju had all the drinks and then went around and finished off whatever was left over. She was last so the liquor had all that time to get all the way in her system.

JUJUBEE: I actually blacked out when I was performing. I don't remember the performance. All I remember is that I went out there and I was like, ooh, ooh, don't throw up, don't throw up. And that was the memory. I'm unsure that I could even stand up after that. It was my one chance to show the world that I could sing and to impress the judges and to sing RuPaul's song in front of RuPaul. And I fucked up the lyrics. I fucked up the whole thing. I just didn't know where I was 'cause I was so fucking hammered.

CHRIS MCKIM: It was a disaster and it was an awful day. We never wanted anyone to get messy and we didn't want people to get drunk and do bullshit fighting or whatever. We had our big wall of screens in the control room and the director sitting right there next to me and Randy and Tom and in the row right behind that and the story folks and I was just slinking, slinking, slinking in my chair because I felt so awful and so responsible because I approved the drinking.

PANDORA BOXX: I didn't actually know what was going on with her until after the challenge had happened. I know that she got in her head because we knew that she could sing so I think it was the pressure of being the one who could sing. I just remember her being onstage and thinking, oh my god, please don't say it, don't say it. 'Cause Ru asked her what was going on, and she said, "I'm drunk." I didn't want her to go home because I love Juju. She was my friend and I was like, fuuuuck.

TATIANNA: We didn't know what happened because we were in the Interior Illusions Lounge. But when she walked back in that room and that lipstick was blown out, I was like ohhh girl. What happened out there?

RANDY BARBATO: I remember going in and having a one-on-one with her and saying, "Girl, you gotta snap out of this and take some deep breaths." Everyone was thinking she was going to give up. She needed a pep talk. I remember her being really apologetic and it was just one of those moments where you connect with someone who is vulnerable and disappointed in themselves, and all I'm wanting is to get her to move forward.

JUJUBEE: I begged for coffee and all my sisters were there—every single one of them. I remember during *Untucked*, everybody was eating and I was still really fucked up.

TATIANNA: I think that we asked production to go grab us some makeup, or one of us ran down and grabbed some makeup and brought it back up. She was lying on the ground and it was Pandora Boxx and me just sitting over her, powdering down her face, reapplying her makeup. I remember making her eat some bread.

PANDORA BOXX: She had cried her lashes off. She was a mess and I remember that she lay on the floor and it was like a drag queen game of Operation. Somebody came in and put her lashes on. Everybody was helping fix her and put her back together so she could go out because I think that we all loved her. And aside from one person, we were all getting along really well. She had a moment where it could have happened to anybody. It wasn't her intention and then her nerves got the best of her and she drank too much. So we were all like, let's help our friend. Let's put her back together so that she can at least go out there and look good and face the consequences of what happened.

JUJUBEE: I was lying on the floor and Raven was doing my makeup for me. Tatianna was applying blush and they were giving me water and they were feeding me. They knew that I had to lip sync and Sahara was there for me, too. She had to lip sync, too, and she was like, it's going to be okay. It was just nice to have a family.

CHRIS MCKIM: There was all this weird tension in the control room because I felt awful. We had to tell the judges and it just felt like the dirty show we were never producing and I felt really bad.

TOM CAMPBELL: We were playing by the seat of our pants. We wanted to represent what was going on, but also respect her. We had an alcohol sponsor so we wanted to make sure we weren't disrespecting that agreement and the laws that go along with that.

RANDY BARBATO: We changed the policy, starting Season 3. They only get one drink.

JUJUBEE: I knew I had to fight for it and remember clicking into that good Juju. Those words *Lip sync for your life* didn't mean shit to me until I had to do it. And I said to myself, if you don't fucking win this, you're going to die. And that's how I drilled it into myself.

TOM CAMPBELL: It shows the tenacity of the human spirit. She had just had her worst day ever and then she killed the lip sync. She was so seductive.

JUJUBEE: "Black Velvet" is such a beautiful song. I knew that that song for me was about emoting and telling you this story. And Alannah Myles's voice is so strong and tender at the same time. It's an emotional voice and because of everything that was going on that day, it was what I was feeling. And I managed to be in the moment.

I managed to use the space and to perform and to get on the ground and to be vulnerable. I think that's what saved me.

PANDORA BOXX: She *was* lip syncing for her life. She wanted to stay in that show. She pulled it out. I think she channeled everything she had into that lip sync. But it was sad, too, because Sahara was lip syncing and I didn't want to see either of them go.

CHRIS MCKIM: She just gave a really fuckin' great performance. She used it. And she saved it. And that's why it's not part of the story. It wasn't appropriate and it wasn't intended and it's just not good.

In the end, the queens were right. Tyra Sanchez was crowned the winner, sparking two more controversies: Did she fake her collapse at being pronounced the winner? And the question that won't die: Was Raven robbed?

RAVEN: Before the show began filming, my friend talked to me about *The Secret*. I knew bullet points and I knew that positive affirmations help to manifest those things in your life. So I remember being in my hotel room every night, and I would just lie there under the blankets thinking, *America's next drag superstar is Raven! You're going to win, you're going to win, you're going to win!*

When we finished filming *RuPaul's Drag Race* on August 10, 2009, I walked away knowing I did not win. It wasn't like it is now where they leave them in limbo for a few months, and then they film the finale, and then you still wait another week to find out which one of you won. It was a done deal. I was crushed. There's always been this dark cloud over Season 2. It wasn't because it was Tyra that I felt robbed. It was because it was anyone else.

MERLE GINSBERG: From the beginning, I knew they loved Tyra. Tyra did some great stuff and she was very glam. But I didn't think Tyra was that original. I thought Tyra was crazy competitive. Tyra to me was just attitude. To me, Season 2 was all about Raven. I thought she was the standout of this season. There was something about Raven's attitude—that kind of goth, kind of rock and roll, kind of fuck-you edgy, I could relate. I saw myself in Raven. She should have won. That was a crime.

JOEY NOLFI: The way Tyra approached the challenges, her attitude, she was real, genuine drag. She was a drag queen. I think that she gave us a real taste of authenticity in her drag, in her attitude, her personality, her interactions with other people. Tyra did not give a fuck and she didn't care if you gave a fuck about her not giving a fuck. She was just there to do her thing and she did it really well and she was a great entertainer. She was old school mixed with new-school grit and it just was really exciting to see that on television because I had never seen anything like it before.

JUJUBEE: To this day, I think it could have gone either way. Raven and Tyra, they brought it. I was there to celebrate it with them and be a cheerleader. I was happy to be part of it.

PANDORA BOXX: I don't negate anything Tyra did in the show. I think that she really was good. There was lots of things that she thrived in. And I think she's beautiful. Had she not been so terrible backstage, then maybe I would be yes, she definitely deserved to win. But Raven came from the bottom and really worked to get back into the top. So I have mixed emotions about that whole thing.

MORGAN MCMICHAELS: I love Raven to death but Ru picked the winner for a reason. I don't want to talk about that entertainer, but that person's package was very well put together. Raven didn't win but she clearly didn't need to because she is the winner. She is an Emmy winner and she really has utilized her position to do great things.

RAVEN: It was a little scary because I went to go say "Congratulations" and she just started hyperventilating. And I remember thinking, is this for show, or are you really hyperventilating? But when I saw her trembling and pull her wig off, I knew. I was standing up there trying to help her but I had nothing. And so that's when they came and helped her. You're looking at a single father who had nothing who had just won and now he has a chance. He's got an opportunity. I don't know how I would have reacted, had I won.

I remember being in the airport in San Francisco with Tyra on one of the moving sidewalks after we had had the Absolut tour stop in San Francisco. And I remember someone coming toward us on the other side and he goes, "Oh my gosh, Raven. You should've won. You were robbed." And Tyra was standing right behind me. And I instantly turned and I said, "Tyra is right here." I was always trying to think about how that would feel to Tyra. I'm sure that it's really difficult.

TOM CAMPBELL: Was Raven robbed? I believe that everything on *Drag Race* happens for a reason. Raven now works on the production and is such an essential part. She brings so much spirit and experience. And she won an Emmy for her work making Ru look beautiful.

ADORE DELANO: I was nineteen at home with my mom and it was midway before the season when I realized Tyra is a force. And I was a big fan of Tyra's for years after that, too. I would go watch her at the eighteen-and-over clubs over here sometimes. But now? Yes. Raven got robbed. After everything that's been going on? Yes, she definitely got robbed.

JOEY NOLFI: Getting robbed implies that someone else deserved bad fortune. I don't think Raven was robbed. I think you can make the case for both of them. I think Raven did really well on the show and has her fans and has her long, successful career because she did so well on the show. But I think that Tyra in some ways felt more pure, in a sense. I always felt like Raven knew she was on TV. In some ways, Tyra, too. I think Tyra felt less polished in a good way. I think Raven was more aware of the camera, was more aware of leaning into the show's aesthetic and vibe a little bit more. Tyra just did Tyra and that's what I think Ru fell in love with—Tyra being Tyra.

CHRIS MCKIM: If Raven had become America's Next Drag Superstar, she would probably have no Emmy. So she won. [Editor's note: Raven won an Emmy in 2020 for Outstanding Contemporary Makeup for a Variety, Nonfiction or Reality Program.]

RAVEN: I was going through a drive-thru with my boyfriend and one of the producers called me and asked me what I was doing tomorrow. I was leaving for Louisville, Kentucky, on a three-city tour. And they said, well, we need to know if you can come in tomorrow to do Ru's makeup. I asked, what about Mathu? And he said Mathu can't do this anymore, can you come in? I said no, I have this tour. So many things were going through my head. We hung up and then he called back, and I could hear Ru in the background. They were basically begging me to come. I said, okay. I got off the phone and I just remember crying and I looked at my boyfriend and I said, they just called me to be Ru's makeup artist. I had to call the promoter and World of Wonder paid the contract, and that's how I became Ru's makeup artist. We always have fun. We listen to such obscure music all day, really loud, and it's like two kids playing around and just having a good time. If you would've told me when I walked on the main stage fourteen years ago to be judged that first day that you will be nominated for an Emmy painting that person there, I would have said, *Shut the fuck up, no way.* It's still very weird.

Chapter 3
SEASON 3

I N MANY WAYS, THE THIRD SEASON OF *RUPAUL'S DRAG RACE* WAS A RE- birth. RuPaul came into his own as a host and judge, bolstered by the presence and laughter of his longtime friend Michelle Visage, who replaced Merle Ginsberg on the judges' panel. The runway be- came more fashion-forward with queens Manila Luzon, Yara Sofia, and—the most avant-garde queen to date—Raja. It was a season of cliques and catchphrases—*Bam! Halleloo! Echa pa'lante!*—and a pro- duction shutdown.

Competing for the third title were Season 2's first eliminated con- testant, Shangela; three New York City queens—Carmen Carrera, Mimi Imfurst, and Manila Luzon, the boyfriend of Season 2's Sahara Davenport; sweet Stacy Layne Matthews of North Carolina; Phoenix, the drag daughter of Nicole Paige Brooks; Madonna impersonator Venus D-Lite; Puerto Rican soul sisters Alexis Mateo and Yara Sofia; Las Vegas queen India Ferrah; glamazon Mariah Paris Balenciaga; and longtime Los Angeles friends Delta Work and Raja. Soon after pro- duction wrapped and months before the third season aired, celebrity blogger Perez Hilton posted the cast list and declared Raja the winner, forever changing the finale format into a live event that is filmed and edited. Queens learn who won the night the episode airs.

RANDY BARBATO: There is tight security for *Drag Race*. It's like the FBI at World of Wonder. It is hard to get access to anything. When we send anything out, it's behind walls of security. Having said that, it is also virtually impossible to keep some things from leaking. This one, though, really pissed us all off.

TOM CAMPBELL: Now we live in a world where everybody who has a phone or a camera or Wi-Fi is a gossip columnist. But at the time it was shocking and dispiriting. Our point of view is that we are the Super Bowl of drag and nobody wants to know how the Super Bowl ends.

RUPAUL: I've never heard of a show being leaked. I guess I don't follow enough shows. I think it's just rotten. I was so angry about it. One morning, I was in between sleep and waking up and it occurred to me to shoot three different endings. *That will fix those motherfuckers!* So I presented it to my partners and they said let's do it.

MANILA LUZON: I had just landed in New York City after we wrapped and it was already in the news. And it was the whole cast list, too. *Drag Race* was still kind of underground and I didn't think that many people cared. But it had an impact because they changed the way the finales are done.

CHRIS MCKIM: The changes were bound to happen anyway. They had been discussed before because we're shooting something that's a secret, so how do we do it? One of the things that had come before was shooting multiple endings, which we didn't want because you want a real reaction. But of course, that's the way we do it now.

RAJA: There was a part of me that was really pissed off because I wanted people to see it. But it all added to some of the press and the sensation of it. Now looking back at it, it's a bummer, but kind of fun for the story.

ALEXIS MATEO: I didn't understand if people were thinking Raja was going to win because of her track record on the show or if there was actually a leak. I mean, I didn't even know what a leak was. But it was leaked and it changed the entire thing. It's still leaking, girl.

Michelle Visage and RuPaul met in the late 1980s in the New York City club scene and ran into each other again in 1992 at a Dance Music Seminar in Times Square where she performed "It's Gonna Be a Lovely Day," from *The Bodyguard* soundtrack. Michelle recalls the electricity in the room as the audience braced for RuPaul's performance of her hit "Supermodel (You Better Work)." When they ended up in the green room together, Michelle asked RuPaul if he remembered her from the clubs. "Bitch, of course, I know who you are. You're a motherfucking superstar," RuPaul replied. They have been friends ever since.

Decades later, after working in radio and TV together, RuPaul imagined Michelle by his side for the launch of his reality competition show. But Michelle was working for a radio station in Florida and she couldn't break her contract.

RUPAUL: Michelle Visage is a girl who is a drag queen. She has earned the right to judge them because she comes from that club world. When I met her a hundred years ago, my first thought was that she was like a cat who will always land on her feet.

RANDY BARBATO: In all honesty, we always wanted Michelle. Michelle was the number one choice. Michelle's life was very different when we started the show and we couldn't make it work for Michelle for her to relocate her whole family. The show wasn't in that place. We had done a hundred episodes of *The RuPaul Show* with Michelle. So Fenton and I worked with her, Ru worked with her. We all really are family.

MICHELLE VISAGE: I remember going to LA, I sit down next to Ru for Season 3, he takes a deep breath, he looks at me, and he goes, "Now the show can begin." So I often joke about Season 3 being the real Season 1. Obviously, I don't want to take anything away from Seasons 1 and 2 because they were magical. I was just distraught about the whole thing because I couldn't do it.

MORGAN MCMICHAELS: Merle was a great addition to the judging panel because she came from the fashion world, she came from a different side. I would like to see Merle on later seasons of *Drag Race* because the fashions have become more fashion. But there's something about getting judged by Michelle. It is like a rite of passage because she is a drag queen. Her hair, her costumes over the seasons, she's a big symbol to cisgender bio queens. Having a strong woman up there who has been such an ally to RuPaul and the community was a great addition to the show.

RANDY BARBATO: I felt badly about it for Merle but I think Merle always understood that there was a natural person for that seat that had a relationship with Ru that frankly made more sense, ultimately. Merle and Santino were too fashion-y. Michelle and Ru are hardwired. They can finish each other's sentences. And that's great for TV.

MERLE GINSBERG: I am thrilled and honored to have been a part of it. How many journalists can say they were in a major TV show? I had nothing but fun. We had a blast. It was never hard. My life changes all the time, but one of the constants is that *RuPaul's Drag Race* always comes up. People are always mentioning it to me.

TOM CAMPBELL: Michelle has become a pillar of the show and is uniquely qualified, like maybe no other cisgender woman...just so happened to be part of the Harlem ball scene, a hitmaking recording artist, a radio personality, and things of that nature. Michelle Visage is someone who has something to say about everything. You could bring up almost any topic and she has read something, she knows something, and she delivers it with such authority.

MICHELLE VISAGE: Oddly enough, I wasn't nervous. I grew up around drag. I grew up around drag queens. I lived the life, I walk the walk, I talk the talk. This is not just Ru's friend sitting there. I would not be sitting there if I did not know what I was talking about.

RUPAUL: I feel so blessed in my lifetime to have found a partner who speaks the same language. She and I can get together and start talking and we never stop. We have such great chemistry together. I've never had that with any other person. I knew that once she joined our judges' table, it was really gonna take off.

ALEXIS MATEO: I did not know anything about Michelle. I was not having her, girl. I was not having her. She was tougher with me than any of the other contestants. I was like, who invited this girl? Can we bring back any of the other judges please?

MANILA LUZON: I was not prepared! I had met Merle Ginsberg at some events with Sahara for Season 2. So I thought maybe I had a little bit of an in. On that first episode, I turned around and there was Michelle. She looked like some kind of ancestor of the evil witch and Snow White. She was just pale with this dark black, raven hair with this blue streak in it. She had these big, smoky eyes and she was very stoic and frightening. I was like, I don't know who that is. She looks mean. And she was also really, really gorgeously done up in drag. She didn't look like a news anchor. She was giving you looks. If she could impress me with a look as a cisgender woman I knew that she was going to have some substantial critiques for the queens.

TOM CAMPBELL: Michelle isn't the mean one, but she is the honest one. And my favorite thing is when she says *I don't like your [blank] and let me tell you why.* Oh, and her nails.

The season opened with a special Christmas present from RuPaul for the queens—another queen in a box. Hint: Halleloo!

TOM CAMPBELL: Shangela has an amazing star quality that we saw, that the world has seen, that Bradley Cooper and Lady Gaga saw, and it is just undeniable. Because she was an LA queen, our casting people kept an eye on her and thought we hadn't seen enough of Shangela.

SHANGELA: I remember coming in the room and they had that box for me backstage, and I got in it but they hadn't put any breathing holes in the box. And I was in there and they said, "Just listen for Ru's key word which is going to be *ridonkulous*, and when Ru says ridonkulous, you push the top off and the front will fall forward and you just do your thing." Miss Ru took about fourteen takes before she did ridonkulous after I had been rolled in. I was so hot and sweaty in that box. And I can hear the girls talking and I can recognize some voices from LA. Raja has a very iconic voice. I knew Manila so I could tell her voice. And finally I came out. I was hot and, baby, I made it.

RAJA: The first thing I thought was that someone had put a camera on my life. Like, how did they even know? She and I had just had a falling-out. I always want to help the new queens. I had seen her on Season 2 and I really liked her. I liked her energy. I liked her talent and she was such a force. When she was on the reunion episode for Season 2, I dressed her head-to-toe. The wig is mine. The dress that she wore is mine. I helped her make the corsage that she had around her wrist. I didn't know her well but I wanted her to look really good since she got kicked off first. When she brought me back the wig and all the stuff, the dress had food stains on it and the wig was messed up, so I was upset and I was feeling like a big old diva. So when she jumped out of the box, there was a lot of tension. I wanted to be there with people who are at the same level and she was so fresh and she was so annoying because she didn't know how to do anything on her own. She had to ask help from everybody. And so we just went with it. I was like, okay, we have issues, let's make this theater.

SHANGELA: When I gave it back to her, she sent me this text saying, "How do you return the wig all ratty into a knot?" I was like, "I didn't return your wig all knotted." And then we didn't talk anymore until we saw each other at *Drag Race*. I didn't know nothing about hair, wigs, and all that back in the day. I didn't know about brushing it out.

RAJA: People still today, eleven years later, tend to think of us as being these rivals when, you know, oftentimes I really just want to make out with her.

YARA SOFIA: I knew Shangela because I used to go on trips with Jessica Wild and they were on the same season. When I saw the box, I didn't expect her at all. But I was excited to know somebody there.

MARIAH PARIS BALENCIAGA: I was disappointed that it wasn't a fine man poppin' out that box. But it was kinda cool to see Shangela because she had already been on the show. I was just like, oh okay girl, welcome back.

ALEXIS MATEO: Oh, boooooo! Booo! Shangela is here! Send her back! Return to sender. She lost, good night, god bless you.

SHANGELA: The only thing on my mind was that this [is] the first time that anyone's ever been brought back on a different season to compete again. I don't want to mess this up. I was the first girl to go home in Season 2. I have worked really hard over the last year to try and become a better drag queen. I didn't want to let Ru down because they brought me back. That was like the biggest thing in my head. That's the reason I was so passionate and on edge.

In the third episode, after completing a challenge in which they shot a trailer for a space movie, the queens retreated to the Interior Illusions Lounge to wait for the judges to deliberate. The friendly trash-talking between Mimi Imfurst and Shangela took a dramatic turn and production was halted.

MARIAH PARIS BALENCIAGA: Absolut was one of the sponsors for the show. We're used to nightclubs and drinking while we work. We just cracked the bottles open. It started off as playful banter but it escalated and then it really got serious.

CHRIS MCKIM: There were two shows going on. We were filming the deliberation on the main stage but the queens are upstairs doing *Untucked*. So we're half listening to deliberation and half watching what is going on upstairs on the screen. But then this crazy fight starts happening.

MARIAH PARIS BALENCIAGA: They stopped filming on set because they could hear the melee happening in the Interior Illusions Lounge from the main stage.

VANESSA VANJIE MATEO: You know all the furniture was white and she threw that cranberry Absolut drink! You know they had to pay for that. It was the early seasons, bitch, we don't got that money! I live. I live.

SHANGELA: They never told us why. They just said we're going on a break and they'll call us to come back. And honestly, I remember thinking oh my gosh, they're shutting down the show. They got canceled or something. I remember going home immediately, going to Google, and I looked up every girl that was there so I can figure out what she did and what her talents were. We were only supposed to take home one bag and bring it back and I stuffed as many things as I could in that bag.

RAJA: When we returned, Ru and the production team had little gifts for us. They were blue-and-white Jonathan Adler ceramic containers with DOLLS on them. I took my ceramic container to my Tic Tac lunch with Ru and I asked her to sign it. I still also have my ten-year-old Tic Tac inside of the container. I have a little altar at home with all my stuff on and I always keep that container there with this old Tic Tac. I opened it recently and the Tic Tac that was once orange is now black.

SHANGELA: The good thing is when we came back to Season 3, Mimi and I both realized that moment had probably gone a little farther than either one of us wanted to. I remember going up to her in the werkroom and apologizing and she apologized as well.

RAJA: Looking back at it twelve years later, I love that. I wish there was more of it. I wish there was more wine and drinks thrown at each other. I like that tension.

ADORE DELANO: They just don't make 'em like that anymore. I wanna see people throw drinks at each other! And "I'm from Chicago, bitch!" You know what I mean?

Production resumed three weeks later. After producing silly workout videos for the challenge, Mimi Imfurst wound up in the bottom with India Ferrah and had to lip sync Thelma Houston's "Don't Leave Me This Way." By the end of the song, RuPaul's famous admonishment had been delivered—"Drag is not a contact sport"—and Mimi Imfurst sashayed away.

You'd think the drama would've ended there but this wasn't the last time a queen would hit below the belt in Season 3. In one corner, there were the Heathers. In the other, we had the Boogers. Except no one told the Boogers they were supposed to be feuding with the Heathers or even that they were Boogers.

MANILA LUZON: Our group was working together in a team in one of the earlier episodes in the space challenge and it created a bond that carried over throughout the weeks. I already had a friendship with Carmen Carrera because we were both doing drag in New York City. We would see each other at the club and would party together and I was familiar with her drag mother. I loved how gorgeous and polished and beautiful and, in a way, delusional Carmen Carrera was. I was also very drawn to Raja because she was just fantastic. She was really creative, really fast, fierce. I was very impressed by her and that motivated me to do better. Raja also was longtime friends with Delta Work from the Southern California scene. They've been performing together and working together for years and they were already friends. And Delta was the first big queen on the show that had the polish of any of the skinny bitches. There was no flaw in her. And so we became this group of friends.

RAJA: We were definitely those girls. We were bratty and we thought we were the shit. We would all have dinner together after the episode was done. We would go back to our hotel and the four of us naturally gravitated to each other, and we were just joking around.

MANILA LUZON: There was a high school vibe. We were like, shit, are we the pretty, popular girls shitting on the girls that don't [have] pretty clothes or pretty wigs? Are we the "mean girls"? But we didn't have internet or our phones and we couldn't remember the names of the characters. I knew Regina George. So then we thought let's do a major throwback since Delta, Raja, and I were a bit older. What about *Heathers*? It has a similar vibe of evil popular girls wearing scrunchies at Westerburg High, which is really crazy because my last name is Westerberg. We thought it was funny because in the movie they all end up dying and eventually we would all get kicked off. We only planned on doing it for one episode. We kept calling each other Heather in the werkroom but then other people started catching on and they started questioning what was going on. The next episode the producers were like, "So what's going on with this Heather thing?" And so we just went with it. We realized that we had the ability to create our own narrative and we were adding to the vernacular of drag.

CHRIS MCKIM: I love *Heathers*. I'm a fan of *Heathers* from way back. If this set of queens and that set of queens want to set up rival girl gangs to go at it in the werkroom, who's to stop them? It's a free world. I liked queens on both sides.

MANILA LUZON: Our other competitors were a little more rough around the edges. Amazing personalities, but this is back in the day when we thought it was a beauty contest. It would frustrate us when we would do these really amazing, elaborate costumes and some of the other costumes weren't as good, but the girls could talk themselves out of the bottom because personality is a big part of the show. So there was rivalry there and we called them Boogers because that's what you'd call a girl that's a drag queen who is a little bit crunchy. She's a little booger-y. There are a lot of derogatory things you can say to a drag queen.

RAJA: If this show is like watching a sport, why not have teams? If you were to watch two teams playing baseball or football or basketball or whatever, you don't want them to all get along and be friends and help each other into the jerseys and guide them to each other's goals. You want to see some fighting. You want to see us against them. And it worked, but it also created a lot of controversy because people talked about us as being bullies, and perhaps we were a little bit.

ALEXIS MATEO: The group was divided at this point between the self-proclaimed popular girls and the girls that were there to have fun and do what we do. It was literally going back to school 101 on a national TV level. Carmen Carrera started it. In the werkroom we did not refer to each other as Heathers and Boogers, but we started to see the separation by the way that they looked at us and the way that they talked to us and things like that. So we created our own clique and I was able to ignore it.

SHANGELA: I wasn't familiar with the movie *Heathers*. Even to this day, I've never seen it. When they called each other Heather, I had no clue. At the time, watching it at viewing parties, up until episode 4, they were saying "She's a Booger, Booger, Booger," but nobody ever said it to my face. So in watching it, it was difficult to see on the screen because up until episode 4 we were all kicking it behind the scenes.

TOM CAMPBELL: What I love about unscripted television and, especially our show—because our show is about queer people and I'm queer—is I can see a little bit of me in every single character. Sometimes you're the mean girl and sometimes you're not and sometimes you're in and sometimes you feel out.

ALEXIS MATEO: The Booger situation—I didn't notice that in the werkroom. As a Puerto Rican, I learned English very literal. When Carmen used to refer to Boogers, I was like, girl, she has got to have the worst sinusitis ever 'cause she's always talking about boogers. I never realized that she was literally calling someone a booger. It was not until I was already home and they were airing the season that I realized that *booger* was a negative term about an unpolished drag queen and that she was referring to us. And then I understood that it was a bully moment in a funny way.

YARA SOFIA: Carmen told me that they could make me into a Heather but I needed to stop talking to the Boogers. I was like, girl, I don't want to be in any group. What the fuck is this? I didn't watch *Heathers*. Who cares? Who is Heather? If you're gonna do a reference, tell some queens. Not even the producers told us it was a movie. I figured out at the end of filming that Heather killed everybody. The thing about the Heathers is they never said "Boogers" to our faces. They said it at the end. I didn't even know what *booger* means.

MICHELLE VISAGE: That stuff never sits well with me. I don't like cliques. That was like *Mean Girls*. But I also didn't know what was happening behind the scenes.

MARIAH PARIS BALENCIAGA: If one of them bitches would've called me a Booger, we woulda had a whole 'nother situation in the werkroom. I can't say I was surprised.

MANILA LUZON: It's a competition. You have to go in there with the idea that everything is a tool to be used as a weapon and, honestly, that's how it works. We're getting on each other's nerves. We're trapped in this thing with cameras, so let's make it interesting. I'm a drag queen. I like drama. I wasn't trying to be mean-spirited but definitely was poking fun and not taking it too seriously. I can laugh at myself and so I can laugh at you, too.

RAJA: I was really cocky on this show and when I watch it now I'm a little embarrassed at it. I had my defenses up a little bit. And I really felt like I needed to prove a point. I don't regret anything that has happened because that certainly has shaped me and I have fans now that are global and I appreciate it. But there are times when I feel like I seemed like an asshole.

SHANGELA: By today's standards, we were all very irresponsible with some of the things that we said about each other. But that's what reality TV was at that time, and just reality in general in the drag world. There were things that Alexis and I said to each other about other people that I watch now and I go, oh my god, Shangie, no, no, no, no, no. But we weren't thinking about cameras. We were just loose-lipped the way that could seem impossible today. But at the time, it made for very interesting popcorn-eating juicy TV. We all have to grow from somewhere. And I think we all have.

RAJA: I think all of Season 3 was controversial. It is something that you would never see on *Drag Race* now. It is definitely a window in time for *Drag Race*. But you know what? We have to forgive each other for those times and learn through the process and realize it might have been funny then but it's not funny now.

ALEXIS MATEO: The Heathers versus Boogers moment of the season was when Shangela and Carmen were on the bottom. I knew that performance was going to prove one more time that it doesn't matter how popular or pretty you think you are, some underdog is gonna come along with bigger dreams than you and send you home, girl. There was something about Shangela that we all knew, and it was that she has the fire to be there and sometimes that's even more important than anything else you can wear on the runway.

MANILA LUZON: Shangela was in a fucking goddamn movie with Lady Gaga and she went to the damn Oscars. So, who's a Booger now?

Not Manila Luzon, who delivered an epic lip sync against her friend Delta Work, bringing the camp, elegance, and face contortions to the "MacArthur Park" party.

MANILA LUZON: I had performed Donna Summer's "MacArthur Park" one time before at The Monster in New York City right before I had gone to film *Drag Race*. So it was in my mind at the time. My style of drag is to always perform the lip sync so I love when I can get to do a song that has a lot of vocal flexing, and Donna Summer just did that. I love that it starts out with a ballad and spins into this big disco number. How else do you perform it? It starts out beautiful and glamorous and I had this big, beautiful dress and I was going to use it to make the performance work.

MICHELLE VISAGE: That's one of my favorites of all time, "MacArthur Park." People ask me all the time what my favorite lip syncs were and there are so many but that's one of the greatest. That face! The insanity of it all is what got me.

MANILA LUZON: The song is freaking crazy, man. It's about trees and Chinese checkers and paper dolls and just the most random poetic whatever-ness. It's recipes of cake and the rain and it's lost love. In that moment, it had a new meaning because I'm in this bottom fighting for my life and having to do it against my new friend, Delta Work. It was like one of us is going home and, bitch, it's not going to be me. So I did feel bad that I had to send my friend home. It was emotional for me.

ALEXIS MATEO: The "MacArthur Park" lip sync was emotional. I knew what Manila was feeling. Manila wanted to stay in the show. Delta kind of gave up at that point but it's still hard to send a friend home. I had just done it when I sent Stacy home. So I knew exactly what Manila was feeling. The whole number felt like a Broadway show. It was a story about friendship and it was sad and powerful. It was a crazy lip sync.

The time had come to pick a top three, and Raja, Manila Luzon, Alexis Mateo, and Yara Sofia were feeling the pressure. The week's challenge was to create three looks: swimsuit, cocktail, and an evening gown, which had to be made out of one million Ru Dollars. The queens also had to perform a choreographed lip sync to "Just Wanna Dance" by La Toya Jackson, who was the guest judge.

Although all four queens had at least one problematic outfit, RuPaul declared best pals Yara Sofia and Alexis Mateo on the bottom. Their lip sync to Patti LaBelle's "I Think About You" would go down in drag herstory for all the wrong reasons.

YARA SOFIA: We had to do three looks from scratch. One had to be from money. I was rushing to glue dollar bills on my dress to finish. The queens were all putting this weight on me, saying I was making them look bad because I finished everything—zippers and everything.

MANILA LUZON: That was a nightmare. Season 3 had a lot of build-your-own-drag moments and that's the kind of shit that I love. That's the stuff that I'm really good at and that's the creative part of drag that I really like. But the fact that we had to do a lot on this one challenge was difficult. We had to make all of the outfits and then we had to do the choreography on top of it.

RAJA: I don't think people realize the stress that goes on behind it. We had a lot of extra anxiety and stress in our season because of the fact that we had to make things. We were filming before a holiday weekend. Production wasn't going to let us finish the outfits until we came back to set three days later and we hadn't finished any of the costumes. We had been rehearsing for the number. So I threw a tantrum. I said, "We need you to allow us to take our things so we can work on our dresses over the weekend. Wouldn't you prefer to see us in wonderful-looking costumes instead of pissed and looking like shit and trash?" They gave us two more hours. We were there until about one o'clock in the morning and I was like fuck this, I'm just going to go home. Why don't you just leave me here and I'm going to pack up my stuff and I'm going to go home because I can't do this?

ALEXIS MATEO: At this point, the competition was so long. I was so tired. The stress was wearing me out. I got assigned to be the choreographer. I was so mentally exhausted and I was very frustrated at that point. I was questioning if I wanted to continue the competition or go home. I was missing home. I was missing my time. The thing that people don't understand about being on *RuPaul's Drag Race* is the hours we put in. We don't sleep the same way. We have to switch our entire diet. But I wasn't going to quit. I took a break. I am very dramatic. I'm a dramatic queen.

RAJA: Eventually, the producers let us take everything. We loaded the vans up and we had all of our sewing machines. On our days off at the hotel, we just sewed. I made outfit after outfit after outfit. I understand why Yara was frustrated because it wasn't about performance as much as it was making stuff. Because I excel at it, it worked in my favor. But it was frustrating.

MANILA LUZON: I had already stuffed all of my drag that I was going to work on into my backpack so that even if they said no I was going to bring it to the hotel anyway.

CHRIS MCKIM: During the holiday weekend break, I was pondering all the episodes and I remember thinking Yara Sofia could win this. I loved that wacky energy and she was funny and sweet, which made what happened next even more crushing, although the world does love when two friends have to lip sync against each other.

YARA SOFIA: I was pissed because time was part of the challenge and I could not redo the money dress because it was already glued and I had run out of dollars to add to it. I was almost mentally quitting and I was bored because everyone else was busy and I was done.

CHRIS MCKIM: Two things happened: She got in her own head, and she couldn't dance in that dress. She had already made the dress and she was really upset that now there was an opportunity to continue working on it. She didn't do anything about it and she ended up in the bottom and couldn't dance in the dress because it was just confining. You could see that she was just in her head. You could see the train wreck coming. She's wearing a box with money, so I'm sure it was a billion degrees in there.

YARA SOFIA: I don't remember anything but I remember that I got so pissed during the lip sync. I was another person. I was crying so hard that they stopped filming because La Toya Jackson was crying, bawling. She was bawling.

TOM CAMPBELL: That was one of the most brutal lip syncs I had ever seen. We don't know what's going to happen, but while the show is being shot, I thought Yara is going to be the top. I just felt it in my bones. She sort of gave up or had a bit of a meltdown in front of all of us. And I'm not saying that gleefully but—again—what a thing to experience. The feeling sticks with me.

ALEXIS MATEO: I looked at Yara when we got to the runway and she already looked sad. I didn't know if she knew the words or not. It was so confusing to me. She was crying a lot. She started taking stuff off. I remember I stopped lip syncing to ask if she was okay because I didn't want her to humiliate herself or just give up in front of everybody's eyes. This was a lip sync against a real sister. We connected on another level because we're both Puerto Ricans. Her childhood was my childhood. Her country is my country. When she pulled her wig out, it broke my heart.

YARA SOFIA: I knew the song. I knew the words. But everything was like "Boom!" I'm not a queen who takes her wig off. I hate it. I superglue my wig sometimes because I always hate when they fall off. I never break the illusion. But at that point, I was done. I knew I was going home. I even wished for it. Everything that I hoped for blew up there. I never cry. I'm always dramatic or hyperactive or crazy, but I know what I'm doing. Right there, I didn't know what I was doing. I was not improvising. It was not me. I would never take off the wig.

MARIAH PARIS BALENCIAGA: That was so heartbreaking to watch. I was already gone, so I saw it on TV. I know how kind Yara was and how much she extended herself to the other competitors even as they were making fun of her accent, even though they were calling her a Booger. She still helped Raja with stuff. She still helped Carmen with stuff. She is such a caring and giving person and the relationship that she and Alexis had was a lot. I had to go to the bathroom during the viewing party because it was heartbreaking to see. It's true what they say: Check on your strong friends. People who are smiling aren't always happy.

MICHELLE VISAGE: I didn't understand. I went and talked to her after because I was sooo into Yara. I thought she was such an amazing queen and she was just getting stronger and stronger. I think she's so kooky and amazing and her aesthetic is just so strong. I just loved her. She is one of the ones who wanted to go out on her terms and she did. I don't understand it because if that were me, I would never give up.

JOEY NOLFI: You don't get Yara Sofia on *Survivor*. You don't get Yara Sofia on *American Idol*. You can only get Yara Sofia on *RuPaul's Drag Race*, at the time, at least. Now, of course, things have changed. But at the time it was just seeing these refreshing personalities doing this incredible artistry, but they are also so funny. It felt like a family that I didn't even know I had.

MANILA LUZON: Alexis swooped in there with a perfect lip-sync performance and she made it to the next week. So I remember it being like oh dang, like, this is really anyone's game at this point. Anything can happen.

ALEXIS MATEO: I watched the episode in Puerto Rico at a bar. When we finished in the bottom together, I remember how quiet the whole bar was. I look around and everybody was crying. The judges were crying. Everybody was crying. Who would have thought that the two little Puerto Rican boys were going to make it to Hollywood to be on one of the best pop-culture TV shows in history?

And the winner is...Raja! After co-starring in RuPaul's "Champion" music video, Alexis Mateo was eliminated, leaving Heather besties Raja and Manila Luzon to compete on the runway one last time and lip sync to "Champion" on the main stage.

RANDY BARBATO: I thought Raja was a bit of a game changer for *Drag Race* because I feel like Raja embodied this sophisticated fashion and she was fully possessed. She was definitely a game changer, next level. And it was pretty clear early on. Raven was like that, too. We have girls that don't edit themselves. They're not self-producing. Bianca was like that as well. They don't need to do that, they trust who they are and they put that out there. If they don't win the trophy, it doesn't matter because they win this deep connection with the audience.

RAJA: There were a lot of times where I questioned myself. I was like, oh my god, if I go on the runway wearing this look, are people going to understand it? Is it going to go over people's heads? I actually thought that I was going to get kicked off about halfway through. I thought my ideas were probably too gender-fuck, I guess. I think I'm what people call nonbinary, and I relate to that and that's how I treated drag and fashion at my stage performances. My idea of drag has always been playing with neither male nor female.

TOM CAMPBELL: I think Raja was jaw-dropping from the start. Raja blew Ru away, blew everyone away, and brought a level of sophistication and humor. She did all of it in a way that was really exciting. And she wasn't afraid to be a little shady. Raja is a real drag queen, a crazy talented makeup artist. There was something about her knowledge and deep roots in drag that set her apart.

RAJA: In hindsight, the only thing that really allowed me to excel and look as great as I did on my season of *Drag Race* is the fact that we had to make so many things. It is the last season of its kind where everybody had to make everything for every challenge. That is what I do. Don't ask me to be anybody's lip-sync assassin because I'm not that person. I'm not that type of stage performer where I'll do splits or a shablam or whatever the kids call it. But if you give me a hot-glue gun, a bag of rhinestones, some good scissors, a sewing machine, and piles of fabric, I will create things. And so I think that's one of the reasons that I won: because we had to make things all the time.

MANILA LUZON: When I found out that I didn't win the show, I was very disappointed. But then it was okay for me because of all the queens that I was competing against the one that I looked up to the most, the one that inspired me to work harder and push myself the most, was Raja. She was deserving and I was very happy for her.

JOEY NOLFI: Growing up, if you're not familiar with the art of drag, if you don't participate in the art of drag, drag queens were always the butt of the joke on mainstream TV—a big, burly man comes in in a glittery dress on some sort of sitcom and cracks a joke. But this show opened up my eyes to an entirely different community that I didn't even know existed. It was the magic of discovery of that artistry that I was seeing. You look at some of the things that Raja was doing on the runway in Season 3, like that Marie Antoinette look, and it's next level. It blows your mind.

MICHELLE VISAGE: Raja was the first queen that we had that was purely fashion. She was untraditional and she just did her own thing. It was more fashion and less drag, and I don't think we'd had a queen like that on the show before that. And listen, I love it all. I love fashion, I love fashion drag, I love drag, I love camp drag, I love comedy drag. I love it all, but I think that was a big thing for *Drag Race*. She was very edgy.

ACID BETTY: When Raja was on it and won Season 3, she was an old friend and also the first drag queen that I had ever seen in my gay life. So I saw her and it sealed my gay deal. I was like, okay, this is a legitimate show. Real fabulous drag queens are winning.

CARSON KRESSLEY: I think Raja brings utter individuality and I think she approaches drag from a very personal and spiritual viewpoint and I thought she brought so much bohemian glamour. But that doesn't even really nail it. Her glamour comes from within and it's very heartfelt. We say this to queens every season—show us how you do drag and bring you to the equation. We don't need to see another Bianca or another Kennedy Davenport or another Ginger Minj. We want to find America's Next Drag Superstar and that individuality is so important. Raja really mastered showcasing that inner light of hers that is so beautiful and so unique.

RAJA: I did drag because it was a subculture. I did drag because it was provocative. It was naughty and it was rough and raw and it was very dangerous. I love that I won coming from that place. As far as *Drag Race* goes, it is the last moment where the queen gets crowned onstage. I was the last person to have it done that way. I feel very thrilled and honored by it because my ugly cry and my genuine reaction to that moment was one of the most realest that I've ever seen myself in. To look back at it, I feel every emotion the same way.

Chapter 4
SEASON 4

I F THE FOURTH SEASON OF *RuPaul's Drag Race* PROVED ANYTHING, IT was that this wasn't just your gay uncle's favorite show anymore. The introduction of super queens Sharon Needles, Latrice Royale, Chad Michaels, Willam, and several other lovable characters—*may I call you Jiggly?*—catapulted the series into pop-culture realness, cementing its place in TV history. Around the country, viewing parties hosted by *Drag Race* alum became a Monday-night destination as fans from all walks of life gathered to learn who would be the next queen to sashay away and what fight would break out next in *Untucked*.

Would it be Puerto Rican queens Alisa Summers, Madame LaQueer, or Kenya Michaels? The Princess, Milan, or lip-sync assassin Dida Ritz? Or Lashauwn Beyond and Jiggly Caliente, whose fight gifted drag culture with one of the most lasting lines of all time in the first week? For fans, it was love at first sight with large and in charge, chunky yet funky, bold and beautiful Latrice Royale, the polished pro Chad Michaels, and spooky original Sharon Needles. For a long time, no one knew what to make of pageant girl Phi Phi O'Hara or bad girl Willam and everyone loved that, too.

It was a season of epic fights and lip syncs, a shocking disqualification, and a surprise change in the finale format. In other words, it was sick'ning, and mainstream culture would never be the same.

RANDY BARBATO: Season 4 was a turning point for a number of reasons. One of them was that Sharon Needles represented a different generation and partially a different type of fan. On the one hand, it seemed less mainstream drag, but on the other hand, it had a broader appeal. It gave more people more permission to watch in some weird way because it was so punk rock and it was incredibly creative. It reminds me a lot of Ru's early drag. I think it made people realize there was a future to the show that they couldn't predict and that there was more to drag than they thought they knew. Raja and Raven laid the groundwork for this and Sharon took it to the next level. When you look at it today, it's not just that all types of drag are represented, but that all different types of people are represented.

FENTON BAILEY: The show itself is like a drag queen that reinvents itself and proves its reason for being.

MANDY SALANGSANG: It blossomed a little bit. It found its way and its following. We were doing challenges that were a little grander and had great payoffs, like the wrestling challenge. That felt bigger than anything we had done before. It was pretty iconic. We had Latrice and little Kenya and we had a large studio audience. We had Rick Fox and John Salley, major NBA stars, present. And the queens had created these really dynamic characters. Professional wrestling is drag. It really, really appealed to people and it was an exciting challenge that we still talk about and we have talked about redoing and we have not touched because I think it's perfect as it is.

MICHELLE VISAGE: Season 4 broke the fuckin' internet! I think Season 3 started to get a lot of attention, but it was still virtually unknown apart from being within the community. And then Season 4 happened and everybody started talking about every part of it—about Sharon, about Phi Phi, about all of it. The Snatch Game was hilarious! There were a lot of memorable people—Latrice, Chad Michaels, Willam, Jiggly, Dida Ritz.

LATRICE ROYALE: It was a pivotal moment for the show because never have you seen such a diverse group of degenerates that all live for something. You know what I'm talking about!

MANDY SALANGSANG: Boy, we had a good group of queens that season. They had had the opportunity to have an understanding of what they were signing up for, what type of talent show this was going to be, and how to do well at it. The stakes of winning were more important than ever because they had seen what that could do for you. There was a legitimacy the show had earned that was an exciting thing for them to compete for.

ALASKA: I think I was dating Sharon when I did the Season 3 audition tape. I snuck away and did it on my own because she didn't think they were gonna cast someone like her. But then for Season 4 she was like, why not? I'll do one for a lark. And then she ends up getting on and I didn't. Ohhh, I was crushed, I was crushed. It was really hard on us because Sharon felt like shit about it, too, because we went through the long audition process. We did follow-up interviews and we were auditioning together. We thought we'll have a romance story line, we'll lip sync against each other, it'll tear our lives apart. It'll be great! I was really bitter and jealous for a while. But then once the first promo aired for Season 4 and I saw them spinning around like robots on a platform, I thought this is the coolest fuckin' thing and I became her biggest fuckin' fan.

RUPAUL: Alaska had auditioned for every season up until then and the other producers really wanted her for Season 3. But I said it wasn't time for her yet. Her style of drag and her approach to drag at the time was a little too esoteric for our audience. It wasn't until after Sharon Needles introduced a gender-fuck style of drag and did it so flawlessly and in a loving, heartfelt way that we could introduce a more esoteric genre of drag. We had to educate our audience as the seasons moved on.

CHAD MICHAELS: I believe that archetypes were formed on Season 4. I represented an era of drag not too long ago, from an in-between time. I'm not old school and I'm not new school. I think that I brought a lot of heart to the show. I think I let people know that you can be on that show and you don't have to shred people to ribbons and you don't have to throw shade and you don't have to be a bitch. I showed people that there's another way to move through that competition.

RAVEN: A lot of people don't know Chad is the reason I wanted to start doing drag. I had been in drag shows. I had thought about it, but when I saw Chad do my friend Vanity's show in 2002 and he came out and did Celine Dion, then he did Cher, then he did Marilyn Manson in a one-hour show, that was it. He's done a lot to his face now obviously, but back then he was redoing his face with makeup and I decided that's what I wanted to do. It wasn't *To Wong Foo* or all this other stuff. It was watching Chad do it.

MORGAN MCMICHAELS: My name came after Chad Michaels. He took me under his wing and taught me the art of celebrity illusion, whether it was Pink, Annie Lennox, David Bowie. He taught me the skills to do the makeup and the little idiosyncrasies that make you an impersonator. We met working in Palm Springs.

LATRICE ROYALE: There was so much heart in our season. And our *Untucked*s were very passionate and heated. Woo! We gave you some *Untucked* situations. But that's when the fans really got to understand the core of who we were as people and individuals and so they connected with us and our stories resonated with them because they saw themselves. And so given that, it really changed the dynamic of what *Drag Race* had been up until that point. People always say to me, "Get those nuts away from my face!" Oh my god. And that "Good god, get a grip, girl." They are iconic moments. "Go back to Party City! This isn't RuPaul's Best Friend Race!" We had the lines! We had the whole thesaurus.

MICHELE "MEESH" MILLS: Latrice emits lovability but in a badass kind of way. She was always just nice and pleasant but also very wise and not taking shit from anyone. I'm still friendly with her to this day.

She was always wonderful on set and she was just always the voice of reason. But it's also her story. She had lost everything, her family disowned her, she ends up in jail, she lost all her drag. She really just hit rock bottom and turned her whole life around. She owns her own company now, she owns a beautiful house, she is married. She is so inspiring.

JIGGLY CALIENTE: We were the turning point where *Drag Race* became the big thing. We were in seventy-five countries. And I think *Drag Race* Season 4 was the first season where they kinda dug into us more and got to know the person behind all that, too. That's why our season was such a big hit and people fell in love with all of us.

But the queens didn't always fall in love with each other. Lashauwn Beyond may have just been learning to paint her face when the competition began, but her way with words lived on in herstory. "I don't have to be your friend to win this show! This is not RuPaul's Best Friend Race!" Lashauwn famously screamed at Jiggly Caliente during an *Untucked* brawl in the first episode over sewing and makeup.

TOM CAMPBELL: Every year, there are new words and new references, but that's one of the lines that will come up forever. From the contestants to Ru, our show has a big influence on drag culture. We self-reference. It becomes its own language, which is really what drag culture and queer culture is about.

JIGGLY CALIENTE: Lashauwn got really good critiques but she didn't like what they had to say about her makeup. I was so annoyed with the fact that she was talking as if she was in the bottom. And I was like, shut up. I was telling the girls—not the judges—that I don't know how to sew. Outside of this, do I need to ever make an outfit? No. I have a designer that works with me. Why would I need to learn how to make an outfit? And so she was aggravated or annoyed by my lack of interest in wanting to sew. And I was like, but that's not my gig. So when she was trying to say shit like that, I was like, well, bitch, your makeup is shit, how are you talking to me? I was so annoyed. I was like whatever, bitch.

DIDA RITZ: I think I might've been in the Gold Bar when that happened. When I watched, I was kinda shocked. But tensions were always high because we knew we had to deliver. So I think that Lashauwn and Jiggly might have let that fight get kinda crazy 'cause they never had a spat like that off camera. So I think that being there and being in the moment, it was like you know what, Season 4 *Untucked*, bitch, you comin' for me, I'm getting yo ass, too. Even when Jiggly told me, she was like, "Me and her got into it in *Untucked*. We just had words." That was more than words, girl!

MICHELE "MEESH" MILLS: Jiggly's a fun, crazy character, kind of like very New York and very Barbie doll gone left. Very mouthy, very mouthy, which is fun on reality TV. Lashauwn was a really fun queen. She made all of her own clothes and she was really good friends with Latrice. She was not as fully baked in her drag as some of the other ones, which is why she didn't last as long, but she was very lovable and honestly will always be forever remembered for her quote.

JIGGLY CALIENTE: I cringe at it now because Lashauwn and I have become friends and we're cool. But I was like, ohh fuuuuck. Every year, it comes up. My legacy on *Drag Race* will forever stand because of my fight with Lashauwn and Ru's "May I call you Jiggly?"

CHRIS MCKIM: It's always sad to see somebody go in that first episode, but Lashauwn lived long beyond his time on *RuPaul's Drag Race*.

VANESSA VANJIE MATEO: I love the *Untucked* lounges, the Interior Illusions Lounges, they need to bring back that. This is not best friends race and all the arguing and fighting and the cocktails and all the slurpy sound effects. Legendary! I live.

. . . .

It turned out that Lashauwn and Jiggly's fight was only the appetizer. When Sharon Needles called Phi Phi "a tired-ass showgirl" during a werkroom fight, Phi Phi replied with some of the most infamous words ever screamed on the show: "At least I'm a showgirl, bitch, go back to Party City where you belong!"

CHAD MICHAELS: It was electrical. The room just lit up. We all just froze like an animal that gets in trouble, and everyone kind of side-looked and no one was saying anything and we all just stayed really still to let it happen and not get in the middle of it.

LATRICE ROYALE: Baby, we all stopped what we were doing. We were all in the mirror doing our thing and they started going back and forth, and we were just like oh my god. No, they ain't for real! And we could not believe how fast it escalated. I was right there when Sharon came over to speak to Phi Phi. She was like, "I said some things on the runway and I wanted to bring it up to you and let you know." And Phi Phi said, "So basically you threw me under the bus?" So Phi Phi wasn't having it from jump street. It just escalated and then those famous words came out of their mouths.

DIDA RITZ: The werkroom that I remember is not a large room. You can hear everything. So when they sat down and started having this talk and it started getting heated, Latrice and I came together and were like, if they start fightin' you'll grab one, I'll grab the other. We don't want no fights, girl. So when she was screaming "Go back to Party City!" I knew this was gonna be the moment of our season. Signed, sealed, and delivered. Sharon had admitted before that she shopped at Party City and that was her gag.

TOM CAMPBELL: I didn't know about Party City until this episode. It's where I get all my wigs now.

CHAD MICHAELS: It was loud and it was dramatic and it was funny, too. It was just funny to see people's personalities start really coming out at that point. You got to see Sharon on the defensive, but then you got to see Sharon recoil a little bit, get a little bit hurt. You got to see Phi Phi really blow those lungs out. It was great. It was good TV. That was just a product of the fishbowl and of the pressure and the stress, and maybe a little bit of getting on each other's nerves, but look at us today, we're all friends.

DIDA RITZ: That entire fight was honestly prompted by Kenya in my opinion. I love Kenya but Kenya told Phi Phi that Sharon basically ratted her out on the runway. Kenya was on the runway with us while we were all getting critiqued and Phi Phi was safe. But I remember that Kenya prompted that whole thing because it was never brought up on the runway. It was brought up in the werkroom. And I think what happened was Phi Phi, wanting to be the villain, decided this was the moment that she could really let the world know how crazy she is.

JIGGLY CALIENTE: We were safe, we won, why is it an issue? That's what I didn't get from Sharon's part—we won and you won the challenge, so why do you have an issue about it? You are clearly on top, why is that an issue? Kenya went and ran and told Phi Phi what Sharon said on the main stage. She low-key started that. I was hoping they were going to fight. I was that girl going, "Hit her! Hit her!" They were both wrong!

MICHELE "MEESH" MILLS: I don't remember that but that's very possible because Kenya was very tight with Phi Phi. She was very sneaky. There is a reason they were friends. But she was a little more stealth than Phi Phi.

TOM CAMPBELL: Sharon was another breakthrough, just pushed the limits. We hadn't seen a spooky queen and her intellect and her commitment to drag and how she saw it as a real art form. And then the rivalry between those two is epic. The whole thing was intense and it was real. We were capturing their dynamic, raw and unfiltered.

VANESSA VANJIE MATEO: After that, everybody made sure their outfits did not look like it was Party City store-bought. It set the tone for picking a side. Are you gonna be on the side of the girls at the pageants? Or the girls that are gonna be doing whatever they wanna do and are the future of drag? It was the gay Super Bowl, one team versus another team. I live!

MICHELE "MEESH" MILLS: Where's the popcorn? We were watching it like a movie.

CHRIS MCKIM: That was so exciting! I loved it because there is a lot going on during the day and it happened in one of those moments. I happened to be sitting there when that happened and just being so excited, thinking about where I was going to cut it. I have fun taking that moment and helping to make it fun with the editors.

MICHELLE VISAGE: I didn't know anything about it until it aired. I think in that pressure cooker of a television show, there is no right or wrong. I think people will fall on either side of the argument but unless you know what it's like to compete like that under the scrutiny of cameras and the pressure that you're under, you don't know what you're feeling. So I think they both had a point to what they were saying and I think they both felt very strongly about what they were saying.

DIDA RITZ: I will tell you the magic of Sharon and Phi Phi is that as much as they fight and argue there was a deep-down love and respect for each other, and hyping that up was part of the fun of that.

CHRIS MCKIM: It's always fun when you drive past a Party City now, right? Had we known ahead of time, we would have been raiding Party City for all the fright wigs they could give us. Nobody wants to give you money but they will give you product.

ADORE DELANO: This was iconic! I was in love with Sharon at the time so I was totally on her side. But watching it back now as a fan, objectively, knowing both of them personally, I'm like this is iconic television. I thoroughly enjoy it now. I have a chip on my shoulder, though. My old wigs!

TOM CAMPBELL: At different times when I'm angry, I've been the one throwing my hands back and going, "Go back to Party City where you belong!" It's somehow cathartic.

Like the queens that came before them, Season 4's girls knew they'd be competing in Snatch Game, which, by then, had become a season highlight for fans across the world. The pressure was on: Tatianna and Pandora had brought the house down when they impersonated Britney Spears and Carol Channing, respectively, in the second season; and Stacy Layne Matthews followed up with Mo'Nique perfection, from her spot-on makeup and hair, to her sweat suit and her nasty grunts. But as flawless as Chad Michaels was as Cher and as bold as Sharon Needles was as Michelle Visage, the taping of Snatch Game quickly devolved into painful pandemonium. Compensating for their lack of character and ingenuity, first-row queens Jiggly Caliente, Phi Phi O'Hara, and Kenya Michaels pulled focus from the game by being as outlandish as possible. The next day in the werkroom, Latrice laid down the shade of it all, calling their unprofessional behavior "Romper Room fuckery."

CHAD MICHAELS: I was honestly a little bit apprehensive and scared because I didn't want to go on and just do the cliché Cher jokes. And I also did not want to offend her because she does keep an eye on me and she's got people around her that make her aware of everything pretty much concerned with her. And, to me, drag has never been a joke and doing Cher has never been a joke. So it was really important for me to get on there and be funny under the rules of the game. It's not to go on there and be Evita and sing from balconies. It's to be funny respectfully.

JIGGLY CALIENTE: When we shot that, we had a couple days off and there was an MTV marathon of *Jersey Shore*. So I was like, good, I'll do Snookie.

DIDA RITZ: I wanted to do Beyoncé but Kenya took Beyoncé. I wanted to do Diana Ross and Milan took Diana Ross. So then my backup is Wendy Williams because at the time I was watching Wendy a lot on TV and I knew that I could reference a lot if I had to. At the time, Wendy would pull a Slim Jim out of her wig. I pulled one out and gave one to Ru. In one quick clip, they have Ru holding the Slim Jim in his hand. I gave the other one to Latrice because, at that point, Latrice was like, "I ain't got no more food." I said, "Oh, I got you right here." They didn't show that, I was really upset about that. I felt confident going into Snatch Game. But all the Romper Room fuckery bullshit happened and it's hard to watch.

TOM CAMPBELL: It was one of the noisiest tapings of Snatch Game ever. There were lots of people and they were crammed together. The magic of Snatch Game is about timing. And Ru goes down the line so you know he's coming. Everybody wanted attention and it became a little chaotic.

JIGGLY CALIENTE: The most chaotic Snatch Game in history.

LATRICE ROYALE: It went left, honey. It didn't even start off right and was left, honey. So yeah, that was hard, that was rough, because I wanted to do well in that but I was distracted. I couldn't believe what I was witnessing. RuPaul was over it. It went on for a while, to the point that they were stepping on his lines where he couldn't get his bit out because they were still acting the fool. And I was like, see now you pissing off Mama Ru, this is not how this is supposed to be.

DIDA RITZ: It became difficult for Ru to do his job, for him to say his lines or get his pun or joke out because there is chaos going around—people are fainting and falling out of their chairs—and I could see the frustration on his face. This was a mess.

TOM CAMPBELL: I remember Chad's incredible wig changes, which was iconic and the first time someone did that.

CHAD MICHAELS: I was with the kids down in front. That shoot was probably about three hours. There's a lot of activity. We were on rolling computer chairs. They had wheels. I don't know who pushed but someone pushed from one end and I literally went wheeling out into the studio. I didn't fall on the ground. They just pushed my chair. I'm like, whoa! Like, fifteen, twenty feet away. How is there that much power coming from Kenya Michaels? It was chaotic. It really was.

JIGGLY CALIENTE: I planned for like four, maybe five questions. And RuPaul threw in one last one and I was like, fuck, what am I gonna do, I was like fuck. *Snookie wants smush smush*, that's exactly where that came from. And then when I was doing that, I knocked over my fucking jar of pickles that spilled all over my legs and my dress. I smelled like pickles for a whole day. There are no showers in the fucking studio so I couldn't wash myself properly. I was so annoyed.

DIDA RITZ: I was dead-ass right in the middle and I was so envious of Chad Michaels 'cause at least Chad was like off to the side and he could do his own thing. I couldn't imagine if Chad was in the middle of that. Oh my god, that would've went a whole different way.

CHAD MICHAELS: I've been planning that my whole life, so I was just trying to be in my bubble because I knew this is what I came there for. I wanted to do my Cher on *Drag Race* and have that platform. I was concentrating really, really hard. My ability to stay in character comes from years of doing it. When I'm onstage, there's so much shit going on. There's a bachelorette here pulling off her shirt, there's a couple guys making out here, there's a fight in the back, so I'm used to chaos while I'm doing my thing.

LATRICE ROYALE: I couldn't believe what was happening. They were all bombing so it was desperate attempts to redeem and try to be funny. So they would go extra and it was just extra. And it didn't work.

MICHELE "MEESH" MILLS: We were watching it in the room and it was everything that you saw plus more with all the queens just acting a mess. We could see Latrice's face, she was not having it. They were pushing each other, they were talking over each other. And the queens who were not a part of that were so irritated with them. And it really was a mess. I don't know what they were thinking.

CHRIS MCKIM: I think they were all in character and just getting messy. Wasn't Phi Phi down there playing on a piano or something?

CHAD MICHAELS: I think it sparked from people not being prepared and using hijinks to get the attention of the judges. That's the only thing that I can figure. We certainly weren't stoned. We weren't drunk. But if you're watching the show, it looked we're having a really crazy good time. I think people's nerves got the best of them.

LATRICE ROYALE: I thought I was gonna go home because I didn't have a good performance because I had shut down. I had really shut down. I couldn't believe that this is what we're doing. Ooh, gurl.

DIDA RITZ: I was also annoyed because Snatch Game is supposed to be fun and everyone is supposed to be able to participate in it off of each other. The front row was just foolishness and Romper Room. I could not deal with it. I could not. Latrice spoke for how I felt, how Chad felt, how Willam felt. We were all kind of shocked and appalled.

JIGGLY CALIENTE: I genuinely felt bad that I was a hindrance and an inconvenience to other people and it was not my intention. I was just trying to make my Snatch Game fun and good. I didn't know that it was affecting other people like that. I felt bad so I apologized to Latrice and everybody. I didn't know I was gonna be the only one that apologized. I wasn't the only one that was a fucking mess that day. Bitch, Beyoncé was manic, what the fuck? And Lady Gaga, too! Child.

CHRIS MCKIM: I loved the fight the next day. Latrice is just so fun to listen to. I was really excited because sometimes it's frustrating that the queens spend all this time in the *Drag Race* world and then they go claw each other's hair out in *Untucked*. Oh, you're fine on set, but then you're crazy people who are just tearing each other apart. So when this was happening in the room, I was like, yes!

MICHELE "MEESH" MILLS: When Latrice read them for Romper Room fuckery, oh my god, that was another delicious moment. You go, Latrice, you tell them. She was not happy. She felt like the whole group of them had been made to look like a fool, including herself. She was really pissed.

TOM CAMPBELL: Romper Room fuckery! Latrice summed it up pretty well.

Willam walked into the empty werkroom on the first day of the season and licked a makeup case so that no one else would use it. By the time she became the first queen to be disqualified in herstory, she had broken so many rules that it's difficult for anyone involved with the show to pinpoint what the final straw was. Years later in media interviews and social media, Willam admitted his goal was never to become America's Next Drag Superstar. He was just "trying to fuck shit up" and make a name for himself. As he intentionally broke rule after rule—leaving the hotel to go to a nearby store, getting drunk and high, having a computer in his room, and stealing from set—Willam said he was waiting to be kicked off.

The day finally arrived during the filming of the eighth episode, "Frenemies." The queens had been paired up to perform a duet to an original song, "So Much Better Than You." Willam and Latrice Royale earned rave reviews from the judges and won the challenge. Then they retreated to the back of the stage to wait for RuPaul to announce the queens that would be lip syncing for their lives. As RuPaul called on Phi Phi and Sharon Needles to place them in the bottom, Willam threw up off the side of the stage, shocking everyone, including guest judge Pamela Anderson. Minutes later, after Phi Phi and Sharon performed

"It's Raining Men (The Sequel)," RuPaul called Willam, considered a front-runner, to the front of the stage to break the news that she was out. To quote a wise drag philosopher the *Drag Race* universe would meet years later, Shea Couleé: "Mama the drama!"

CHAD MICHAELS: I knew Willam from before. We were both running around West Hollywood doing different gigs and he worked the door at Micky's when we did *Dreamgirls* so we saw him every Monday night. He was very quiet. He had really super-long beautiful hair. It was mid-back. And you know how curly his hair is? It was just like giant blond locks of curls. That's how I remember Willam from that time—kind of reserved but also will cut you.

JIGGLY CALIENTE: I'm in my cute little rockabilly outfit, I walk into the werkroom, and I see Willam. I was watching her movie *Ticked-Off Trannies with Knives* on Netflix before I left for *Drag Race* so she looked really familiar. I said, "I know you," and she threw that in my face: "Oh, you must own a television." In my head, I was going, *Bitch, your movie went straight to DVD, calm down.*

DIDA RITZ: In the beginning, Willam was a really hard person for people to understand on our cast. I never took her to heart.

JIGGLY CALIENTE: I thought Willam was annoying because I thought she was so smug. *I've done this, I've done this, I've done this.* Now that I work in television, I get that she is just proud of her body of work. But at the time she was fuckin' annoying.

LATRICE ROYALE: I had been calling her Snatch Willam because she was just talking too much shit, like she was all that and a bag of chips. She had her shoes with the labels. I was over her. Then I started to get to know her during the boat challenge the week before. And when they paired us up for this challenge, I was like, okay, she's not bad. She's just misunderstood.

RANDY BARBATO: It was still very early in this series. Even though the show was growing and it wasn't shot in a closet, it was still on Logo. It is still a small-budget competitive reality show. There is no question it is stressful. It is hard, unbelievable work and unbelievable pressure. We cast him because we loved him. I remember his casting tape. There's footage of him all in blue in a bathtub. We were so excited about having him on the show.

DIDA RITZ: That day, it was taking a very long time for everything to run. And we were getting really concerned because it was longer than normal and we were still in drag. We didn't know who was gonna lip sync. We didn't really know if we were gonna be judged individually or as a group. I remember sitting down on the couch and seeing production going back and forth. You could feel it in the air that something wasn't right.

CHAD MICHAELS: Willam kept leaving the werkroom. But Willam's weird every day.

TOM CAMPBELL: There were a lot of issues that were coming up, like production issues that aren't part of the show. And so all this stuff was happening in those peripheral places that don't belong in the show.

LATRICE ROYALE: We had heard her computer was missing and we're like, wait a minute, what is she doing with a computer? So the stories were unfolding. We heard her husband came. We were more scared that production was going to find out that we were hanging out and our little social gatherings were gonna go away because of this bitch. Everybody was like she's doing shit that we're going to get in trouble for.

CHAD MICHAELS: I think his room was at the other end of the hall from mine. So I didn't really see anything but that time we got to still eat together and hang out in each other's rooms. So I wasn't really hanging out with him. I was more hanging with Sharon and I'd drop in on Kenya and Madame. I wasn't looking for anything so I wasn't Nancy-Drew-ing it.

LATRICE ROYALE: The night before the performance, everyone was staying up, rehearsing, trying to get it together. Willam and I never did. We just talked through what we were gonna do. She was off. She said she was going through some stuff. She was not her normal self.

DIDA RITZ: Chad Michaels and I stayed up all night rehearsing that number to make sure that it was just right. By the time we were ready to perform, we were so ready. We were having fun out there onstage by that point because we had rehearsed all night.

LATRICE ROYALE: Because they never saw us rehearse, the other girls were counting us out. And they were saying if we ended up on the bottom, I needed to send Willam home. Phi Phi was saying we should make it so bad that we're gonna be in the bottom no matter what. But I was not about to go out there and make a fool of myself. We're going to do the best we can. And, honey, we made our little dresses, and we got onstage and blocked out what we were gonna do, just talking our way through it.

TOM CAMPBELL: We do the challenge. Then they change, we have lunch, then they come back onstage, then there's a critique. The period of time gets shrunken for the TV show, but it was during this time span we were juggling shooting the show and managing stuff off camera. And it was difficult.

JIGGLY CALIENTE: Willam decided to have a meal that day. Willam usually didn't eat when we were filming. She would have little snacks here and there, but she wouldn't have lunch. And then the dumb bitch asked Latrice to tie her back into her corset. That's not smart. You're gonna have a full meal and then you're gonna have this big, brawling bitch tie you back in a corset? Yeah, that's smart, bitch!

DIDA RITZ: Before we went out on the main stage, Willam took me aside quickly and said she told them everything that she did. She said she told the producers she went out and whatever but she didn't tell them that I was with her and I shouldn't say anything.

TOM CAMPBELL: So we were trying to decide, is this happening tonight? Are we doing this tomorrow? How do we deal with the exit of a queen? How do we even begin to explain it in the story of the show? There's no foreshadowing in the mini challenge. There was no interview. It was something we needed to address, so let's do it here in front of everyone.

LATRICE ROYALE: When she first started jerking her head, I was like, "Are you okay?" And she's like, "Mm mm." And she had this corset on. All of a sudden, there's puke at my feet. We are literally gagged.

JIGGLY CALIENTE: That's what Latrice gets. You shouldn't have tied it that tight, bitch.

CHAD MICHAELS: You just heard "Get camera number 2 on Willam!" Those cameras are on giant tripods. They got it all, baby. It was funny. It was a little bit alarming, too, because we didn't know what was going on. And it was just quite a day.

DIDA RITZ: When Willam threw up, I got fearful. And I just told myself, if they say something and they ask just tell them that you did go with her. You don't wanna be caught lying on camera.

LATRICE ROYALE: And then when Ru was like, "Willam, front and center," we're like, well, where is this going?

CHAD MICHAELS: That caught everybody off guard. We had no idea why Ru was calling her up to the front of the runway after everything had already been decided for the day, basically.

DIDA RITZ: My heart dropped into my butt. It was just fear. Why is Willam getting called up there? Am I next?

LATRICE ROYALE: And then the famous, "It has been brought to my attention...and I'm sorry, Willam, I'm going to have to ask you to leave the competition immediately." We were all gagged.

JOEY NOLFI: It's what we come to reality television for—a juicy moment like that, especially when it happens to someone who was as popular with the fans as Willam was and still is to this day. I think Willam is fabulous, I think Willam is so funny and smart and has navigated this industry in a really unique way. But seeing that was shocking. You feel bad that someone is being disqualified but you're also like, okay, give me the tea, what is really going down? It was all kinds of emotions.

TOM CAMPBELL: This is the thing about Willam—he is an incredibly talented drag artist. But when it comes to a competition show, he is not meant for captivity. He is a free-range queen, and needs to be running wild in a field of clover. When you try to tell Willam what to do—even in the most constructive way—he doesn't want to hear it.

CHRIS MCKIM: When a queen got eliminated, they would do their little goodbye thing and we would usher them out to do their last interview and then they'd have to pack their stuff up. This had never happened before on *Drag Race* herstory so we had to deal with it. After she was kicked off, we went to go talk to her. If you recall, she put lipstick on her ass and put the print on the mirror. So she was upstairs in the Interior Illusions Lounge sitting on a Kleenex because she still had lipstick all over her ass.

LATRICE ROYALE: Everybody was shooketh.

CHRIS MCKIM: I honestly cannot remember the final reason why she got kicked off.

TOM CAMPBELL: It's hard to know now if what Willam did behind the scenes really happened. Some of it really happened. Some of them he lied about so that you think they happened. It's an impossible story to tell in a sound bite and, ultimately, it was distracting from production and the other queens.

DIDA RITZ: Drag queens need a lot of things in order to do this on a

daily basis—multiple cans of hair spray, lots of nail glue and under-
garments, all these little things that we naturally pack [for] shows to
bring with us but this is for a month and a half or two months. I was
very light on resources and I didn't want to have that in my story
line—that I didn't have this or that. Willam knew that I was new to
all this and I really needed stuff from the store. So, I admit it. We
went to the store.

JIGGLY CALIENTE: I had a cell phone. I handed them a dummy phone
and I kept my cell phone. I didn't even really get to use it 'cause the
schedule of *Drag Race* is like boom, boom, boom. I was exhausted. It
was like, get back to the hotel room, eat something, and sleep.

CHRIS MCKIM: I think part of it was like it felt like she didn't want to
be there and there were multiple times of leaving the hotel. There is
a game element of fairness to consider. There's also an element of us
being responsible for these people. What if somebody gets hit by a car?
There had been a lot of that kind of bullshit throughout. There was
such an umbrella of bullshit.

DIDA RITZ: When she told them everything that she was doing, I think
she knew she was taking the bad-girl role. I think she accepted being a
bad girl and being disqualified. That's why when she gets disqualified
you can see my face like, oh my god. If Ru would've called me up and
asked me about it, I would've openly admitted it. But it didn't happen.

JIGGLY CALIENTE: Season 4-ever is thick as thieves, we are not gonna
rat each other out. I feel bad that she got disqualified but it was like
well, bitch, you got caught. I found out when we all got home.

RANDY BARBATO: I know stories have changed and I know that there
have been stories about how other people broke other rules and I'm
sure there have been. But it's about the spirit of—are you in this? Do
you want to do this? Are you going to play by the rules? Or are you going to be disruptive to the whole process?

TOM CAMPBELL: We gave him this epic send-off and purposefully invited him back to the reunion so he could tell his story. We always want to end on a good place with the queens.

JIGGLY CALIENTE: At the reunion, she was talking about having sex with her husband and I was like, is that all you did? That's all you wanna say? Okay. But Willam didn't rat any of us out, so I wasn't gonna say anything. I was just like, go ahead, bitch, go ahead.

CHRIS MCKIM: We didn't even know she had slept with her husband. That could very well be true, but we didn't know that. That wasn't why she got kicked out. It really felt like she just wanted to get kicked off.

CHAD MICHAELS: I think that Willam worked everybody's nerves individually. So him being gone was just kind of like an element that was taken away that would let us all maybe focus on what we were doing a little bit more without having to be like, goddamn, Willam, quiet down!

DIDA RITZ: Willam can turn it on for a camera but she really took the friendship we were forming seriously.

LATRICE ROYALE: Willam is my good Judy, actually. If there was ever some shit to really go down and I needed someone, I know I could call her.

CHAD MICHAELS: If Willam hadn't gotten disqualified for whatever reason, he would have gone really far on the show. Willam's super talented, he's original and funny as hell. He can pretty much channel anything you throw at him so I think he would have gone far.

TOM CAMPBELL: Willam seemed top-three material to me. Top four, for sure. We never want anyone to leave. We've watched their tapes. We've sent them plane tickets. We root for them every week. We want them to stay.

MICHELLE VISAGE: I actually really enjoyed Willam. I thought he was really funny and he always made me laugh. The one word I can use to describe it is *confusion*. I had no idea what was going on. I still to this day don't know what happened. There are many theories online and I think Willam himself has said a few different things. So I really don't know what the truth is. But I remember going, what the fuck is happening?

JIGGLY CALIENTE: We were the worst season ever. We broke so many rules and I'm one of the people that broke rules. But Willam took the whole blame for himself and didn't rat any of us out.

CHRIS MCKIM: We're all just trying to make a show and we're not here for these antics.

LATRICE ROYALE: We are the reason that the queens are on lockdown now so securely. Season 4 was definitely the pivotal moment for that. We really hung out and we watched TV and ate dinner together. We were social. But the deal was you don't talk production and we always had a chaperone to make sure that that was not going on.

Now your hotel room door is taped shut so they know that you've not broken the seal. They slide a note under the door if you need something. In our season, it was just a normal closed door.

JIGGLY CALIENTE: Hell no, I don't feel bad! We got to eat dinner together in the hallway like a family. They don't do that now. They can't even look out the peephole nowadays.

DIDA RITZ: One of the things I've learned from Willam is to do what you gotta do and have fun and apologize for the things that you have to after if you've gone too far.

LATRICE ROYALE: But then the question lingered. Who would have went home out of Sharon and Phi Phi if that did not happen? I have always wondered how different the season would have turned out. That would've changed the whole game.

. . . .

The season was bookended by lip syncs that became instant classics. The first was a third-episode battle between The Princess and Dida Ritz to Natalie Cole's first hit "This Will Be (An Everlasting Love)," a battle sweetened by the presence of the late singer at the judge's table.

DIDA RITZ: Lip syncing against The Princess was very hard. But to do it in front of Natalie Cole, that makes up for it a little bit. Natalie Cole is an icon, so to be able to do her song in front of her, that is something that still sits in my head all the time. I think about her smile and how when she came out to sit down she had this gorgeous black dress on that touched the ground and they were holding the back of her dress as she was walking. So adorable! She had her little white slippers on to go sit down.

TOM CAMPBELL: One of the beautiful things we've learned is a good song is timeless. I remember watching the Grammys with my sister as a young Natalie Cole performed "This Will Be." I was like eleven years old and I bought that single. It was her first hit. Flash-forward three decades and Natalie Cole is our guest judge. I recall that she wanted us to use a different song. Maybe she had a new song. We were like can you tell Miss Cole that there are a lot of gay people here who love that song? Randy felt exactly the same way about Natalie Cole and that song. It's just one of those songs that really touches people.

CHRIS MCKIM: Those were always very exciting lip syncs when the queens got to perform in front of the artist. A couple times we had a great star and we were not able to clear the best song they have, but that was amazing. Dida was just fabulous.

JOHN POLLY: It was epic. Dida fully embodied the spirit and energy of the song.

JIGGLY CALIENTE: We were watching it from the back, but Dida was getting it. I feel bad to say this but poor Princess didn't have a prayer in hell. Like, as soon as Dida started doing the shuffle I was like *ohh that's it*. Dida did that! And in front of Natalie Cole, it was just iconic.

TOM CAMPBELL: And Randy said let's give all the judges handkerchiefs. That was one of the only times we ever added a prop to the lip sync. But we had no idea. Dida Ritz was a great queen but no one saw that coming. And that is maaaaybe the best lip sync in *Drag Race* herstory because that lip sync was amazing and electric and fueled by the Holy Spirit. And the great Natalie Cole was there watching it.

RANDY BARBATO: My favorite lip sync of all time of *RuPaul's Drag Race*. I have a personal connection to that song. I have such warm feelings that connect it to my childhood. I love Natalie Cole and she was on the panel and she took her handkerchief out. Princess did a good job, too, but Dida killed it. It was like the Lord was running through her veins. She was possessed.

MICHELLE VISAGE: One of the absolute greats.

DIDA RITZ: That was always the piece, the one thing I feel that I, as a Ru girl, can hold on to that no other Ru girl can hold on to. There's been so many great lip syncs on the show but no one of y'all have made RuPaul and the judges and Michelle pick up handkerchiefs and start havin' church. I'm a little cocky about that because that to me is iconic. The judges normally sit there, very prim and proper and together. And for them to really lose it at a performance lets me know the energy that I am blessed to give off onstage.

In a stunning juxtaposition, Latrice Royale faced off with Kenya Michaels in the tenth episode in a lip-sync battle of Aretha Franklin's "(You Make Me Feel Like) A Natural Woman." Wearing their baby bumps from the pregnant diva challenge, the season's largest and tiniest drag queens approached the song in completely different ways. Latrice stood still; Kenya danced ballet all around her, creating one of the series' most indelible moments.

LATRICE ROYALE: It came to me in the moment, as I was standing.

I had no shoes on, I got this baby bump, it's Aretha and "Natural Woman." This song is about this baby and how it makes her feel like a woman, like this is what makes you feel whole. And so I really channeled and tried to be that mom. Maybe it's her firstborn and she's singing to her. That's just old-school drag coming out, honey, and telling the story. And that's what we do as drag queens: We try to tell stories.

TOM CAMPBELL: Shut up! The weirdest, best lip sync of all time because they all had baby bumps. I love when you watch it online without knowing the context. What's going on? Who are these people dressed as women with baby bumps? And Latrice sooo won that lip sync. But I have to say the counterpoint of little Kenya Michaels, like a ballerina in a jewelry box, was so beautiful. It was an epic performance. Sometimes there's too much shablamming and death drops and histrionics. That was just pure feeling and embodiment of the lyrics.

CHRIS MCKIM: Latrice didn't move an inch. She just stood there. There was such a contrast. Sometimes you'll have two queens and they both do death drops. This was exciting because they couldn't have been more different.

RANDY BARBATO: That was one of those lip syncs where you're like, what is going on? It was so freakishly compelling 'cause Latrice was pregnant, just standing there and singing "You Make Me Feel Like a Natural Woman" with her hands on her belly and then Kenya doing ballet in the background. It was the other magical lip sync of the season.

CHAD MICHAELS: That lip sync has aged well.

MICHELLE VISAGE: That lip sync is one of my favorites of all time. Latrice was always a great personality, always a great sense of humor. I just fucking love her.

JOEY NOLFI: That lip sync was a culmination of Latrice just doing what Latrice does really well, simultaneously approaching the competition in a way that was very strategic because she knew what Kenya was gonna do and she purposely did the exact opposite. There is genuine emotion from Latrice going into that song. So it is such a unique blend of things that you can literally only get on *RuPaul's Drag Race*.

LATRICE ROYALE: I can't tell you how many cisgender women have written and told me how that performance moved them and inspired them and how I captured really the essence of a mother's love and they really related. I do drag...to pay homage to women. I respect them and want to be the glamorous side of that.

As the season headed toward a glossy finish, RuPaul and the producers had a few surprises for the queens and fans alike. For the first time, three finalists—Sharon Needles, Phi Phi O'Hara, and Chad Michaels—competed for the crown. Their last challenge was to shoot the music video for RuPaul's "Glamazon" and lip sync the song in front of the judges. But as they waited for RuPaul to declare the winner, the host ruvealed a change in the show's format: The winner of the season would be announced at the reunion, which would be filmed nearly a year later at El Portal Theatre in Los Angeles in front of an audience.

At the reunion, Sharon, Phi Phi, and Chad learned there were even more surprises in store for them.

JIGGLY CALIENTE: All the people screaming in the theater and seeing how huge *Drag Race* was. That was really fucking cool.

THAIRIN SMOTHERS: People were screaming like they were at a sports event for Sharon Needles and I thought oh my god this is different. And then that's when it took off.

CHAD MICHAELS: At the finale, they were walking us onstage in our final looks and they said, "Hey, guys, listen, we've got something to tell you. We're going to go ahead and film three endings tonight. And we're going to crown each and every one of you. And then we're going to announce the real winner on the show when it airs." And we were all, are you fucking kidding me? We were pissed because they sprung it on us last-minute. It wouldn't have been an issue if they had prepped us for it. But to break protocol and switch the rules up and change the format the second before you walk onstage?

TOM CAMPBELL: More than anything, we just wanted to make it bigger and better. We were still on Logo, and the numbers were small, but we still felt like we had created a cultural juggernaut. It kept growing each year and we wanted to bring our tribe together. But once you're in public, how do you keep the crowning a secret? That's when we came up with the idea of multiple endings.

CHAD MICHAELS: Imagine being in the middle of all that but having to fake through two other crownings. And in your mind going I'm fucking pissed off right now because they switched the rules. It was a lot mentally to absorb in a very short amount of time with an acting challenge on top of it, which was acting like a winner and then acting like a first and second runner-up minutes after they told you that. So to me that was the probably the biggest challenge of Season 4. I do understand why they do it. They have to protect the security of the show and the secret. It just sucks that that's the climate we live in. Whenever I see a winner get crowned now on the show, I know the real tea. And I always look to see what a good actress they are. That's their final acting challenge right there. So it's interesting for me to see. I'm a great actress. I carried Sharon's train for her ass.

TOM CAMPBELL: Once the name is announced, boom, it's a celebration and then the competition is over. So it's as real as can be. As a by-product we've created a very meta moment when the viewers get to watch the top queens as they're watching the show to see who really won. It's really the only way to do it.

JIGGLY CALIENTE: Because of the feedback of the fans, I did feel like Sharon was gonna win. Phi Phi was public enemy number one.

DIDA RITZ: I knew Sharon was going to win because they all loved her, even when Sharon had questionable things on or looked a mess or was unkempt, they always gave her such praise and credit because she had a good personality. Also, drag was evolving at that point. It was becoming what Sharon was—that whole darker creative artsy vibe.

LATRICE ROYALE: I was completely happy with it. People thought that I wouldn't be but no, she was the one to beat. So the fact that she won was completely correct and so necessary because it changed the perception of what drag was and it broke down a lot of barriers and gave a lot of permissions to a lot of people who didn't fit in that mold. And there are people who like to be gothic and freaky and witchy and creepy and it's all beautiful and it's all art and it's all expressions and extensions of your inner workings. And I think that is what drag is and should be. Sharon gave people more freedom to express who they are.

MICHELLE VISAGE: Sharon is very glamorous. She is just one of the smartest people I know. She is so well rounded when it comes to pop culture. Her winning showed people that *Drag Race* was for them, too. It showed there are scary drag queens that do spooky and horror and that's their thing but they are also amazingly creative and inventive and glamorous.

AQUARIA: *Drag mom* is definitely more of a term we use to make our relationship make sense to other people. Sharon was doing a show in Philadelphia, which I couldn't scam my way into, so she invited me over to her hotel room with my mom. She clearly saw something in me and wanted to make this little kid's day. Her manager was sitting there with his laptop on the toilet while she's getting ready, asking her all her interview questions. I was there for fifteen minutes because she had to bounce.

ALASKA: It was electrifying. The fan response to the phenomenon of Sharon was ridiculous. Even though we were sort of on the inside of that, we could still see that and feel that. That being said, we still didn't think she was going to win. We didn't think at any point that we got this in the bag because she was up against Chad Michaels, who was drag perfection. We didn't think it was for her, this crown. And then it ended up happening. It was definitely palpable. It galvanized the fans and the fan base in a way that hadn't really been harnessed the seasons previous to that.

CHAD MICHAELS: Sharon was the winner the world needed at that time for the people that weren't seeing themselves in the competition, for the people who considered themselves outsiders, outcasts, nerds, not your average, run-of-the-mill gay. He represented a lot of people who didn't have a voice, and for that reason I happily lost to Sharon.

ADORE DELANO: Sharon winning made a lot of weird people become powerful. My normal shit was flannel because of Sharon or a punk shirt because of Sharon. But they would book me for the pretty or tell me to put my hair in a ponytail and contour a little more, don't do the white contacts. But when Sharon represented that, I was like, it's full-force now. I reverted when I went on the show in order to play the game. But I saw the shift in the drag community because of Sharon.

ACID BETTY: Sharon Needles slayed and put the nail in the coffin with the show. It became world-famous. That's when *RuPaul's Drag Race* discovered its true audience and it was this alternative, maybe-not-beautiful-all-the-time kid that has a little something and if they throw a little makeup and wig on and Vaseline on the lens they, too, can be Lady Gaga. A lot of people I think recognized themselves in that person. For all the freaks and the weirdos, like me at a young age, who didn't have a real voice or a place to call home, she was blowing the siren.

JINKX MONSOON: Sharon Needles's drag on *Drag Race* was not shocking to me because I came from a performance art community. In Portland, there were plenty of drag queens doing the same kind of stuff that Sharon was doing on television. But Sharon's the first one to bring horror-themed drag and drag that is edgy and gross sometimes to television. And it really shifted the drag community. The drag community turned a huge corner at that point. Performance artist drag queens weren't being taken seriously by the pageant drag queens or the bar drag queens, but all of a sudden, everyone was respecting everyone else's style of drag in a new way that I hadn't seen within my own communities. That was what inspired me to submit my audition tape.

Chapter 5
SEASON 5

S EASON 4 WAS THE TURNING POINT, BUT THE FOLLOWING CYCLE, with its pageant superstars, one-of-a-kind winner, first celebrity roast, and stale and fresh dramas, cemented *Drag Race* as must-watch TV. Epic lip syncs took a back seat to sleeping disorders, back rolls, a new clique, and "Hieeeee!" (sorry, Ongina). Supersized with fourteen queens, the season launched in 2013 and featured the series' first double elimination, first double save, poignant stage confessions, and an exciting finish. Fans were gooped by the inscrutable Seattle MILF Jinkx Monsoon; Alyssa Edwards, a pageant darling and sick'ning dancer from Texas; Florida pageant divas Coco Montrese and Roxxxy Andrews; flexible-jawed Detox; Sharon Needles's then boyfriend Alaska; cute Jade Jolie and her back roll attacks; the season's Miss Congeniality Ivy (Iveeee) Winters; Puerto Rican queen Lineysha Sparx, who birthed Lil' Poundcake with Alaska; San Francisco community activist Honey Mahogany; Panamanian American entrepreneur Serena ChaCha; beautiful queen Vivienne Pinay; Facebook fan choice Penny Tration, who went home first; and Monica Beverly Hillz, who touched fans and queens alike when she opened up on the main stage about being a trans woman. It was everything but a snoozer.

JINKX MONSOON: When I have a sleep attack, it feels like how you feel when you take sleeping pills. All of a sudden, your eyes become extremely heavy and you can't keep your eyes open and all you think about is going to sleep. Right before I started college, I was diagnosed with narcolepsy by doing a sleep study that monitored the way that I slept. In college, my symptoms were very severe mainly because I was burning the candle at both ends. I worked as a janitor at my college, which meant I got up every day at about 5:00 a.m., went and cleaned the school, took my classes all day, and then at night I had rehearsals for whatever project I was working on. On the weekends, I had my improv troupe and anything else I had taken on. My symptoms were extremely severe because I wasn't doing the things to help alleviate my symptoms. I went on *Drag Race* shortly after graduating so I had forewarned them about my symptoms.

ALYSSA EDWARDS: Did they ever see papers? Did she have a doctor's note saying she's narcoleptic? Because that lady is an actress.

THAIRIN SMOTHERS: She didn't fall asleep on her audition. Not that I remember! But she mentioned it. I think she saved that for the cameras on set.

IVY WINTERS: At the time, I wasn't sure if it was an act for TV. I felt like if it were a real disease, it would have been in control by that point with medications. She would not have been falling asleep when she was. I know filming *Drag Race* was incredibly tiring and I know we all wanted to sleep. Maybe she just fell asleep and it was edited that way. But I thought she was playing it up a little bit. I should have thought of that.

ALYSSA EDWARDS: In my first interview, I was telling the producer, "That poor lady, she keeps fallin' asleep. I'm concerned for her." He said that she's a narcoleptic. I said, "A who?" I honestly thought he was saying narcotics. Y'all need to drug-test the girls. No! She has narcolepsy. Well, what exactly is that? He said it's when someone just falls asleep. She's always sleepy? He's like, no, you can just fall asleep. I said,

"She's probably getting sent home." She's not gonna make it around this track that many times. This is a race. Ha! Whoo girl, honey.

ROXXXY ANDREWS: I never saw that ho fall asleep.

JINKX MONSOON: I think, because I had forewarned them of narcolepsy and because of what they saw as narcolepsy being portrayed in mainstream media, they were prepared for someone who was going to pass out all the time. And they had already started preparing the story for my track on *Drag Race* as a person with narcolepsy. At one point, the producer asked me about it because they hadn't seen me fall asleep.

ALYSSA EDWARDS: Call the Academy because I thought she was really falling asleep. I think I offered her a Red Bull one time. I said, girl, I got some go-go juice over there, do you need a sip?

TOM CAMPBELL: I didn't know that. Jinkx is such an amazing character and that happens to be something that she deals with, too. It's not to be made fun of. It's just rich. Everybody comes with stories; everybody comes with things that get in their way.

COCO MONTRESE: One of the girls explained it to me because I was like, why does Jinkx keep falling asleep? That's so weird. This is exciting, why is she falling asleep all the time? At first, I thought she was acting.

DETOX: It wasn't as crazy as they made it seem. Yes, she has narcolepsy, but it was more like whenever she felt like she had a tired spell coming on, she would find a little place to take a little nap. It wasn't constant and she would push herself, too, to make sure that she was trying to be as present as possible and to do the work. It's exhausting not only physically but also mentally and spiritually being there. So anytime I would see her resting I would be like, goals, bitch!

MICHELE "MEESH" MILLS: She actually fell asleep in interview. She would fall asleep all the time off camera. When they're waiting in the rafters, she would fall asleep in the hallway. Now, what she did tell us is that she has learned to control it but that here it's hard because they are under more stress and they don't get enough sleep. She can't just run off and schedule a nap. So sometimes things would hit her in a way that generally was not really happening to her in her recent normal life.

JINKX MONSOON: It's no secret that editing is done to make the story clearer and to enhance the experience of watching the show. So there were times when I would fall asleep in my interviews. And I remember one time, specifically, they told me we have to change the battery, and I fell asleep in my chair during my interview. But I never fell asleep in the middle of a sentence. I never told everyone it's time for me to take a nap. There were moments when it was authentic and there were moments when it was played up. And, to me, the moments are obvious. When I'm falling asleep trying to write my jokes for the roast, that was real. When I'm seated in a chair and I start dozing off, that's real. When I'm in the middle of a sentence and then, all of a sudden, it cuts to me and I'm asleep, that was played up.

ALYSSA EDWARDS: I was oblivious to all of that, okay? Truth be told, I was self-centered. I was in the mirror, I didn't have time to worry about Jinkx Monsoon falling asleep, nor did I have the energy. Nor was I that worried! I was just like, girl, you gotta make it through these challenges! If she's tired, honey, she needs to take a damn nap. Did y'all not see me over there on the couch, eating potato chips, minding my own business with my shawl on? Go ahead, damn Jinkx Monsoon!

ALASKA: I always make this joke with Jinkx—I have this terrible illness where sometimes I feel sleepy and have to take a nap. Ohhh my gosh, it's horrible. If that's narcolepsy, Tina, I've had narcolepsy my whole damn life. I guess I'm undiagnosed. It was a compelling story line. I think I have more narcoleptic qualities than Jinkx. I literally sometimes get so exhausted and I go fall asleep on the floor. This happens all the time. I can fall asleep at the drop of a hat.

ALYSSA EDWARDS: Oh girl, well, I got a mild form of narcolepsy! 'Cause I'm sleepy right now! Jinkx Monsoon done pulled a sting on all of us. Oh my gosh! Shit, that Jinkx Monsoon. Well, it was Monsoon season, baby.

Known as the Vanessa Williams of the gay community, Alyssa Edwards won Miss Gay America in 2010 only to be dethroned two months later because she wasn't fulfilling her official duties. As the first runner-up, Alyssa's good friend Coco Montrese took over the title, which caused a rift in their relationship. When they made their grand entrances in the werkroom, they hadn't spoken in two years. Their estrangement made no sense to the rest of the cast and lasted longer than all of Jinkx's naps.

ALYSSA EDWARDS: I'm a Southern lady and I found success early on. I won Miss Gay USofA my first attempt in '06. I won Miss Gay Texas my fourth attempt. Went right on to Miss Gay America and won. I was surrounded by so much love and positive energy and people that believed in me. I was the baby sweetheart of Texas and here I am in Hollywood, going on national television, oh my gosh! And then Coco walks in? I said, uh-uh, no ma'am, I'm not losing this one. How's this gonna play out? What's she gonna say, what am I gonna say? What are we gonna say to each other? And then we did it, honey, we seen it. That will go down in history, okay? *Drag Race* herstory, Season 5, unforgettable, the rivalry between Alyssa Edwards and Coco Montrese, honey.

COCO MONTRESE: When I saw Alyssa, I was so shocked. I had to keep remembering we're filming because at the time I wanted to go oh my god, girl, why didn't you talk to me? Why didn't you pick up the phone? That was my first thing.

ALYSSA EDWARDS: I was very much surprised. I'm not that good of an actress. We've all seen that. If you watch it back, I'm trying to hold it together and I'm fidgeting. I keep running my fingers through my hair. And mind you, my hair is kinky curly so I keep fluffing it out. I'm competitive. It lit that fire.

JINKX MONSOON: Drag is very much a community-building thing but at the same time the people that you call sister, you're also in competition with them. And I'm not just talking about *Drag Race*. In every show you perform in, you want to be the best performer. You want to make the most tips. You want to be the person who gets hired again. You want to be the person that the audience loves.

ROXXXY ANDREWS: I'm a pageant girl, so I remember when Alyssa won Miss Gay America. I knew her but I was friends with Coco. Miss Gay America is very by the book. You've always got to have fingernails on, you always have to have pantyhose on, that's not a choice. Alyssa was like strike one, strike two, strike three with that system. So by the time it got to whatever strikes she got, they dethroned her. As the pageant girl, I hate when they pass it down to the first runner-up. But that was Coco's job. She got a lot of slack for it in the beginning but then she ended up an amazing Miss Gay America. She finished her reign. She looked phenomenal at all the prelims. She put in all the hard work.

ALYSSA EDWARDS: At first, I was so embarrassed, humiliated. This is something I worked really hard for. I competed four years for this and I won and these guys are taking it away because they don't think that I'm gonna be worthy. It was a little disheartening. But you know what? Like everything else in life, I picked up and carried on, honey, like Martha Wash. When the valley was deep, baby, I kept it movin'. And that was really the end of that.

COCO MONTRESE: We were really, really good friends. Alyssa won Miss Gay America. She was absolutely incredible and there was six points between us and she won and I was gonna come back the next year and win. But then she ended up getting dethroned by the owners of the pageant. And it created a huge divide between her and I. I gained a crown but I lost a friend at the time because she was going through so much with the owners of the pageant. And that was a really hard time because Alyssa was not only a friend but was somebody I looked up to as an entertainer.

ALYSSA EDWARDS: I remember when I won, the night I won, I remember tellin' her, I'm gonna help you win this next year. And she said, Alyssa, if you choreograph my number I know that I'll do well, and I told her don't worry, I got it. I think people got in the way and got in her head and got in my head. So I just turned my phone off, it was easy for me. I said, baby, I got a dance class to teach. I ain't got time to deal with this foolishness. And all communication stopped.

COCO MONTRESE: I think the rift was mostly because of social media. People didn't understand there was a contract that if something should happen during a certain time frame, the first runner-up would be required to step into that role. I didn't have a choice, but everybody came up with theories about why Alyssa was losing the title that were wrong. Alyssa was going through what she was going through personally because they took a title from her. And we went from talking on the phone every day before the pageant to I couldn't even get her on the phone because it was a devastating, traumatic experience for her. And I was feeling like she didn't step up and defend me and say to everybody it's not her fault, just let her do her reign. It was a hard reign for me. We didn't talk again until we saw each other on *Drag Race*. I felt I was abandoned. It was really one of the hardest things ever to experience.

ROXXXY ANDREWS: Alyssa walked into the werkroom first. I hadn't even heard that Coco got accepted to be on the show. So when Coco walked in, that's the first thing I thought was, oh bitch, they're gonna have it out. That's why it started, "Oh, we'll talk." "Oh no, there's nothing to talk about." "Yes, we'll talk, we'll have our time." As the time rolled on, there were many opportunities to talk about it. I think they definitely used it for their advantage on the television, to stay a little longer until their story was told because you're not going to have a feud and then one of them goes home and they never even talked about it.

COCO MONTRESE: I felt like it was going to be a distraction and I wanted to have the conversation with her right away so we could get it out of the way. She didn't want to have the conversation on camera because I think seeing me brought up the old feelings of everything that had happened with the pageant. I think we were at a different place in our lives at that point and she didn't want to talk about it anymore. But in order for us to move forward, we needed to talk about it. I always knew that at some point we were going to end up having to work together. And I knew that with her ability and her creativity that if we got this out of the way we'd be fine.

DETOX: It was one of the longest story lines ever in *Drag Race*. People who know about the drag world knew already the drama because back in the day the pageant world was the *Drag Race*. Pageant girls were it. It's very rare that something happens where a crown gets stripped from somebody and it has to be re-awarded to the first runner-up. So when it did happen with Alyssa and Coco, it was obviously a lot of confusion and a lot of drama. It was very Alyssa to be like, well, mama, you're the second choice, don't forget that. It was exhausting. Eye roll.

ALASKA: I was like this is dumb. They were trying to be clever about it. Everyone in the room was like what happened between you guys? We don't know the pageant world. What are you talking about? Oh, we'll talk about that later. I was like, ohhh very clever, not obviously trying to manipulate TV drama at all.

JINKX MONSOON: It's this thing where when you're there, and you're in the process of doing it, and you're like, oh, this is an exaggeration of the truth, but it's going to make great TV.

TOM CAMPBELL: I don't know what's inside someone's heart. But it didn't feel fake to me. The whole thing didn't make sense, but the world of pageants and rivalries is something *Drag Race* only captures a sliver of. That rivalry fueled their performances and it made for intense lip syncs.

ALASKA: Alyssa was kind of throwing it in Coco's face a little bit, which I didn't like. And so I understand why it was upsetting to Coco. 'Cause she felt probably overshadowed.

JINKX MONSOON: The evidence that it was being played up for television is the fact that every time we said, can you guys talk this out? One of them would say, "Oh we'll figure this out later." That was what they said eight times.

MICHELE "MEESH" MILLS: We did want to play the story line because it was a real thing that happened and when you talk to them individually there clearly was some animosity. Now, those two probably also hammed it up on top of the real animosity because, even through the years, I have continued to hear about it. We definitely wanted to have this big draggy story but we didn't want to monopolize the first episode with it. I feel like it definitely needed to be talked out because they never really did really talk it out in real life. But it was definitely not something that was meant to become something we were going to talk about in every episode. The queens mostly did that on their own.

JINKX MONSOON: Alyssa is hands-down one of the most enigmatic naturally funny people you'll ever meet. When you work with Alyssa Edwards, you are just a guest star on the Alyssa Edwards show, no matter what it is. If Alyssa Edwards is at the gig, it's the Alyssa Edwards show and we're all just stock characters in it. At the same time, it is endlessly entertaining to watch.

COCO MONTRESE: She really did not want to talk about it on camera. She was like, girl, really, let's not do it. But I told her I'm not going to be able to walk away from this show and then go three more years without talking to my friend. I don't care about the money. I don't care about winning this competition, if I can find a way to talk to her and let her know what I was feeling and get my friend back that was more important to me at the time. I think she didn't want the general public to see her in a certain way.

ALYSSA EDWARDS: I talked to her but I felt like it was dragging on. She wanted something from me that I couldn't give her. I felt like, what do you want from me? What do you want for me to say to you? You want me to say that I'm sorry that I have a successful life outside of this? You want me to say that I'm sorry that I built a studio in the city that I didn't even know would embrace me? I'm sorry that the pageant owners didn't think that I could do this? I'm sorry that you didn't get the reign that you wanted? Like, I don't know what is wanted from me. It kept dragging on, I'm like, girl, we're here to have a good time and compete for another title. You gotta let it go, honey. And it was very hard for her just to let it go. She kept saying she wanted our friendship back. Well, then let's move on, let's scrap it, and keep this party jumpin', girl. Because everybody in the room was like, what is really going on? And I'm like, I know! I am still trying to figure this out my damn self.

Meanwhile, in the smokers' zone outside, alliances were forming, secrets were being traded, and a new sorority was born. Or not. Whatever it was, it had a name: Rolaskatox.

TOM CAMPBELL: The Heathers of their season.

DETOX: Roxxxy and I essentially grew up in the drag scene together. We started doing drag in different circles but we were always very close so it was amazing to see somebody who I was so familiar with walk in and who I just love and adore and who does such amazing drag. I was so excited.

ROXXXY ANDREWS: When I walked in and saw Detox, it was just like perfection. Oh my god, I get to go through this with my sister! And then the walk-ins start. Alyssa, Jade, Coco, I'm like, what? Is this like a Florida pageant girls takeover? And immediately, I thought me and Detox—top two. It's a wrap. I thought our only competition was going to be Alyssa because of lip syncs. Detox and I are performers but she's a trained dancer. So, depending on the song, Alyssa could be trouble for us.

DETOX: As soon as I got on my flight to LA, I hear somebody go, "Faggot!" I was hung over. I was about to pop off on the plane. I look up and it's Alaska in her big fur coat, hidden with these sunglasses, having a Bloody Mary. And she's just like *he he he*. We landed and we were kiki-ing obviously. And then we went down to the baggage claim and there's two PAs sitting there looking out for the drag queen that they're supposed to be picking up. They were like, "You're not supposed to know each other yet."

ALASKA: Detox and Roxxxy and I were the smokers, so we were always hanging out together. We were always going out and smoking.

ROXXXY ANDREWS: And Detox was friends with Alaska so that's how Rolaskatox started because we both had Detox as friends. I was a fan of Sharon's so I thought, okay, we're a little trio.

ALASKA: We just made it up. I don't know who coined it. I think I probably did, honestly.

DETOX: I couldn't even pinpoint exactly when it became a thing 'cause to us we were just the smokers. But I think Alaska came up with it. Smoking was the only way you could get a break from what was going on or to even have a moment just to sneakily talk to the girls. We were sequestered and you're supposed to be on ice, which means you can't talk to anybody during the whole filming. Season 4 ruined that for us, thanks to Willam! So it was really our only time that we got to spend time together. And even then they were like vultures on us so we had to be really quick. We didn't really think more of it until Alaska started putting hidden messages on her shirt. It didn't even dawn on me that she was doing that until maybe halfway through the show. We didn't really think anything of it more than just the bad-girls group.

ROXXXY ANDREWS: We wanted to be a little clique 'cause in our minds we're the bad bitches here. Coco and Alyssa had their drama, Jinkx was no competition, Serena was about to go home, we were the It girls.

MICHELLE VISAGE: It's like Heathers and Boogers all over again. I don't like a clique. Cliques are dangerous. Friendships are one thing. You're gonna meet people that you like, you're gonna connect with them, and that's totally fine. But it's when you start only connecting with them and not including others where it can become a problem.

ALYSSA EDWARDS: Did you say Rolaskatox? I don't know her! I love to talk about me. My favorite subject is me. Very Mariah Carey, honey. I don't know what that was. I don't think I was invested in it. If those girls wanna put tape on their shirts and say they're a girl group, well, girl, do it. You can, honey, you do you, baby! Whatever your spirit is telling you to do, honey. In other words, Iwasntbothereddotcom.

JINKX MONSOON: It was annoying and it was frustrating and I'll tell you why. We were all in competition with each other and then suddenly there was a team. You have two people rooting for you while everyone else in the room had everyone rooting against them. The annoying part was, simultaneously hating the fact that this team had formed and then being jealous that you weren't part of it. That was a difficult thing.

JOEY NOLFI: I think Rolaskatox was maybe more detrimental to the other people who were not in the group than the Heathers and Boogers was. Jinkx was in a very isolated place on Season 5. Seeing the way that it impacted Jinkx in the context of a competition, I think there was definitely an element of darkness to it that you can't understand unless you are in that room, experiencing it.

COCO MONTRESE: To be honest with you, at that time, we were saying okay, these girls have created an alliance and they are not even hiding it. It was off-putting.

TOM CAMPBELL: I used to go away to Boys State in high school, I have been to rehab in my life. I have been locked up in situations where it can quickly become *Lord of the Flies.* You do create systems and alliances. It sounds like it's all made up for TV but that's what happens. They knew each other and had a certain commonality and they got together for better and for worse.

MICHELE "MEESH" MILLS: It backfired because the main person who ended up being the brunt of negativity from them was Jinkx, who was sweet and did not really fight back. I mean she would speak up for herself here and there, but she was just this sweet, really talented character.

DETOX: I was so oblivious, to be honest. We're not a crutch or anything like that. I was just being a supportive friend. I never really saw it as a problem until I watched it. It was cringe-y. It was like eeewww. Because it wasn't really what I thought was going on. I didn't realize that people were annoyed. I didn't realize that it looked like we were like some kind of alliance. It didn't dawn on me until I watched it. And maybe it's just because of the way the editing was or whatever but I didn't see us as anything more than just friends.

ROXXXY ANDREWS: Alaska didn't do well one week and Michelle told her, "What's going on? Leave the clique!" And that's when it started bothering her. For me and Detox, it didn't hinder our performance. It was just a group, but we still did our things. I think she was leaning on it more.

ALASKA: The judges kept telling us don't do that. So I thought we have to listen to the judges, guys. If they're telling us that we are a clique, which we didn't believe that we were, we should listen to them so that we can do better. That was good advice because my role in my drag family in Pittsburgh was I was there to support everybody else and make everybody look their best. That was my preferred, comfortable spot. *Drag Race* is about pushing yourself beyond where you're comfortable. So they wanted to see what I can do if I'm not worried about making my friends look good and making my friends have a great time.

MICHELE "MEESH" MILLS: Alaska was great but she would freak out a lot. So I'm sure she probably found comfort in her little group. I think she had her little bit of competitive thing with Jinkx but I think she felt like her and Jinkx were more similar in terms of doing this kind of kooky drag. I think she both loved Rolaskatox but also related to Jinkx somewhat so she was in a little bit of a weird situation.

COCO MONTRESE: We were not having it. The sad part about it is we loved the Beyoncé of that group. It was the Kelly and the Michelle that were really, really wearing us thin. Everybody had their own personal relationship with Alaska, so it was kind of odd for us to see Alaska as a part of the group. I felt like they were using Alaska and her connection to Sharon Needles to try to get to the top. I told her, "Alaska, you don't even need them. You're Beyoncé and you're gonna be a hit all by yourself."

Perhaps all Alaska needed was a mantra.

JINKX MONSOON: Every time I'm on that stage saying "water off a duck's back," it's because I was convinced I was going to be eliminated that day. Even when I did great in the challenge, the critiques on the runway would still be very harsh. I performed well in almost every challenge and was torn apart almost every time on the runway for my styling and presentation, so every single episode I had this fear of will today be the day when my styling is so bad that it outweighs the good work that I did.

ALASKA: I think Jinkx deserves a producer credit on this season 'cause she really gave herself some really interesting character points. But that's kind of what you have to do. I don't know if it was done in a conniving way or anything. It was very smart of her to bring it up on the runway while there are eighteen cameras on. That's not my style but then I'm not particularly good at reality TV. That's why she fuckin' won the show. She is extremely vulnerable and extremely open. She is a completely open book. And that's why America fell in love with her.

JINKX MONSOON: I told everyone I was going to a nature retreat with my aunt for her health and no one believed this. But we all played that game of pretending that I was going off to a nature retreat so that I wouldn't get into trouble for talking about *Drag Race*. So Robbie Turner, who was in Season 8, was driving me to the airport and I said, "I'm really nervous about this nature retreat, Robbie. I'm nervous that other people at the nature retreat are going to hate me and they're going to make my life living hell." And Robbie said, "Well, if they do that, just say, 'Water off a duck's back.' Convince yourself that you don't care."

DETOX: There was a lot of water off a duck's back, period.

JINKX MONSOON: "Water off a duck's back" was a thing that I did for myself. But when I noticed that it irritated other people, of course I started saying it constantly. Because if I knew that they were frustrated that I was bolstering myself, and that was causing them to be thinking about that rather than thinking about their performance, of course I'm going to fucking do it. It's a competition. I probably said it about three thousand more times than I needed to say it to myself. But it was real. It was a mantra that saved me.

When Alaska and Lineysha Sparx teamed up in the third episode to drag up a doll into the next Miss Junior Drag Superstar, a "mother fucking dick pig" legend with her own very catchphrase was born: "You're not my real dad and you never will be!" Introducing Lil' Poundcake.

ALASKA: Lineysha Sparx was in charge of the hair and the dress. The dress was gorgeous. That was a world-class dress that she made in ten minutes on this miniature doll. I was in charge of the makeup and I gave her these really angry eyebrows and this scowling frown, because she hates this. She doesn't want to be doing this pageant. And then I took on the character of the overbearing stage mother who was putting words in the mouth of the child and forcing her to be there.

COCO MONTRESE: That was a really genius move for Alaska. Lil' Poundcake became a staple. She was picking at pageant girls and what we do and who we were and it was a little take on the Honey Boo Boo type but a lot raunchier. I thought it was really, really funny.

JINKX MONSOON: I thought it was hilarious! I felt this way many times throughout the competition. I felt like I have a great idea and then Alaska's idea was just a little bit better. I thought that Jade and I had done a really good job of doing a satire of pageant moms and a satire of what those kids are like. And then Alaska turned around and did the same thing but better. That was the beginning of my own internal rivalry with Alaska. I didn't know then that Lil' Poundcake would become such a thing.

DETOX: It was hilarious. We were dying during the speeches. We were losing our shit 'cause it was just so stupid. We know those girls.

ROXXXY ANDREWS: When I saw them making that doll, I would have never in the world thought that that thing was going to fucking go off the way it did. She had the pretty dress that Lineysha put on her and she was giving the middle finger. She had mean makeup but it was just hilarious. And the way they described her, it was just genius. To me, that was when Alaska came into her own on that season. That's when she showed who Alaska is.

JINKX MONSOON: Alaska's one of my best friends and I love her. But when people want me to be really excited about Lil' Poundcake, I saw her when she was born. I've already had this experience. I don't need to still care about Lil' Poundcake.

Each season, the Snatch Game is typically one of the memorable episodes, and Jinkx Monsoon didn't disappoint with her spot-on Little Edie impersonation. But the moment that lives on in infamy took place in *Untucked* when Alyssa Edwards and Jade Jolie continued their werkroom fight. Alyssa called Jade "a phony amateur girl" and Jade retorted with "You're a mean girl." Then Jade stunned Alyssa into silence when she told her she had "rolls all over the place in the back" and it "was disgusting." While discussing the incident in her interview later, Alyssa craned her neck, stared at the camera asking, "Back rolls?" in a move that launched a thousand memes and positioned her as one of the franchise's most unforgettable characters.

ALYSSA EDWARDS: Bankrolls! That's what I say now. I took some back rolls, honey, and turned 'em into bankrolls. Honestly, at the time that was a trigger. Y'all saw me on there, I said, "Now, hold up, what she just say to me?" And you know what I said to her off camera? I was real funny about that, the back roll jokes. I went up to her and I said, "Lemme tell you something, you know how you knew I had back rolls?" And she said, "How?" I said, "Because when they called the winner, you were behind me."

COCO MONTRESE: Here is the thing with the outfit: Alyssa put on the outfit and I was like, "Are you gonna wear that?" And that was her cue to say no. I wasn't gonna say don't wear that or you need to do this. And Jade was there. When we got on *Untucked*, Jade talked about the back rolls and I was sitting in the corner. And Alyssa said, "Coco, you weren't gonna tell me?" I told her she didn't take the hint. I had nothing to do with Jade saying that. Alyssa is a character all unto herself. To see her upset about the back rolls, I was like, girl, there were back rolls. It was funny. It was really, really funny.

ADORE DELANO: Jade Jolie is iconic!

ALYSSA EDWARDS: Nothin' else bothered me. Not the fact of her saying well, girl, you weren't funny, da da da. But, girl, you have back rolls! Back rolls? Well, hold up. Stop everything right now. Y'all can push pause on this camcorder. Now you gone too far, Miss Thing. I don't think I ever thought I'd be remembered for saying back rolls on television but it's been a big part of my legacy, right? For real, for real. You gotta take it where you can get it these days.

ROXXXY ANDREWS: I was not present but Alyssa told me later, "Bitch, she said back rolls!" And I was thinking to myself, well, bitch, you did walk in with a low-cut outfit, with back rolls showing, girl. Jade was younger than her and Jade was like a baby to drag, where Alyssa was a pageant queen royalty. So it was like, bitch, you're not going to demean me like that or downplay me. Know your place, bitch.

THAIRIN SMOTHERS: I didn't even see those back rolls, but those cameras sure did.

ALYSSA EDWARDS: Full, freakin' back rolls, girl! Can you believe that? As I sit here and eat my french fries.

When Roxxxy and Alyssa landed on the bottom together, neither queen had lip synced for her life yet but both knew they were in for an intense battle from their previous pageant experiences. During the "Whip My Hair" performance, Alyssa underwent some wardrobe malfunctions—her stiletto fell off, some jewelry flew away—but her dance moves were on fire. In the end, the night belonged to Roxxxy who shocked everyone with her wig reveal—a first in *Drag Race* herstory—and then followed up with a surprising personal revelation on the main stage.

ROXXXY ANDREWS: It was my first time on the bottom. My heart sank when Ru told me, "You're up for elimination." Following that, we go film *Untucked*.

TOM CAMPBELL: In *Untucked*, we used to play fun games and stuff. That day, they had baby pictures of the queens and it was a guessing game for the queens to figure out who was which queen. I think Roxxxy saw a picture of himself as a little boy.

ROXXXY ANDREWS: In *Untucked*, we talked about families and it came up. I said I was left at a bus stop when I was three and got adopted by my grandparents, blah, blah, blah. But I was so mad about the challenge that I just threw it out there and I said, "Oh, let's go to the fucking stage 'cause now I'm going to have to lip sync." But at the same time that's running in my mind—talking about family. I feel like I look stupid and look like somebody's who's not worth it. I just told all these girls that my mom denied us basically and so that's on my mind and weighing heavy.

JINKX MONSOON: In my head as a competitor, I wanted nothing more than for Roxxxy to go home and I knew that she wasn't going to. I said, well, at least I'll get one person out of the werkroom who makes me feel small.

ROXXXY ANDREWS: When we finished filming *Untucked*, I told the PA I have to go to the werkroom. I had to put another wig on. The wig that I had on for the challenge was a really long wig but it was ponytails that were sewn together. The song is "Whip My Hair" so I needed to put something on that flips. I took the hair that I wore for the pink runway and I flat-ironed it real quick, twisted it, and I put it underneath the other wig. And since it was ponytails, it had little claws, so I just clawed it without pinning on top of the other wig. I was trying to get Alyssa not to see me doing it because Alyssa's the type of person that if she would see me do it, she would do it herself. So I wanted nobody to know what I was doing.

TOM CAMPBELL: So then we go to the lip sync. You could watch both of these queens lip sync all day and never get tired of it. Alyssa is a star beyond belief. They're up against each other and "Whip My Hair" is just such a weird, fun choice. And then it happened—Roxxxy's wig-under-the-wig reveal, which has created the expression "Never remove your wig while performing, unless you're wearing another wig underneath." Ru's reaction, Michelle's reaction, all of it was real and iconic.

ALYSSA EDWARDS: I whip my hair back and forth. I whip my hair! Oh my gosh, it was fierce. It was fire. I thought it was such a fun lip sync. We turned it out, all right.

ROXXXY ANDREWS: The lip sync is done and I feel amazing. I feel like I kicked her ass, and all the girls are like, "Bitch, you did it!" I knew Alyssa fell apart, like her shoe came off, her wig slid back. I flipped my hair from every corner to the corner.

JINKX MONSOON: Roxxxy changed the *Drag Race* zeitgeist forever. They both did an amazing lip sync.

ALASKA: Roxxxy was on fire. She did the wig underneath the wig. Roxxxy is good at drag. She is excellent. Alyssa was less so. We were like, this is Alyssa's time to go. Her shoe was coming off. She didn't know the words. Her jewelry was flying all over the place. Roxxxy was amazing. Alyssa was a little bit of a disaster.

DETOX: They're both phenomenal entertainers and they do such similar drag. But the wig reveal was over the top!

VANESSA VANJIE MATEO: When she pulled the wig, I thought, is she gonna be bald? I used to go see Roxxxy all the time at Pulse, the nightclub in Orlando, and Roxxxy don't really dance a lot. I remember sitting on the edge of my bed, having the TV all the way to the highest volume. My mom is telling me to shut the hell up 'cause I was screaming in the room. It was so good.

MICHELLE VISAGE: That was legendary! Listen, all my years of going to drag shows and seeing drag shows, this is what I love about *RuPaul's Drag Race*. I have seen pretty much everything so when you do things that I haven't seen it blows my fucking mind. When we saw that wig reveal, you saw the reaction. That reaction was real.

ROXXXY ANDREWS: Because we always take a second to drink water and stuff before we film the ending, as soon as I started sipping that water, there were so many emotions. And Ru looks at me and goes, "Are we filming? Roxxxy, what's wrong?" I said, "I feel great, let's go." And she kept drilling me, "What's wrong? We're not going to continue until you tell me what's wrong." They got it out of me, girl, and that's where it starts and the story came out.

TOM CAMPBELL: The main stage is a magical place where people are under pressure and things come out. Ongina shared that she had HIV, Monica Beverly Hillz revealed that she was transgender, and then there's Roxxxy. We were in the booth and everything's running on schedule. We're trying to figure out who is going home. I cry when I talk about it because you hear that sound that Roxxxy made. People are like, oh Roxxxy was faking it, Roxxxy was acting up so she could save herself. There is no way in my experience as a human being that that is possible. It was like the sound I made when my mother died, a deep, primal wail. The control booth went silent.

ADORE DELANO: If you're not used to being on camera or being filmed all the time, it exposes your vulnerability. Well, not Bianca, but most people. She would not talk about her family or nothin'. If you are already in a vulnerable position and you're going through ups and downs and your emotions are being pulled every which way, it can be something as simple as like, "You look sad, Roxxxy, why do you look sad?" And that's the trigger.

ALYSSA EDWARDS: I remember that emotional breakdown. I was so touched, I was like, I need to go home. She needs to stay. This lady is deeply hurt. She'd been doing so good in the competition. Listen, as much as I love to win, I teach kids every day that winning isn't everything, wanting to is. I could recognize that she was in her feelings. There was a lot of emotion, oh my gosh.

ROXXXY ANDREWS: I wasn't even thinking and I just blurted out—I was left at a bus stop. That's not something I want to share on national television. I'm glad I did but I regret it at the same time because the people who ended up not liking me used it to their advantage to send me messages of that's why you were left at a bus stop, that's why you lost the show. They used it so improperly. That's what makes me regret it. But I loved that I shared it because that's what matters to me the most, is the people who wrote me that I've also been left or disowned for being gay or whatnot. I got to share those experiences with people because I told my story.

MICHELLE VISAGE: It was the one time I ever cried on that judge's table because I'm an adopted kid. I know what it feels like to not feel loved. And being a mother now, I couldn't imagine abandoning my child at three years old and leaving. I can't even imagine when people leave their dog. You see all these people abandoning their dogs and dropping them off and leaving them and walking away. I cry when I look at that. Imagine doing that to your child.

JINKX MONSOON: When we would open up about personal experiences, there were constant reminders that even if you're in competition, even if this person is being rude to you, even if this person is your biggest rival, they have their own story. They have their own experiences and you have no way of knowing what other people have gone through. In one moment, I'm wishing Roxxxy will go home and then in the next moment, she's sharing this painful, traumatic experience. And all I could think was thank god she gets to stay another day.

ALASKA: Being on *Drag Race* is such a pressure cooker and anything that you've got going on makes its way to the surface. And you never know how it's going to come out or when it's going to come out but it just does. It was really a moment of seeing how vulnerable Roxxxy is capable of being because she is this drag machine. She's drag excellence and drag perfection. So it was very sad. I felt for my friend going through it and crying but it was also really touching to see her vulnerable side.

DETOX: Knowing her for so long, she is such a stoic person and she does maintain this exterior where she is impenetrable. So to see her so vulnerable was so surprising to me because it was something that I had never witnessed before. Obviously, while it was happening, all I wanted to do was run up there and hold her and hug her 'cause it was heartbreaking to see her be so devastated and to have all that raw emotion come out. I knew that made her uncomfortable because she never wanted to be seen in that way. But I think that's the magic about this program—it is a way to cathartically deal with past traumas that we go through. Things come up in the process of filming and being sequestered and being put into this pressure cooker environment that you all don't really expect.

COCO MONTRESE: Everybody had that feeling there was going to be a showdown between Alyssa and Coco. So when Roxxxy was lip syncing against Alyssa, I don't think that she felt like she was going to survive it regardless, because we didn't expect for Alyssa to go home. So I think that at that point all her emotions were poured into that lip sync. And because she thought she might be going home, everything came out. A lot of the girls were skeptical about it later. They thought it was interesting that she waited to say it then, when she thought that it would save her.

ROXXXY ANDREWS: I have such a tough exterior. Like even now, I can talk about it and not get emotional. That's just how I am. I've always put that wall up of not caring. But it was something about that moment of being on the bottom, being defeated, being disowned, being not good enough, all that went into my story of my childhood, how I felt. It was like a therapy session, something snapped.

JINKX MONSOON: We all respond to trauma in different ways, but for some people responding to the trauma of being abandoned is to become self-reliant. And that air of confidence that I saw in Roxxxy, she confessed, was something that she put on as a defense mechanism to keep herself from being hurt the way she had been hurt in the past. So it was such a profound moment because it was a reminder that even the person that's giving me the hardest time right now has had an extreme amount of pain in their life.

IVY WINTERS: It was hard to hear. That her mother decided to do that was incredibly sad, and I feel bad for her mother that she'd feel like she had to do that. And I feel bad for Roxxxy that that happened to her, to him. Clearly he's doing well now. But what do you say to something like that? It's hard to relate. I think the stress got to her. No one knows until you lip sync for your life and you're in front of those cameras, producers, and a room full of people looking at you. The emotions were probably right at the surface and she had to let it out.

RANDY BARBATO: The most memorable moments are the ones that just happen. We produce the entertainment, we produce the challenges, but we don't produce the emotional moments and the things that really connect people to the show.

ALASKA: That's an important element of the show and I'm glad that they're not afraid to take it there. I think a huge part of that is that RuPaul is at the center of this and RuPaul's message is about love and love for yourself, no matter what and no matter what you've been through. So that spills over and translates to everybody who goes into the thunder dome. Everyone is on the same journey, ultimately. It's a huge part of why the show is such a huge phenomenon, because that story translates to everybody—that story of overcoming the things that are holding you back.

JINKX MONSOON: And then neither of them went home! In the episode, I'm like yeeeesss, and in my head I'm going fuuuuckk! Why couldn't this be the double elimination? No, this is the double save!

You got rid of my friend Honey, but you kept both the bitches that I really can't stand at this point.

ALASKA: I was pissed because you're counting down the weeks and we were thinking we are going to be final five. And then it was like, we're final six again. Great. But you know, as a viewer, I guess it was exciting.

IVY WINTERS: Watching that from behind, Roxxxy was killing it. Alyssa, her shoes were breaking. And then she kept turning around to us when she didn't know the words. I feel like all of us were, like, oh, Alyssa's going to go home. And I was like, fuck yeah, right, Alyssa's going home! And Roxxxy had the wig change! When RuPaul said they're both staying, it was very dumbfounding to all of us.

DETOX: I wasn't surprised that it was a double save but Roxxxy blew me away. She performed like I've never seen her perform before. I thought that was amazing. We were all really excited to see that it was a double save. And I think it was really deserved.

ROXXXY ANDREWS: Everybody thought Alyssa lost the lip sync and that she should have went home. But it never makes the air.

COCO MONTRESE: I actually thought they got it right. It was one of the most amazing performances of the season. I think there were really good lip syncs during our season because we had so many well-rounded entertainers that it always climaxed at a point where it was going to be something pretty amazing.

TOM CAMPBELL: We are all capable of being good and bad and evil and nice. In that dark moment, through tears, Ru reminded us that as gay people, we get to choose our families, and everyone came together and melted into a group hug. You couldn't send anybody home after that. You just couldn't. When people ask what *Drag Race* is, I say watch that episode because it's kind of everything and more. From our first raunchy roast to that epic lip sync, to Roxxxy's heartbreaking moment, to everyone coming together to share in her grief.

Before Jinkx Monsoon was crowned America's Next Drag Superstar, she faced off against Detox, who had already slayed two other queens with her famous jaw wobble. Although Jinkx blew the judges away with her comedic shtick, dance moves, and flawless lip syncing, and she did send the Rolaskatox queen home, the glory didn't come without a price.

ROXXXY: The first day of filming, we go to the holding area and then they're just ushering us into rooms, one at a time. We sat in the rooms for like an hour waiting for our big entrance. It was like a warehouse.

DETOX: When they had us all sequestered before our entrances, they gave us little iPod Nanos, so we could not hear anything. We were told to listen to music and it was already loaded. One contestant was blaring that song and singing that song so loud that we could all hear it.

ROXXXY: While we are waiting, you could hear somebody screaming, singing from the top of their lungs, "Wow, wow, wow, wow, wow." And I'm like, who the hell is singing so goddamn loud? It's so annoying. It was Jinkx! I may not have liked you on the season, but I didn't like you before we even walked in the room, girl. Your singing was too loud, obnoxious, and just too much. They had to go tell her to shut up because she just had them in and was singing so loud. It was the song she ended up doing for the lip sync.

JINKX MONSOON: And now we come to yet another conspiracy theory, one that I cannot deny. They always tell us what the lip-sync song would be in case we wanted to start listening to it. They had told us at the beginning of that day that it was going to be En Vogue's "Free Your Mind." And then by the end of the day, they told us that they had made a choice to change the song because of the licensing agreement.

They changed it to "Malambo No. 1" and that was my song. I don't know why they made the decision, but here are the facts: The facts are we have an iPod that has all the songs that we could potentially lip sync on them. We couldn't have our own musical devices. A lot of the songs were pop songs that I didn't care for. But the two songs I really loved were "Defying Gravity" from *Wicked* and "Malambo No. 1."

ROXXXY ANDREWS: As soon as they saw what Jinkx's outfit looked like, the Miss Reindeer Santa Claus, they came in the werkroom the day of the runway and said the song is changed. And we're like, bitch, we're ready to do "Free Your Mind" whoever's on the bottom. Why are you all changing the song? And then we knew. When they saw her outfit, they changed it because they knew she knew it and that she would do well. Nothing against the show or whatever, but she's going to be on the bottom and you want to give her something she can do to stay. I got you, television.

JINKX MONSOON: Do I think they were trying to stack it in my favor? Possibly. I do know that I was listening to "Malambo No. 1" constantly not because I thought it was going to be a lip-sync song. I loved the song. At one point, we were all in the werkroom talking about the songs on the iPod that we knew we would win if it was our lip sync. And I said, "You all talk about 'Malambo No. 1' like it's the worst song on the iPod but I swear to god, if you have to lip sync against me, you better hope that it's not 'Malambo No. 1.'" I said that out loud in the werkroom for everyone to hear early in the competition.

DETOX: I was annoyed going into it. As soon as they changed the song, I knew I was gonna go home. It was like, well that was nice. I started packing my bags. I saw where this is going. It's been fun, everybody. Nice to see ya!

TOM CAMPBELL: Untrue! Especially back then, we were always waiting for songs to clear. If we changed it, it would've been around a clearance issue. A song didn't come through. I like that conspiracy theory, though.

ALASKA: Detox is insane at lip syncing. She is so good. She has that mouth that's just a Muppet character. She knows every nuance of a song and can deliver it in a way that's fierce but also funny when it has to be. She is gorgeous and so smart and so hilarious.

MICHELLE VISAGE: That was soooo good. What a great song to lip sync to.

TOM CAMPBELL: I thought that was a really good lip sync. That fact that we could do Yma Sumac was everything. That's a classic drag song.

JINKX MONSOON: I would have still won the lip sync, even if it was "Free Your Mind" by En Vogue. There was no way I was going to lose the lip sync. It could have been "Toxic" by Britney Spears. It could have been fucking "Fuck the Police." I'm not a bad lip syncer. I'm a talented performer and so is Detox. But I was so galvanized. I was going to do my best no matter what. Detox was a fierce lip syncer and she had already won two lip syncs. She wasn't going to go without a fight.

DETOX: It was emotional because obviously I didn't go as far as I wanted to. But it was also just such a rewarding experience and to be able to have the critiques that we got and to meet the people that we did and to go through the whole experience with some of my closest friends was a really awesome opportunity. And then to also have somebody like Ru and Michelle validate what I do was really rewarding and something that not many people get to experience. It's still one of everyone's favorite lip syncs.

In the aptly titled "Drama Queens" episode, viewers finally got the confrontation they'd been clamoring for, and it wasn't an *Untucked* brawl. It was two pageant superstars, Alyssa Edwards and Coco Montrese, in a classic Paula Abdul lip-sync battle.

COCO MONTRESE: I remember Alyssa being very self-conscious in the werkroom and I think she forgot that we were mic'd. She didn't know the words and she said she was gonna dance her way through the number. I kept covering my mic and saying they're gonna know you don't know the words. I know this song like the back of my hand. I perform this song. Paula Abdul was Janet Jackson's choreographer so I loved Paula. "Forever Your Girl," "Cold Hearted," I loved everything about Paula Abdul. I knew her music like the back of my hand. Dance-wise, Alyssa is going to dance me into the floor, but I can embody this song and allow them to understand the words to this song and perform it. I gave it all I got. I think at that point I was giving it everything that I had.

ALASKA: The ultimate showdown! Yeah. It was a wild moment and I thought it was really vindicating for Coco because she finally got to come face-to-face with someone who she had felt overshadowed by her whole career and she finally got to really face that head-on. And she came out on top and deservedly so. I thought she really was amazing.

DETOX: It was a pretty iconic lip sync, too, and it was finally this moment that we had all been waiting for the entire season of the head-to-head between Alyssa and Coco, it was finally here. We're all living in the back. That song is amazing. It was in Coco's repertoire that she would do all the time.

ROXXXY ANDREWS: Finally! Thank god, because it was miserable with both of them there, attacking each other every moment. Detox and I were talking about it, and we're like, wouldn't it be awesome if after all this Miss Gay America stuff, if Coco could finally have her winning moment of beating Alyssa? And she did. Coco had that yellow pantsuit with the sleeves that swirled. It was sick'ning.

ALYSSA EDWARDS: And I'll tell you right now, going home to her I was totally okay with that 'cause I said if I go home to anybody, I hope it's to Coco 'cause she's a fierce lip syncer, even though I secretly wanted to beat her.

COCO MONTRESE: It was bittersweet because I wanted to go all the way to the end with Alyssa because I wanted that friendship back. But even after she left, I knew that we were gonna be fine at that point. And she even said to me later, if I have to lose to anybody, girl, I would've wanted to lose to you. And that meant the world to me because we have always been competitive and it felt really, really good. But I wanted to go all the way to the end with her.

ALYSSA EDWARDS: This is how I really feel about this whole experience. It is so far beyond flamboyant men galivanting around in high wigs and long nails, popping, pumping, and death dropping. It really is a journey of courageous souls sharing their stories. And that is my takeaway from it all. But my very favorite part of all of it is the lip sync for your life. When you're standing there at that stage looking at RuPaul dead in the eyes and them lights go down and that spotlight comes on, it is the biggest adrenaline rush I have ever experienced. It was everything. I was like, this is it! I was like, give it your all, girl, give it your all.

MANDY SALANGSANG: Something I first recognized in that season was how you can fall so in love with a queen even when their performance within the challenge is kind of a train wreck, but they are so charming that it's impossible not to love and laugh with them. Someone like Alyssa Edwards comes to mind, who doesn't nail every challenge but steals your heart in every single one of them.

For much of the second half of the season, Roxxxy Andrews focused a lot of her energy on bringing down Jinkx Monsoon. Although it felt personal, and sometimes it was, a lot of Roxxxy's negative feelings were rooted in changes to the artistry of drag brought on by the ascent of Sharon Needles in the drag community after she won her crown. The bullying was uncomfortable to watch, but Jinkx Monsoon held her own.

JINKX MONSOON: I really think that Sharon Needles winning shook the drag community. In a way, the queens who had always been celebrated were suddenly being criticized. I think the pageant queens went into Season 5 with a certain level of defensiveness. What was popular was deconstructing drag and rethinking drag where it doesn't always have to be pretty, where it doesn't always have to be glamorous, where it can be disgusting and shocking. The balance of power had shifted in the world and they had to fight to get back on top.

RONAN FARROW: The mainstream cultural interpretation of drag was still crystallizing and there was a still-evolving discourse about what drag is. Is it a pageant queen world? Is it for people like Roxxxy? Is it for more multifaceted performers, like Jinkx? And the answer clearly is all of the above. But I do think part of how the show changed the culture was to further cement and institutionalize the idea that performers who are comedians first, who are more intellectual first, who are more art house first, that that is drag and very much the heart of drag. The Jinkxes and the Sasha Velours—that feels right, but it also happens to be Ru's taste. You can sense as you watch the show, season after season, that Ru loves those queens that are a little more cerebral.

ALASKA: Drag is so many things. There are so many different types of drag. But *Drag Race* is all of those things. So you have to be able to draw from the elements of pageant drag, which are very important. Things have to look nice and be aesthetically pleasing but that's not all it is. You also have to be able to tell a joke and land a punch line and be funny on your feet. *Drag Race* is all of those things.

JINKX MONSOON: Roxxxy's consistent criticism was, "You're lucky that all of these challenges have played to your strong suits because you're looking like the stronger competitor but I know I'm the stronger drag queen." To which I said every single time: "These are the challenges that they always do. Don't act like this season has been customized and specially tailored to me. Every season there's a singing challenge, there's an acting challenge, and there is a comedy challenge." And she'd say they're all comedy challenges. This TV show in and of itself is a parody. Everything we do is a parody. And it wasn't just Roxxxy. Coco and Alyssa also would say they we were being given an unfair advantage because we were comedy queens.

ALASKA: Roxxxy is lovely. She's very down-to-earth. She is very funny. It is a difficult process being in there and I think that the judges were pushing her buttons. She was reading Jinkx for filth. Roxxxy was feeling frustrated because she felt like she was doing a really great job but she kept getting criticized and pushed and needled.

JINKX MONSOON: A lot of things happened in those last days. Even though Roxxxy really came for me, there was a moment. Alaska left the werkroom because she needed to go shave before she started her makeup. So I asked Roxxxy, what was your favorite part of this competition? And she said, "Seeing you in the bottom." It was so cold and so emotionless and so pointed. I had written off a lot of Roxxxy's behavior as competition and it really didn't get to me but that got to me.

ALASKA: So rude!

JINKX MONSOON: I was really honest with her about that. I said, "I just don't understand how after everything we've been through, I don't hate you. But how do you hate me enough to say that to me? After all the amazing things we've experienced, and all the amazing celebrities that we've met, and all of the opportunities and moments that we've had that have profoundly changed us and made us better people and made us stronger drag queens, with all of that, the only thing you can focus on is your hatred for me?" She then turned around and apologized to me. At the time, I thought it was a tactic. And maybe it was. But Roxxxy, from the moment the competition was done, was one of my very good friends. I care about her a lot. And I believe that she cares about me, too.

ROXXXY ANDREWS: I started really going in for Jinkx because I was thinking if I can't beat her, throw her off of her game. I started throwing jabs and making her upset so that she wouldn't perform to the highest of her ability. I was playing dirty. I watch a lot of *Survivor* and *Big Brother*, and I know how to play mind games as far as the competition goes.

DETOX: It was interesting because there was parts of me that agreed with Roxxxy because throughout the competition there was a lot of times that I felt like people were getting away with things that other people wouldn't have been able to get away with, which goes to a lot of the self-production, I think, and playing a game really, really smart. But I feel like Roxxxy could've been a little nicer. There were definitely times where I was like all right, reel it in. But I also feel like it wasn't as bad as it was portrayed. It made it seem like everybody was gunning for Jinkx, but I don't remember it being as bad as it was portrayed while we were there.

IVY WINTERS: It did not happen often. If it had been blatantly in my face, I probably would have said something about it. But I think a lot of it was on the one-on-one interviews where a lot of us couldn't hear what was going on. Jinkx is a very kooky, creative character, and she may not jive with a lot of people. But that's no way to act negatively toward someone. Jinkx was very unique and interesting and I think it intimidated some of the other queens and maybe they felt like they had to put her down a little bit in their interviews to make her seem smaller or to make themselves feel bigger. She's a very lovable person.

ROXXXY ANDREWS: I feel like Jinkx played a character the entire time. On and off with makeup, she was always Jinkx Monsoon. With everybody else, I could see the two different people. She was Jinkx the whole time. I think I made a comment to her about the Little Edie and that's when our little tiffs started. I was seeing a girl catching attention and that was bothering me because of my game. I didn't like that. That's where it started.

RONAN FARROW: They totally bullied Jinkx. There's plenty to be learned from Jinkx's arc across the seasons on the show where the cross she has to bear is that she is just so good and people really resent how successful she is. And she handles that role with a lot of grace. She makes it as hard as possible for people to hate her in the process because there is no bullshit there.

JINKX MONSOON: I remember Roxxxy saying she thought it was a tactic when I said I was afraid I was going to be eliminated because I performed well in the challenge. Maybe subconsciously, it was a tactic, but in those moments, the fear was real. Sometimes I watch episodes and I think, you really do seem like you're doing that, Jinkx. You really do seem like you're trying to paint yourself as this wounded little lamb so that people won't want to criticize you.

ROXXXY ANDREWS: The real me would creep up and feel bad and knew what I was doing and I would want her to know that I apologized because I was wrong. And I was apologizing throughout the show, even on the reunion. Girl, I'm being stupid, I apologize. And then the old me just kicks right back in because we're still competing. I felt dumb at times and that's why I wanted her to know that I genuinely did feel bad. Oh girl, I was the water and she was the duck. Anything I did rolled right off her back. It did not work for me.

It sure didn't. And as the *Drag Race* fandom soon learned, it was time to "get ready, bitches," because Monsoon season had arrived. What viewers didn't know was that behind the scenes, there was also an Alaska cyclone brewing.

ALASKA: When we taped the finale, the audience was very nice. They applauded for each of us. But there's an energy you can feel in the room. You could feel that it was Jinkx's moment. It was her year; it was her season.

RONAN FARROW: I tend to gravitate a little more toward to the thinking man's queens, if you will. The cerebral queens who often can do great comedy. I'm a big Bob The Drag Queen, I'm a big Monét fan, Sasha Velour obviously. They and Jinkx are some of the smartest queens who have been on the show. They are so charming and have such comedic chops but also bring to bear such thoughtful cultural references in their looks, are pulling from interesting places in both their own experiences and in the wider world, and are clearly giving a lot of thought to how their performances fit in with advance the wider field that they are in. I like how smart Jinkx is but also just Jinkx's total package as a performer. This is somebody that can sing, and a little bit like Ru, Jinkx also has some wisdom. You can feel it even in that initial season when she is so young and vulnerable, you can feel even then that there is a Ru-esque quality in terms of the level of authenticity and truth there. Across her two seasons Jinkx is never stooping to being bitchy or mean or getting embroiled in the drama. Jinkx is fun on set but Jinkx is also there to work, like Ru, and to not get distracted in the process.

JINKX MONSOON: I felt like there was no way for me to truly express in that moment what winning meant to me because I knew that it might not be real. It was hard to have an authentic response. I smiled huge, I said my catchphrase: "Get ready, bitches, it's Monsoon season." I knew when that crown was on my head I was going to bow down to the audience the same way I bowed to Detox. I had made all these decisions about how I was going to do it. The only thing that wasn't planned out was I couldn't summon the actual emotion I was feeling in that moment because it felt like it wasn't real yet. The night that they aired the episode, that's when I had my true reaction to it.

ROXXXY ANDREWS: We were in the room. Oh my god, I was so happy for her. I'm telling you, we had become friends and I was just so happy that we had a queen and it was so well deserved and, you know, at the end of the day, it's just overall happiness for them.

JINKX MONSOON: I was in New York with the entire cast. We were all staying at the Out Hotel in New York, which doesn't exist anymore.

It had a nightclub attached to it called XL and we all were performing in a show. And we went in order of elimination, so that meant I was last. All of the other queens were in this big suite watching the final episode together, but they had Alaska and Roxxxy and me in a separate room watching.

ALYSSA EDWARDS: I think Jinkx proved that she could rise up to any challenge. She had the charisma, the uniqueness, the nerve, and the talent. She was funny. She was theatrical. She had all the qualities.

DETOX: I was obviously rooting for Roxxxy because, to me, she's the best drag queen in the world. But I wasn't surprised at all. By the time everything happened and the finale took place, we were all so close and we'd all become such great friends that you have nothing but love and support for everybody.

ROXXXY ANDREWS: People are probably going to read me for this, but I felt like I won the season. I felt like I had to go out the furthest on a limb on a lot of the challenges. I felt like I jumped through the hurdles that they gave me. Although Jinkx and Alaska were amazing, the Alaska that was on *All Stars* is the one we were waiting for. To me, it was between me and Jinkx and I felt like we both had a great game. We had the same amount of challenge wins. I just felt like I had to go further than she did for a lot of those challenges. But she won. She was a great queen, well deserved.

MICHELLE VISAGE: What I loved about Jinkx was her openness to growing. I never want these queens to change. I just want them to venture out of their comfort zone. I want them to try something new but to keep themselves in it. Jinkx, from the very beginning, was open to all my criticism and she tried harder and harder every week. So when they go on a real metamorphosis and a real journey, it is so impressive to me.

JINKX MONSOON: When the finale aired, Roxxxy was there to hug me and hold me as I screamed and cried. Alaska sank down into the couch and was completely deflated, crying her eyes out, and then goes, "I'm so happy for yoooou!" She was clearly in a lot of pain. I know that she was happy for me but she was also feeling her own emotions, going through her own thing. I don't hold this against her but Alaska went through a whole emotional roller coaster that completely overshadowed my winning.

ALASKA: It was really difficult for me because I knew that I wasn't going to win in my heart of hearts. However, I couldn't go around saying that because it goes against the integrity of the show. It was also insulting to Pittsburgh and everyone at the Blue Moon and at home who were supporting me, and my family and my mom who really believed that I had a chance of going in there and winning. I knew that there was literally no chance that that was going to happen.

JINKX MONSOON: Alaska told me that morning, "Jinkx, I'm a very sore loser. And if I lose, I'm probably going to throw a temper tantrum and it has nothing to do with you. I'm not going to be nice and I'm not going to take it graciously. I'm going to be a very sore loser when I lose tonight." So then she begins crying and we go out into the little courtyard outside of this room we were in. And she wants to go into her hotel room but she doesn't have a key to her room and no one can find her assistant, who has the key. So Alaska starts going on a tirade. She starts storming around the courtyard. Producers are there, her mom's there, all of our friends and family are there. She's yelling at everyone. She's throwing this huge temper tantrum. She's throwing things. She's yelling swear words at everyone. And then her assistant comes running in with the key to her room. And I'm standing right next to her room and I didn't realize it was her room. He runs and opens the door and she walks toward her room, storming, angry, pushing everyone off, and at the very last second before she went into the room and closed the door, she turned to me, looked me straight in the eyes, and winked at me.

ALASKA: When it finally happened and Jinkx won, it was a release. The outside is finally matching what is happening on the inside. So there was a release of a lot of emotion and I was crying and throwing a fit.

JINKX MONSOON: She was the second-to-last performer that night, so she went onstage and performed her song and then flopped down on the stage and wouldn't leave. And Mimi Imfurst, who was the deejay, played the next track. So Alaska sits back up and starts performing the other song, which happened to be "Don't Cry Out Loud." And she starts scream singing, "Don't Cry Out Loud" from the ground. The whole thing was just so epic. And then flops back down on the stage and won't move again. Her assistant and her mom came out and tried to help her up and she wouldn't stand up. So they each grabbed an ankle and just dragged her offstage. I kid you not. They dragged her limp body offstage. And then I had to go onstage and perform my song. There is no way I can top everything that just happened. That's why I say Alaska's temper tantrum overshadowed my crowning. But I'm not upset about it. It was an amazing thing to witness firsthand.

ALASKA: It was fabulous.

Chapter 6
SEASON 6

From Monsoon season to Hurricane Bianca, *RuPaul's Drag Race* soared into its sixth season with an eclectic cast that quickly flourished into some of the most successful drag queens in the world. To kick things off, producers chose to shake things up and divide the queens into two groups for a two-part premiere, but didn't explain the new rules to the cast. While the queens who were selected for the first part jumped off a platform for a photo shoot and designed outfits inspired by a TV show, the rest remained sequestered in their hotel rooms with no information. The shade of it all.

First up were Adore Delano, whom TV fans knew from *American Idol*; Seattle queen and BFF of Jinkx Monsoon, BenDeLaCreme; oats-feeling Gia Gunn; Puerto Rican sexy queen April Carrión; and actor Kelly Mantle, who was the first to go home. In addition, two queens made unforgettable entrances: drama queen Laganja Estranja, a protégé of Alyssa Edwards who gagged with her entrance dip, and Jamaican queen Vivacious who confused everyone with the awkward-hilarious reveal of her famous headpiece Ornacia.

The second group holed up in the hotel were insult comic Bianca Del Rio, *Australian Idol* contestant Courtney Act, comedy queen Darienne Lake, figure skater Milk, sweetie pie Joslyn Fox, YouTube personality Magnolia Crawford, and Atlanta pageant queen Trinity K. Bonet.

204 Maria Elena Fernandez

ADORE DELANO: I remember walking in and I was like, "Where the fuck is everybody? This is stupid!" And they're like, can we maybe do that again? And I'm like okay, fine. I'm like, I'm home! Fuck yeah, I'm first! I knew Laganja was gonna be on and I thought she was already gonna be in there and I just wanted to be like yay, we're all here, but I was like *ohhhh*. But I was a fan of Willam so I was like, okay, maybe I'm cool enough to be the first one then 'cause she was first, too.

TOM CAMPBELL: Ru was like, "What's better than one big opening? Two big openings!" We live to make ourselves laugh. Fourteen is a lot of queens to meet in one episode and to send somebody home. It feels unfair.

LAGANJA ESTRANJA: Why on earth is it my season they had to switch up the format that I have practiced so hard to win? That was not a part of my plan, okay? I had planned my makeup, my nails were in a book, I was very organized, and this whole twist was not in my book. I thought this is going to be a lot of work if it's only going to be six of us in thirteen episodes. But I also thought I'd get more camera time, so that's great.

ADORE DELANO: I hated it. I even told RuPaul that. I was so in shock that I even got on the show, like walking in it was so surreal that I didn't even hear what he was saying. I thought he was saying we're doing a mini season. And I was just so mad. I was like, wait, am I a Booger? I have ADHD. They were telling me, no, it's not like that. I'm like, so one of us stays to go into the real competition? And they're like, were you listening? And I was like, no! I was so traumatized. And when he started doing the walk-through I said to RuPaul I was so confused. And then he explained it and I was like ohhhh and I still hated it. I was like, why can't we all just get to know each other in the beginning? We're gonna start rivalries like this. I didn't want that.

BENDELACREME: That was wild and unexpected and definitely a surprise and it put a little bit of a hitch in my giddy-up around my big plan to make a connection with everybody the first day. But once we all got in there, I really just tried to make the same effort.

ADORE DELANO: I was always into makeup and I grew up watching the show. I think I was eighteen or nineteen when Season 1 came out. I had makeup skills and I was already living my life as a girl in high school before this even came out so I was like, wow, there's a competition show like *America's Next Top Model* but with drag queens? I could beat that up. I could fuck that up. Yeah! I just wanted a year experience first and I auditioned for Season 5. And like low-key, I think they gave it to Penny Tration because I didn't have any clothes. I was that close to getting on but I had no wardrobe to fulfill the challenges needed.

BIANCA DEL RIO: I got there on a Thursday, and they took my phone, and I did not know anything until the Monday after. We're not given any information. We're trapped in our hotel room. That whole time, I was in my room sewing snaps on stuff. I cut my Judge Judy wig. I couldn't drink so, yeah, it was wild.

MILK: I wondered why they made us be here by this date and then you're just gonna sit in your hotel.

DARIENNE LAKE: I figured they had stuff to set up. I remember them coming in and giving us our music and they said to pay attention to these two songs, "Express Yourself" and "Turn the Beat Around." Music was a huge part of my life growing up. I love music. I held my tape recorder to the radio to tape songs. Music was always my escape. I knew every one of their songs forward and backward except for "Fancy," even though I've seen so many drag queens do it over the years. For some reason, I can't get that fucking song. That one would've been tough. But I learned it.

PANDORA BOXX: My first time seeing a drag show I went to see Darienne Lake. I had met her in a club. I was introduced to her and she was named after a theme park, and I thought why does she have such a horrible nickname? People are calling her a theme park because she's a big girl? I didn't get it. Then I saw her perform at this outdoor festival in Rochester and I went, oooh, that! I want to do that! People were giving her money to lip sync, which I did all the time in my bedroom. I was like, you can do this?

BENDELACREME: I had never been in front of TV cameras before. I remember running out, being very nervous, but being very excited and expecting to go in and see a gaggle of girls and not seeing anyone. Adore was there in the room but she was kind of hiding in the corner. I'm blinded by the lights and seeing all the cameras and what's going on and I'm taking in the fact that the walls are fabric and not really brick and that was blowing my mind. Holy crap, TV is different on the inside! And then I saw Adore. I felt like I clicked with Adore immediately. Our friendship was very strong and she was really there for me in hard moments. She has got such a stylized way of being and speaking and moving through the world but there is so much genuine energy there.

ADORE DELANO: I've never met somebody like Ben. Still, to this day. I was confused because my drag is pretty vulnerable. I pull my inspiration from growing up and I try to apply that to myself but still trying to be a human. And she was just like, "Hi!" And I was just like, whoa. I was like, what's your sign? "Oh I don't have one of those." What are you? I'm trying to vibe with you, bro. And then when the drag is all off, she's like, "I really think I'm overthinking things." I'm like, who the fuck are you? Like a whole different human! I'm like, where is Ben and where is DeLaCreme?

LAGANJA ESTRANJA: The entrance was something that I had planned long before I even ever auditioned. I think as someone who watches *The Real Housewives of Atlanta*, where you have to have a catchphrase, this was something that I had already wrapped my brain around long before auditioning. Being able to do it and to nail it the way I had envisioned felt great. That is an incredible, powerful feeling.

ADORE DELANO: Laganja is so extra. Like, all right, we all knew she was gonna do something. I thought she was gonna climb on the ceiling and do a backflip and break her knee. But I knew she was going to make a difference and stand out. She's always been known to do that for sure.

BENDELACREME: I am glad that Vivacious's reveal moment made it onto TV because that was a truly classic moment. When she first walked in with her face covered and Ornacia on her head, I was like okay, this is my kind of queen, total weirdo.

Ornacia is still one of the very best things to come out of *Drag Race*. I was obsessed and continue to be.

MANDY SALANGSANG: The first time that I spoke with Vivacious I thought what an interesting personality, what a colorful character with such a unique and specific artistry. I was not that surprised to see that that's what she was wearing on day one because she was such an interesting queen. I knew she had planned for this reveal and she had even run it for me. I knew how it was meant to execute and I knew we would stay with her until it did.

LAGANJA ESTRANJA: I thought this girl is kooky and I'm here for it. I love people who are a little off. Vivacious was struggling so much with the reveal that I knew that this person underneath was going to be a unique individual with creative ideas and someone who maybe wasn't the most typical drag queen. I gravitate toward those people.

ADORE DELANO: My favorite moment of the whole season! It was longer than what you saw. She couldn't find it. I remember I said, "What in the Michael Jackson?" And then everybody started laughing. We were tripping out. I was like what is going on? And then she was like, "Mother has arrived." And I was like ohhh, my god this bitch is gonna be so kooky. You would never see that on the new seasons. They're too worried about looking like Naomi Campbell. We need freaks back! We were all freaks. We were wild.

MANDY SALANGSANG: Even as she struggled, seeing that there is a perseverance there and a purpose, that is really special. It's sort of an unexpected gift in the presentation because in succeeding finally with it and never breaking her character, we actually captured something unexpected and all the more endearing. That was a magical entrance, an iconic entrance.

DARIENNE LAKE: Vivacious took the last of the hot Cheetos and I was really mad about that. We didn't even get to see Ornacia. She was just in episode 1.

STEVEN CORFE: I remember giving the note in the episode to give Ornacia her own little graphic where we put the name on it. It's still one of my favorite gifs—that isolated shot of the Ornacia wig head with her name on it. Bow down to Ornacia. She is a star.

MANDY SALANGSANG: And then for Vivacious to proceed with the photo challenge for that day with the Ornacia head on, jumping into the foam pit, made that challenge all the more special, too. Of course, Ornacia has visited us many other times throughout the subsequent seasons.

JOEY NOLFI: Did you know that there are Ornacias for every holiday? Vivacious sells Pridenacias, she sells Fourth of Julynacias, she sells Hallownacias, she sells a nacia for everything. Ornacia is for everything.

When the second group walked into the werkroom, they were greeted by a lipstick message on the mirror, BEWARE BITCHEZ, and the remnants of a party: half-eaten cupcakes, champagne, balloons, and streamers. The queens were gagged when Ru explained a group had already come and gone, and a queen they never met had sashayed away.

BIANCA DEL RIO: Sunday night, a note was passed under my door. "6:00 a.m. tomorrow, camera ready." And of course I couldn't sleep then because I'm like, oh now I get a fuckin' warning? They took us in separate cars. We had been told to wear something that you're not upset if it gets damaged. I didn't know what I was walking into. A producer says, "What are you going to say when you enter?" And I said, "Oh my god, I must be in someone's nose because this room is full of boogers." And he said, "What if you're the first one?" And I said, "Well, you wouldn't be telling me that unless I am the first one." I walked in and I was the first one. That son of a bitch!

MILK: No joke, when I walked in and saw things hanging up, like the other queens' garments and dresses, wigs and shoes, I was like hold up, do they provide looks on this show? I thought that I had been duped this whole time, that all of these looks were provided by the show. But then once it was just six other girls and I, I figured out oh, other girls have set up their stuff. The other girls had thrown some sort of soiree to welcome us with dirty dishes.

DARIENNE LAKE: When we were first sitting there, we all started talking to each other and we're like it looks like there was a party that already happened and there are only seven of us. That's when we started thinking that something was up.

JOSLYN FOX: One by one, all the queens were doing their entrances and we all just had different theories of what this all means. I think I was very optimistic about it. I thought that there were queens from previous seasons returning and that made me nervous. I thought they had a welcome back kind of party.

BIANCA DEL RIO: I was waiting for Courtney Act because there were many sites online that were saying she was on the show. The night before I flew to Los Angeles, I was on Facebook and I can't remember if it was me first, or Courtney, that sent a message saying "See you tomorrow." So I knew that she was going to be there in some capacity. Luckily, she was in my group. When I saw her I was like, okay, it's on. She's glamorous like RuPaul, she is a pretty queen, she is super talented, an established performer. I thought she's got this in the bag.

And Darienne Lake was a hoot. She had me cackling, she was so damn funny. I loved her.

JOSLYN FOX: I saw the back of Trinity's head and it looked like a drag queen that I do not get along with back home and my heart sank. But then Trinity turned around and I was so excited to see her. That was when we first became friends. And then Bianca opened her mouth and it was like, oh crap, she's gonna tear me apart and eat me alive. She was eyeing me up and down and cracking jokes at me and I was just trying to ditz it up like it's not bothering me, but really I'm going to cry myself to sleep tonight. She ended up becoming one of my best friends.

BIANCA DEL RIO: I remember calling people out. Magnolia Crawford was the first one because she was a complete pain in the ass and I wasn't a fan of her right off the bat. She basically wasn't interested in putting in the work. It's episode 1, you fuckin' troll, what is wrong with you? I'm always bothered by people that don't rise to the occasion. You got all the way here. So many people would have wanted to be there.

MILK: It was very nerve-racking. You're walking into the set of this show that you've loved for so long and then you are supposed to say this line that will make the first impression last forever and ever and ever. So, you know, a little pressure. But seeing that there were other girls there already made me feel comfortable. But you're also meeting new competitors for the first time. A lot is buzzing through your brain.

DARIENNE LAKE: Milk didn't remind me of a drag queen performer. She reminded me of a fixture, like the club kids that you would see but they don't perform. They'd be at a club, or at a party and they were just decoration. So I thought she's great and a lot of fun but I don't think she is built for the competition. But that was just because she wasn't really a performer.

BENDELACREME: I think I just lay flat on my back in my hotel room and hyperventilated. I don't quite remember what I was doing when they were filming the second episode. We were not told anything.

BIANCA DEL RIO: I had a room with an adjoining door. When they're going around, taking our orders for food, I knew someone was next door that was part of the show. So I sent a Post-it note underneath the adjoining door saying, "Who's here?" And I had a message back saying it was Milk. So on many nights we'd come back to the hotel after we finished filming, and Milk and I would open our doors and we'd talk. We were not allowed to talk to anybody so Milk and I became this therapy group every night. It was so sad when he left! When I got back to my room that night, there was a Post-it under the door saying, "I love you. You're going to win, Milk." Which was very sweet. I missed him! He became a really sweet friend of mine. He was very genuine and down-to-earth and in the moment it was just great to talk to somebody outside of producers.

After Magnolia Crawford went home, the twelve queens met for the first time in the werkroom, and nobody was having it. Cue: gagging, reading, and eye rolling.

LAGANJA ESTRANJA: Dun dun dun! The girls come in and we are gagged and I just remember thinking Courtney Act is fucking beautiful and Bianca Del Rio is an old, crusty bitch. I don't like her and she's gonna be trouble and what's her tea and why is she so fierce and everyone is living for her? I didn't know who she was so I was just like ohh please, this is one of them Dallas pageant queens who swears they're the tea and just wait till you see this young hot thing, mama.

BIANCA DEL RIO: I kept thinking some shady shit is up. Shockingly, within those two or two and a half days of filming, we kind of became a clique so when we met the other group it was completely *West Side Story*. We spent a day with each other and we already hated the other group.

ADORE DELANO: I felt protective of the girls that I was already forming bonds with but then, I'm not kidding, it only took a day to start liking the other group more. I was like, okay, I love Ben so much, I fell in love with Bianca, I thought Milk was interesting and cool. I thought they had a stronger cast for sure. That was my honest opinion. We were younger, more immature. I would see it on the bus that we were separating ourselves. Why are we doing that? We are merged. Let's sit together.

BENDELACREME: Figuring out how to come into that space and start to connect with queens who have already connected with each other was tricky. But I did actually feel like people got on board pretty quickly. I definitely remember Courtney Act feeling terrifying to me just in terms of how insanely beautiful she is. It's almost surreal and it's weird to see close-up because it's like, how are you Photoshopped in real life? I'm campy and don't really think of DeLa as a woman so much as a cartoon or a Muppet. And then I see this other drag queen who is just this stunning beauty.

JOSLYN FOX: Bianca, Courtney, and I were thick as thieves from day one. And the rest of us got along pretty well. When we walked in the werkroom and the other girls were there, I felt like the energy was us against them. I wanted to cry. I felt like I was getting bullied. It felt very real and intense. It's funny in hindsight because I ended up being closer with some of those girls than the girls in my first group. Courtney was like another species of drag queen.

DARIENNE LAKE: I'm a huge lover of reality TV so I also notice what's going on and who is getting close to who. I'm really into alliances and all that stuff. When I saw Bianca and Courtney getting close, I was like I need to get close to that group so I could position myself to be with the winners. I love *Survivor*, I love *Big Brother*, and all those reality shows.

MILK: There were three young girls that seemed on the verge of aggressive or could be aggressive. They seemed like a very strong presence. They all had strong stares. Death stares.

JOSLYN FOX: Gia was making some mean comments to the group. That's so not me so it made me feel really nervous and feeling like I was getting bullied in middle school all over again. Laganja was doing that, too. I was scared of Gia. It wasn't like I didn't like her, but she was just so intense.

DARIENNE LAKE: I definitely got that nasty vibe from some of the girls. Gia Gunn and Vivacious also seemed very grand. I don't know. They wanted to start something. I thought April was so beautiful and so sweet. I loved Adore instantly because of her energy. Ben-DeLaCreme and I connected together as well. There was this great energy that we had. She reminded me a little bit of Kasha Davis in a way, that campy character queen. But when we were having our van rides back to the hotel, they were still keeping us in separate vans so we were all talking about each other.

LAGANJA ESTRANJA: I have always wanted to be beautiful so I remember thinking wow, Courtney looks better than me, I'm jealous of that. And I knew who she was, of course, from WeHo. I just knew Bianca is going to run this. The minute I met her I just knew. There was no telling her she wasn't the one. You could just tell she knew she was the one and that's because she was the one.

ADORE DELANO: I've never been wrong about my winners. I'm obsessed with the show and I always clocked them: Jinkx, Raja, Sharon, and as soon as I met Bianca, I was like, fuuuuck.

BENDELACREME: Bianca carries a ferocious storm cloud around her at all times. It was this energetic electricity. Bianca is truly one of the kindest, most generous people I know but she came into *Drag Race* to win and that was clear from the moment she stepped in.

ADORE DELANO: I told the producers to keep Bianca away from me because I hated her and I thought I was gonna fight her. We were split into two different episodes in the beginning so she came in when we were already bonding and I didn't know she was an insult comic. I didn't know anything about her but her hosting the finale shows on YouTube and I didn't really know her personality. But she was really just blunt and I didn't catch the insult comic vibe yet. There was an interaction we had on *Untucked* that I was like, oh she's gonna be a problem. I would say something and she would cut my charm in half. And I'm like fuck, my charm's not working!

BIANCA DEL RIO: That was my nasty drag queen behavior. My instincts were like, oh please, these children. But I ended up liking everybody for different reasons. I'm not the easiest pill to swallow so I think it took a minute for them to adjust to me. And then we kind of clicked.

ADORE DELANO: I had called our group eccentric. And she was like, well if you're eccentric, you can't even win a fuckin' acting challenge. And I was like, okay, we're gonna have a problem, girl. And I told her that, too. I don't think they aired it. I was like, oh, you and me are gonna have a problem. And she was like, why do you say that? I'm like, we are not gonna get along if this is gonna be you twenty-four hours. And then we started warming up because my Scorpio came out and I was kind of blocking her through my vibes. We started warming up on the rides home in the van. And by episode 3, I was in love with her. I was like, oh she is so fuckin' cool.

BIANCA DEL RIO: Adore, especially, grew on me. As I got to know her, there's something about her that I love, and if I get it, the audience will get it. I just thought there was something charming and fun and great and not annoying like some of the other contestants. Adore was the only one from that group that lasted 'til the end.

MICHELE "MEESH" MILLS: Bianca started to realize that Adore could take the joke and could give the joke back. And I think Adore went from hating her to just thinking oh she's this funny old queen.

ADORE DELANO: It changed because I understood. She doesn't mean to be hateful. She's reading the eyes out of you. She's not cutting you down to make you feel like shit. She's homegirling you. You have to laugh at yourself in order to be read by somebody like that. You can't take yourself too seriously but you have to get to know a person before you can banter with them on the same level. So I was like bitches get punched where I'm from talking to me like that.

MANDY SALANGSANG: They are both very smart and they're both very passionate about their artistry. They have more in common than their differences. I think that Bianca appreciated the youthfulness that Adore had. She was a little rougher around the edges but what is not to love about Adore's youthful enthusiasm? And I think that Adore could appreciate the polished, more seasoned nature of Bianca's drag, but also her maturity as a person.

To experience Gia Gunn de-dragging is to be thoroughly entertained. Or annoyed. Just ask Bianca Del Rio, who after watching Gia feeling up her own boobs and flipping her long tresses, wondered if Gia was performing in a White Snake video. The response became a dragverse classic: "I'm feeling my oats! Let me feel my oats."

BIANCA DEL RIO: I didn't know oats needed to be felt. I think my oats were dried up. Gia is a magical creature and emphasis on the word *creature*. I was fascinated by this grand behavior. Outside of the challenges, there was grand behavior and this idea that she was more than what she was. And what I thought was interesting is that during the challenges she didn't produce. She was all about being sexy for the cameras and flipping her hair. That's when I realized in my head, oh my god, I'm old. I'm not used to being around these children. If this is what drag is I need to quit.

JOSLYN FOX: When I watch reality TV shows and they mess up phrases and sayings, it irritates the life out of me. I remember in that moment thinking to myself isn't it sowing my oats? To this day, when I hear a fan say I'm feeling my oats, I'm like that's not how you say it.

ADORE DELANO: She kept saying oats and berries. I remember she explained it to me but I was like, what? I forgot what it is.

BIANCA DEL RIO: Gia and I would go back and forth and be catty with one another. We were allowed five bags under fifty pounds for all of our drag to travel with. But Gia had a box that she brought with a lot of costumes in it and midway through the show I realized there was a sticker on the side of the box for a porcelain toilet. So all her expensive drag was in a Home Depot toilet box. I called it out one day and that's when we hit it off. It didn't air, but I was like, how dare you try to be cunty with your fuckin' drag in a toilet box? She was like, "Aaaa! I hate you." At least take the sticker off your big porcelain toilet box before you pack.

If you're going to create an original musical, you might as well do it when you have two stealth singers on the cast. Introducing..."Shade: The Rusical," the musical that launched a dozen other drag musicals.

JOHN POLLY: The drag ballet telling Ru's life story that we did in Season 5 led to us doing our first full-on Rusical. I feel like Tom Campbell probably came up with most of that. It was so much fun to do because it was a pastiche of many Broadway shows. It's still one of my favorites because we had amazing singers for it, Adore and Courtney Act. We write all the musicals. We help contribute to the songs and write the lyrics and have so much fun doing them.

TOM CAMPBELL: The Rusical story line has been so exciting. I am very involved in them. Whether it was Lucian Piane at the beginning or David Steinberg or Leland and Freddy Scott, it is so much fun. Musicals are such a part of gay life and queer life. We parodied *Dreamgirls* and *Cats* and all these different things with silly, silly plotlines and we loved it. We thought we'd do one and move on but it did really well. When you look back, it was a little rough in comparison to the others that came after. But we try not to super polish. We just try to learn and make them better each year.

JOHN POLLY: It was up to us producers to somehow build the framework of the choreography that night. And then the choreographer took it and added the flourish and made it choreography. So I have a soft spot for this one because it felt like we were putting on a show in our high school gym—except it's a global TV show.

JOSLYN FOX: My favorite thing about being on the show was that it was like a daily seminar. I was a theater kid so it was neat to sit with a script and work on singing and all that choreography. We had a lot of fun with it. I was the butch queen.

BIANCA DEL RIO: In that segment, there were comedy queens and pageant queens. And I thought if I'm a comedy queen, I don't know if that's going to work in my favor or work against me. Am I gonna be told I'm not experimenting? It would have been me and Darienne as the comedy queens and Trinity and Gia as pageant queens. So I suggested we break up the teams. It ended up being fun but it was testy because we were trying to learn choreography and that's where Trinity and I had a couple of moments. Throughout all of it, I thought I was helping. I didn't understand her reaction to it. I was just trying to find the best way to make it work. And she was just busy trying to say I'm wrong.

DARIENNE LAKE: We were in Ben's team and I remember Bianca said she should probably help Trinity and told me to help Gia so that we don't suck and we're not in the bottom. They kept doing the choreography for Trinity and Bianca, over and over. So by the time it got to us, there was no time left. And then I remembered on the judging panel, Lucian said we didn't stand out. I'm like, "'Cause you put me in the fuckin' corner in the dark!" I was biting my tongue and being nice. I didn't wanna go off on anybody on my third day. But I was like fuck this! And they put me in the bottom three. That definitely lit a fire under me to then be more vocal about what I deserved.

BENDELACREME: It was such an obvious decision to cast Courtney in the role of Good Penny. She was already that person so that was perfect. And I loved getting to play the villain, Shady Lady. I felt like I was really getting to mix it up and show different sides of myself. Shady Lady was a really fun role. It was a blast. When it aired, Jinkx turned to me when we were watching, she was like I'm so jealous that you got to do this musical. This is the best.

ADORE DELANO: At the time, I really didn't like Courtney, either. She was very condescending and she gave backhanded compliments. I think she was also confused at how I was making it that far. She would say little things. I liked her when we started touring together. I remember telling Bianca, why does she always say stupid shit to me? We are all very close now but it was like, Courtney, Courtney, Courtney. I was scared to go up against Courtney because she sounds like an actual cis woman when she sings. And then I had this huge wig that I borrowed from my friend April and I was super reckless with handing out the roles. But I had fun. I mean, it was a moment.

MILK: My part was the old, wizened woman on Adore's team. I hadn't sung routinely in a long time. I grew up in music so I knew that I wouldn't necessarily be a flop and that I could keep rhythm. But learning lyrics and having to sing them live and having to do choreography and having to be funny and wink, wink, nod at the judges at some point in time is a lot. *Drag Race* is a lot. There are so many things going through your brain at every single moment on that show, even if it's just being locked away in your hotel. It's always something, as Roseanne Roseannadanna said.

LAGANJA ESTRANJA: Now I'm back in my vibe thinking this show is made for me. This is my challenge. I'm supposed to win. And then I get cast as one of three showgirls. So I remember being bummed a little bit. How am I gonna stand out amongst the others? I just remember thinking that, like, oh dang, always a bridesmaid, never a bride.

BIANCA DEL RIO: I found that their inner madness or insecurity was getting the best of them. I was just kind of trying to find the best way to say that doesn't fuckin' matter, just do the job. But I also learned that everyone doesn't think like me so it can be problematic. Generationally, it's different. The younger generation really expresses their feelings all the time. I don't wanna hear it. I don't care about your feelings.

JOEY NOLFI: I think when you see the younger queens that were raised on the show and their drag is molded entirely based on what they see on the show, there is a weird sense of entitlement that comes along with it. They are often queens who are doing this from their bedrooms, they are on Instagram, they are watching beauty influencers. It's a very internalized process and not having that kind of feedback or energy in the room I think really changes how you approach the art form and see yourself as an artist. You're not getting any external feedback outside of clicks on a computer screen. I think it's great that the show is fostering people to explore themselves and do this artistry however way is comfortable for them, but it adds an interesting element to the competition when you have old-school queens like Bianca Del Rio, Darienne Lake, Latrice Royale, people who have been doing this for years, partnered with queens performing only on Instagram. We are definitely seeing even more of a divide between the types of drag that were birthed in different eras.

MICHELE "MEESH" MILLS: I think it was interesting because between Laganja and Adore you saw two different ways that they handled it and it resulted in very different relationships that each one of them had with the others.

MANDY SALANGSANG: It was just like life. Bianca had been there, done that, was someone who had been around the block and then Auntie Bianca had something to say, whether you wanted to hear it or not. It's also the culture of drag. She had a career and some of these baby queens maybe were going to parties in drag or going out with their friends in drag or performing here or there. But they didn't have the decades of experience Bianca had. Throughout time, they've come up through these drag houses, these families, where there's been lessons to be learned and stories to be told by elders, and that's what Bianca was on Season 6.

Little did Bianca know she was about to unleash a whole lot of feelings in the *Untucked* lounge. After a video message from Laganja's parents expressing their pride and confidence that she'd win the competition, Bianca joked about how wrong they were. The result was the first of Laganja's tantrums and the birth of one of her lasting catchphrases: "This is my moment!"

LAGANJA ESTRANJA: The last thing we did when we got to *Drag Race* was hand over our phones. So when the PA came to pick me up, I was allowed to make that last phone call. I called my mom and she didn't pick up. So I was already crying in the van before we even got to the show. I'm sure World of Wonder was like, mama, this queen is TV. We haven't even gotten her in the van and she is already hysterically losing it. I was perfect for TV. I was young.

BIANCA DEL RIO: I felt a huge disconnect with the younger queens because that wasn't my drag world. And anytime I was around younger queens prior to *Drag Race* I was always in charge. I was always the one kind of guiding people through it or making suggestions because someone had done that for me when I was younger. That's just how I knew drag to be. When they came in, the Laganjas and the Gias, I was completely like what the fuck? And I thought oh god, she's performing when she doesn't need to perform.

LAGANJA ESTRANJA: When I finally admitted to my parents that I had won the Micky's showgirl contest and that I was going to do drag full-time, they cut me off financially. They had paid for everything up to that point, my entire education, $50,000 a year. They felt they were paying for this dance degree and now I wanted to go flip around in heels? So, needless to say, when I saw my mother and father appear on that screen and I knew World of Wonder had actually facilitated this happening, I knew there had been a shift in their consciousness. I just remember feeling overwhelmed. I just couldn't believe that they would come on a national television show and be like, well, babe, we did some research and we found out this shit is hard so we're proud of you. I mean, I couldn't ask for something better.

ADORE DELANO: I was onstage when that happened, so Bianca told me on the ride home and I was like, what? And then the next day the tension was weird. And then she started noticing that Bianca and I and Courtney were kinda hanging out a bit and I think she was like, oh, I'm gonna get her. I was like, what are you doing? That's when it started to get ugly because she started trying to make me look bad on camera. I would see her face in the werkroom when Ru would laugh at my jokes. I don't know if she thought he was favoring me because I didn't have any of my stuff made. I had leftovers from Sonique's drag. All my stuff was given to me. This was back when you could carry your ass through the season with your personality and your talent and your charm.

JOSLYN FOX: We were supposed to be on ice in the vans. But there were a few times where we would chat. And the conversation would always lead to Laganja and the shows that she does in LA and how she knows these people and blah, blah, blah. So it just got kind of annoying to the point where she was showboating. Every morning, we would go into the werkroom and she was having to make a big scene. And it was just so opposite me. I just like fly under the radar. But it was always the Laganja show and so everyone got annoyed. I got to the point where I felt like I was seeing a broken soul. And I felt bad but I was still annoyed.

LAGANJA ESTRANJA: I was trying to have my moment. I guess people didn't really understand how big this was for me. The TV people were trying to have my moment and the other girls were not having it. So now I'm famous for saying "This is my moment!" It was such a serious moment to me at that time. Can't we be gay men here for a second? Can y'all calm down and can we have a moment? I'm actually experiencing something real here. I know you're gonna win and all that but, bitch, chill the fuck out and let me have my moment! But I hated watching that. Oh my god, I hate it, what a cringe. But I know what my intentions were and I know at the end of the day it made great TV. So I choose to own it and, mama, I've sold "This is my moment" merch, so cheers to that.

MILK: It came as a shocker that she felt so hurt and put on display by us because it did feel like a room full of support. Laganja got quiet. So to keep energy up for the cameras we just started talking about other people's families. In that moment, with emotions and feelings...wires got crossed and people came for people.

BIANCA DEL RIO: And that's when I started to see the dual-personality thing that eventually was just a lot of insecurity, unfortunately, that got the best of her. But this was also a young girl who was not used to being without her phone, without her computer, without talking to her parents every day. I lived a different life. I think it messed with her head at the time, which was sad to see but I didn't know why in the moment.

LAGANJA ESTRANJA: This is when it started getting dark for me. I started to feel the tension from the other girls. At this point, I was getting nervous about the challenges, too, because we'd already done the musical theater, we'd already done the picture, so we'd done the things I was good at. I felt like comedy was coming up and Bianca was already clearly coming for me. I was nervous.

MILK: I was happy to get on Season 6 to experience that because then on Season 7 they took the Gold Bar and Silver Lounge away. Those were iconic places in queer history. The things that went down in those lounges! Which, by the way, looked much bigger on TV.

The next day to self-soothe, Laganja Estranja wore a macramé pot holder as a headpiece to the werkroom. After stretching her leg on the table, as if it were a ballet barre, Laganja said apropos of nothing: "Well, girl, I'm young and hung and clearly march to the sound of my own drum. So props to you, mama!" A bewildered Bianca responded by asking what happened to the plant that had been hanging in her hotel room.

LAGANJA ESTRANJA: Oh girl, she came for me that day when I had the macramé pot holder on my head.

JOSLYN FOX: Bianca was like, "What the hell is on your head?" I think Laganja just had the mindset of I'm here to make good TV.

ADORE DELANO: I liked it. I thought it was cool. I know they made it look like I didn't but I thought it was cute. I even told them in the morning, bitch, that's cute. I would wear that in drag. But Bianca hated it! I'm like, leave her alone!

LAGANJA ESTRANJA: That's another moment I totally planned. I knew I was going to go in one day and put my leg up on the table and start doing ballet. And people perceived that as fake whereas I just perceive it as a well-rehearsed individual who cares about what they're doing, who wanted to give a good performance.

MICHELE "MEESH" MILLS: Every year, it's harder and harder to not have people who come in thinking they're gonna play a role. Because of social media, because queens tend to really have big stakes, bigger than just winning but how much their drag careers actually flourish in the world, a lot of queens come now either totally clammed up, not wanting to say anything because they are afraid that anything that they say is gonna make them sound like a bitch. Or they self-produce and offer story lines or produce fights. I discourage all of that because none of them is Meryl Streep. You don't have to do anything extra. You're a drag queen. Just be yourself and talk about your feelings.

LAGANJA ESTRANJA: At the end of the day, I'm sorry, coming in there in that macramé pot [holder] and doing ballet up on that thing was hysterical and it made great TV. I'm sorry you don't like it, bitch, and you're bitter because I'm stealing your moment, but there are two of us here, so let's play. I've never worn it again. I believe it broke apart a year later. My friend James made it. I thought it was amazing fashion and I went after it.

The stand-up comedy challenge arrived and, naturally, this meant that while everyone worked on their scripts, Laganja Estranja huddled under the werkroom table with a NO SMOKING sign from their hotel on her forehead.

JOSLYN FOX: We're all in the werkroom and we know cameras are everywhere and we're trying to be creative with our art. Was this her kid fort kind of thing? Or are people going to say I'm weird because I'm sitting under the table and I'll get more camera time? She was also wearing the NO SMOKING sign on her forehead. No one knew why. I think Laganja was very smart.

LAGANJA ESTRANJA: At that point, the queens were so over me that they were just like oh whatever, let her do her fuckin' antics to get camera time. Everyone was just like whatever, cuckoo.

JOSLYN FOX: I wanted to have a big opener and a big closer and then just spread everyone else out. I wanted who I thought was going to be the worst to go before me and then I wanted the closer to follow me so that way I would not have a tough act to follow.

Darienne is one of the funniest people on the planet, so I put her first. I thought I was being strategic by putting myself last after the weakest before the strongest, Bianca.

BIANCA DEL RIO: We were finally getting to do something in front of a live audience and it was stand-up comedy. And I was very concerned about this because it's what I do so I didn't know how it was going to be perceived. I wrote all kinds of random shit about everyone that was in the show. Joslyn Fox, who I loved, was in charge. No one wanted to go last. She put me last, which was fine.

DARIENNE LAKE: I was so ready for this. This is gonna be fun. I love telling jokes, writing jokes and coming up with one-liners and stuff. And when they were saying it's in front of old people, I'm like, perfect! I've done shows in front of old people at bowling banquets. I know what can make them laugh and make 'em pee their Depends and have a good time.

BIANCA DEL RIO: I love a specific audience. We had the man that was asleep. We had all those old ladies knitting, and I thought that's my life, that's what I'm used to! My captive audience is a senior citizen home. This might be the last show they see! It was one of the few challenges that we were able to sit and watch each other perform. As each person went down this rabbit hole, I started to think they're all talking about each other. I can't do this. I just need to wing it like I normally would. That's when I switched my whole set and just owned it. If I go home for being myself, fuck it.

ADORE DELANO: That was probably the hardest challenge—that one and the makeover challenge. I had the raunchiest, most before-cancel-culture jokes that I was gonna tell. But even back then they were like, you can't say that. I was like, damn it! So I just was scared to say the wrong thing that I decided to just make fun of my family and myself 'cause I know my mom has a sense of humor. I really wish I could redo that and do a roast or something.

LAGANJA ESTRANJA: I'm very lucky that mine was so bad it was funny and it became iconic. So I now sell merch with my entire comedy on it. My whole speech with emojis and everything. It's dirty. People have grown to love that stand-up and to think it was very funny. Even though it sent me home, I still am very proud of it. I still think dry as your vagina is hysterical and I don't care what anyone tells me.

BENDELACREME: This one was super devastating to me. That was a really hard episode because so much of what I do onstage is I'm a comedian and a writer. While I don't do stand-up specifically, it's adjacent to what I do. I felt so awful that I bombed on this thing. Part of what happened to me is that the night before I thought I was going home. So the next day, it's time to get onstage and be hilarious. I was still crying backstage before I went on to deliver that. And then getting heckled by that audience member just made me dive off the stage. I was like all right, let's cut our losses. I'm not gonna stay up here and just keep flailing.

ADORE DELANO: Ben's so sweet. Ben is more of a Libra than I am. I'm more of a Scorpio.

BIANCA DEL RIO: I think that the audience had the opportunity to say whatever they wanted, just to throw us and see how we were going to react under pressure. I think that's where that came from. Or he just hated Ben, which is highly possible.

JOSLYN FOX: I don't know if most people recognize the heckler but he was actually in the makeover challenge. I forget who made him over. I also think he was on another season.

ADORE DELANO: Thank god he didn't fuck with me because I don't give a fuck how old they are, I probably would've cussed them out. That guy was the heckler from Jinkx's season! He was heckling Jinkx. And then Bianca ended up attacking him and I was like, yeah, fatality!

BIANCA DEL RIO: I don't know what he was doing but he was trying to get my attention, which is what set me off. That kind of thing, that's just what I'm used to. I worked in a bar with drunk people. I ain't afraid of him. I also saw he was mean to Ben during her moment. Ben didn't respond to him. So I was already like, oh I'm gonna get her. I dare you to say something! And sure enough he did. Wearing horizontal stripes in his third trimester, yep, that was it. That bastard!

It was all fun and games, until it wasn't. As the judges deliberated, the queens went upstairs to film *Untucked*. Soon it was everyone against Laganja, who delivered the most famous words she ever spoke.

BIANCA DEL RIO: This was a very tense *Untucked*. A few episodes back, Laganja had a big crying moment where she was saying her family didn't speak to her because she did drag. And I made the joke, oh it's very sweet that your parents love you the one thing they're wrong about is you winning, ha ha ha. And she had her big crying moment. Later on, I saw that she was milking the situation but that her story was conflicted. She said she hadn't spoken to her parents and they didn't like her being gay. But then it was oh just since she's been doing drag, which she had only been doing drag for two years. So my little investigative brain was putting all this together. So cut to us being in *Untucked* after the comedy challenge and I'm sitting there and she is having this meltdown. She might be going home tonight and I'm holding on to this information that I had to get out because she might go home and I need to let her know she's full of shit because her story didn't add up.

ADORE DELANO: I remember having a discussion with one of the producers, and he asked what's the tension? I'm like, she is a whole 'nother human, bro. I think she studied Alyssa and is trying to do that vibe but back home she was so chill, a little competitive but talks how we're talking right now. Looking at new seasons now, they all talk like she did. But back then, we were like what are you doing?

JOSLYN FOX: I was pissed because that was when I got my video from my husband. We had the pink furry box and I pulled the card out and it had all these Jennifer Lopez song titles so I knew it was for me. And then my husband popped up on the screen. I was crying and he was talking about our nephew had passed away, so I'm crying more. My lashes are falling off. And then he showed me our dog who was like our daughter. I had been away from home for four weeks so it was just a really nice moment and I loved that I got to share it with my sisters. The second the video ended, they all gave me hugs and then Bianca was just like, "So, Laganja, I've been thinking." And then Adore gets into it. And she's saying, "This isn't you." I had the feeling that we're ganging up on her and this doesn't feel right. And she had her "I feel very attacked!" moment. And I told everyone after she left that I felt like a piece of shit now. And they said, "Yeah, that was shitty, but still go out there and eliminate her."

ADORE DELANO: What a lot of people don't understand is that prior to this happening, Ganja and I had celebrated my twenty-second birthday and she spent the whole weekend. She was like the homegirl but she did not speak like that. Stop trying to be Alyssa! Alyssa doesn't even try to be Alyssa. Stop, Jesus!

LAGANJA ESTRANJA: Adore and I were in lots of contests together and we were really good friends. Well, when I say really good friends, it doesn't mean we were having lunch and kikis on the side all the time but we did have lunches. There was a real friendly rapport and a healthy, competitive nature between the two of us. We definitely supported one another.

ADORE DELANO: I was nervous to do this with her because we always got along very well but there was an underlying competitive nature.

BIANCA DEL RIO: I think that's when everybody was finally reacting to her antics and her behavior. When we did have authentic moments, she was lovely but a lot of it was for the camera. I think she was just someone who had witnessed friends on the show, Alyssa, being close to her, and maybe she just thought she could control the narrative and she could be full of one-liners and performing—which really didn't translate.

LAGANJA ESTRANJA: I felt like the rug had been pulled out from underneath me. It was clear to me that people thought I was a lot but what wasn't clear to me was that people thought I was being a character—not that I was being an extension of myself. When they're all telling me that, I'm just like, but you guys never told me this. It just felt like, oh my god, I have been duped and I'm an idiot and I need to go home and get out of here. It really did take me aback. You saw how I really felt. I felt like those girls had preorganized this attack on me. And it felt really shitty.

VANESSA VANJIE MATEO: You do not want to go against fucking Bianca in any kind of verbal anything, bitch. If you annoy Bianca, you better come ready with the knock-knock jokes 'cause it's gonna go down.

DARIENNE LAKE: When the whole confrontation thing happened, I said, when we're at the club and we're all drinking and having a good time, I'm into it. Give me that personality. Yesss girl, let's have some fun. But when we're just being real, can you just be real for a minute? I liked her.

BENDELACREME: She clearly came into *Drag Race* feeling like she had to perform a certain way and give a certain type of personality because of her connection to Alyssa. I can understand that because I felt similarly because of Jinkx. I felt like it was something to live up to. It was easy to see that she was being really hard on herself and that she was really going through a very difficult mental and emotional experience, which is something I can really empathize with hard as somebody who has had my own mental health struggles. But it was very hard to watch. It was difficult to watch somebody have to go through that publicly. I wouldn't wish that on anybody.

ADORE DELANO: I had even asked her privately what was going on and telling her I am her friend. And she's like, well probably not. The whole thing was overdue and I think she thought that Bianca was trying to make a moment and be mean or cruel. So that's when I was like we're not trying to make it so like we're attacking you right now. I'm really not coming for you. I'm telling you what's going on and what the judges are saying because she kept saying she doesn't know what they're talking about. It seemed like she was just kind of losing it. Maybe 'cause she wasn't smoking, either. That will do it.

BIANCA DEL RIO: I don't have a problem with Laganja at all as a person. I think some people are good under pressure and some people weren't. And I think in those moments, I think she kind of struggled with identity and what is the right thing to say, how do I make this work? And a lot of queens in particular see something successfully working for another queen and feel the need to do the same. I think that's where it came from. In the moment, it was a hard pill to swallow for all of us.

LAGANJA ESTRANJA: Knock on wood, it's really the only panic attack I have ever had in my life. I'll never forget being outside and having a producer just trying to calm me down because I was hyperventilating. I was just freaked out. It was horrible. I had just been publicly humiliated and everyone just told me they hate me. What am I doing here? This is horrible. Send me home. I don't want to be a part of this. If this is what you guys think and feel about me, then I'd rather go home with my friends.

BIANCA DEL RIO: My favorite line at the end of *Untucked* is after Laganja storms out and there is a pause and Courtney goes, "I don't think that was the best way we should've handled that." I fucking cackled. This girl is being taken out in a stretcher and we're all like mmm, well. It's the pressure cooker of the show. It makes people crazy.

ADORE DELANO: I heard Courtney say that and I was like, you witnessed what she's been doing to me all season, trying to make me look bad on camera. I'm gonna confront her if she's gonna act dumb. I just remember distinctly like yelling to keep her away from me because she's just going off the edge. I remember her yelling, too. It got really bad. I remember watching her leave and her throwing her shoes and fucking being like, I'm done! And I'm like, Jesus Christ.

BIANCA DEL RIO: Oh honey, that was a wild episode.

MANDY SALANGSANG: When Laganja was upset and she was struggling with coping with the emotions that the competition brought on and the relationships brought on, we obviously are very concerned about their mental and social and emotional well-being. We were extraordinarily moved by her vulnerability and empathetic to the circumstances that she found herself in and supportive of her both then in those moments and to this day.

LAGANJA ESTRANJA: It's like Alyssa's back rolls. It's one of those things where it's very hard when it happens, and it's very hard to relive, but at some point for me at least as a human and an individual, it's like, are you going to allow that pain to tell your story or are you going to take that pain and turn it into something? And that's what I did. I carried a whole line of "I feel very attacked" merch and now it's one of those used memes in *Drag Race* history and I just feel like it has lived on. In that moment, it was awful and sad and I felt alone and broken. But now it's a way for people to openly express when they are not feeling very well with humor. And I think that's the most incredible gift that I could have given to the world—to be able to have something that now we use.

MICHELE "MEESH" MILLS: I really had high hopes for her because by this time I was madly in love with Alyssa and that was Alyssa's drag daughter. She'd be like, now I'm gonna make a scene or now it's time for the apology scene. I would say no! I talked to her and I told her I thought she was trying to be like Alyssa but Alyssa is naturally like this and she's not.

BENDELACREME: Laganja has grown to be one of my favorite people from that season. We talk very regularly and I think she has done such an incredible job taking a situation that was really, really hard and figuring out how to grow from it.

DARIENNE LAKE: I thought when the cameras were off she was really sweet. When she wasn't using the fake voice and the fake affectations and stuff, I thought she was really cool.

THAIRIN SMOTHERS: She gave drama. Uncensored drama. She was the queen of the catchphrase and trends.

ADORE DELANO: We've talked about it so many times now. Even at DragCon, at the hotel, we laugh about it now. But it still makes me feel bad because, I mean, not to be a Tyra Banks and make it about me but I know how it feels to have a panic attack. I can't imagine having that on camera, you know what I mean? I'm a grown-ass human now but back then I was just like, what are you doing?

LAGANJA ESTRANJA: I own exactly who I was. I know I went in there at twenty-three years old with a plan, with rehearsed things, and people can say that makes me fake but I know my intentions. Even in those dark moments and in those moments where maybe I didn't say it the best way or said things like "This is my moment" and came off really diva and cunt-y, I am proud of them because they part of *Drag Race* history. And, to me, that is the ultimate win. Walking away from the whole thing, I am just so proud that I was young enough and dumb enough to be that over the top.

BIANCA DEL RIO: Those *Untucked* moments, it was really where you got to see who we really were because we weren't interrupted by a challenge or producers or the activities. It's just sitting in a room. So either you're sitting there feeling cool as a cucumber or you're sitting there with some pent-up bullshit and you're ready to unleash it. And with her, I didn't know where she was coming from. At the beginning, I thought it was just an act for the camera. I didn't know she was really struggling. I'm not good with pity to begin with so don't ask me for pity. I'm not the one.

By the time the Glitter Ball challenge arrived, frenemies BenDeLaCreme and Darienne Lake had already faced off in a lip sync to Exposé's "Point of No Return" after landing in the bottom as a team during the cosmetics infomercial challenge. That time, they both got to shantay.

DARIENNE LAKE: For the infomercial challenge, they put us in groups and it didn't dawn on me at all that they were putting people in groups who had some sort of beef. I was like, I get to be with Ben, this is cool, we're gonna rock this challenge. We're gonna be crazy and memorable and do something wacky and fun. We thought we're doing a great job. We're showing the product. I definitely didn't think that we would be in the bottom at all.

BENDELACREME: I felt like our concept was pretty strong and I felt really good about it but the hardest part of challenges like that are having no idea what the judges are actually looking for. We had to make a decision: Are we really trying to sell this? Or are we making the funniest idea we can come up with? Turns out, we chose the wrong thing. We decided let's make the best comedy sketch we can come up with and then we got on the runway and everybody was like well that's not gonna sell anything.

MICHELLE VISAGE: We went through a lot to get Ben to drop the act and give us some vulnerability. And the issue is Ben, the human, is fully engrossed in BenDeLaCreme when Ben transforms into Ben-DeLa. So BenDeLa doesn't like to bring Ben into BenDeLa—and that's not necessarily a problem, but when we see drag queens onstage performing we like to feel the crusty bits, the rough edges. That's what makes us fall in love with someone.

BENDELACREME: DeLa is a character and I'm a character queen and I am not a queen who is just Ben in a dress. I'm a character. So I made a very conscious choice when I went on *Drag Race* to be in character when I'm in drag. I knew that that might be a thing. I knew what Michelle meant. DeLa is this aspect of who I am. I'm introducing you to my drag and if you don't know who Ben is, then you can watch the confessionals when it airs on TV. I'm not trying to show you who Ben is. I'm trying to show you my art.

BIANCA DEL RIO: I knew early on not to argue with the judges. No matter what they say, you just go mm-hmm, great, and then do whatever the fuck you wanted. But I wasn't gonna give them the, *Oh, how dare you?* Because I'd seen that ruin everyone else. You're not gonna see some emotional mess or me lose my mind over a critique. They have to say something. But I'm also questioning things Michelle was wearing. Give me a break! She's judging us? What the hell is that? That's when she had those tits that were just propped up on the desk.

JOSLYN FOX: Darienne and Ben had had a little tiff before so there was a tense vibe for the lip sync.

DARIENNE LAKE: Ben won Snatch Game and Ben was like ohhh did anybody else win two challenges? I was like, wow, somebody's getting a big head pretty quickly. I think it was definitely played up more on TV. That just rubbed me the wrong way but it didn't affect how I felt about her.

BENDELACREME: I don't know if I've ever been so nervous. My throat was dry and my hands were shaking and clammy. It's this moment of you've come so far and maybe it's just suddenly over. It is so dramatic. When you're there in the moment, and Ru says that you're going to lip sync for your life and then the lights shift, and all the crazy show lights go on you, it is terrifying.

DARIENNE LAKE: I love that song. Bianca said in her interview that I probably had it on cassette tape. She was right. I did! I loved it and I think I have a really great musicality so I know all the words and I know all the ins and outs. When you're performing that song specifically onstage, the musical interlude is when you take tips from the crowd. So that's exactly what I did. I'm gonna be like, oh thank you, thank you! I'm taking tips. And it got a great reaction. To make Ru laugh, that's the goal. And then just to see the way that Michelle and Leah Remini were reacting to my dance moves, I was like, this is great. Palm of my hand.

BENDELACREME: I was definitely wearing the wrong dress. I could not move in that dress and I could not move my hair. I really wasn't expecting to lip sync tonight and I really would have worn a different outfit if I was. I knew Darienne was thwarting me in that lip sync. There was no part of me that thought I was winning, but I was still fighting for my life. My stomach fell into my butt. I thought I was going home.

DARIENNE LAKE: We thought whoever lost the lip sync would go home. I still liked her, so I thought it was good that they kept her.

BENDELACREME: The pause between Ru saying Darienne was safe and then saying I wasn't going home was maybe eight years long. I knew the competition was stiff and I was never of the mindset that I am going to win this. I knew it was a struggle but it was so unexpected because I actually didn't think we had done the challenge so badly. So by the time she said that I was actually staying I had gone through such a crazy mental spiral that it was hard to even take in what she was saying. It was really wild.

BIANCA DEL RIO: Oh, Darienne kicked Miss BenDeLaCreme's ass, honey. Ohhhh, it was good, it was good. That bitch Darienne Lake would always find a way to turn around to show us she knew the words. She was the only one. But I was horrified. I thought if I have to go against Darienne in a lip sync, I'm going home. If I had to go against Trinity, I'm going home. So I was always fearful of them. It was quite shocking because I didn't think they were going to get rid of Ben so quickly and then they were like, oh you can stay. And now no one's going home. Oh, great. Thanks!

But now lip syncing again to Kelly Clarkson's "Stronger," the stakes were higher for Darienne and Ben. The winner, Darienne Lake, moved on to top four. But once the episode aired, BenDeLaCreme's fans created an online competition to bring back their favorite queen.

BIANCA DEL RIO: That was the episode where Ben and I had a moment because Ru does that shady thing where she asks who should go home. In that moment, we all named Darienne, who struggled with the challenge. Darienne fully admitted it and said yes, she should go home. And then Ben made a snide comment saying, "Well, we all can't just sail through the competition like Bianca." I was furious.

ADORE DELANO: I think what Ben was saying was that Bianca's silhouettes were very similar. I remember her mentioning that a lot. But yeah, Bianca did not like that at all. I think she called her the C-word, I remember, and onstage. I didn't agree with Ben on that one. Bianca was the strongest contender and I smelled that from the beginning even when I didn't like her for the first three episodes. I think that Courtney had a more dumb answer. Do you remember her coming for me onstage for no reason? Like, well I'm surprised that Adore has made it this far. And Ru was like the question wasn't who you're surprised is still here, my question is who do you think should go home tonight?

BIANCA DEL RIO: I took it as something nasty in the moment because I helped Ben with her costume and I thought how dare you fuckin' come after me after I helped all of you for this challenge. And I took it completely as a diss. I was not a happy camper. I was happy Ben went home. This bitch has got nerve after I cut out her skirt that she's wearing.

BENDELACREME: I couldn't hear that song for a looong time afterward. I really felt good about what I had delivered and I was really surprised I was on the bottom. I was fully unprepared to deliver a lip sync. As far as all the things we do on *Drag Race*, the one that pertains least to what I do in my normal life is lip syncing. I never felt like I was a super-strong lip-sync competitor and I knew Darienne was incredible. So when I knew that I was going up against Darienne a second time, I did not have high hopes for how that was going to turn out. I fought my hardest.

DARIENNE LAKE: I twisted my ankle during the banjee runway. I remember icing my ankle and being like okay, now I have to perform and I'm tired and I'm exhausted and feeling defeated and stuff but what doesn't kill you makes you stronger and you just gotta do it. I love Kelly Clarkson. I was definitely sad to see Ben go but at the same time you're like, okay, now I'm in the top four, this is amazing. One step closer. You gotta crack a couple of eggs if you're gonna make an omelet.

ADORE DELANO: Darienne out-lip-synced her. Ben was one of my other best friends on that season. I wasn't even that close to Darienne during filming. We got close after. But if I'm being honest, I thought Darienne out-lip-synced her.

BENDELACREME: Any of the animosity between us just came out of the stress of that competition and everyone wanting to do and show their best work. So once that was all out of the way, I feel like it just freed us up to have a good time together on the road. We have done a few tours together and always had a really fun time being on a tour bus and traveling around and entertaining. I am grateful for that friendship.

DARIENNE LAKE: The way that I came across on the show, there was definitely a lot of fans who did not like me at all. Whether it's for my weight, whether it's for my shadiness, whether it's for sending Ben-DeLa home, whatever it was. Of course, I didn't send her home. It's not "The Darienne Lake Drag Race," it's *RuPaul's Drag Race*. She sent her home. But I got a lot of hate.

BENDELACREME: It was edifying to have so many fans asking what I did wrong. I was really nervous to watch and see that there was something that I didn't see that was a misstep. And so when that didn't happen, it felt really amazing to have so many people identify so strongly with me and be rooting for me and want me to succeed. The flip side of that was that I know Darienne got a lot of really negative attention and messaging and she was bullied. And that was a thing that was a really sad side effect of it and that I spoke up about at the time. We were all just there to do the best job we could and to try to make it to the end of this competition and that's all that Darienne was doing, too. So that was a bummer that that happened. But I was really, really grateful for all the support and love and surprised by it and very overwhelmed by it. It felt like a real phenomenon.

MANDY SALANGSANG: We had hit some sort of a stride in terms of popularity and awareness around the show, so we were reaching people beyond who we'd reached in the first few seasons. There were people paying attention and becoming invested, and not just watching one or two episodes. There were people knowing and recognizing who BenDeLaCreme was, who weren't just the young, gay audience we had prior. The audience now included a large straight female fan base, whose boyfriends and partners also got into it. Teenagers and young adults were engaging their families by introducing it to their parents. BenDeLa had been performing really well in the challenges, had an iconic Snatch Game performance, and was really relatable to the expanding fan base.

However controversial the decision, Darienne Lake, Bianca Del Rio, Adore Delano, and Courtney Act excelled in the music video for "Sissy That Walk," their final challenge. Then RuPaul hit them with another twist.

BIANCA DEL RIO: That was a marathon. Aside from it being a mental fuck, it was a physical fuck that you finally get to the end and you can see the light but there's this challenge in different parts. We had an acting challenge. We had choreography. We had to learn the song. We had to make the music video. So it was intense and we had a modeling montage we had to do. The choreography was the toughest part. My style is to not be sexy or youthful, and here it is: We're having to do this choreography in a line and to be seductive and wind blowing and be on a treadmill. Oh girl. That's challenging for my old ass. I struggled with that. It wasn't natural for me to be as seductive as Darienne,

Adore, or Courtney would be. It definitely threw me and I thought this is it. I'm going home.

DARIENNE LAKE: I knew that I was different than everybody else. I'm the big girl. I've got my own little niche and nobody can compete with me on that. I know I have experience, I know I have fun and humor and shade and all that stuff. I went in there with a winning attitude of like I'm gonna win this completely.

BIANCA DEL RIO: We had to lip sync "Sissy That Walk" against each other in pairs: Adore and Darienne, and then it was Courtney and me. Then Ru said she had made a decision. We were standing there and the first person eliminated was Courtney Act. And I just looked around and thought, oh, wait, this is serious, this is it. Courtney left the stage. And Ru goes, "This is my top three."

ADORE DELANO: Do you know what I did that we had to record again because Michelle couldn't stop laughing? Again, I'm not paying attention because I am so shocked that I'm in the top four. I'm just looking around and whatever. Some producer goes, "All right, so now we're gonna film the winner's reaction." That's all I heard. And they go, "The winner of *RuPaul's Drag Race* is Adore Delano!" And I really started crying because I thought it was real. I was like, are you fucking kidding me? And I looked at Michelle's face—she's like, what is she doing? I started crying and I hugged all the girls. And they're like, "What are you doing? Did you not hear what we said? We are filming the winners' reaction!" I was like, I thought you were crowning one! And then Michelle was screaming. She was like, are you fucking kidding me? It was so funny though. I got so red. And then I was so sad.

BIANCA DEL RIO: Courtney came back and they said, "We're going to do this again." And then they eliminated Adore. And I was like ohhh I see what they're doing. And then they eliminated Darienne. So by the time they eliminated me, I was just like okay, whatever, this is fuckery! We were top four and we had to wait months to find out who was in the top three.

DARIENNE LAKE: They filmed each of us leaving, so we had no idea. In the months we were waiting, some of us were talking and Bianca told me she thought maybe Courtney was coming off like Detox, a bit arrogant.

BIANCA DEL RIO: We filmed in June and July and then it started airing in February, so we didn't find out until May a night or two before we filmed the finale. We went back to real life and that's where Courtney, Darienne, and I started our endless group text that we still have to this day. We were planning merch and dealing with management and waiting for this big moment when they reveal us in December. And all hell broke loose. It was wild.

DARIENNE LAKE: I remember Mandy called me and said the good news is you don't have to make two dresses for the finale. The bad news is you're not in the top three. By that time, I had a feeling because Courtney, Adore, and Bianca had the biggest followings on Instagram. They were the popular ones.

BIANCA DEL RIO: We were in a finale rehearsal and they pulled us aside and they said they had written a song for the top three and that's when they told us Darienne would not be in the top. So Adore, Courtney, and I had three different verses. We rehearsed it, and then they announced to the other girls off camera that we were the top three, which was just wild. We didn't have much time to process it.

And then the top three had to wait some more.

BIANCA DEL RIO: When we were done with the season and I went home, I told a friend of mine, "You're going to be very proud of me, I was very nice. I wasn't really mean until episode 5." And all of a sudden, the show starts airing and I'm like oh my god, I'm a cunt the first day! I mean I didn't realize how often I rolled my eyes, how many faces I made.

Through the process, I had gone through every one of the story producers. For some reason, I was constantly being moved around. One day, I asked Jacqueline Wilson, who became my final story producer, why I kept getting shuffled around and everybody still has their same person? She said as people get eliminated, they have to shuffle us around, and they decided I was easy to move around because I didn't care. Which was true. I would talk to a potted plant, I don't give a shit.

MICHELE "MEESH" MILLS: Jacqueline was such a heart of the show. Jacqueline has been on the show since Season 2 and she was the main supervising story producer. She hired me on and she had this whole structure down that I came into. She was on the show until she passed away, which was right after we finished filming Season 12. She had cancer for a year and a half, approximately. When she first got diagnosed with cancer, I was the only one that she told, including her family. She just very much wanted to keep working and she was doing treatments that she was hoping were going to work. It was a traumatic thing. As soon as we stopped filming, she went into the hospital and passed away within a couple of weeks. She had this thing that both of us do where we're really invested with the queens. Some you connect with more because they reciprocate that bond. We'd continue talking to the queens after the season is done and go to their shows. We're invested in what they're doing.

BOB THE DRAG QUEEN: The story producer weaves all the stories together. It's not manipulation or some trickster thing like what people have come to think it is. It's just making sense of you and helping you to tell your story to the world. Jacqueline Wilson was mine and she helped humanize me to people because I do come off as very arrogant and very "I'm great." But Jacqueline helped ground me and let people realize that it wasn't just me being some pompous asshole. She helped people see why I feel it's so important to believe in yourself. I have a picture of me and Jacqueline that I keep in my home because she was really my rock on the show.

RANDY BARBATO: The relationships they build with their story producers are kind of everything because they come to the set and they can't talk unless the cameras are rolling. Then they are under pressure for whatever challenge it is and then they go home and they can't pick up the phone. They are in isolation. So, when they sit down with their story producer, it is a really intense connection.

BIANCA DEL RIO: In the end, I was paired up with Miss Jacqueline, who I adored. I miss her. In those moments, she could get the best out of me by phrasing a question properly. That's where a lot of the comebacks and the nasty comments or the face-making would come in. My goal was anytime I could make her laugh I was set.

STEVEN CORFE: Bianca comes from this unsanitized world of drag. She grew up in the comedy clubs, and I just think that filthy, dangerous edge is something that is so important in drag and, in a lot of ways, it has to be cleaned up for television or for other forms of mainstream media. And she is just an old-school, filthy cunt and that's why I love her.

MICHELLE VISAGE: I knew Bianca and I was the one who encouraged Bianca to audition because Bianca thought they don't have queens like her on *Drag Race*. And I said, "That is exactly why you should audition for *Drag Race*." That's kind of how that happened. Even if we pushed her and gave her a critique, she was like, okay. She could take it and she was willing to give me what I wanted and that's what was amazing. Whereas a critique would hurt Laganja or make Adore laugh, Bianca was like, all right, I'll do it next week.

JOSLYN FOX: The top three are my best friends from the show. I was so excited. I would have been happy with any of them winning. But Bianca is the perfect example of a drag superstar. I think we all should look up to Bianca and learn a thing or two about the way she handles her business and how she handles her relationships, her persona, her art form. She is so smart. She's been in the game for so long and she has that mean personality but she is the sweetest person on the whole planet.

BIANCA DEL RIO: Up until the end, I thought for sure Adore was going to win, without a doubt. I didn't think I was going to win because I wasn't crying about my life. I wasn't struggling. I didn't go through this caterpillar butterfly moment. I was just plowing through it as best as I knew how. We had just come off the season with Jinkx. I just assumed I was going to get the bad-girl edit that I would have to explain later and that Adore was going to win because she had the journey. Adore's got a great way of being chilled and relaxed and we clicked. She was really, really funny with comments and with moments and very welcoming to exchanging conversations with me or barbs or jokes. I really liked her personality a lot. It just clicked.

MICHELLE VISAGE: Everybody kinda knew Courtney from around LA. Adore was new to me and Adore was fucking magical. We knew what Courtney did and we knew what Bianca did, but we didn't know what Adore did. I'm not sure Adore knew what Adore did. And that's what made her so magical with the ill-fitting clothing, the funny sayings. She is so LA. She is so funny. Her Latina pride—everything about her. She is so lovable. You can't help but to love Adore Delano.

MICHELE "MEESH" MILLS: Adore has that natural star quality and she is relatable. I am Mexican and she has this whole chola vibe, which I love that right off the bat. She is sweet. She is lovable, she gives the best hugs, and she is just so funny. She is also not afraid to say her real feelings of people, but somehow it always comes off as endearing and funny, even when she's kind of insulting you a little bit.

STEVEN CORFE: Adore just has this effervescent charm. I'll always remember this one sound bite, we cackled about it in post-production for way too long. Episode 1, she said, "I may have or may have not glued my dress to the mannequin." And that just cracked us up. Every turn of phrase with her had us rolling on the floor when we were editing Adore. She is so likable.

JOSLYN FOX: Every single challenge, Bianca would be the first one to be done with her makeup and then she would go to each queen and help them finish their makeup. She deserves Miss Congeniality. She set everybody's sewing machines up. She would help them if they got stuck. She really is a very kind person.

BIANCA DEL RIO: We were filming the finale and they had not announced to the audience yet that we were going to do multiple winners. So Ru says, "The time has come." I think she says Adore Delano or something. And it was this weird moment where they crown her and then we got back in line and that's when Ru says we're going to do multiple winners. Everybody's like argh! Then Ru says we need to do Adore again because they got the name wrong or something. So immediately I thought if they have to do Adore a second time it's because she won. Then they did me. Then Courtney, who we knew was not going to win. Then Ru says, "Wait a minute." She talks to producers and they come back and film a tie between Adore and me. Adore was ecstatic. The whole time in my head I'm thinking, do we have to split this money? Oh fuck this! And Adore was like, "Oh this is amazing! I love Bianca." And they said, "Bianca, how do you feel?" And I said, "Party."

TOM CAMPBELL: Bianca is such a strong, fully developed entertainer. She was not a kid when she came to *Drag Race*. Whether she was playing the game or just being smart, she had a heart of gold. She's tireless, a nice person, and a grown-up. She is a star.

JOEY NOLFI: Bianca really spoke to me as somebody who represented the essence of New York City drag, that old-school vibe, and so smart, so hilarious. Just no bullshit. You can't get anything past her, almost like an old schoolteacher or something. Bianca was teaching the kids. You listen to Mother, she is just giving you tough love. And I really loved that.

BIANCA DEL RIO: We walk out and we go to meet our family and friends and stuff and as we're there my phone rings and it's Courtney who is in her car going, "They couldn't even include me in the fucking tie?!" So I walked away knowing there was a huge possibility that...Adore was going to win when it aired, because of the mix-up, or having a tie.

But it was Hurricane Bianca in the end. Since winning *Drag Race* in 2014, Bianca Del Rio has become a drag monarch, selling out arenas worldwide, appearing in a West End musical, and becoming an author. When it comes to Bianca's global stage presence, fans around the world are in agreement: Yes, today, Satan.

BIANCA DEL RIO: We were all together in Las Vegas when it happened. We were at the Flamingo Hotel. Courtney, Adore, and I had gotten close, obviously, through this whole process so we were there with our assistants and managers in this hotel suite doing press all day. And it was my suggestion to include Darienne. So she came in the room with us and she hung out with us that day. We were cackling and having a good time. At one point, I saw Adore's people being taken into a room and they were talking and then they came out of the room and I thought they told her she won. This is mind games! I turned into Laganja all of a sudden. Laganja with conspiracy theories and craziness. But I knew within a couple of hours we were going to find out. And then we were all three together sitting on a couch when they announced the winner.

ADORE DELANO: I love them so much. We're going on tour together. I have such a bond with all four of them. We still have the same text thread with us all. They're like my brothers.

DARIENNE LAKE: Bianca totally deserved it, 100 percent. She was great TV. She was so funny and quick-witted, very much like Ru.

LAGANJA ESTRANJA: Good for you, boo, we all knew you were winning. Do you really need it? Aren't you some world-renowned queen already? I was bitter, I was bitter, of course I was bitter. But I am very happy for her now. She was the best. She deserved it. I don't feel anything but grateful to be a part of the season that in my mind has the best winner. I mean Bianca has gone on to play Wembley Arena. She is the most iconic queen and I'm a part of that and I'm a part of her journey and that makes me feel really great.

RANDY BARBATO: Adore was the people's princess and Courtney was first-rate, an international superstar, but in the end, what Bianca had was so consistent. She was polished, delivered dimension, and possessed undeniable wisdom. On top of all that, she was funny as hell and had a heart of gold.

STEVEN CORFE: A lot of Bianca's brilliance was in her sit-down interviews. No one gets to see that while we're on set, producers or queens. It's not until you get back into post that I think the sheer brilliance of Bianca was fully realized. Perhaps from that point on, it was a no-brainer for us. But Season 6, one of its many joys, was that it was a tight horse race with some incredibly popular and different and talented queens.

ADORE DELANO: It was the last season before Instagram girls started getting on. I got to experience the importance of different personalities when it came to work ethic and how their personalities turned on when the camera came on. Even now that I have a little bit of money, I wouldn't spend ten grand on an outfit. Pay your taxes. I'm not spending that money on an outfit I'm gonna wear once or twice. There is no way. It's more focused on look than talent, and you have to have both.

BIANCA DEL RIO: We live in a world now with celebrities that we don't know why they're celebrities. They don't have any talent, but they're known and seen and they're exposed and there's nothing wrong with that. To keep things alive, you have to keep the young and the new people interested. I'm a live performer. I don't look good in Instagram photos, but they can't perform live. It's a different element. Winning was surreal but in the end I felt like fuck, we all won. We all really had this amazing opportunity. Little did I know that it was just the start of the insanity and the crazy life journey that began after that.

Chapter 7
SEASON 7

IS SEASON 7'S BAD REP REALLY DESERVED? IT INTRODUCED FANS TO drag superstars Trixie Mattel and Katya of Russia, Ginger Minj and Kennedy Davenport, and Violet Chachki and her teeny-tiny waist. "She'd already done had herses." Pearl coined *flazéda* and slept through half of the competition, though she wasn't narcoleptic. And Ross Mathews and Carson Kressley replaced Santino Rice as alternating permanent judges.

Despite those highs, the season drew a lot of hate from fans, mostly because the first cast of fashion powerhouses, several of whom grew up watching *Drag Race*, like Miss Fame, was wasted on scripted comedy challenges that, in the hands of acting amateurs, fell as flat as Violet's chest in the first runway challenge. The season also featured mature queens Tempest DuJour, Mrs. Kasha Davis, and Jasmine Masters; Iowa queen Sasha Belle and Kandy Ho of Puerto Rico; Nashville queen Jaidynn Diore Fierce; and Max and her indiscernible accent.

TOM CAMPBELL: It's called the worst season of *RuPaul's Drag Race* and yet some of the biggest queens with the biggest followings were in it. I thought it was amazing.

MICHELLE VISAGE: This was the millennial season. Nothing wrong with that but it was the first season that it was like, oh, you guys are young.

LATRICE ROYALE: Season 7 is where everyone's like ooooh, they have the most stars. When you think about Trixie and Katya and Ginger and Kennedy, they have some good girls that came on. But the season was so horrible! That was bad. They *know* it was bad. Put that on the record, exclamation point three times.

MANDY SALANGSANG: I think that is such nonsense. I have never understood that. At the time, I remember being so perplexed by that especially because the fans were rabid for Katya. They were just crazy about her. When you look back on it, the stars that were created from that season—Katya and Trixie, Violet from a fashion standpoint, and Ginger Minj from a performance standpoint—those are some really talented queens.

VIOLET CHACHKI: My season gets a lot of weird opinions because it is a weird season. They cast really iconic "look queens." I hate that term, by the way. There was me, there was Max, there was Miss Fame, there was Pearl. To me, that was set up to be the supermodels of *Drag Race*.

KENNEDY DAVENPORT: During my season, we had more acting than we did actual entertaining. That was the discouraging part for me because I really wanted to be known for being an entertainer because that's what I was doing at the time. I had taken a few acting classes and some improv but I wasn't heavily into that. I did drag for survival.

MANDY SALANGSANG: This was also the season that Ross and Carson came on board. Santino was great, but I think Ross and Carson have brought another magic, both of them, that has only been positive. They are both such professionals in their fields and such experts as it pertains to just evaluating drag—the fashion and performances.

They provide such knowledgeable critiques and when they are coaches they've got so much value in their advice for the queens. Plus, they are both so funny.

GINGER MINJ: Season 7 gets a lot of flak for being a boring season. It has undeniably one of the most successful casts from any season across the board. There are more of us from Season 7 who have gone on to do TV and movies and Broadway and this and that and the other thing. We're still working. We're still really successful. And that wouldn't have happened if it was the most boring season ever. It has aged like a fine wine, I believe.

The queens arrived on set expecting the usual opening photo shoot and a maxi challenge. Instead, producers melded the mini and main challenges and tasked the fourteen queens with three runway looks: spring, fall, and a resort-wear tearaway to reveal a nude illusion. Violet Chachki's decision to show off her naked male body drew Michelle Visage's immediate ire—"I would have liked to have seen it zhuzhed a little because I'm getting boy"—and the support of Ross Mathews, who loved the risk, and guest judge Kathy Griffin: "I enjoyed seeing your boy body. You kind of had that essence of those crazy skinny models that may or may not have boobs."

VIOLET CHACHKI: I decided I was going to do drag after Sharon Needles won. Season 4 was the turning point of the entire series. It went from a show about drag queens that was silly and fun and under the radar and took off. I saw that there were so many different ways to do drag. In Atlanta, I was going out to bars and I wouldn't really see anything from other local drag performers that inspired me at all. I wanted to go out and see someone doing something sexy and '50s or something really glamorous. And it was more like real girl, passable type of stuff. Atlanta's really pageant-heavy and there are a lot of trans performers. So it wasn't really like giving me what I wanted to see. With Sharon, it was very clear that there were no rules on how to do drag. And I think that's really what connected everyone to the show.

STEVEN CORFE: This was the season that the girls really brought the fashion. We knew that going into pre-production. We had seen the auditions of Violet Chachki and Miss Fame and we devised a premiere that had two fashion shows right off the bat. We thought that was gonna be such a good way to get to know a little bit more about the queens' aesthetics because we knew they were all packing such killer looks. It also was the season where the fashion world started to notice *RuPaul's Drag Race*. Designers started clamoring to be on the guest judge panel and queens were being invited to Paris to sit front row at the fashion shows.

CARSON KRESSLEY: Sitting in that chair for the first time, I thought, did they change the format of the show? Is it all about fashion now? I was thrilled because they were all really fashionable but in a very editorial and edgy way that we hadn't seen on the show before. Never in the history of the show did we have so many on one season who were real fashion queens and could walk in anybody's fashion show tomorrow and really had a great point of view with fashion, a great sense of edge and originality. My first day at work, they had that runway show and Violet Chachki had the reversible, sequined black jumpsuit. There's a meme of that moment where I'm just losing my mind. I don't know where to look or what to do. It's funny but that look was iconic.

VIOLET CHACHKI: It makes sense that they did this three-look runway on the first episode but it almost seems like they did it to get that aspect out of the way because the rest of the season was all acting challenges. It was a weird season as far as production, story line, the challenges, the writing, and the casting was concerned. All of that together is a very strange situation.

KATYA: I remember thinking holy shit, that's a lot on the first challenge. And then it was about sizing other's people's drag up because you really got a sense of where people were at with their aesthetic and where they were with their budget and where they were with their ability. That was wild. And then we had to make something.

TRIXIE MATTEL: That was psycho. The mini challenge was two runways. The mini challenge! Crazy.

GINGER MINJ: To be completely candid, I didn't put a whole lot of thought into any of my runways for Season 7 because to me that was never the focus of my drag. My focus was always on performing. And I didn't realize that that was something that went hand in hand with drag. That is something I definitely learned from Violet and from Miss Fame, from Max, from Pearl, all of these girls who were called the look queens.

At first, I wanted to dismiss them and write them off because their viewpoint of drag was the polar opposite of mine but I really ended up learning so much, not necessarily in the room but watching it back, I learned a little more insight into why they make the choices they do and like what it means to create these outfits. My drag has evolved so much because it has become more about me and more about what I like and how I feel and what I want to portray.

KATYA: The craziest thing was walking out onto the runway the first time with no practice. I think it is diabolical that they do that. You do it twice but it was daunting. It was so scary, it was so daunting, and it was so bizarre to see the judges over there.

GINGER MINJ: I thought it was such a random thing, the nude illusion. The nude delusion is what I call it. I get the concept—we're all born naked and the rest is drag. But to me it felt like it's a bunch of body stockings. If we actually had to be naked, I think it would've been a little more meaningful. I don't know that I would have wanted to do it at all, but the fact that we were more covered in a body stocking, it felt a little strange to me, almost like a letdown.

VIOLET CHACHKI: If there was anyone who has a complex about femininity as it relates to being flat-chested, it's clearly Michelle Visage.

It just felt like she was really projecting her own insecurity about her chest onto me. That whole episode was weird.

MICHELLE VISAGE: Violet was always amazing to look at. Violet was not nice. She was cold. That's what I didn't like about her and I was trying to break her out of that.

VIOLET CHACHKI: It really did piss me off. I talked about gender neutrality and being gender fluid on the show and what that looks like and how I think that women who have smaller chests should embrace them. Of course, in the moment I said I hate Michelle Visage. I was playing into the idea of me being cast as the bitchy one but I was still speaking from a place of truth in that moment.

MICHELLE VISAGE: She said, "I hate Michelle Visage" because she was a child. At twenty-one years old, if you told me you didn't like something I would tell you to fuck off because I knew everything. But one thing is for sure: Every time Violet was on the runway, she might not have been sweet but she was fierce. She looked amazing. She killed every challenge.

VIOLET CHACHKI: Michelle and I are good friends now and she's had her breasts removed. I think Michelle has a better understanding of what drag is like now. Drag has changed so much. I don't know who was the first to go flat-chested. Maybe it was me. But that was definitely a defining moment for queens going flat-chested and embracing their androgyny and their boy body.

Ginger Minj was the self-declared leader of the Bitter Old Lady Brigade, even though at twenty-nine she and Miss Fame were the same age, and they were only seven years older than Violet Chachki. But as an experienced queen herself, Ginger related more to the older contestants and when prompted by producers to come up with a name for her clique, she came up with the Bitter Old Lady Brigade.

GINGER MINJ: I regret it to this day because that was supposed be just a joke. We were making fun of the fact that they were viewing us as this clique. And I was like, oh yeah, we're the Bitter Old Lady Brigade. It was something that was said in jest and it never dawned on me that anybody would take it seriously because it is something that is so silly. They thought that we were on this vendetta to get rid of all of the young skinny girls and to make their lives hell because we didn't feel like they were worthy. Girl, nobody felt like that ever. Ever. It was more the thought of old-school drag versus new-school drag. We weren't really trying to force a rivalry.

KENNEDY DAVENPORT: Older people relate more with older people. It don't mean you are old as dirt, but we were older. We had more experience in drag than they did so we had more to talk about than they did. We kinda laughed at ourselves for being that way so we just named it that way.

GINGER MINJ: I didn't know what the hell to think about Katya. I just knew that I loved her. I knew Kennedy for years because of pageants, so there was a level of familiarity, and then we ended up getting very close because we worked together so much on the season. She and Katya ended up becoming friends because Katya intrigued Kennedy. And Mrs. Kasha Davis is definitely from the same type of drag world that I'm from—that retro, almost housewifey kind of drag, very theatrical. We bonded over the fact that we had both done musical theater for so long. And Jasmine Masters is just funny. That bitch deserves her own sitcom where it's just people following her around with a video camera in the middle of the street. I don't think enough of the world really got to see that. She opened up her suitcase and had a whole suitcase full of food. She brought hot sauce, bread, cold cuts. It made me laugh. And it made me hungry but it also made me laugh.

KENNEDY DAVENPORT: This new generation of drag did not like me because I stuck to my guns and I was opinionated. I felt strong about what drag was and what drag should be and I was vocal about that. The fans called me bitter and I got called so many names for attacking the younger queens, which I never did. And of course, I experienced being called [N-word] and got told why I haven't died yet.

By the time the queens were divided into three girl groups to spoof RuPaul music videos, Pearl's subdued nature was getting a lot of attention. Was she sleepy? Or just aloof? It was hard to tell but after her team's messy parody of "Dance with U," she ended up lip syncing for her life against Trixie Mattel. And the world got to see her signature move, aka The Pearl Smash.

GINGER MINJ: Pearl has this whole demeanor that is very laid-back. It's very sleepy, for lack of a better word. I think a lot of times that that can be misconstrued as being bored or not wanting to be a part of what's going on around you. And after getting to know her more, I don't really think that's it. I think that's just genuinely how she is. That's just what her personality is. And it's something that's really funny to me. A lot of the girls were thinking that Pearl was kind of just coasting by and not taking anything seriously. They felt like she was too cool for it. And it was frustrating because it didn't seem like she was being held accountable for not caring when everybody else was working so hard.

VIOLET CHACHKI: The thing about Pearl is that she is a cute guy. And there is something about this that I really don't like. I love Pearl as a person, as a drag queen, as a friend, but the whole reason that I do drag is to escape being judged on natural looks or being judged on how masculine I am or being perceived as masculine or any of those things. So when people start taking into account somebody's aesthetic and somebody's sex appeal outside of their art, outside of their drag, it's annoying. If there was anyplace in the world where you should not be judged on your natural beauty or your boy beauty, or your male sex appeal, it would be *Drag Race*. You even have RuPaul saying in podcasts recently that she knew that Pearl was going to be well liked because of how attractive she was out of drag. So I feel that was a big factor in her staying. I think that Pearl is wildly talented. I think she's hilarious. I just hate that male out-of-drag aesthetics are part of the game.

KATYA: She was doing the drowsy thing, which I think people interpreted as an I-don't-care attitude, which hadn't really been seen on *Drag Race*. You never had somebody who was chill on *Drag Race* before, ever. Everybody was just like, "Uuuuaaah!" And Pearl was just like, you know, so.

KENNEDY DAVENPORT: This was the time where they were really trying to figure out who Pearl was 'cause she was really just starting to fade in the background. And during this time, she really did not care.

KATYA: I thought she was horrible on the lip sync. I'm telling you I thought she was hoorrrrible. We saw the whole thing and I couldn't believe they sent Trixie home. I didn't know what the hell Pearl was doing. What the fuck is that? I mean I've seen all types of drag performance. A lot of times the pageant girls don't understand the kooky girls or whatever. But I've seen it all, and I've done it all, and I was like, what the fuck is she doing 'cause I don't know what the hell that is. The Pearl Smash!

TRIXIE MATTEL: I love Pearl and I'm here to celebrate drag queens for their strengths. She is not a fabulous lip syncer and I knew I was gonna let her have it. When RuPaul said, "Sashay away," I was like what? What did you say? I couldn't believe it. But also, Pearl was so much prettier than me and still is to this day. She's very attractive out of drag. At the time, she really represented a type of personality that people hadn't seen in drag. Somebody a little more soft-spoken, kinda over it. She's kind of punk rock. I'm a Pearl fan forever. So looking back I'm like, great, she was amazing. Winning *Drag Race* later makes it so easy to look back and be fine with it.

Then came the RuPaul v. Pearl staredown in the werkroom. After RuPaul wondered how Pearl would stand out in a comedy challenge without a big personality, Pearl said telling him so breaks his confidence. "I hope it will light a fire under your ass," RuPaul replied. After they stared at each other for a few seconds, Pearl asked her most famous question: "Do I have something on my face?" RuPaul replied, "No, I'm just not convinced, and I want you to do well. That's why I brought your ass here." And sashayed away.

KATYA: One of the most cliché story lines at this point is the "I have to get out of my own head." With Pearl, that was just so heavy-handed and obvious. Wake up, Pearl! Wake up! Or like oh, Sleeping Beauty's gonna wake up at some point and the judges are going to gag. And at the end they're going to be, oh look how far you've come, Pearl. Whoa, the power of *Drag Race*! Pearl hasn't fucking changed at all.

KENNEDY DAVENPORT: I didn't hear it when it happened. This is something that I really never said anything about because it seemed like every time a Black girl says something we are bitter about it. But, for instance, Pearl was the one that had the most problems but they were still praising her. They were still liking her looks when she was doing the same stuff. And she made it all the way to the top three. I never understood that.

MISS FAME: Everybody just got quiet because you realized it's taken a turn in that RuPaul's response was from a very pissed-off place. RuPaul responded like, *Listen, bitch*, without saying *Listen, bitch*. But it came across like that. And I thought that Pearl was in a weird position because she was trying to defend herself through these kinds of responses, but also was sitting in a chair and RuPaul was like seven feet tall looking down from this point of power. We all felt this tension and it was very uncomfortable and scared the shit out of all of us. The last thing you want is RuPaul to be really upset or mad at you.

GINGER MINJ: I was not in the room for that. Kandy and I were working with Kathy Griffin on the main stage. When I came back into the room, everything had just happened. Pearl had started smoking with Katya and myself so a producer asked if I wanted to talk to Pearl outside. So I walk up and I'm having a cigarette and she's filling me in on what happened. It was really interesting to see the switch in Pearl. Even though she was mad at the situation, you could tell it was starting to make sense to her. It was sinking in that if she wanted to stay she needed to step up and be an active participant. It gave her that kick in the ass to slay the Despy Award challenge. She was hysterical.

GINGER MINJ: I didn't know what had actually happened until I watched it on TV. I just knew that they had gotten into an argument. I was just as gagged as the rest of the world. That's like going to somebody's house and criticizing what they have made and how they run their household and looking them in the eye and saying, "Come at me, bitch." You don't do that to RuPaul in the house that she built.

VIOLET CHACHKI: The whole season I was just worried about myself. I don't remember it. I was teamed up with Miss Fame and we were trying to be funny. That's what I was worried about. I was worried about my outfit, and my routine, and I really wasn't focused on it at all. I had blinders on the whole time. I was so determined to win that I was focused on a lot of these horrible challenges.

KATYA: Ru talked about it in her podcast and she admitted that in that moment she wanted to can the bitch. She wanted to say, okay, well, let me help packing your bags 'cause you're fucking out of here! But she didn't do that because, as an executive producer on this show, she knows this contestant's going to be popular. She's a really cute boy. People are going to love her so I need to chill and just ride this moment out. I'm shocked that she admitted that.

MISS FAME: We just went to talk and have cigarettes out back and she was venting and having to step away. It gets in your head and you still have a challenge to follow up on.

MICHELLE VISAGE: Ru is much more even-keeled than I am. I would have lost my shit if that were me. I wasn't there so I don't know where it came from. I don't know what the context was. But it all seemed to come out of nowhere. And Ru was able to rise above it. I've been told this by my therapist many times, even with my own children, you have to fight your inner teenager because your inner teenager wants to come out and go what the fuck did you just say? I would have had to fight. Or I would have fell out laughing because it's so stupid. But she said it and Ru handled it like a champ. And it was really ballsy on Pearl's part. I just don't know why she needed to say it.

Max's elimination from *Drag Race* caused a tremor in the dragverse, and not because fans necessarily disagreed with her departure. Her Snatch Game Sharon Needles impersonation had, in fact, spooked everyone for all of the wrong reasons. Before her lip-sync battle against Jaidynn Diore Fierce, Max asked for a moment onstage that led to some awkward singing on the steps that may or may not have been prompted by RuPaul. Later after the show aired, and Max explained the missing context in interviews, fans were irate with production. But what had happened was...

VIOLET CHACHKI: Max is a prime example of what not to do. That sounds bad, but he was such a strong contender. He was really fierce competition, one of the best fashion queens of the show. And then he let one bad week destroy him. It might have been overconfidence. I was confident on the outside, but on the inside, I was really calculated and I was constantly weighing out the possibilities. I was always ready to lip sync.

GINGER MINJ: That entire episode, Max didn't seem to be present. It seemed like she was starting to fall out of the game. Max just wasn't acting like herself. She seemed very out of sorts.

KATYA: Max asked for a moment to loosen his corset. And then he sat down on the runway and I remember thinking, what are you doing?

Granted, a week or two before, Violet had cinched her waist down to fifteen inches and did actually have a moment backstage where we were all afraid for her.

VIOLET CHACHKI: I have the smallest waist in *RuPaul's Drag Race* history. I want people to see it. I love that exaggerated silhouette. I think corsets are just beautiful garments, the way they're constructed, the detail and the time it takes. And I think there's something really disciplinary about corset training. I think drag is very disciplinary, and it does take lots of practice and skill and time. And so it's just another layer to appreciate when someone can get their waist trained and can get snatched like that. It doesn't really matter about size. People, especially after the show, were really harping on me being super skinny. But it's really just about exaggerated shapes.

GINGER MINJ: Your waist is the size of my neck, cool. I thought that there were other things that Violet did that were so incredible that to skip over those just to talk about how tiny her waist is was really a discredit to the actual work she was putting in. She would walk out on the main stage in anything and look absolutely incredible. She really raised the bar as far as runway looks went. In person, it was even more beautiful. For the Death Becomes Her runway, she wanted her corset really tight, so I volunteered to help her. I didn't do it on purpose but I laced her in so tight she ended up almost passing out before we went out for the runway. We had to stop and loosen it up. I felt so bad.

VIOLET CHACHKI: You have to walk the runway twice, once with music and once without. I did the corset right before I went on, and I had been sleeping in the corset at the hotel. So in between the two runways, I was just thinking I'd stay tight and loosen it up after the second runway. But it was taking so long to have the girls walk. There were probably like ten or eleven contestants still left and everyone had to cycle through again. I just started feeling faint and had to sit down and took the corset off a bit. It's not super painful but what was painful was the amount of time that I was in it because filming just takes so long. When I wear corsets in reality, if I am feeling uncomfortable, I go to the bathroom and I take a little break and then I tighten it back up. But when you're in a full outfit on TV, you have your press-on nails on, you have your dick tucked away, you have everything done, you can't just take a break. So I fucked the whole order up and I got lots of attention and everyone was all worried about it and for the rest of the season they'd ask if I needed a break.

KENNEDY DAVENPORT: We were really concerned about her. It may have been presented that the older girls was against the newer girls and things like that but it was never that way. We really cared about each other. So we were really concerned because you could almost wrap one hand around her waist.

KATYA: So now Max had to take this moment and I thought he was being a diva. No, stand up. We're all in pain, bitch, get a grip. You're not in any more pain than we are. We're all in front of the camera. You don't get to take a break. Max was late every fucking time. She was the last person ready. She was really young so she didn't have a lot of experience. She wasn't used to being ready at a certain time for a show.

GINGER MINJ: Out of nowhere, she goes, "Oh, this is too tight, I need to take it off. I need some water." So they brought her some water, took the corset off, and sat her down on the stairs to catch her breath. It happened during Jaidynn's critiques. RuPaul said that she looked like Judy Garland down there. And Max started singing so Ru said, "Do you take requests? How about a little 'Over the Rainbow'?" And so she sang a Judy Garland song. It was a cute moment. It wasn't as big of a thing as it became.

KATYA: The way all of that was edited does not give a really accurate picture because she didn't just start singing. She didn't just take a break and say well, since I'm down here, does anybody want to hear any Judy Garland? It wasn't like that. Ru asked her to sing the song. And she did. It was weird.

KENNEDY DAVENPORT: Why would RuPaul ask her to sing if the bitch can't breathe?

TOM CAMPBELL: I think she was just trying to make an awkward moment feel less awkward.

KENNEDY DAVENPORT: They just edited it down. That's all.

GINGER MINJ: The fans were like, oh that was so weird and Max went crazy. And then Max explained what happened. But the fans took that and started saying RuPaul and production set Max up. It aired as a weird moment, but I don't think that makes RuPaul and production monsters and I don't think it makes Max this whackadoodle crazy person.

Something else that seems crazy: From the moment Violet Chachki entered the werkroom, she proved she was fiercely creative and determined. So why was she always picked last?

RANDY BARBATO: I remember thinking that Violet Chachki was extraordinary and that she should be cast because her fashion is to die for. When they arrived and we talked to them in their hotel rooms, I remember our first chat with Violet. I was impressed. I saw then that she was way more than a fashion queen. That's when I realized she really could be a contender.

KATYA: She was not very social. She wasn't very friendly and she was kind of a bitch. Everybody besides Max and Violet were very friendly. They were very in their own worlds. Ginger was the opposite. She was very gregarious, very outspoken, and she smoked so we smoked together. The smokers got to know each other really quickly, me, Pearl, and Ginger. And I got to know Trixie a little bit 'cause she was friendly, and Kasha Davis.

GINGER MINJ: I don't think the audience really got to see a lot of

262 Maria Elena Fernandez

the fact that Violet was not a very pleasant person in the werkroom. She always had something negative to say about everybody and everything. People have asked me, is Violet a bitch? She's not a bitch. She is a brat. You can tell that she worked hard for the things that she had but she wasn't used to hearing no. Whenever we would get into group situations, it would always have to be how she wanted it, when she wanted it. She was the one voice that had to be heard and listened to. Or she would just randomly go up to the other girls and point out their body flaws. Violet and I get pitted against each other from the fan base because we were in the finale and we were both deserving of winning but we represented very opposite ends of the drag spectrum. She had an attitude problem.

KENNEDY DAVENPORT: Violet was not good at acting. She was not. And I'm not gonna say I was a damn Denzel Washington but at least I gave more character than she did. Violet was dead when it came to acting.

KATYA: I got to work with her in a challenge, which was helpful. She's just very driven. She's the opposite of me, she's very confident and she was very focused and she wanted to win.

VIOLET CHACHKI: I have a really hard time being fake. I'm not good at acting or at faking it, as you can see on the show. I guess I am unfiltered and I say what's on my mind and that is definitely bratty sometimes and mildly offensive. That actually is who I am, and I knew that I was cast partly for that reason. So I was really just being myself. If you look back at the footage, what did I really do that was bad? I told people what I thought honestly and openly all the time to their face whereas I was being called names behind my back. I got called horse face; I got called no talent, all behind my back. It's just funny to me how those people aren't really remembered as being bitchy. I guess I did say that I didn't have any fat to push together and I was jealous of Kasha Davis but I said it to her. But I was jealous. I did want fat to push together and now I have fat to push together on my boobs.

. . . .

Every season of *Drag Race* features a makeover challenge involving new faces on set, including brides and grooms, senior gay men, and jocks. This season, all of the eliminated queens returned for a conjoined-twins challenge that paired them up with the remaining queens and gave them a shot to return to the competition. Because Kennedy Davenport won the mini challenge, she assigned the pairings. By the time the challenge was over, Trixie Mattel was back in business and twins Ginger Minj and Sasha Belle faced off with Jaidynn Diore Fierce and Tempest DuJour in an epic lip-sync battle of Tiffany's "I Think We're Alone Now."

TRIXIE MATTEL: When I got sent home, it was so disappointing. I pictured my home bar, all of the bartenders watching and being disappointed. I thought I let everyone down. It hurts because you think of all your fans who want you to win. And by fans, at that point, I mean your friends who come to your Wednesday-night show and tip you a dollar. You think you've let them down. It's deeper than just losing. But then production told me not to unpack my bags. And then they brought us back and we had to compete for the spot. That was crazy.

GINGER MINJ: When Kennedy set up the teams, she thought she was doing me a favor because she knew that Sasha and I had been friends and she thought Sasha was a seamstress, not realizing that our skill set was about the same. And then Sasha and I came up with a great idea. I think it was the best idea out of all of the conjoined twins because it was different. It's very easy to join hip-to-hip but to take it and turn it on its head and amp it up and make it drag, like, why wouldn't you be conjoined at the breasts or the hair or something like that? So even if the execution wasn't fantastic, I thought the idea was spectacular.

KATYA: I was happy that the makeover episode was going to be with somebody we knew because I didn't want to make over a stranger or something like that. And it wasn't even really a makeover. It was more of a collaboration. I thought it was a really fun episode. It's one of my favorite challenges from the show. Kasha and I came up with these two characters. I think their names were Trish and Gloria, and I think we were cousins, which is funny 'cause we're twins. It was like we're both drunks, like Vegas barflies, trashy, it was so fun. It was so difficult being attached at the pussy all day. We had a blast.

KENNEDY DAVENPORT: I was glad that they came back. I was glad to see Jasmine. And of course, I had to partner everybody up. I knew Jasmine could sew, so everything was my idea. Jasmine was just there to sew the costumes and do what I tell her to do. My whole idea was like a Billie-Holiday-and-Ella-become-sisters type thing. Like jazz singers coming out. So that's why we had the flower in our hair and stuff like that. We were supposed to be singers, not pageant. I can't say that I understood how I could've taken it further.

TRIXIE MATTEL: Pearl and I worked together in Chicago in bars and clubs and circuit parties. She was definitely my friend from the season outside of the show. She had this idea for prom queens and then I was like no, let's do like teen pageant twins. They say one twin is always prettier than the other. Let's exaggerate that. Let's make you gorgeous and me not meant for beauty pageants. And I knew I could probably figure out how to make braces. So I made those braces from a nail file, some hair clips, some wire, a paperclip I unfurled, and I stuck beads on it and superglued it to the teeth so when I smiled I had real train tracks on my teeth. And once we were in drag and the character of me as this monster developed, I was like we're winning this. The competition was really good but ours was a really good match between beauty and comedy.

GINGER MINJ: I think that we could've done a lot better had Sasha Belle been more interested in the challenge at hand than running around the room catching up with people. It was so frustrating because I had been doing very well in the competition, so far. I had won two challenges, and just coming off of a Snatch Game win, I felt like there was a target on my back. I didn't want to get too comfortable and I knew that design challenges were not my strong suit. It wasn't exciting for me. It was just nerve-racking. I knew we were gonna end up in the bottom because the construction wasn't great.

TRIXIE MATTEL: It was probably the most iconic runway of our season, the conjoined twins. And it was so joyous. I remember RuPaul off camera looking at us and going, "By the way, it's rare after the first episode that we get to have everyone back and it really is just nice to have all you girls back." And then she hit me! You can put that on the record. I'm just kidding.

GINGER MINJ: They told us stay in your costumes. We already knew that Sasha Belle had no chance of coming back because we ended up in the bottom. So I said, well, it's not like they can punish you for bringing scissors. So we snuck the scissors into her breastplate and she took 'em out and I started cutting. Luckily, it was so funny and Ru laughed so hard. But I also knew that since we had to face each other the way our costumes were built, there would have been no way for us to lip sync effectively because we couldn't even turn out to the judges. So we gave ourselves a double mastectomy right onstage. Everyone had a good time and it really took what was a bad experience for me and redeemed that entire episode for me. In hindsight, I'm glad we ended up in the bottom because that lip sync is iconic. Even though it was horrible for me, I think it was one of the best makeover challenges that there have been.

TRIXIE MATTEL: It was very exciting to return with Pearl. The fact that we won that challenge and got me back in, that was crazy. That was one of the happiest days of my life.

Seven months after Sharon Needles won *Drag Race*, her bejeweled crown was stolen during an appearance she made at an Atlanta pageant. Logo turned the mystery into a "Ru-Dunnit" starring Michelle Visage that aired as commercials during the fifth season. Detective Visage didn't crack the case, but the baby queen who *Drag Race* fans would watch win the show two years later has confessed to her hilarious role in the caper. Sort of.

VIOLET CHACHKI: There was a pageant in Atlanta at a place called

The Jungle and I was doing a special performance with the cast. Sharon was a judge. After the show, I went with my friends to a bar and my friends said they had a surprise present for me in their car. My friends at that time were very mischievous and they were basically obsessed with me doing drag and getting on *Drag Race*. We were all obsessed with Sharon Needles, too. So we go outside and I'm thinking in my head before they popped the trunk, if they have Sharon Needles's crown in this trunk, I will lose my shit. They popped the trunk, and Sharon Needles's rhinestone crown is sparkling in the parking-lot lights, staring at me. She had worn her crown to the pageant and they stole it! I guess she took it off in the dressing room and my friends were backstage with me helping me to pack my suitcase, and they just snatched her crown. I was gagged, of course.

STEVEN CORFE: I know the version of the story that doesn't have "friends" in it.

ADORE DELANO: If Violet denied it, then I'd be like, well, maybe that's true. But if Violet was saying it's her friends, though, it's Violet.

MICHELE "MEESH" MILLS: I think she had friends that were with her but Violet told me she stole the crown. And she was very proud about it, too.

VIOLET CHACHKI: A couple of months go by, we're watching Season 5 and there's this whole campaign with Absolut that came out called "Ru-Dunnit" and it is basically who stole Sharon Needles's crown? So all this stuff is happening behind the scenes, Sharon's manager is talking to the owner of Jungle, where I performed every week, yelling at him about this crown being stolen. And the crown is sitting in my friend's apartment. Sometimes they'd be walking around wearing her crown casually, being funny. One night after one of my shows, we went back to their apartment and I ended up putting on Sharon's crown, getting naked, and taking photos of myself in her crown naked with a disposable camera. I decided it's a smart idea to leak a photo of myself wearing the crown naked.

I posted the photo of me wearing the crown on my Facebook, and this gay gossip rag in Atlanta called *Project Q* figures it out. This article runs about how I stole Sharon's crown in Atlanta and I'm getting hate mail and people are saying that I stole it. At this point, she already has her crown back. My friends got in touch with her and somehow got it back to her.

ADORE DELANO: I was on tour when Sharon showed me the picture of Violet naked with the crown and she was like, "This bitch is probably gonna get on the next season." And I was like, wait, what? She actually stole your crown? Like, how do you let that happen, loser?

VIOLET CHACHKI: I just kept going on in my life but, of course, everyone thought I was a thief now, which was really fun, locally. I did get in trouble at the bar. I was guilty by association. Sharon and I never talked about it until after I won. Now it's a joke. The important thing is she has her crown back.

And, of course, Violet Chachki also has one of her own.

Chapter 8
SEASON 8

A LOT WAS RIDING ON THE EIGHTH CYCLE OF *RuPaul's Drag Race*. It was no longer the newbie on the TV schedule, and fans wondered if it had peaked. Now marking its one hundredth episode, a distinguished achievement in television, *Drag Race* returned in the spring of 2016 with a dozen queens and a shorter season.

From the moment they entered the werkroom, it was obvious New York City queens Bob The Drag Queen, Thorgy Thor, and Acid Betty were going to dominate.

Laila McQueen and Dax ExclamationPoint were eliminated together in the second episode, prompting RuPaul to bring back Puerto Rican queen Naysha Lopez, who left first. Cynthia Lee Fontaine, the "Cucu" queen, enchanted with her warmth but also went home early. Seattle queen Robbie Turner, a close friend of Jinkx Monsoon and BenDeLaCreme, slayed on roller skates. Country dancing queen Chi Chi DeVayne split, cartwheeled, and death dropped, but won fans over with her sweet charm. Supermodel striver Naomi Smalls and Instagram fashion and anime sensation Kim Chi both made it to the top three. As the season's prime instigator, Britney Spears impersonator Derrick Barry proved why he's popular worldwide and became the hundredth queen to make a grand entrance into the werkroom.

BOB THE DRAG QUEEN: The day Season 8 got cast was the day that marriage equality passed across the nation. So it was really an overwhelming day! I was at Boots and Saddles, which is a bar that is now closed, in the West Village. We couldn't get into the Stonewall to celebrate marriage equality because it was just packed. The whole block, you couldn't get near it. So we went into a nearby gay bar and we were just hanging out. And then I got *the* call. It was Steven Corfe. He has a very cute British accent and he talks really slowly. And he goes, "All right, Bob The Drag Queen, I'm just calling to tell you, you're a Ru girl now." It was a lovely day.

NAOMI SMALLS: Walking into the werkroom on Season 8 was an out-of-body experience. I would consider the first twenty minutes of being on set with the other queens, before production began filming, the most fun and foreign feeling I ever had filming *Drag Race*. Everything was so new to me and it was inspiring to see so many different walks of drag at the highest level of the time. I have a fascination with innocence and perception. Who was I to go on national television in a sheer swimsuit with my toes hanging over the edge of my platform?

CYNTHIA LEE FONTAINE: When I accessed the werkroom, I saw everything in slow motion. I saw the werkroom, I saw the fifteen cameramen in front of me, I see the techs from the other side, and I see everybody. This was the moment it was real. I believe I am here. I don't have to pinch myself. There was a longer version of what I said, but they cut it to: "How you doing, *mis amores*? Do you want to see my cucu?" When I was four years old, I tried to tell my mom that I needed to go to the bathroom. I had heard one of my siblings say the bad word in Spanish, *culo*, which means 'ass.' So I told my mom, "*Mamá, caca, peepee, culo*" and she slapped me with a *chancleta* (flip-flop). So me, just trying to figure out how to not get the *chancleta* in my cucu, the next time I said, "*Mamá, caca, peepee*" and she was already giving me the evil Latina mom eyes, so I'm like, "Cucu!" She dropped the *chancleta* and since that day it was cucu. And today everybody calls me Cucu, even Mama RuPaul.

ACID BETTY: I knew Thorgy was going to be on, I didn't know Bob was going to be on. I got wind of Thorgles because all of her friends said she was going to makeup school, and I knew she wasn't going to no makeup school.

BOB THE DRAG QUEEN: I had been in LA for five days already. So you go and then you're in the hotel for three, four days, seeing only producers, and two or three at a time. Bitch, we were quarantined before the world quarantined. And after not seeing anyone who would hang out with me for more than thirty minutes—remember, I love attention—once I got released into the werkroom, it felt like taking the chain off a dog. I had an idea that one of my best friends Thorgy would be there because she started being weird back in New York City but I didn't know.

THORGY THOR: The producers came in to check on me in our own little private room before I walked in. And I was eating fruit snacks. I get tagged every day with that! And then I walked into the room and I saw Acid Betty. And then Bob came in and we made a lot of noise. The other girls hated us, immediately hated us. Loved it! Oh I loved that the other girls were like ugh, they know each other? And we were loud. The three of us—our personalities, ooof.

BOB THE DRAG QUEEN: You feel like the baddest bitch on the planet because you're like, girl, I'm walking into the werkroom, and you're told to ignore all these drag queens and stand and say your line. But then as soon they give me a break, I just started screaming, I'm diving on the table. I also recognized two New York City drag queens who are already there, Thorgy and I knew of Acid Betty. I couldn't contain myself. I was just so excited. I couldn't articulate it. I was on my favorite show! And not only that, but I was sure I was going to win it.

DERRICK BARRY: I came in and I said, "It's Derrick, bitch," and started dancing. It was exciting, butterflies and everything. I heard so many woooooo! A lot of the cast had known who I was because of *America's Got Talent* or just being on the road for almost ten years at that point. When Ru first said Derrick Barry and that I'm the hundredth queen to walk in, I was like, oh my god, what did I win? Do I get a crown? A sash? Something? But it was just so exciting to feel right away noticed and welcomed. You want to be the first person in the room because you get more camera time but in this case I was so happy to be the last.

THORGY THOR: Bob called me up recently and he goes, "Do you know you are my longest drag friend? I have known you the longest." I always knew that! Because he started drag a little after I did and I used to book him at Saliva Tuesdays at The Ritz. He had his own show around the corner. And we were just hitting the streets of New York and he was just brilliant. He said, "I just want you to know that I love you and you are just incredible and we are such good friends." I thought that was very cool. So when we walked into the werkroom, I was like, this is just like hanging out in New York to us. And Acid Betty, I've known for twenty years. She was extra but I love her. Acid Betty is one of those very rare, brilliant minds. She can figure out something that no one else can figure out. A month ago we had just been working in New York and now we're on television.

KIM CHI: I was a nervous wreck. The whole thing just feels surreal. The whole time you feel you're getting punked or kidnapped until you walk into the werkroom and then you see RuPaul.

TOM CAMPBELL: I sit at home a lot googling *RuPaul's Drag Race*. I wish I had a bigger life but I don't. I think I'm the one who discovered it. I wonder where we are? And we were approaching a hundred and then someone else did the math, and we're at a hundred queens. It's just like holy shit! As Ru says, the real test in showbiz is achieving some kind of longevity. It's not about becoming famous, it's about longevity. Are you still working? Are you still creating? And the hundredth thing was big. We weren't just a drop in the bucket. There was one time when an executive said that *Drag Race* isn't the kind of show that defines a network. It's kind of a filler show until a network figures out its brand. When you reach one hundred, you're like, I think we're doing okay.

. . . .

To commemorate the special hundredth episode, the queens were tasked to a photo shoot with past winners, including a clown who stood in for Bianca Del Rio.

KIM CHI: Luckily, all we had to do was pose in front of people. They didn't dump us in a water tank or anything, and I was like oh, thank god. But it was definitely intimidating. Can I see myself next to these legends? Probably not, so I just kept posing.

ACID BETTY: I watched every single episode of every season before I went on. I knew that they could throw anything at us and that the first week is always underwater or under a power fan or upside down. Like this is all cool, but soon they're going to throw mud in our faces. But they didn't. They threw us in a room of piranhas.

THORGY THOR: It was all right. I knew half of them. I was like, oh hey, oh hey, and they didn't move and they tried to create this cold atmosphere and I was just like, hey could we just have more fun? Why is it so sterile in here? I'm dressed like a clown for a reason so let's get to work. You can stare at me; you can stand in silence, I'm fine.

DERRICK BARRY: I think we had ten shots. I saw that they were all in their spots and not moving. So I started picking different areas and grabbing props. I don't know if it was the judges or if it was queens but people started saying that the cast looked like my backup dancers in my Vegas show. I was absolutely comfortable in my costume and my hair and just the feeling of being there. I knew almost all of those queens so it didn't feel scary.

ACID BETTY: I loved it because Raja is an old friend of mine and she was sitting next to me and she was whispering in my ear. I'd met Sharon Needles at club gigs and stuff. It was funny seeing those people there in work mode. At first, I thought Violet Chachki was reading me. She was like, "What's up with your shoulder pads?" I'm like, huh? And she was like, "I love them. Where'd you get them?" Oh, I made them.

THORGY THOR: The only one that I noticed that made me laugh and was laughing was Mathu Andersen. He was the director of the photo shoot. He was saying, "Bigger! Bigger!" I was like, how about this cartwheel? How about jumping in the air? And then I left. I talked to Sharon Needles later, and she goes, "Thorgy, what the fuck were you wearing? This was your entrance look on the show? Garbage." I'm like, "You're a monster."

For their acting challenge, the queens performed in scenes inspired by the TV drama *Empire*, a huge hit that year. Bob The Drag Queen and Thorgy Thor played Chocolate Chip Cookie, the star of the show, for their respective teams.

ACID BETTY: They played us an eight-minute trailer of *Empire*. And then someone came in and was like, "You do it like that." I didn't even know the reference. It was untethered. Like, how do I make fun of it if I don't even know what it is? It was also weird because we were a group of all white-skinned actors and the show was Black people. The other cast had Black people, Bob and Chi Chi. So that was also awkward.

THORGY THOR: There was a lot that happened during that episode. I was supposed to get Kim Chi's role, Vanilla Wafer, in my group because Naysha was in charge of it and gave the roles out. We literally spent 75 percent of our rehearsal time reading the lines and memorizing them. And then right before it, Kim Chi stands up and goes, "I don't know how comfortable I feel with the Cookie role because I have a lisp and I have an accent and it's really wordy and I just don't know." And Naysha makes an executive decision and says you and Thorgy are going to switch. And I thought to myself, I didn't have any time to memorize these lines. Wow, you're really putting me on the spot.

DERRICK BARRY: The *Empire* challenge was so uncomfortable. I wanted to be Cookie, of course. I wanted to be the star of that number. And I ended up with Ginger Snap. I wish I would've just went there and been like super crazy, sassy. They warned us RuPaul just wants us to make him laugh. And Kim Chi was so over the top 'cause Ru had wanted more tongue pops and things like that. I think I was trying to be so politically correct so that was not easy for me to convey that.

KIM CHI: This episode is kind of a blur. I don't have any acting experience either so that was also new to me. I actually don't remember much from this episode. Vanilla Wafer was supposed to be overacting, so I guessed I had to be as over the top as possible.

CYNTHIA LEE FONTAINE: At the end of the previous episode, they called a primary care doctor because I wasn't feeling well. I was losing my appetite. I'm very tired and I don't know what is happening. They were saying I looked pale and yellowish. World of Wonder immediately called a doctor and they came before we started filming the acting challenge. The doctor told me I needed to see a specialist. So I had to get dressed for the acting challenge in twenty-five minutes, real quick. And I was feeling really, really bad that day—dizziness, vertigo, nausea. I didn't look super healthy in front of the cameras.

BOB THE DRAG QUEEN: While sewing for the show, I watched all of *Empire* to prepare. I had already been watching it kind of on and off because I love Taraji P. Henson. And then when I saw there was an *Empire*-based challenge, I was like, well now I've gotta amp up my skills because I realized I could have been any character. I was looking at them all and I don't know why they gave me Taraji. It feels like giving me the chocolate Cookie character was like handing me the win. Or maybe they wanted to uplift the whole team.

STEVEN CORFE: Bob did maybe three different takes. Every one was hilariously different in its own way and hilariously usable. Bob, whether he was throwing water in the queens' faces on the floor or saying "Is the bus still running?"—improvising that on his way out the door—literally had us in stitches from beginning to end of that challenge. I think that is when we knew here is a powerhouse. Here is someone with acting chops, comedy, and smarts.

THORGY THOR: I learned it and I did the Cookie role and it was funny and I think RuPaul loved it. But then she would get really nitty-gritty with me, which I didn't appreciate. She wanted it word for word. If you watch Bob's thing, girl, he made up his own script completely. So why was I being held to a different standard? I knew if I spoke up, it would've made me look like a sore loser so I kept my mouth shut. I messed up one word in the script but he can make up any words he wants and he won? What is this bullshit? I learned it in five minutes. So, whatever, I'm a little bitter, I'm a little bitter.

ACID BETTY: Bob's acting was incredible but the weird part about is that they gave us a script and they were like, stand here, do the lines. And then Bob was telling us, girl, I couldn't remember the lines so I was just improv-ing. What made the cut was all of his great improv-ing, which was amazing. I know Thorgy was off-the-wall frustrated because she didn't improv. Had I known that I could have gone more crazy and not stuck with "I'm every woman" or whatever these lines are, maybe I could've done better.

JOHN POLLY: Watching Bob The Drag Queen in the *Empire* challenge, every single person on the set was dying because Bob just walked onto the set and blew the doors off of it. Ad-libbing throughout, the sparkly bodysuit reveal, which was all her own. She just breathed life and joy into that and I feel like that's one of the moments on the set when everyone was just like bowled over in laughter the entire time because she was just great.

BOB THE DRAG QUEEN: Queens were being funny before Bianca and Jinkx, but Jinkx really made it a thing on *Drag Race* to be insanely funny.

DERRICK BARRY: I had changed the lyrics to the song, and then I forgot them, and Faith Evans was not having it. It's intimidating. I wish I would have been as crazy and as manic as possible to steal a scene. I loved *Empire*. I wanted to kill it but it was uncomfortable.

· · · · · · · · · · · · · · · · · · · ·

When that challenge ended, the queens transformed into rollergirls and skated down the runway, some more successful than others.

NAOMI SMALLS: Whose idea was it to have a group of clumsy queens wearing wigs in roller skates? I did not pack the best outfit for roller-skating but I still loved how the glam of my runway came together. I felt so fierce in my poorly styled lace front that I had no idea how to glue down.

THORGY THOR: That was so much fun! They said roller-skating, so I'm like let's do '70s porno, blond. And I made those headphones backstage out of foam and cardboard. And then the cord was some computer wire that they didn't need so I cut it and glued it onto my headphones. I will never forget Carson, who I freakin' love, he goes, "Yeah, it's just a little done and expected so I don't like it." And I'm like, okay. Didn't Bob win this one wearing a $10 silver robot Amazondotcom jumpsuit?

DERRICK BARRY: I haven't roller-skated since I was a kid. I got Rollerblades in high school and I Rollerbladed. It's a little stage. I was super intimidated. And knowing that Robbie was a professional and then finding out that Ru loves to roller-skate and he is really good at it, I thought, ohhh man. With my candy land, fairy princess dress, I just wanted to feel like I was roller-skating in the clouds. I knew if I fell I would be padded enough around me with all my bubble wrap, alternative materials. I did okay. A lot of people did worse. I would definitely not say that I am doing any Roller Derby competitions in the future unless it would be on Rollerblades.

ACID BETTY: I know how to competition roller-skate, not as good as Robbie Turner. It was funny because Robbie and I were the only two that they were yelling at because they had this whole insurance thing and a stunt man to help us. They wanted to make sure that we knew the safety hazards of skating. And Robbie and I were like, give us these skates, oh my god, and, bitch, let's skate. The rebel in me is like let me roller-skate, I'm gonna go crazy. Bob won that challenge and Bob cannot skate. And that onesie, I have that in the trash bin. I couldn't believe he won it off of a onesie that I bought from Halloween Adventure with $20 and he couldn't skate.

KIM CHI: I roller-skate all the time so that was really fun for me. The runway itself is too small to be on roller skates so I was telling myself not to skate off the runway. I had my parrot look. My idea was to be free with the skates and fly like a parrot.

BOB THE DRAG QUEEN: To quote Barack Obama, let me be clear. I never thought that our roller look was going to be a runway. I thought they were going to take us to a Roller Derby and that we were going to race or do some sort of a challenge. I didn't think it was going to be for the runway. So my outfit was just so basic. I bought it off Amazon. I also saw this Transformers thing on YouTube. This kid had a Transformers outfit made out of cardboard. It was so cool looking, and I tried to re-create it but we have such a limited amount of time in there.

CYNTHIA LEE FONTAINE: The costume that I wore for the roller-skate runway look, I filled the pants just two weeks earlier. I was looking like a living skeleton walking around everywhere. In a week, I lost forty-seven pounds. I was experiencing symptoms of stage one liver cancer but I didn't know it. I was having severe nausea, I was not eating, my skin was all yellowish, my eyes, and I had diarrhea. During the two weeks I was preparing for the show, I didn't feel like eating and I was feeling a little bit tired. But I had to put together twenty-eight to thirty-two looks, shoes and hair, so I thought it was just stress.

THORGY THOR: This is why I love Bob. This is why he's my favorite person. He could not skate to save his life. He kept falling. So he joked with me and he goes, girl, I'm just gonna pretend like I'm a robot. And then he won and I felt like, really? You ad-lib and you wore a cheap thing and you still won. I really felt like that was the second time that I was in the top where I was like, *okay*. Shut up, Bob, shut up. Shut up.

BOB THE DRAG QUEEN: It felt great. It felt really lovely. It didn't feel out of place. It didn't feel like, what's going on? It felt like this feels right and it feels good.

The episode ended with Cynthia Lee Fontaine and Robbie Turner battling it out over Faith Evans's "Mesmerized" and Cucu going home, which turned out to be a blessing for her.

DERRICK BARRY: Cynthia's outfit was a wreck. It was like a country western, Hooters showgirl. She was mixing reds and oranges with a black stoned belt and a cowboy hat. I was like, what is this? I am all for someone not wanting to be a normal rollergirl from the '70s, like Naysha and Thorg. But I think she had red tights or red fishnets on. It was all just a wreck. And Robbie looked like he was stepping out of a '70s movie. He looked incredible in the denim outfit and he could skate. I knew that Cynthia didn't have as much pep or pizzazz as she had in the beginning, but I also thought maybe she's getting beat down throughout the competition.

BOB THE DRAG QUEEN: I love Cynthia but she could not get it together. But girl, Robbie Turner was so bad, oh my god. And I thought that Robbie was going to be a threat up until that moment. I was like, oh this bitch is really just here for fluff, girl.

CYNTHIA LEE FONTAINE: After my lip sync, I asked for a chair. They ran and got me a chair. I almost fainted on the floor. That's why I decided to do the lip sync in high heels, not in roller skates, because already when I was doing the runway, I was having trouble with balance. I've been roller-skating since I was a kid but that day even my balance was off.

BOB THE DRAG QUEEN: We did get to see that amazing lip sync between Robbie and Cynthia. Robbie fucking turned it out on those fucking roller skates. I was like, go off, girl. I'm glad it wasn't me. Can you see me on roller skates, trying to navigate?

CYNTHIA LEE FONTAINE: It was a mix of emotions because it was a combination of everything at once. Finally, I get my dream come true to go to the TV show, and then I'm experiencing health issues. It was devastating, to be very honest. When I got eliminated, I was a little bit in shock but at the same time I was so tired and I was feeling so bad physically. Mentally, I was exhausted. I was diagnosed with stage one liver cancer two or three weeks after I came home. I went through chemo for two months and I was ready.

From the day Bob The Drag Queen got the call that he had been cast on the show, he knew he would take home the crown. It didn't take long before the rest of the cast caught on—they were living in Bob's world and they were just lucky to be a part of it. But did he have to talk so much?

BOB THE DRAG QUEEN: I'm just really confident and my mom always told me I was the best and I believed her. My mom wouldn't lie to me.

RUPAUL: One night, I was incognegro at The Monster in Sheridan Square, the oldest club in the country. Nobody was paying attention to me at all. It was so freeing, because these bitches were slaying and Bob was actually running the place. The show was fabulous. I'd heard of Bob before that. The deejay played "Sissy That Walk" and I had never heard it at a disco before and it just killed me when the children all got into formation and made a runway on the dance floor. I was so happy to be incognegro to watch this! And Bob and I tweeted at each other after this. So when Bob's audition tape came around, I said oh yeah, we gotta get this bitch on the show.

DERRICK BARRY: The whole cast started calling it The Bob Show. We were all loving the show. I know Thorgy had a big problem with this because she would come up to me and she'd be like, "Look at them, they're eating him up. Everything he says they're laughing at." And she had a problem with that because that's her friend and Thorgy is also like, I'm a clown, ha ha. I'm assuming, because they worked together a lot in New York, that they both had to fight for the same amount of attention. Thorgy was a comedy queen and so she has to kind of figure out how to fit in with Bob in this new space.

ACID BETTY: I knew Bob was winning. We all did. There were so many reasons. RuPaul never talks about or tweets about anybody before the show. She already talked about Bob and tweeted his stuff before we got there. He is from New York. And there is energy. When you have people like us who are empaths and witches, and you put us in the room with sixty producers, two of them could be poker players and fifty-eight are not. You can start smelling the blood in the water.

DERRICK BARRY: Bob was so popular in New York. People knew that Ru had come to see his show. So that was a no-brainer. And he was so funny. And everyone loved Bob. The judges did. The crew did. We did. Even if I was mad at Bob for anything he said, I got over it in 1.5 seconds and then we would move on.

BOB THE DRAG QUEEN: I really love attention. I fucking eat that shit for breakfast, lunch, and dinner.

ACID BETTY: We were all in the van the first week or second week, and we literally all said okay, we all know that we are fighting for top two because Bob is top three. We're like, okay, Chi Chi is gonna be the dancer, she's gonna send people home. I knew my competition was going to be Kim Chi because she is talented, creative, stunning, and gorgeous. I love origami, I use origami, and someone who has the same skills as me, I'm afraid of. So I was afraid of her and Bob. That was pretty much it. I really thought I could fight my way. Robbie Turner, I wasn't too concerned about.

THORGY THOR: It's not like I hate Bob or really want him to shut up.

It's just part of my personality. I'm like ugh, shut up. Out of love, just stop talking! Lovingly, shut up. I said it *a lot*.

KIM CHI: I'm sure part of it was jealousy that he's hogging so much of the camera. Some people just are made for television and Bob is definitely made for television. Some people just take the spotlight effortlessly and Bob is one of those people. I'm sure a lot of other girls were jealous that Bob was doing that.

THORGY THOR: I said a lot of other things but somehow they edited this big feud between Bob and me. I was like, what? Even Bob texted me, she goes, girl? I'm like, yeah. I tell him to shut up all the time because he never stops talking because I like to be the one to talk all the time.

MICHELE "MEESH" MILLS: Thorgy, from day one, had an extremely competitive feeling with Bob. And they have that weird thing where they're friends but Bob is not competitive back. They make digs at each other the same way. But I feel like Bob would have been a hard one to beat for any of them.

KIM CHI: Especially after knowing Bob off the show, Bob was and is talking. But also that's part of the reason why he is such a great stand-up comedian. A lot of stand-up comedians, when you're talking with them one-on-one, they're testing out their materials on you constantly. And that's how Bob is. He's always cracking jokes. He's always making statements with a punch line. That's just who he is. And that's what makes him so great.

BOB THE DRAG QUEEN: I talk a lot and I'm really loud and I don't mind taking up space, which really irritates some people, especially when everyone is fighting for camera time. But I never had to fight for it. The camera just would find its way to me. And that's just always been part of my life. I draw a lot of attention and it's been happening my whole life. And when you're in a show where you also want attention, I guess you're like, Bob, I wish you would stop talking so that

The first set in Burbank
[Season 1]

Ongina behind the scenes
[Season 1]

Raven's autobiography
challenge [Season 2]

YOUNG, BROKE, & FABULOUS

YOUNG, BROKE, & FABULOUS

THE PURSUIT OF FINDING YOUR INNER TRUST FUND

RAVEN

BY RAVEN

Michelle Visage joins the cast [Season 3]

Shangela, who pioneered the lipstick message, says goodbye for the second time. [Season 3]

Raja was known for her fashion-forward drag on the runway. [Season 3]

"Go back to Party City where you belong!" Season 4's top three [Season 4]

Rolaskatox in the werkroom [Season 5]

Roxxxy Andrews recording "We Are the World" [Season 5]

Jinkx in her iconic Little Edie
look [Season 5]

Alyssa Edwards and Roxxxy
Andrews before Roxxxy's
emotional revelation
[Season 5]

Alyssa Edwards and Coco
Montrese finally face off.
[Season 5]

Internet superstar, Lil' Poundcake [Season 5]

Vivacious's Ornacia reveal [Season 6]

Laganja Estranja in her macramé pot holder [Season 6]

Joslyn Fox, Laganja Estranja (and her aforementioned pot holder), and Darienne Lake in the werkroom [Season 6]

The first lip-sync musical, "Shade: The Rusical" [Season 6]

Adore Delano and Bianca
Del Rio lip sync to "Sissy
That Walk" in the semifinal.
[Season 6]

Violet Chachki's waist
[Season 7]

Miss Fame's and Violet Chachki's fall looks from Season 7's epic three-part runway challenge [Season 7]

Max in her "Leather and Lace" look [Season 7]

arl and Trixie Mattel in the conjoined-twins makeover
allenge [Season 7]

Bob The Drag Queen going Purse First
[Season 8]

Derrick Barry, the hundredth queen on *RuPaul's Drag Race*, posing with previous winners
[Season 8]

Chi Chi DeVayne's necklace breaks during her lip sync to "And I Am Telling You I'm Not Going."
[Season 8]

Team Naomi Smalls in the RuCo's *Empire* challenge
[Season 8]

Peppermint makes her entrance.
[Season 9]

"I'd like to keep it on, please." Valentina's mask moment [Season 9]

The infamous cheerleading challenge [Season 9]

Trinity vs. Charlie lip sync [Season 9]

Eureka's lipstick sign-off after her injury removes her from the competition [Season 9]

Sasha Velour's rose-petal wig reveal [Season 9]

Monét X Change's sponge dress
[Season 10]

"Miss Vanjie. Miss
Vaaanjie." Vanessa Vanjie
Mateo's notorious exit
[Season 10]

Aquaria's crowning moment [Season 10]

Yuhua Hamasaki as Samara at the reunion
[Season 10]

Monét X Change
and Kameron
Michaels at the
controversial
reunion
[Season 10]

Tammie Brown's "Team Unity" runway [*All Stars* Season 1]

After Jujubee and Raven's emotional lip sync to "Dancing On My Own" [*All Stars* Season 1]

BenDeLaCreme's self-elimination [*All Stars* Season 3]

Trixie Mattel's victory
[*All Stars* Season 3]

Ru looking over her kingdom

some of us could also have our moment. I got it mostly from Derrick and Thorgy.

DERRICK BARRY: Thorgy had it out for Bob. But I love their friendship. And it would've been so fun for me to be there with someone that I had worked with so closely. If any one of my *Divas* cast members, like if Coco Montrese and I were on a season together, it would've been so much fun because we know each other so well and we were both such highlights in the *Divas* show as Janet and Britney.

MICHELE "MEESH" MILLS: I'm okay with how much Bob talks. We've had girls in the werkroom who talked more than her before. But I think she was definitely felt to be the one to beat for sure from early on. In a conversation with you, if you try to come for her, she'll outgun you. She is just smart and funny.

JOEY NOLFI: I think it's the same energy [as] Bianca—that complete unabashed confidence, literally unshakable confidence. If there was a lack of confidence, they were really great at hiding it. Complete comfort in their artistry and knowing what they do so well and doing it in a way that meets what *Drag Race* is looking for but preserves their individuality. Bob is just one of the quickest, wittiest artists on this planet. So while Bob's fashions were maybe not the best, with somebody like Bob it doesn't matter because Bob is not here to serve you. You don't need to be impressed by Bob's runway because you're focused on Bob's mouth and what is coming out of Bob's mouth.

In the fourth episode, the queens teamed up in three '80s-style New Wave girl bands and performed in front of guest judge Debbie Harry. During the critiques, Michelle Visage paid Bob The Drag Queen a backhanded compliment when she said she loved his neon realness look, even though "I think ratchet drag is your thing." Later, Derrick Barry pulled the same punch during one of his many arguments with Bob The Drag Queen in the werkroom.

DERRICK BARRY: Bob said that he wanted Blondie to be drug-tested because she said I was the best singer, which now I laugh at. Why did I take it so seriously? I think it's because I was not getting the recognition or the compliments that maybe he was getting or other people and I think he was used to being complimented and so the fact that he really didn't that episode, it was easy for him to take a jab at me. And I gave it right back.

BOB THE DRAG QUEEN: I made a joke about Debbie Harry. And I guess Derrick didn't like my joke. I made a joke, and it did not land well. Welcome to my life.

DERRICK BARRY: Bob was very easy to fight with because I think we both knew how to push each other's buttons and we both are shady and we both like to do digs, obviously. So I think that I had absolutely found my counterpart. Sometimes it's hard to look at your own reflection, and Bob and I were so similar to me—maybe not to everyone else. We both really like the attention. And I never had to fight for attention with my brother because he was very behind the scenes. He doesn't want attention. So I felt like I had found someone that was very similar to me, and I thought we were going to be better friends because of that. And then on the first episode of *Untucked*, when I came for Naomi and he defended her, it threw a wrench in what I thought we were building. And then from there on out, anything he said would piss me off.

THORGY THOR: Bob is very smart and Bob knows how to push people's buttons and so do I and this is why we get along so much. But there are certain times where I'm like just leave it alone because Derrick is smart but she took Bob's bait every time. All they did was fight and I loved every second of it. Every second!

KIM CHI: At the time, I didn't understand the full context of why they were fighting. I was just a random person off to the side watching it go down. And to all of us it almost looked like Bob was ganging up on Derrick because we didn't see how the fight was started. It just escalated out of nowhere. But part of me also was thinking they're making television. They're making a memorable moment for TV. Let it go on. Bob is a very passionate person. Derrick Barry and Bob The Drag Queen both have to get the last word.

ACID BETTY: Britney was always on these tangents, always picking at people, always picking on people. It was a great night and we had just had pizza. Then I recall Britney getting in Bob's face. It was very random because Britney holds on to grudges, I feel like. And so I think once she finally starts to connect them, she brings up the ratchet stuff.

BOB THE DRAG QUEEN: It turned into an argument when she brought up the ratchet thing, which kept coming up as a strange thing. You look at a Black person and you tell them that they're ratchet. I don't identify as ratchet.

I think that what Michelle was trying to say was that she didn't think I was polished. But I didn't think I had presented anything that was particularly ratchet the entire season, quite frankly. I wore that gown on the second episode. I wore a cocktail dress on the first episode, I wore palazzo pants on the third episode and I was told that I was ratchet. And I didn't think that was ratchet. I thought that I looked really nice.

Do people even know what ratchet is? Ironically, the phrase *ratchet* comes from Shreveport, which is where Chi Chi DeVayne is from. It is called Ratchet City. Shreveport has a lot of Black people and there's a lot of Black culture in Shreveport. So if you're being very Shreveport, you're being very ratchet because Shreveport is Ratchet City. After a while, it went from acting like you're from Shreveport or Ratchet City to just being ghetto. The short answer is I don't think I'm ghetto. I think that I act and sound Black and I think it's clear that I'm Black.

DERRICK BARRY: Michelle said that he does ratchet drag so, of course, I'm gonna repeat it because I'm a parrot. And I definitely got myself into a lot of trouble for saying something like that. But it's TV. It's elevated emotions and it's high stress. If someone looks at me the wrong way, it is not easy for me to have a poker face. Being from Vegas you'd think I would be a better actor. But if he pissed me off, I gave it right back to him. That's why I said it really was more of like fighting with a brother, not fighting with someone you hate or having an enemy. We both would say things that would get under each other's skin and then we were fine because in Snatch Game I loved working with him. It was super fun. He was fun to vibe off of.

BOB THE DRAG QUEEN: I can laugh at it now. But in the moment, I was not laughing. In the moment I didn't think it was funny. You know that tingly feeling you get when you're mad and you're just irritated and it almost feels like fear. Anger and fear feel so similar to each other sometimes. And I just remember being like, I'm going to snap on this bitch and I did snap on her. It was a white person calling me ghetto on TV. I don't think Derrick saw it as a microaggression. Derrick thinks he just being sassy. But for me he just weaponized my race against me on international television. I was too mad to say much. All I said was, "If I wanted to make you cry, you'd be crying right now." I felt like I was on *Bad Girls Club*.

After a historic Snatch Game in which Bob The Drag Queen surprised everyone and soared playing two different characters, Crazy Eyes from *Orange Is the New Black* and Carol Channing, Michelle Visage warned the comedian he sometimes showboats. Thorgy Thor also cracked up RuPaul as Michael Jackson, Derrick Barry shined with a different side of his Britney impersonation, Chi Chi DeVayne played a hilarious Eartha Kitt, and Kim Chi created hysterical Kimmy Jong-Un, the sister of the Korean dictator, at RuPaul's request. On the runway, Bob The Drag Queen also stood out with his Madonna Scout look for the iconic Madonna runway.

THORGY THOR: Here we go. What did they call it? Kimonodon't! Kimonogeddon! Oh god.

DERRICK BARRY: That episode was the Madonna runway. Bob was the Cub Scout Madonna and we were the four kimono Madonnas. I had the kimono made by Coco Vega, and Nick [my partner] painted Madonnas on it so it would be different from what she wore and add an artistic flair to it. And then I find out that there are three other kimonos and two kimonos had already been eliminated. So out of twelve of us, six were going to be the same. Like, how? Great minds think alike and so that is very easy to imagine that so many people thought oh, I'm doing "Nothing Really Matters" 'cause no one is going to do it. What I wish I would've done is have a tearaway under the kimono and ripped the wig off and been a completely different Madonna underneath the kimono. Like the bride Madonna, the boy toy Madonna. Backfired!

KIM CHI: It was already a joke among us. If you're one of the girls that brought a kimono, you're probably going home. One thing that frustrated me was when we were doing our makeup, the crews supplied the inspiration shots for different Madonnas. They went and printed out the photos. The Madonna I chose was from "Paradise," her tour. Everyone else chose "Nothing Really Matters" Madonna. But they supplied the reference images from Paradise to the girls with "Nothing Really Matters," which is how we ended up looking so similar.

THORGY THOR: I didn't really care at the end because I knew my kimono was cool. But I really thought somebody was going to change. At the last second, I was like, I think I can throw together "Frozen" but I needed a crow because the video for "Frozen" was all about those dark crows. I was like, if somebody from the production team can just go to Michaels arts and crafts and buy me a crow I will attach it on my shoulder and I'll do "Frozen." And they were like nooo we can't do that. But then we did these kimonos and I didn't know it was going to become this huge joke. But my kimono was still really good and all the judges loved it. And then I didn't win. Again. I love Bob, but it did make me feel like I'm not in this competition. I'm just not getting any amount of fair shake.

ACID BETTY: The night I heard the challenge was Madonna, I thought do not do kimono, do not do cone tits, do not do a wedding dress. What's iconic of hers? And then I land and everyone was like oh, I'm doing a kimono but different, I'm gonna do a different kimono. I was like, oohhhkay. "Bedtime Stories" is one of her best albums and music and that music video is actually in a museum somewhere. I was a big fan of Madonna. It was one of the first times that a music video captured a dreamlike feeling. That's why I'm Acid Betty. I like trying to explore these things that are beyond mind and physical. I've had a few visions of that video that have stuck with me. There was one where there's a still of her hair that's going like this and then there's the one where she is pregnant and the doves come out of her belly. And I was like, oh, if I could have doves coming out of my belly, that's really what I would do. They were ushering me around and treating me kind of special because I didn't fit through certain doorways. I'm glad I did it. It was a good choice.

BOB THE DRAG QUEEN: Legendary challenge, honey, legendary runway! Half the cast had kimonos! I chose Madonna's Boy Scout outfit from the HRC gala. I always thought it was a cute look and I just thought it was really cute. It also reminded me a little bit of Troop Beverley Hills. It was subversive, it was a statement, and also I thought it looked nice.

ACID BETTY: I had thought I was going to lip sync the last three previous times because they didn't like me. I knew I was going to be going home soon. Backstage, I was trying to let Naomi know that I wasn't going to go out there and throw knives at her or something because she was freaking out. Let's just have a lot of fun and give them the best show that they've ever seen. That is the best thing we can do. I'm not going to try to knock you over with my belly and I'm not going to trip you, we're just gonna fucking slay the house down. The only reason I didn't have a baby is because the only one who had a baby was Naomi and I couldn't ask the girl that was going up against me to borrow a prop and be like, can I borrow this to send you home?

Of course, production paired up Bob The Drag Queen and Derrick Barry for an acting challenge in which they had to shoot presidential campaign ads and smear their partner in a race for first drag president of the United States. RuPaul advised them to tear each other up. They won the challenge.

DERRICK BARRY: That's good TV! It was The Bob Show so if I could make it The Bob and Derrick Show I was all for that. I definitely know that when we were paired together we were gonna win. I didn't even second-guess it. I had just lip synced. I felt like I had set myself free and I was not going to hold myself back.

BOB THE DRAG QUEEN: Every four years, on election year, *Drag Race* does a political challenge. They've done two debates and political campaigns. I wish I'd done a debate. Knowing that Derrick also did a great job on the Snatch Game and Derrick was great at long-form improv and a great performer, I was actually happy to be Derrick's teammate. For the sake of having a productive competition, and going forward, we were talking and I don't know if it made the cut or not, but we were just over time realizing that we were both just really competitive.

DERRICK BARRY: The challenge was a smear campaign, so it was the perfect partner to have because I wasn't going to feel guilty, I didn't feel like I needed to be PC. When Ru came around to our tables, he said I want you guys to go there. I want everything that you guys have wanted to say to each other to come out. And that was so easy. I was basically given a green light to say anything I want about Bob.

MICHELLE VISAGE: Derrick was fun to watch because Derrick went through trials and tribulations trying to figure out who Derrick was, apart from Britney Spears. So Derrick is the world's foremost Britney impersonator and still is and is amazing but she really wants to be her own queen. She wants to be a pop star. She wants to do other things apart from stealing Britney's face. And going through it with her has been very interesting. And she loves a bit of drama. She likes to stir the pot. If you're going to stir with Bob, you better be ready for the outcome. Bob is very quick and very smart.

DERRICK BARRY: I was like what can I say that is going to offend everybody? And I got a lot of shit for it. I put Bob in a hoodie and that's a stereotype. Say what you want, but it's called a smear campaign. And if you have ever seen a real smear campaign, especially during a presidential election, the amount of corruption that they talk about is beyond me. So when we got the go-ahead from Ru to take it there, then that's all I needed. And Bob was a great partner. I mean, anything I said, he would do. And same with me. He wanted me to eat a baby. Why am I eating a baby? I'm eating a baby because Bob told me to. So I think that that is where you really come full circle with an archnemesis is you work together and you realize that you're stronger together. I had already changed my perception of Bob in the Snatch Game because I loved working with him on Snatch Game. So I was already Team Bob at that point. But the political challenge definitely brought us so much closer. We knew when we were filming it that we won. I was covered in fake blood and I walked in and the other girls were like what the fuck? What did you guys do? And I said, "We just won, what did you guys do?"

TOM CAMPBELL: Bob is the real deal. Bob is a personality that dominates. He has that "it." Derrick is a whole other case study. Derrick in captivity can't adjust. If you ever put a turtle in a cage, it'll always walk east or something. He just sees things a certain way and he just goes into it. I love Derrick Barry. There is no one who will work harder for the franchise. There's nobody who loves what they do more and is more appreciative of the opportunities. But his thinking is very Derrick. We learn things when we learn things in life.

BOB THE DRAG QUEEN: I never did get to discuss microaggressions and why what Derrick did was really offensive. But also, at the same time, I did not have time to go through *RuPaul's Drag Race* and teach Derrick about the politics of race relations. I had a crown to win.

. . . .

Thorgy Thor and Chi Chi DeVayne's teamwork went in the opposite direction and led to one of the series' most memorable lip syncs, with Chi Chi DeVayne commanding the stage from beginning to end. The *Drag Race* universe was heartbroken four years later when Chi Chi tragically died from scleroderma.

THORGY THOR: I knew I was going home. The song was supposed to be "You Make Me Feel (Mighty Real)." They came in the back and, all of a sudden, the song was "And I'm Telling You" from *Dreamgirls*. Last second, right before we lip synced. I knew Chi Chi was going to send me home because she is a real-life Dreamgirl. I got it. So I literally said my goodbyes. But I wasn't gonna do a Tammie Brown and be all bitter about it. I literally looked inside myself and I said you know what, if it's my time to go tonight, which it is, because there is no way I was gonna win lip syncing a *Dreamgirl* number next to a real-life Dreamgirl from Shreveport, Louisiana. It didn't matter if I grew wings out of my flesh and flew across the stage. I said my goodbyes and I was at peace because I did my best. I made it seven episodes and I showed who I really am. I felt good. I made friends for life and this was a great dream of mine and I'm really happy. I just told myself to lip sync my ass off because it's a great song.

BOB THE DRAG QUEEN: "And I'm Telling You" is *the* drag queen song. This is the song you want to get for a lip sync. It was a full-on brutal massacre. I knew Thorgy didn't stand a chance, Thorgy knew Thorgy didn't stand a chance, Chi Chi knew Thorgy didn't stand a chance. If you look at the very end of the lip sync, Thorgy is literally holding Chi Chi's hand and being like, "Here's your winner."

DERRICK BARRY: I did love Thorgy's look. I thought it was really cool. It was a *Sex and the City*, black-and-white character. And Chi Chi looked like she was walking out of a black-and-white film of *Dreamgirls*. It's funny because she didn't want to be *Dreamgirls* with us for the New Wave challenge but yet she ended up winning the lip sync on a *Dreamgirls* song.

NAOMI SMALLS: Chi Chi was such a fluid performer. You could really tell that's where she felt the most comfortable and confident. A true showgirl who will be forever missed.

BOB THE DRAG QUEEN: I miss Chi Chi so much. Chi Chi was one of those people on the show who really reminded me of a lot of people from back home. She had a real earnestness and charm to her personality. She was so funny. It's heartbreaking. Chi Chi was a year older than me. Scleroderma is such an insane disease and sickness. She was such an optimistic person. I remember the last Insta story she posted was, "Hey guys, keep me in your thoughts and I'll see you when I get out of here."

DERRICK BARRY: When Chi Chi's beads went everywhere, it was dramatic and effortless. We knew Chi Chi could tumble and that is an amazing part of a lip sync, to be able to do back handsprings and splits. We'd seen her do that upside-down split but to see her lip sync in that gown. She couldn't do tricks or cartwheels but to still command the room like she did, it was unbelievable. It was so real. She was telling us she's not going. When it came to performing or dancing, Chi Chi was the best of our season.

TOM CAMPBELL: I'm a cornball but I believe that everything on *Drag Race* happens for a reason. That was not a stunt. Those pearls breaking at that moment, on that stage, falling to the ground was unbelievable.

JOEY NOLFI: Thorgy's eliminations on both of her seasons stand out to me as some of the biggest what-the-fuck eliminations. She shouldn't have been in the bottom but it's a game and that's how it goes. The lip sync with Chi Chi and the breaking of the beads was so dramatic and it's one of my favorite lip syncs. It has extra poignance when you re-watch it because it encapsulated everything that is so great about Chi Chi. Yes, Chi Chi won the lip sync but Thorgy should not have been in the bottom.

KIM CHI: At the time, I was holding Bob's hand crying. You never see it on the episode. But when they were lip syncing, I was crying the entire time saying to Bob that I didn't realize this was going to be this hard when I'm not even in the bottom two. I thought I was going to be in the bottom two. At that point, it's so close and so down to the wire, I think that we're all overly stressed out. And then I saw Chi Chi when she was lip syncing and I saw Chi Chi's garment break and the beads flying everywhere. It looked amazing. 'Cause all the beads were reflecting up the light, shining as Chi Chi was belting it out. As soon as I heard the song choice, I knew she would win.

MICHELE "MEESH" MILLS: I talked to her a week or two before she passed, when she was in the hospital. She was lovely to the end. She was extremely talented and a beautiful drag queen, but really very real. She was one of the ones who stayed the most real as she became famous. She had a lot to deal with in her life.

KIM CHI: Chi Chi was always amazing to work with. Every show we did together, she's always stoned out of her mind and she's always sleeping till literally ten seconds before she goes onstage. Like she'll fully be taking a nap backstage in full drag. And they're like, Chi Chi, your song is about to start. And then she wakes right up, goes onstage and does ten cartwheels, a backflip, and a split, and turns the party. Then after that, she's back to napping again.

BENDELACREME: I don't think I have wrapped my mind around the fact that she is gone yet. The relationship and bond that you have with someone from *Drag Race* is unique. I felt very close to her when we were filming, I loved seeing her when I would see her on tour. We were all part of a group thread from *All Stars*. Chi Chi was a drag queen's drag queen. There are casual drag queens and there are drag queens deep in their soul and Chi Chi was one of those. I also had a major crush on her on set. I came home and told my partner immediately that I had a big crush on Chi Chi.

TOM CAMPBELL: We learned she had passed as we were filming Season 13. It left us empty. It's still hard to believe, actually.

MICHELLE VISAGE: What I loved about Chi Chi is that Chi Chi had a love of life. She wanted to get better. She wanted to try things, she wanted to improve her drag, and she was never afraid to ask. I was able to do one of the cruises with Chi Chi and she had never been out of the country. I remember being in Dubrovnik, Croatia, with her and Shangela and there were a bunch of us walking around and exploring. And I knew Chi Chi had never been out of the country before so watching her with her headphones in and seeing the world and exploring, I felt like a mother watching her do that. She was just a really kind, loving soul. She kept to herself, kind of quiet, but when you got to sit and talk to her, she was really sweet and really loving. And I really dug her drag.

TOM CAMPBELL: There's one queen every year that grabs your heartstrings. There's somebody who comes up and you love them, just love, love, love, love, love them. They can do no wrong whether they have flaws or not. And Chi Chi DeVayne was the heart of that season. Such a humble person, such a genuine person. I loved his relationship with Ru. There is no better message than just lean into who you are. Don't try to present a different version of yourself. Give us who you are. And Chi Chi was so Southern-fried and delicious and a great lip syncer.

The following week, it was Bob The Drag Queen's turn to lip sync against Derrick Barry after they landed in the bottom for their lackluster Book Ball looks. By the end of their performance of "You Make Me Feel (Mighty Real)," Bob The Drag Queen was poised to win it all.

BOB THE DRAG QUEEN: When you're in *RuPaul's Drag Race* and RuPaul says the time has come to lip sync for your life, everyone at the bar is laughing and chanting along. But when you're there, it's not funny. When RuPaul says, "The time has come," the air in the room is so dense, it is scary. It feels like someone's going to die. And when people walk through that archway, you don't see them again until the fucking reunion because they literally go through the archway and they make us wait while the person goes back and packs, then we can go back into the werkroom. So they are actually gone. They are erased from our memory. We don't see them at the hotel, we don't cross paths, we don't run into each other in the hallway, you're not at the lunch table eating with us, you are gone. I was not nervous. I knew the song, and I knew Derrick didn't stand a chance. We had already made amends so we were cool.

DERRICK BARRY: I would rather it have been Bob than anyone else. We had come so far from just winning into the bottom now. I was actually hoping that Ru would say I love this top five and you guys are all amazing and you're all gonna be in the music video. That would have been a dream. But I made it to the second-to-last episode and I was sent home by the winner. In my eyes at that point it had to be Bob as much as I thought it could be Kim Chi for the look or Chi Chi or Naomi for the growth, Bob had three wins and it was clear that Bob was gonna be in the top three and most likely win the entire season. The Bob Show turned into The Bob Win, which Thorgy probably still hates.

The top four—Bob The Drag Queen, Kim Chi, Naomi Smalls, and Chi Chi DeVayne—spent the last two days of the season filming the music video for RuPaul's "The Realness." As production had done in the past, all four queens filmed their eliminations and waited to learn who would make it to the finale about a week before it was filmed.

NAOMI SMALLS: One of the most fun days ever was filming "The Realness" with Bob, Kim, and Chi Chi. Not having to make a joke or make a costume with limited time or memorize a script or be on edge made the day so memorable. We had the opportunity to be part of a music video for a song we listened to multiple times a day on the runway. I love music videos. You get to tell a story using music, fashion, visuals, makeup, and glam.

KIM CHI: Filming the video wasn't hard. What was annoying was the stylists they brought on. They had to help us put together these avant-garde looks, but they only brought non-starch items that only fit a size zero. Like Naomi, who's skinny, didn't even fit into 90 percent of the costumes they brought in. I was even more annoyed because everyone else found out what color they were wearing for the floating scene so they could style accordingly. But I was the only person that they didn't have an outfit for or a color. And they couldn't even tell me until right before I went on.

BOB THE DRAG QUEEN: It was one of the sweetest moments of the season when Chi Chi, Kim, Naomi, and I all decided to do this one unified move. When we sing, "Gonna move into the house," we said, we made a pact. We're going to do this one thing together, put our hands over your head like a little house, and then after that, it's a free-for-all. It was just a nice moment of solidarity between all of us.

NAOMI SMALLS: Making it to the top three of Season 8 was such an awesome feeling. I felt seen, and I was really excited to not have to write a mirror message.

BOB THE DRAG QUEEN: We did not know the top three until about a week before it happened because all four of us got filmed being eliminated. It's a fucking acting challenge so it makes it less emotional than it would be. They gave each of us calls individually and said we're going to eliminate Chi Chi. She won't be going on to the finale. Mostly, I was glad it wasn't me. Everyone brought something different to the table. Chi Chi could have easily gone on to the finale and no one would have questioned it because she was that amazing.

KIM CHI: In retrospect, all of us could have been in the top three. But if we're just going strictly based on track record, Naomi had been in the bottom once, while Chi Chi had been in the bottom twice. And Bob had three wins, I had two wins, and Naomi and Chi Chi both had one win. Technically, Chi Chi had a worse track record.

NAOMI SMALLS: Filming the finale was a lot. I had just finished six straight days of gigs and flights, followed by our first DragCon. Just two days later was the finale. Rehearsals and no sleep, a lot of pressure and a lot of drag to prepare.

KIM CHI: At first when I got my song, "Fat, Fem & Asian," I wasn't sure about it. But then upon listening to it over and over, I saw the message was very positive. Around the time I got this song, not only were we rehearsing and practicing for the finale, but we were also doing DragCon at the same time, so it was just a very stressful weekend. I wanted to continue to represent Korean culture so I thought let me make the biggest henbo that I possibly could find. My friend Tiger Lily made the whole garment for me with boning and everything.

TOM CAMPBELL: Kim Chi was so beautiful, so funny, so wry, and horrible at choreography. I think Jamal Sims needs a special award for staging Kim Chi's grand finale number.

NAOMI SMALLS: "Legs" was the best song for sure. I have never seen an episode of *Game of Thrones* so I'm still curious about why I received a video message from Lena Headey. Kimberly and I knew Bob would win but we still came in our fiercest drag at the time. Bob deserved to win.

BOB THE DRAG QUEEN: They called me and they said they wanted to do a song about purses. And I was like, please don't 'cause I have a plan to release my own song about purses. The whole Purse First thing happened because Thorgy asked me how I worked the runway. And I said, "Well, I came out like this. I came out purse first." And then if you watch the first episode of *Untucked*, you can see literally the moment where Purse First is born. I have always been into being really silly. So I started carrying the purse every day because I just thought it was funny. It was my security blanket. And then the purse started to annoy other people, which made me love it even more. It was really a hideous purse. I would just carry the purse every day everywhere. I

298 Maria Elena Fernandez

would put my stuff in it. It was falling apart. It was made of cardboard and curtains. It was really not keeping well. The purse was a great idea but they just kept seeing it over and over again, and I think it just started driving them a little bit crazy.

KIM CHI: I think all of the songs that were created fit all of us really well. I'm very partial to "Legs" in particular. I just think it's a fun song.

BOB THE DRAG QUEEN: They agreed not to do one about purses, so I said yes, I'd love a song about me being arrogant. It was called "I Don't Like to Show Off." It was very in the vein of "Show Off" from *The Drowsy Chaperone* with Sutton Foster. That is the nerdiest, gayest reference that you're gonna hear all day.

KIM CHI: We all knew Bob was going to win so we all went into the finale with the mindset to have fun. Bob had the most wins so it made sense for Bob to win. Naomi and I knew we weren't going to win, but also we didn't want to win because the backlash from the fandom would have been huge and insane. And we didn't want to deal with that at all.

BOB THE DRAG QUEEN: We all filmed winning and I treated like it was real. I tried to go through the motions of feeling like I was really, really winning. But I did not know how emotional it would be until I actually won. I believe that Kim Chi said, "When's dinner?" And I believe that Naomi Smalls said, "It's about time a big girl won."

TOM CAMPBELL: Bob was great on camera and in person he owns the room. He is funny and charming and clever and it was a pleasure. He was a little bit of an attention hog but only because he is so fuckin' talented.

CYNTHIA LEE FONTAINE: I was there in the theater, of course. In the interview with Mama RuPaul, Bob spoke from the heart. It was beautiful. I do believe the sister that wins *RuPaul's Drag Race* represents a brand, represents Mama RuPaul, represents the production and herself. But she also represents a community. When Bob did his number and the interview, in the theater, people were crying and gave him a standing ovation because he spoke from the heart. He was ready and he was prepared to receive that crown but with humbleness.

BOB THE DRAG QUEEN: Every once in a while, I'll click in and watch it and be like what fun it was. I was so skinny. I was not wearing a corset. That's how skinny I was. I was not wearing a corset like, bitch, go off. Dancing in huge heels. Like I was so happy that I have this moment documented that I can just go back and look at it. That's a great thing about being on reality TV because a chunk of your life is just documented.

ACID BETTY: I was glad Michelle told Bob he was bordering on showboating because yes, you're amazing, yes, you're funny, but girl, you're bulldozing over everybody. You're funny. Yes. Work. I love that he won because it was the first time someone ever did multiple characters on Snatch Game and he was nervous about that. I also love that he was a Black Carol Channing. That's really fierce. His Carol Channing is on point. He should have won.

THORGY THOR: I think it was well deserved. I think he's hilarious and he is a good crown holder. He just walked the walk and talked the talk for so long. Ever since we started being friends in New York, he talked about this show and how he's gonna get on the show and he's gonna win the show. And he did. I was so proud of him. I was so happy for him.

BOB THE DRAG QUEEN: When the episode aired, we were all together. It was a big party in New York City at Stage 48. I cried like a little baby. If I had actually won that night at the theater, you would have seen the crying version of me.

Chapter 9
SEASON 9

I N ITS NINTH SEASON, *RuPaul's Drag Race* TRANSFORMED FROM TASTE-maker to cultural juggernaut, bolstered by Lady Gaga's gag-worthy premiere appearance and Viacom's expert decision to move the series from niche Logo TV to its more popular sister network VH1. Heading into the season, RuPaul had earned his first of seven Emmys for outstanding reality show host, and his reality competition garnered the kind of show-business acceptance it never anticipated: a *Saturday Night Live* spoof featuring Chris Pine, followed by a whopping eight Emmy nominations that fall, including one for outstanding reality competition. In a season of stunts and injuries, drag queen bromances, illuminating gender conversations, and the one and only Valentina, of course it did.

TOM CAMPBELL: We had all of Season 9 in the can when Chris Mc-Carthy, who had taken over VH1, said he wanted to move the show. He's very strategic and has had great success in scheduling and bringing up the ratings at MTV. He really had the foresight and the courage to say I want to take this little gay show on this little gay channel and I'm gonna put it on VH1. I do believe that Lady Gaga helped us get there.

STEVEN CORFE: I think we have a lot to be grateful for, for Lady Gaga. I think she really did help tip us into this level of visibility that has just helped with the runaway success ever since.

TOM CAMPBELL: Lady Gaga was doing a Thanksgiving special for ABC and we got a call. They said Lady Gaga would love Ru to come tomorrow and be a part of her special. Ru's pal Elton John had been with Lady Gaga and they thought it would be a great idea. Ru just happened to have an extra gown hanging in his closet and said, let's do it. We got to this massive set and Lady Gaga was rehearsing with the Muppets. She stopped rehearsal, walked over to Ru, and told him how, as a teenager, listening to "Supermodel" got her through really hard times and that she loved that song and performed it in front of the mirror. She also told him she wanted to be a guest on *Drag Race*.

RONAN FARROW: From the beginning, the show worked because it is, in some ways, a send-up and a pastiche of reality show tropes but it also was something new in the drag world and you can feel the queens at times being quite real in those early seasons and figuring it out as the public was. And then something happens as the show gets bigger and as it moves to VH1 where the culture in the wider world has changed because of the show and then also inside the show the expectations and the culture have shifted.

TRINITY THE TUCK: Over the years, you just see production get more creative on how they tell our stories. It makes our art more valid. It makes our people in our community more valid and seen as human versus freaks. I think that's the biggest thing that has evolved throughout the years with *Drag Race*—how they have fine-tuned how they are able to tell these stories. I also think they have upped the ante year after year with how they produce the show. Season 9 was the first season on VH1 and it was also the first season that they did a grand finale the way that they did with the final lip sync. And that was a major shift in the way that the show was seen.

RONAN FARROW: Now the queens are more polished by the time they are getting on. They've seen these stories, the way the editing works, the intricacies of the format, and they've learned it or they have failed to at their peril—see e.g. every werkroom exchange where Ru says, "Why didn't you learn to sew?" But they also are playing character types to a greater extent. The drama is bleaker and the pacing is better and the performances are bigger. It is a very, very different show now.

MICHELLE VISAGE: People think *Drag Race* was an overnight success and what they don't realize is that it took years to get it made and then it took nine years for us to get recognized. Nine years. I am grateful for every single one.

RANDY BARBATO: I do think *Drag Race* has always offered hope. It's a show that people go to for laughs and walk away with inspiration. During dark times, that inspiration reached beyond the fan base and even seemed to inspire the industry a little. It might be part of why people might have been more motivated to include us and invite us to the big kids' table.

Before the queens stepped into the werkroom, they received a treat no other cast has been gifted to date: riding around Los Angeles in a Range Rover with a special chauffeur.

SHEA COULEÉ: Oh my god, the Ruber!

EUREKA: They came and got me and took me outside and said, "We're gonna stop you here at the corner and then you're gonna walk up and you're gonna get in the car. There is a surprise guest that's gonna drive you around and interview you." Okay, work, this sounds fine. I thought it might have been one of those late-night shows. Before I saw who was in the car, I was already saying, "Hey sexy, you wanna date tonight?" And I poke my head in the window and it's RuPaul. I literally said, "Oh shit!" She was like, oh you're giving dates, are you, girl? And I was like, well if that's what it takes, Mama, to make it to this show, honey. And then we rode around and chitchatted and I was sweatin' 'cause it was hot in LA. I wasn't used to the heat. That was a lot.

TRINITY THE TUCK: You know how they do the meet the queens? We did Car Ride Karaoke with Ru. You're going into a car with just you and Ru and she is driving you 'round and you are literally shoulder-to-shoulder with RuPaul. And so I was terrified. I was shaking in my boots. They opened the car door, I get in this small SUV, and there's these little mounted, tiny cameras and RuPaul is there and she's like "Hi!" So you're having to immediately be like, hi, and not be scared to death. I was terrified because this was *the* RuPaul.

MANDY SALANGSANG: Ru had a show where he interviewed celebrities on WOW Presents Plus and he drove his red Volvo around town and interviewed celebrities in it. There was a trend there in doing that type of content with James Corden, Jerry Seinfeld. So we thought how fun would that be? They will get in the car with RuPaul. They'll lip sync to one of his songs, and they will be asked some questions. It'll be a quick meet and greet.

AJA: I was like, oh well, this is happening. I'm very socially awkward. In person, it's really difficult for me to talk to people because I don't want to come off a certain way. So when I was getting told I had to sit next to RuPaul and talk to him, I was like, well, damn, I'm going to have to engage in conversation, shit. I was nervous. I didn't know how to feel, to be honest. I was intrigued. I was excited to see what he was really like in person. We spoke a little bit about religion and I remember Trixie Mattel in the street or something. That was the punch line.

SHEA COULEÉ: I remember that morning getting ready in my little outfit, feeling so cute, and they brought me out down to where we were going to get picked up by RuPaul. I could hear them on the walkies saying that RuPaul was pulling up. I could see it was a Range Rover and it had lashes on it. I remember I got so nervous that I stood purposely behind this pillar so that I was out of RuPaul's sight line because until they say "Action" I don't even want to try and look over there. When I go in there, I want that to be the first time that I lay eyes on RuPaul in person. I get in and RuPaul just goes Shea Cou-leé! The way RuPaul said my name, immediately, I was like, okay, I'm in love. And then I had this orange ostrich feather coat and RuPaul said orange was her favorite color. And orange is also my favorite color. And all the nerves, everything, went away.

VALENTINA: I thought that was really interesting because it individually gave us all our moment to connect with Ru in a way that other queens hadn't done before. At the same time, I was really honored to do that because I knew it was gonna be daytime drag in a car. I know most queens look terrible in daylight and up close but I don't. So I was really honored for the opportunity to sit there looking gorgeous and being like, yeah, touch my skin, I look pretty up close, too. Whenever I perform, I love to get all up in your face so you could smell my perfume and see my flawless textures and everything, honey. So that was fun. I didn't know what to expect and I knew that at any time that the camera was on that I had to deliver authenticity and I had to sparkle and I had been waiting for it. I knew all the things that I wanted to project and to say and I was so excited to get it out. I was really excited to be that close to RuPaul and to have that kind of connection. I think from the very beginning he told me that I had the energy of an old Mexican cinema actress. For him to clock all that I was projecting from the very beginning, I was super excited about that.

PEPPERMINT: It was great to see Ru. I actually had met Ru before. We filmed it in August, the hottest month of the year. It was hot and, honey, I was just like, get out of this car!

TRINITY THE TUCK: And before anything, before you meet the cast, before anything, you're face-to-face with RuPaul and it was just a good old time. She had me laughing, I had her laughing. By the end of the car ride, I just felt like a connection with Ru. I felt like she was really genuine. She was so professional. She knew when to turn it on because we were filming a TV show and she had genuine moments. She brought up my body work and I'm not ashamed of any of that stuff. It made me laugh. We had made up lyrics to one of her songs with pumping references. I felt so fortunate because no other cast has done that with Ru.

SASHA VELOUR: To start off with a private car ride with Ru felt insane. I had had a vivid dream about driving in a car with RuPaul like six months prior, before I had put together my audition. And I dreamt that RuPaul was driving through the streets of LA and was a very dangerous driver. I had to tell her about this in the car ride, of course, sounding like an absolute crazy person. She thought it was hilarious that she was a bad driver in the dream and kept pretending to drive us off the road.

FARRAH MOAN: The car malfunctioned while I was in the car with him, and we had to drive back to the hotel and start all over. There were all these cameras attached to the car. And you know when a car is trying to tell you something's wrong and it just starts beeping incessantly? That happened. RuPaul was like, "Oh, this isn't normal, let's go back." And I was like, huh? I'm already so starstruck that I was sitting next to RuPaul.

SHEA COULEÉ: It was so weird to me because I had been watching RuPaul on television since I was four years old. I'm talking about *In the House*, *Sister Sister*, all of those great cameos, the *Brady Bunch* movies, all of them. I felt like I was catching up with an old friend. It felt so natural and easy and I remember we drove around for twenty minutes. When we got back, they asked how it went. I said it was like going to meet the Wizard of Oz. It was everything!

The next day, the queens dragged it up again in their same looks to make their grand entrances.

PEPPERMINT: I was expecting to see everybody—my mom, seeds that bloomed into flowers, everything. I had been waiting for hours. When

I went in the room, I was in shock. There was nobody to talk to! Going into an empty room to say and make a statement to the camera, that's not me. Sigh. I went and sat down. I was already on edge. Valentina and Eureka were the two that I felt were extremely together. It was a surprise to me to find out that Valentina was so new at drag. Eureka had this extremely conservative, polished, womanly look on. I remember thinking she means business. Trinity was really scary to me because she just came in and seemed so bitchy. But now I know she was hiding her prowess as a pageant queen because you can get judged really quickly from being a pageant queen. I was thrown off. I thought she was going to be the bitch of the season.

VALENTINA: I have one of the most iconic entrances. I think the most iconic is hands-down Laganja Estranja. But everybody knows "Hello, it's me, Valentina." It's one of my phrases that I still use to this day anytime I do a performance. It's the first thing you hear me say on the mic. If ever I do a track with somebody big, an artist, instead of saying my name I'm gonna say, "Hello, it's me." Walking into the werkroom for the first time, it's not as beautiful as it looks on TV. It's the gag. The walls are not real. It's really fucking cold in there. When I saw all the girls, I was like, all right, girl, have fun but don't enjoy this too much because I think that you have to send all these bitches home. That's where my mentality was.

EUREKA: I walked in and was just like work, I don't know who Peppermint or Valentina are but they seemed to know each other. I was just happy to be there, to be honest. And I was like, you know what I'm gonna do? I'm gonna show out and I'm gonna be funny. I'm gonna be big and jolly. I was just so worried about myself. Girl, I didn't even care they were there.

FARRAH MOAN: I remember I had a whole thing planned on what I was going to say and then when they actually told me to walk into the set I had seen on TV for so many years, I blanked and the only thing I could think of was "So this is what it looks like." I was going to say, "Look, Mom, I made it." Or something stupid like that. The first queen

I noticed was Eureka. I instantly felt drawn to her probably because my whole life I've always been friends with big girls. I just had this feeling that we were going to vibe. I remember seeing Valentina and I was like I know her from somewhere. My biggest thought was holy shit, Peppermint is here because I had seen her doing music video parodies with Sherry Vine when I was in high school. She's a drag legend. I was real shook to be in the same contest as Peppermint.

SASHA VELOUR: I wanted to express what I felt on the inside. I feel like I come across as composed and that is not how I feel inside. So I'm just going to introduce myself as the way I feel with this ridiculous scream and then a very humble cough. And I thought it was going to be a riot but it guess it really freaked out the queens who were in the room, which is not something I'd thought about. I was visualizing how it was going to come across on TV but it had this element of actually scaring them. That was my introduction.

FARRAH MOAN: Sasha Velour walked in and screamed. I almost had a heart attack because I was already so on edge and so full of anxiety of being in this trippy universe TV room. But I loved it.

VALENTINA: When Sasha Velour walked in and started yelling, I just was like, what? And to this day, I'm still like, what? Because Sasha Velour is actually very poised and collected and together and she is very like wise and sophisticated. And even to this day it is a little bit off-brand. She must have been nervous, girl.

SHEA COULEÉ: There were four people that jumped out at me immediately. Peppermint, Alexis, Sasha, and Farrah. I had just met Farrah Moan at a party we worked at together in Chicago. I remember Sasha's unibrow and her crown. Fierce. And then Alexis and Peppermint both just had the friendliest, warmest smiles. When I walked in, the way that both of them turned and smiled, I felt very welcomed by both of them. I knew that Peppermint would be competition because she's a New York legend and I had seen her perform many times in Chicago.

TRINITY THE TUCK: When I saw Valentina for the first time, I was starstruck. I thought she looked like a goddess. She was so well put together. She was so beautiful. Her poise, the way she stood there. I just was like, that's the winner, she's gonna win. And when I saw Shea Couleé and she had this fashion, banjee attitude, her makeup was very sharp, I was like, she is fierce. And then I remember seeing Peppermint in this really satin trench coat that was really bright with her dreads. She looked cool. And then I saw Charlie Hides with this really campy, oversize shirtdress with the huge glasses that was like a necklace. Everyone had such a unique perspective of their drag and I was so blown away.

EUREKA: Girl, drama! That's what it felt like when I saw Trinity then. I love her now, of course. We have grown out of all of that. But I had been on rotating cast with her in Louisville, Kentucky. She won Entertainer of the Year. I was her second runner-up. I always felt like she was a little fat-phobic to me, like she just always treated me worse than everybody else and she had one of those grander-than-thou attitudes but that's just her personality. I don't mesh well with that because I'm more of the humble, everybody belongs and has a place. I'm a jolly country fish. I don't like people that think they're better than me, especially then.

TRINITY THE TUCK: Our relationship has definitely changed now but I'm speaking in terms of at that moment. We had competed in several pageants together and Eureka, at that time in her life, she was the type of person who liked attention. She liked to make it all about her and it sucked the air out of the room. And being around her, competing against her, she did the same thing. When we're doing registration for the pageant, she is the loudest one in the room out of twenty to thirty contestants. She's got to make it all about herself. She doesn't know how to share the spotlight. I competed against her in two pageants and in both pageants I won and in both pageants she was one of my runners-up. And she was very bitter about it. I respected her for her drag and her art because she was always great at drag. But sure enough, she did all of that stuff that irritated me on the show. So that caused conflict for me. I did really try to be as professional as I could and try to pull back as much as I could.

EUREKA: There was always an underlying tension with her even when I worked with her before the show. But it was like a frenemy situation. It's where you're really friends and you appreciate each other in a weird way but you also can't stand each other at the same time. Honestly, my mind immediately was I'm sending that bitch home ASAP.

AJA: Child, when I got there, I had a sinus infection, so I was sick. I couldn't even feel excited, 'cause I was like, oh my god, I'm dying. The closer I got to the set, my heart just started racing. I heard people talking and that's what made it nerve-racking. I heard so many voices. I didn't know I was last until I walked in. And can you believe, I fucked up the take? I walked in and I saw a bald head. And in my mind, and this is me being very New York, I was like, who is this bald-ass bitch? And then I looked, and saw her unibrow. Sasha does a little wave at me. And I just screamed! I was gagged. I had to do it again.

As the queens waited for RuPaul, a Lady Gaga impersonator from New Jersey named Ronnie arrived in the werkroom.

TOM CAMPBELL: Every year after Ru appeared on Lady Gaga's special, we'd ask if she was available to judge. It never worked out based on the dates we were shooting and her availability. A few weeks before we started shooting Season 9, her manager said she wants to do it and she has this one day open. Usually episodes take two days, but we had already designed the first episode of Season 9 to be shot in one day. And it just so happened to be the same day Lady Gaga was available. It was a pageant challenge and we changed the second look to a Lady Gaga tribute and it became the now iconic Lady Gaga episode.

MICHELLE VISAGE: I didn't know that was happening until day of and I was like, oh my god, are you kidding me? And I thought you know what? This is a superstar and I'm just gonna be me. I got to talk to her and I remember at one point she was calling my name and saying, "Michelle, you are crazy." I was like Lady Gaga thinks I'm crazy. Life is very good. It was really fun. She was wonderful. She was so down to have a good time.

STEVEN CORFE: It was my job to interview her in drag as Ronnie. Those little interview rooms are so tiny in real life. You're so crunched together that the interviewer is basically knee-to-knee with the drag queen or, in this case, Lady Gaga. I remember being pretty nervous about it because it's fuckin' Lady Gaga! And I crossed my legs to try and keep my knees from touching her knees as she's doing this interview and I gave her a massive kick in the shins. She said, "Oww" in that kind of deadpan, Lady Gaga voice. And I just thought oh my god, my career is over, I just kicked Lady Gaga.

TOM CAMPBELL: She was so much fun because she was willing to come into the werkroom as a Lady Gaga impersonator. Also, seeing her interview in "Ronnie from Jersey" boy drag was everything. She is the most professional and she is the most generous. It was very uplifting to be around her. She respects the art of drag, and she means a lot to a generation of queer fans.

SHEA COULEÉ: Nice try, World of Wonder. At first, I thought perhaps she was this French drag queen named Betty Bitch who does a really great Lady Gaga. But Lady Gaga is so fucking small and when she walked over toward us and I saw how tall the shoes were and how short she still was in comparison, I was like, that is not a man. I said that is Stefani Germanotta in the flesh. Y'all ain't foolin'.

TRINITY THE TUCK: I didn't know what to think at first because it looked like Gaga and it sounded like Gaga but I wasn't sure if it was her or not to begin with. I quickly realized it was her before everybody else really realized it was her. I'm not one of those people that wants to rush to people. I'm more one of those people that steps back. I have a Southern thought process. When you're raised how I was raised, my grandmother instilled respect and I didn't want to overstep my boundaries because she is a celebrity and I didn't want to rush to her and paw all over her like some of the other people did. I wanted to step back. Eureka was over here like fake crying and sucking the air out of the room. And everybody else was screaming and stuff. I didn't want to do all that. I wanted to observe her, so that's what I did. I was in awe but in my own way.

EUREKA: Lady Gaga walking in was just too much for me, obviously. It just took me right over the edge. I didn't think it was her. I thought it was some little gay guy, a little twink-type guy, who just was really fishy and pretty. I've seen queens pull off a fierce Gaga impersonation so I just assumed it was that. She's got this mask on, y'all are gonna look stupid. And then I'm the one that ended up crying. Being a small-town person and a queer person, when Gaga came on the scene, she was such a statement for people that were different. She was our queen very quickly. I was one of the monsters of Mother Monster, honey. A huge stan. Every song she came out with I performed it, you know? It was like fierce and empowering and different and edgy and young and it was my generation's queen bee. It was my generation's Madonna, really.

VALENTINA: Right away, I knew her. I have been surrounded by a lot of celebrities because of my work and being in LA so that stuff was normal to me. I was quite bothered that the other girls were just freaking out so damn much and they were all up on her and Eureka was crying. I'm like, my goodness, can you let her talk and let us enjoy this experience and let her enjoy it, too? You guys are all up on her. My goodness.

SASHA VELOUR: I don't think I could form a thought at the time. I was so already overwhelmed by everything. I don't know if I thought it was Lady Gaga or not. And as soon as it became clear that it really was Lady Gaga, it was like I know even less what to think of this whole moment. But I loved that she was with us right from the beginning. She communicated in every way that she wanted to hang out with the queens that day and that was really sweet. I have never performed to a Gaga song. I almost feel too connected to her, I don't want to lip sync to her music. I'm a huge fan. She's her own drag act, too.

TRINITY THE TUCK: I was overwhelmed inside because I had never been that close to a celebrity other than RuPaul. It was the first time I ever met somebody like that. And Gaga was one of my idols. That's when it hit me that this is real. We are really here, filming this damn TV show. I am part of this. It's not just a TV show, it's my reality now. To see her in person was a mind-blowing experience inside. I was more reserved. I don't always show what I feel on the outside. But it was definitely a moment.

SHEA COULEÉ: I remember Kimora Blac having a conversation with her and still not knowing. I remember just staring at Kimora like you're really buying that this is a drag queen from New Jersey and not Lady Gaga talking to you right now? Classic.

AJA: Kimora comes up to me and she goes, girl, that's Gaga. And I'm like, girl, I think that's a Gaga impersonator. I kept saying different ideas of who I thought it was. But I really did not know it was her. And sometimes I feel stupid because everyone's like it's obvious. I don't get starstruck. I'm very like, oh hey girl, what's up? A lot of drag is influenced by people like Lady Gaga. She also was really fun on set.

PEPPERMINT: I think I was the first person to know that it was Gaga. And then when Ronnie spoke, I was like, okay, that's definitely Gaga's voice. She said, "Mother has arrived." I was like, what's these shenanigans? It was so bizarre because Gaga was still really, really tiny even in these huge heels. Is it a child? I was thoroughly confused for a minute. But I'm convinced I'm the first one to realize this is Gaga.

FARRAH MOAN: Lady Gaga walks in and instantly you can see it on my face. This is the gag of the season, they just brought Lady Gaga in. I was terrified. It was too much. Little pieces of her costume actually broke off and several of us girls noticed and we grabbed it. It's like a little piece of crystal. I've been so crazy to any roommates about not fucking touching it.

SHEA COULEÉ: I was trippin'. I was like, god, I picked the wrong place to stand. I'm not close enough. This is the biggest celebrity we have seen in a first episode of *RuPaul's Drag Race* ever. I kept thinking about all my friends that made it onto *Drag Race* seasons prior and I was like they can suck it!

EUREKA: Seeing her there, I really understood the level that I was at in the entertainment industry, like the fact that I was really in Hollywood. Lady Gaga is touching your body. That was my eureka moment. It just took me over. Lady Gaga had saved my life when I was in an abusive relationship for three years with someone who was on drugs. A song of hers, "Dope," saved my life when we broke up. I was very suicidal at one point and that song pulled me out of it. It gave me something to cry to. She gave me someone to relate to.

CARSON KRESSLEY: This was the start of oh, holy shit, this is major. But what's interesting is the show didn't really change. I think the heart of the show is absolutely the same—the campiness, the callbacks to pop culture, the gay inside themes. It was on VH1, we had all these celebrity fans who were in the know, who were appearing on the show, and it just built that momentum and I think the culture finally caught up to it and everybody was like, wow, this is so good, where has this been? I'm like, it's been on Logo for the last nine years, okay?

As if the Lady Gaga surprise wasn't enough, RuPaul told the queens they were going to compete in a pageant but no one would go home at the end of the episode. Each queen was asked to present a hometown look and a Lady Gaga–inspired look on the runway before they learned a fourteenth competitor would be joining them.

CYNTHIA LEE FONTAINE: They told me I was going to be crashing a pageant. I was going to be walking up and scream as loud as possible, "How you doing, *mis amores*, you wanna see my cucu again?" They said we also don't want you to have a heart attack or anything but our first star guest is going to be Lady Gaga. Before we filmed the entrance, I got a moment with all of them and I got to talk with Lady Gaga. I also talked with RuPaul and Michelle Visage and I had a really nice beautiful candid moment with all of them.

SHEA COULEÉ: After we did the pageant, she made a point to come backstage and give us notes. They were running into overtime. It was such a long day, but she still insisted on coming back to talk to us. And I remember her telling me that I was beautiful and that I had a great energy, like Grace Jones, who I love. And then she told me that I didn't need to wear so much makeup and I appreciate that note because my makeup has changed since then. She said, "You have such a beautiful face. You don't really need all of that." And I was like, work, girl, I see you. I remember giving her a hug and my chin coming into contact with the shoulder of her little YSL jumpsuit and my foundation getting on it and just me being like ohh fuck. Jesus, you can't hug somebody properly without fucking up their fashion.

FARRAH MOAN: Since we only had a couple of days to put our Gaga look together, Judas the satanic priestess seemed the easiest thing. I wore a latex reveal underneath that I didn't end up revealing because a mic person told me that they didn't want me breaking the equipment and they didn't know how to mic me in my latex without getting lube all over the equipment. That scared me out of not doing my reveal. But Lady Gaga told me I should have done a reveal in *Untucked*. And I was like, there was! It was a black latex leotard with bullet boobs that had spikes that came out of the boobs. She gave me some advice that I'll never forget. She said, "I can understand that this is a whole new experience, and you don't want to break the rules or whatever. But fuck rules. This is your time to be a star. Fuck their equipment. Ask for forgiveness, don't ask for permission. If anything like this comes up again, say fuck it and break their shit because they can't do anything."

PEPPERMINT: She came back to talk to us and spend time. And then she pulled out a book that she was writing all of the notes in and she went down all of our names, our looks, she recorded everything. And she gave us each a negative and positive critique, advice that she thinks that we should work on.

VALENTINA: She literally took the time to write down notes. I saw her handwritten notes in her little handbook. There was lots of writing, lots of scribbles. She was really prepared to come in and talk about every single person and make us feel seen. She really had this way of making us feel like she was paying attention to us and that we mattered. I was really honored.

AJA: She was very nice. I think that that was very gracious and beautiful. The best part of it for me was to engage in conversation with her and realize oh, you are a regular person. That type of thing made me navigate *Drag Race* better. I was like, wow, I can't wait to go out and try to be nice.

TRINITY THE TUCK: I had such a great experience with Gaga, especially in *Untucked*. Gaga was so personable in *Untucked*. It made me even more of a fan because she came in there and she actually gave us each really good critiques and it seemed heartfelt and it seemed like a moment.

FARRAH MOAN: I still to this day wish I could have really absorbed that moment wholeheartedly and completely. However, this was at one in the morning after we had been on set all day. And while she was talking to me especially, I had to pee so, so, so unimaginably, irrevocably bad, I was so uncomfortable. And they're like, "We'll let you go, just let Lady Gaga finish talking to everybody and you can go. We don't want you to disappear while the camera is rolling." So I was sitting there just trying so hard to hold it in. I'm so glad I was able to retain everything that Lady Gaga told me but if you asked me a single thing she said to anybody else, I would not be able to tell you. I sprinted through that studio and literally almost peed all over myself 'cause I forgot: As soon as you get to the bathroom, you're like, oh yeah, I'm duct-taped.

It did not take long for the queens to lose their Lady Gaga–induced highs. And all it took was the riskiest challenge in *Drag Race* history— a cheerleading battle.

SHEA COULEÉ: Giiirrlll. Girl. They thought that they cast some athletic girls on Season 9. I am naturally athletic. I was a gymnast when I was younger, did dance, never did any cheerleading but I didn't feel intimidated because I was like, we're just gonna do floor work and we're gonna rah, rah, rah and bounce around and have some pompoms and that's it. And then, when they started describing that we would be doing stunts, that's when things got really real. I do not know these girls and now I have to trust them with my safety and vice versa. I have to literally catch somebody when they fall.

CYNTHIA LEE FONTAINE: Ohhh Lord Jesus. *¡Jesús Cristo!* Before we filmed that challenge, it was three days straight of learning all the choreography and the routine. People were injured. Guess what, I was one of them.

AJA: My god, I hate that challenge. People don't realize what I went through, the three-day fucking rehearsal, and I passed out. I was like gone, pshhhhhh. One morning they took me to the Easy Care because I fainted in my hotel room and they didn't know what it was. And I guess it was because I was recovering from the sinusitis, and then I'm over here doing acrobatic stunts. The things we do for TV, girl. And of course I was one of the thinner girls, so I was one of the fliers and they threw me in the air. I thought I was going to die. It was one of the trainers 'cause do you think I would trust one of these bitches to throw me in the air? I would have been like, Miss Thing, Miss RuPaul, Miss World of Wonder, I don't trust these hoes so please do not have them throw me.

FARRAH MOAN: That was the crazy-as-fuck challenge. It was so ambitious for them to try to get us into professional cheerleading in three days. And since I was so small and skinny, I was obviously selected to be flier. They had us doing tumbling, they had us being thrown in the air, they had us creating human pyramids with each other, and having to hold other girls and be held up in the air. They made us do full *Bring It On* and I think it's kind of cool that I can say I did that. But, whew!

EUREKA: It was hard and they wanted us to tumble. I knew the cartwheel wasn't gonna be a good idea but I pushed myself to do it anyway. And honestly, I was excited and anxious and wanted to do a good job so I just pushed my body to the limit. And as a big person, I was the anchor of the pyramid so I had to catch Trinity, of all people. I had to support Trinity Taylor's sandbag ass up in the air and catch her fifty million times when we rehearsed.

VALENTINA: It was such a challenge but at the same time I was like if anything this is where I've got to show my dance experience, this is where I've got to show my tricks and my flips. The only ones that were actually going full-throttle were Shea Couleé and me. I always felt like Shea Couleé was the queen to beat in challenges because her level of focus was very similar to my level of focus. I could see eye-to-eye on her that she didn't come here to play.

SASHA VELOUR: I didn't go up in the air, which I was very disappointed about. I wanted to be thrown into the air but I was not petite enough apparently. I didn't get any of the cool jobs actually on the cheerleading.

EUREKA: My knees were weak and hurting and I kept stretching and by the time it came to performance day when I did the cartwheel, the first rotation it was kind of okay. I landed everything okay. But the second time we went through it, everything went wrong. My knee popped during the cartwheel, my wig came off completely. They didn't even show that part. I jumped into the split anyway. They paused filming, all the girls came over to help me get my wig back on, they didn't even show that part.

FARRAH MOAN: We were doing our tumbling segments. They were very courteous to not air the exact moment that she fell. They created that moment with her good take. But she was on the ground and couldn't move and we all had to stop our routines to render aid to her. Especially because we had become so close already, I just couldn't believe it. I just knew she really hurt herself. What a crazy thing.

TRINITY THE TUCK: It wasn't until a few minutes later that she had complained about her knee. And even then I didn't think it was as bad as what it was because she was a trouper. She powered through it. She didn't make it a big deal. One thing I will say about Eureka, even back then, I respected the fact that she was a competitor just like myself and she was there to win just like myself, so she was going to do whatever she had to do to win. And for her to power through made me respect her even more because she didn't let it get the best of her in that moment.

SHEA COULEÉ: It sucks that Eureka hurt herself so severely. Eureka has done splits and things like that a million times. I felt like her body was fatigued and she didn't really prep herself for that split properly. The weight came down wrong. And those things can happen when you are in an environment like that, challenging your body to do so many different and new things, something that you've done a million times before can go wrong because you are not thinking about it properly. It was tough to see her struggling and in pain as a result of that challenge.

EUREKA: It felt like when you pop your knuckles but it was in my knee. And then my knee got really weak. I wasn't sure what it was. It didn't really hurt immediately. There was so much adrenaline going. It was just numb and went weak. So I just pushed myself through. But after everything was done and I got out of drag, it was really tight and it was hurting. I thought I needed to get in a hot bath. But I didn't say anything the day of.

CYNTHIA LEE FONTAINE: When I saw her do the split, I saw the impact when she hit the floor. I saw that knee. I'm like oh ayyyyyy. It was a seven-minute routine and you just only saw on TV one minute. So I grabbed her, *mamí*, are you okay? And she was all pale. We were lining up on the sides, waiting for the performance and all the filming to finish. And she was like, oh girl, I hit my knee and it's a lot of pain. I said, "Let's stop this." And she said, "No, no, I'm a professional."

MANDY SALANGSANG: It's unfortunate that anyone did get hurt. But we have queens who injure themselves occasionally, unfortunately, in dance challenges and other things of that nature. Drag takes a toll on the body. They want it so badly. They push themselves and their bodies to their limits. They are all passionate about what they are doing.

EUREKA: The next day I came in and my knee was double swollen and everyone noticed it. And I told them I was struggling a little bit with it so they were like, let's put some ice on it and stuff. I was like, I'm fine, I'll crutch my way to the end. I don't give a shit.

VALENTINA: I think Eureka was trying to deny it. We had walked in to Lady Gaga being on the first episode. We had walked in to a diverse cast of girls. We were ready to live out the entire experience. You go and you sacrifice your whole life to be there. So to be sent home because of an injury? Nobody would want that. She tried to keep that secret.

TOM CAMPBELL: We did put them through a lot of physical exertion in that challenge, more than maybe we should have with the best of intentions. That was a lowlight. I'm so glad Eureka's okay. That was heartbreaking.

SHEA COULEÉ: That experience forced us to really depend on each other in such a way that I feel united us and brought us together as a cast in such an impactful way. I know that we got some critiques from fans saying that they felt like we were too nice to each other. I felt like Season 9 was different because we were forced to be sisters and look out for each other from that first real challenge because there was real risk and danger there.

After the cheerleading challenge, the queens were thrilled to move on to an acting challenge and found plenty of joy in creating fairy-tale drag princesses and their sassy sidekicks. Trinity the Tuck's Princess Aquapussy and her sidekick Stanky the Starfish won the week.

AJA: I was excited about it because I knew that I had not brought anything that was extravagant because I couldn't afford it, but I knew how to sew. And I was being provided the materials to do so, so I didn't have to run crazy to the garment district at 3:00 p.m. with no meal and running the sewing machine. I have the resources and I can do this comfortably, I was excited.

FARRAH MOAN: Arrrrgggh! This was the bane of my existence. To this day, I have PTSD from that challenge.

EUREKA: I kind of got inspired by Cynthia because when we were talking, she was like well, I'm gonna be Princess Cuculina of Cuculand. So I was like, who could be her archnemesis other than Princess You-Reek-of-Daria who lives in the sewers of Cuculand? And what would be a fun play on words for a sidekick? I was like, a mangy dog named Roof Trade, anything I could do to make it campy and comical.

SASHA VELOUR: This is my challenge. I write kids' comic books. I totally stand by my fairy tale but I had a hard time making it funny for the challenge. I underestimated how important the humor was. I really wish I could go back and have another stab at that challenge because I loved the concept.

TRINITY THE TUCK: Looking around, all these freakin' people were doing underwater themes and mine was underwater. There was no way I could get around it because it was shells and stuff. Originally, I had thought about doing a mermaid but since there were so many other people that were doing mermaid themes, I just decided to do the princess of the coral. So her sidekick ended up being a guy starfish because I noticed that a lot of people were doing girl sidekicks. I really hammed it up.

SHEA COULEÉ: I almost didn't finish that look because I was ambitious and wanted to make this big mermaid hoop skirt moment. They said we had eight hours to do this challenge. In my mind, I knew I could do that but that's eight hours uninterrupted. I was not computing that this is production and when RuPaul did a walkthrough, we would have to move and be out of the shot so that took about an hour of time away. And then we had to go on a green screen and do our sidekicks but they were recording sound for the sidekicks, and because the walls were paper thin, we couldn't run the sewing machines while they were doing a girl's scene. There were thirteen of us so you'd sew for two minutes and then have to stop for three and then sew for two and then stop for three. I was not prepared for how much my workflow would be affected by the production of the show and I was scrambling to finish that dress on time and to get ready for the runway that day. They don't call it a challenge for nothing.

VALENTINA: I totally cheated on making my outfit that we were supposed to be sewing ourselves because I had this bathing suit that had a top to it, a neckpiece that sparkled. I saw another fabric that looked similar to mine so I just retraced the other one and stuck the top it to it and sewed the two sides together and it was a bodysuit. I did put it through the sewing machine but I had an easy pattern.

AJA: A princess don't have to be in a gown. I'm from Brooklyn, and our princesses are the girls with the Baby Phat jeans. I'm going to do something a little more fashion, a little more edgy. And I did this fiery princess with chaps, a panty, a bra in a fur coat. I looked kind of like a pimp or like I was going to tell the weather. The deal was that I was erupting and I'm a natural disaster. The sidekick was the sistah of disastah! She's from Bay Ridge and she was also a smoker. She has a raspy voice. She was giving very Big Ang energy. If I'm the explosion, she's the gas. She's the soot that comes out the volcano.

PEPPERMINT: I wanted to draw from my own personal past and turn tragedy into comedy. I damn near died in a fire when I was a teenager. And so I wanted to use that in some way. And so I created Petey the Pilot Light and Princess Carcinogenita is how I pronounce it.

VALENTINA: That's the episode where Cheyenne Jackson told me that I looked like Linda Evangelista. That's what started *You're perfect, you're beautiful, you look like a model, you're smiling, everything about you is perfect, did you stone those tights?* That's the episode!

SHEA COULEÉ: Oh girl, I got dragged for Princess Aquaria, too. Lord have mercy! Oh my god! I am an Aquarius, too. I love my sign, too. And I thought it would be cute. [Season 10 winner] Aquaria dragged my ass. She was like, bitch, how dare you use my name? She went online and she was like, what the fuck? I had met her prior and I told her we did a challenge and I had a character and I named her Aquaria. I'm an Aquarius and that was what her tea was. And she was like, thank you for letting me know. And then she went on Instagram Live and let me have it after that episode aired. And her fans were dragging me and being like, how dare you steal from her? I was like, oh fuck.

When Valentina walked into the werkroom with her expensive designer costumes, she said she had only been a drag artist for ten months. But when the season started airing, Valentina amassed the largest fan base the show had ever seen, especially among the Latinx community. A polarizing beauty who made her own rules and was poised to win it all, Valentina was so popular that Alaska made a hilarious music video parody titled "Valentina" to the tune of the global hit "Despacito."

VALENTINA: Since I was little, I was interviewing myself in the mirror. The world is my stage and I'm living my life as a movie so it was only going to benefit me that I have that mentality in my everyday life already. So coming to do the show, it's like, oh well, sweetie, hold on, let me put the production on for you. I definitely came with my own story line and I've always described myself as a complex character.

SASHA VELOUR: Understanding to what degree Valentina is in a fantasy has helped me really understand her. I love her so much more deeply because I, too, love to escape to a fantasy world. She seemed very LA to me. I'll say that. On day two, she came up and was like, "The fans are going to love you, Sasha. You are exactly the type of queen that the fans get really excited about." And I was excited but those were not things I was thinking about necessarily.

RANDY BARBATO: I think they all live in their own worlds and we are just visiting. Valentina is the queen who sketched everything she was going to wear. She is building these pieces of art and it is all about perfection. I am so obsessed when I watch those sorts of people do their thing because it is just unbelievable to watch that.

AJA: At the time, I thought she was very mean. She was very quirky and she would have her cute moments but then there were times where I felt she was being a little off-putting. Notably, she came up to Shea and me in the first episode, and I remember we were talking about stuff, and she was trying to give us skin care routines. I was like, really? But I admired the stuff she brought. I admired her drag. I just thought that she was being pushed a little forward with favoritism and I didn't see the hype about her. I thought she was standoffish. I did feel bad that I had went off on her on *Untucked* and I apologized to her about that.

VALENTINA: Aja was always digging at me. She was always being a true New Yorker, catty girl. She was always digging at me but she always had this admiration for me. Same with Farrah Moan. There was always this love/hate tense energy between us. I think a lot of it has to do with my attitude of not caring or not trying to connect with any of them because I was so worried about getting ready on time. I was so worried about finishing what I had to finish that I was not connecting with them. But I think, eventually, when I won the first challenge and when I was getting the kind of commentary that I was getting from the judges, I think a lot of the girls came to realize that having me on their team is an advantage.

SHEA COULEÉ: My impression of Valentina early on was that she was stunning and sweet. I really enjoyed Valentina. The judges really loved her.

FARRAH MOAN: I actually really liked her. We got ready next to each other the whole season. But being with her in *Drag Race* in general is stressful because she lives in her own time. She works on her time. She's very able to shut her anxiety about being late off because her attitude is, the show will start when I'm ready. So she was always the last one ready. She was always the one taking the longest, which made all of us really uncomfortable because they would make us put our makeup brushes down go stand in line but then she just wouldn't, which was so ballsy, honestly, in retrospect. I think so many of us are a little bit scared to step on anyone's toes or be inconvenient or whatever. And she really just gave no fucks and, sorry love, you can't force me to be done 'cause I'm not. Which in hindsight is kind of iconic.

VALENTINA: Production would be trying it sometimes, girl. They would say we only had one hour left when we'd only been painting for thirty minutes. I was always just struggling and all the other girls were like done, hoping I'd go onstage with one eyelash. They were always hating. I would always, in the last minute, pull it together and they'd be like oh fuck.

PEPPERMINT: The only person who was sort of the outlier was Valentina because she seemed to be the favorite. She didn't seem to have the same connection to the group as many of the other girls. Valentina's actually one of the girls that I'm the closest with to this day.

SHEA COULEÉ: Back then, it was obvious RuPaul really likes her and is going to let her slide through. But the princess/sidekick challenge was the tipping point. She got really praised for her sidekick character and for her outfit. And the thing that was aggravating to the girls was that she didn't make it. We were told this is a construction look challenge. That was a swimsuit she already had. She cut the lavender fabric and glued it over the swimsuit that she already had. The girls watched her do this. I doubt that production was even privy to it but she cut a lot of corners. And there were girls really working hard on their outfits, building things and working on things in their rooms overnight, and I felt like that is where the tension really came from because she didn't work as hard as everybody else. Here's the thing, though: Work smarter, not harder. I felt like people were in their feelings because Valentina was working smarter, not harder, than they were, and she was getting a lot of attention. That is when people started to change toward her. But I don't hate the player. I hate the game.

SASHA VELOUR: I felt like she arrived to film *Drag Race* understanding how to show up for a TV show in ways that I had to learn in order keep up. There were people there who knew how to play the TV game, which isn't necessarily a bad thing. There was fierce competition for that.

VALENTINA: I would always know how to flip the script on how to not be depicted or to be edited because I was not having it. I think that's another thing that maybe the queens didn't like about me is that I always knew how to control everybody on set. I was so in my own world, filming my own show.

Trinity the Tuck and Charlie Hides bombed their team morning talk show challenge and ended up lip syncing against each other. At least, that was the plan. By the time Britney Spears's "I Wanna Go" was over, Trinity had established herself as a lip-sync assassin and Charlie, well, no one really knows.

AJA: Charlie told me in the morning in the car, "I have a feeling this is not gonna go good. I think if they tell me to lip sync, I'm not going to do anything." I said, well, girl, you should if you want to stay. But if you don't, I ain't going to stop you.

EUREKA: Oh girl, poor Charlie. I have always been told to respect my elders so I ain't gonna say nothing negative about her. And apparently that day, she let everyone know she wasn't a lip-sync girl. But I also felt a little bit like she had given up earlier in that day and I think that showed in her performance, to be honest. She was so paranoid she was gonna look stupid or they were gonna make her look bad that it ended up making her look that way.

FARRAH MOAN: She can deny this all day but I have it all written in my journal that she told us in the werkroom that if she had to lip sync for her life that she wasn't going to do it because she didn't like the song. And then after the fact, she tried to say that she cracked her rib. And it's like, look, baby girl, if you want us to lie for you, tell us beforehand because once we start getting asked in interviews how was Charlie's rib broken? We're like, what broken rib? You know, I'm that friend where I'm like if you tell me beforehand 'cause you don't want to be embarrassed, I will be there for you. She ended up being caught in a whole lot of controversy for that because she didn't want to admit that she gave up.

EUREKA: Trinity always slays. I know she's a fierce queen, that's why I hate her.

FARRAH MOAN: I actually had started to develop a friendship with Charlie Hides and she was telling me what her history working in the drag industry was like. And I think she kind of saw a younger version of herself in me. It was extremely disappointing and also extremely sad because Trinity killed it and watching someone get murdered was really sad.

TRINITY THE TUCK: I had never seen Charlie perform. Yes, she was a lot older than me, but you never know what people can pull out. I performed that song like my life depended on it. I was performing to the judges. I was looking at RuPaul, Michelle, and the other judges in the eye as I was lip syncing when my ass wasn't shaking in their face. I was totally in a zone and had a mission on slaying this lip sync so I could stay. I'm glad that I went full ham because it showed the contestants and the production that if we put Trinity in the bottom, people are going to go home. I was happy about that.

AJA: Trinity is going mad hard, shaking her ass everywhere. Literally, on one side we have a strip club. He denied he threw it at the reunion, but I remember.

SHEA COULEÉ: It was lovely to watch Trinity. Trinity was fantastic. At one point, I was cheering for Charlie in the background. You can hear me being like come on, "Charlie, come on, Charlie!" And Charlie just gave up. I don't root for people that give up so I switched and said let's celebrate Trinity the Tuck for being a badass bitch and having to lip sync against a log and turn it out regardless. It was so disappointing because there's so many people that want that opportunity and for Charlie being the oldest contestant to ever come through the doors of *RuPaul's Drag Race* and say that she's gonna be there to show that you can be this age and do it. All you did was show us is that you can be that age and give up.

SASHA VELOUR: I underestimated Trinity from the beginning. I've talked to her about it. Something about my biases about drag, I just did not understand how fierce she was at first. Watching her perform cleared it up for me because she delivered. It was so good. At the same time that I was screaming at Charlie to turn it up a little bit, I was losing my head because I felt like that had been the best lip sync so far. She was flipping and it was really sharp and she knew the words and it was purposeful and that's what I love to see in a lip sync. I didn't feel like she necessarily should have been there but I was thankful that they had a good lip syncer. It was crazy that we had some lip syncs where one person was not delivering. That's not fun.

PEPPERMINT: Charlie and I knew each other before. And so I was upset. I was not surprised that Trinity was going to turn it out. But Charlie was not fighting and that was upsetting to me because we had all been through so much. We all wanted each other to do well and fight. But Charlie was giving up.

TRINITY THE TUCK: I love Charlie. I think that Charlie is great at drag. I think they really need to consider putting Charlie on *All Stars* because she does comedy very well. She does characters very well. Her fashion is great and she is an era of drag that we need to show more of because she is from the old, old school. I thought that she gave way too many excuses. She literally had fifteen excuses of why she didn't lip sync properly. I'm like, girl, pick one or just own it. Own that you just aren't a lip syncer.

PEPPERMINT: I didn't open her up and look at her rib but she fell. She was lifting and she got hurt. We all had moments when we had to take a minute. And then afterward, I think some of us tried to power through it.

SHEA COULEÉ: That bitch does not have a broken rib! See, that was the part that killed me. I was like, wait a second, you broke your rib by lifting up the back half of my left foot? Girl, come on. Why was that my fault? Why did I break her rib?

SASHA VELOUR: Maybe. I don't know. But how old was she, fifty-four? I mean, that's pretty taxing.

AJA: I don't know, I ain't a doctor. She used to wear those demonic boots and come out seven feet tall, but she can't do the lip sync? Girl, I woulda took them shoes off. She didn't have no cracked rib because if she had a cracked rib, how do you walk in those eight- or nine-inch platform heels?

VALENTINA: I remember thinking come on, Charlie. She just was done. She was not having it. I have so much respect for Charlie because she has been doing drag for so long and she already had her career and her YouTube stuff. I don't want to go speaking against her because I have always had a lot of respect for her but I really don't think that her rib was broken.

SHEA COULEÉ: I feel like our drag sisters who have been in this industry, who have been a part of this culture for a long time, are very important and valuable and I guess Charlie just didn't see their own value. But, honestly, I really don't give a fuck about Charlie Hides. I do not like that bitch, so I don't care.

FARRAH MOAN: Not only did she lie about having a cracked rib, she also blamed it on picking up Shea. Now she's trying to tear other people down with her lies. I hope that if you're reading this book, Charlie, please don't hate! I will lie for you in the future. Just tell me before.

After the Reality Stars Rusical, Farrah Moan and Cynthia Lee Fontaine become the new Sharon Needles and Phi Phi O'Hara when RuPaul was forced to send another contestant home.

EUREKA: They took Cynthia Lee Fontaine and me to the doctor. She had hurt her ankle. I had an MRI and found out that I had an ACL tear. They brought me these little flats to rhinestone and they brought me crutches and they said that I couldn't be active without the crutches. I was definitely in some pain and just trying to push through. It was really awful, honestly. It really had me irritable. Producers asked me how I felt and I said I will crutch my way to the end. I will do every challenge on crutches. This is my chance and I can't mess it up.

SHEA COULEÉ: I remember she had gone to the doctor and she had to wear these crutches for the runway. Ooooh umm, that seems kind of bad. This seems serious. It's a big red flag.

FARRAH MOAN: It was really emotional because Cynthia was the one queen that I knew when I lived in Texas who didn't feel threatened by me and didn't talk shit about me and stood up for me to other girls.

SHEA COULEÉ: A lot of people don't know this but Farrah is the girl from Season 9 that I talk to and see the most. We talk all the time, alllll the time. I had so much fun with Farrah because she's just a little baby sister to me. I feel protective over her. I don't think a lot of people get a chance to see Farrah's sense of humor. Farrah is really funny. But I feel like people are too busy laughing at her misfortune [rather] than laughing with her about her misfortune because she can make fun of herself really well. But people are too busy laughing at her.

CYNTHIA LEE FONTAINE: I was not focused that whole episode, with everything that was happening. I got distracted and my lip sync was not as accurate and synchronized as I want it to be. My execution for the Kardashians Rusical, too—that's why I ended up looking like Celine Dion.

FARRAH MOAN: I was trying to perform for the judges but as soon as I made eye contact with RuPaul, I felt like I was going to faint. So then I just looked at the imaginary audience behind them. I remember at some point seeing Cynthia's dress that looked like a blanket fly off and looking over at her and seeing that her bra and her panties didn't match and I was like, okay, I got this. But, of course, we were singing for Meghan Trainor in front of Meghan Trainor so that was really intimidating.

AJA: Cynthia and Farrah did that long lip sync to Meghan Trainor and then Ru left the room and was gone for a good fifteen minutes and nobody knew what was going to happen.

EUREKA: When I was called safe, I was like, yes, okay, bitch, survived another week, we gonna make it through on crutches, I don't give a shit, I'll be the first queen crowned on crutches, you know what I mean? And then RuPaul said she had some thinking to do and she left the set. They brought me a stool to sit on. We waited for a long time. It felt like forever but it was probably like thirty minutes.

CYNTHIA LEE FONTAINE: During the break when we were waiting for RuPaul, Eureka told me she thought it was her going home. She said this knee is bothering me so much and it sucks because this situation is the one probably sending me home. All the girls were like, Eureka, don't say that, we love you. It was like a big swollen turkey leg.

FARRAH MOAN: That was the dramatic pause of the century because RuPaul got up and left the room. The producers ended up bringing us out stools and poor Cynthia is still in bra and panties from taking off her dress. And RuPaul came back and I could just feel it coming. I could feel her about to open her mouth. Maybe I got a glimpse into an alternate universe or something but I could feel her about to say she was going to send me home. And she said Eureka.

EUREKA: I thought she rewatched the tape and was like, no, Eureka did terrible, we messed up. When she gave me the news, I was genuinely shocked. But I also at the same time knew something was coming because I was really hurting. I really was going through it even though I was pretending like I wasn't. It was a lot. It was emotional. But when she told me that I got an open invitation to come back, it gave me a little hope. I was just so bummed out and depressed and sad and upset with myself really. I was really upset at my body. I felt like my body gave out during this huge moment in my life. I was trying to be humble as I exited but I was really sad and hurt.

FARRAH MOAN: That was just the last thing I expected. And obviously, being in the competition with her and being friends with her, I knew about all the different times she had to go to the doctor. I watched her knee swell four times its size. I just felt so sad that her dream was taken away because of this injury.

CYNTHIA LEE FONTAINE: In my heart I knew that it was Eureka.

Filming in pain is not the best way to continue and express yourself artistically. It is not. And it's not safe. Anything can happen. That's why you see me crying like a baby. Of course, Eureka and Farrah, they were super close and it was heartbreaking for her. Even Farrah was saying I wish it was me. After we finished filming and we saw Eureka leaving, we needed two hours. All of us were crying for an hour straight. It was really, really heartbreaking not just only for me, for all the rest of the cast.

SHEA COULEÉ: When RuPaul called Eureka up, I was like, oh shit. I feel like I know how this is going to go and it was exactly what I thought was about to happen. But it still was such a surprise because she was doing so well. The judges really liked her personality. It was sad because it was something that was out of her control and it sucked to see her go home over something that she had no control over when just last week Charlie gave up.

AJA: We all gagged, I gagged. I was happy for Eureka because she was in pain. But also she was big competition. So less people is better.

VALENTINA: I was devastated. Oh my god, I cried so much for Eureka, I couldn't control my tears. I hadn't eaten all day. We were allowed one cocktail in *Untucked*. I could either be a really fun and energetic drunk or I could be a real emotional *señora*, pass me the bottle, crying drunk, and I think I must have been crying drunk at that moment. Truly, I didn't know anything about Eureka's leg and in a way it felt like somebody was shaming her, eliminating her, crushing her dream. She was so eager to be there. She'd worked so hard to be there. To me, it was dream crushing and I couldn't stop crying because it was so unfair. I was really sad. I ruined my makeup.

PEPPERMINT: When Ru called Eureka forward, it was very scary. This was one of the moments that was unorthodox because Ru had got up and left and had a conference in the back. And when she came back, she made the announcement about Eureka. Eureka had been a threat but I wasn't happy by any means. They had been wheeling her around and I just didn't understand. But with the injury she had, it obviously made sense. I was so happy that they said she could come back next year when she was healed. I was like, oh, okay, they have a heart.

SASHA VELOUR: I thought Eureka would make it to the top. I thought she was going to do every runway on crutches and it was going to be historic. Look how glamorous this can be! It wasn't really clear how injured she was, like a torn ACL. She couldn't stay. It was shocking. But at the same time, I had been struggling with Miss Eureka so I was like, whew, what a relief. Now that I've gotten to love her, what a terrible thing to have thought. But at the time, mm-mm, I was glad. Eureka's such a camera-grabbing personality, and I was still learning how to even be comfortable in front of the cameras, let alone grab them. It's hard to compete against such ham camera, theatrical ham energy. But now I've learned.

TRINITY THE TUCK: When they did the lip sync between Cynthia and Farrah, we were all thinking they are both gonna go home because the lip sync was awful. I think that Farrah and Cynthia were damn lucky that Eureka was sent home, for sure.

FARRAH MOAN: I didn't deserve to be there as much as her and it's just crazy and I just had to take the signs of the universe as they were and put my head back on and realize, I'm still here, and I still have much to show the world what I'm capable of and can do. That cry that I did, that wail noise that I made, was me literally crying so hard that my airwaves were closing, I could barely breathe. I felt so bad.

SASHA VELOUR: After Eureka got sent home, everyone was like, we are fine, everyone's healthy. I will die here of whatever injury I got rather than be sent home.

Although Peppermint wound up in the bottom for her poor impersonation of NeNe Leakes on Snatch Game, it was a doubly triumphant week for her. First, she approached the cast to talk about her gender identity and was heartened to find plenty of common ground with them. Then she slayed her lip sync against Cynthia Lee Fontaine, who never stood a chance.

PEPPERMINT: My first time announcing to the world that I'm a trans woman was on national TV. About a year before *Drag Race*, I was on *The Daily Show* with Trevor Noah. I was on a panel talking about being trans. So going to *Drag Race*, my thinking was this is something I'm doing as a trans woman and it's a drag competition. I just wanted to focus on being the best drag entertainer. But the first chance I got to talk about being trans, I took it. I don't really like to call it coming out. It's more that I was disclosing to the other queens in the room. I want to be clear because it's murky and I want to advocate on behalf of the other trans ladies. There were other performers that are associated with the show who came out either on the show or after the show. In my opinion, they've been trans their whole lives. It's just that they weren't out. The difference was I was out publicly before I got cast.

AJA: I identify as nonbinary, so I fall under the trans umbrella. People should know that the trans umbrella itself is just a group of terms that resonate with not feeling that you are the gender assigned at birth. It's very important to me for there to be trans representation on the show because I feel like drag was pioneered by trans women. And I feel like a lot of my favorite and big idols from drag were a lot of trans performers. It's wrong to deny trans performers the platform they cultivated.

JIGGLY CALIENTE: I was never told to not disclose my trans-ness. That was never an issue. I chose to not speak on it at the time. I was early in my transition. If they were reading me for my teeth, could you imagine if they were trying to read me for my trans-ness, too? That wouldn't have been good for me. Peppermint was trans when she was on the show. Let's be real, the gay revolution would not have existed if it wasn't for a Latina trans woman and a Black trans woman. So we have always been part of the fold.

SASHA VELOUR: We all have experienced queerness around our gender identities in ways that we should be in conversation with each other about it. And not just joking about it, but actually going deep, too. And then we can joke. I thought it would be a pretty profound political statement just because as Peppermint herself said, there's still so much conversation in the world of drag and especially back then about whether trans women had the same validity as drag artists. It's in the history. It's in our traditions, like, trans women and men, nonbinary people, are part of what makes drag so great. And so I felt like celebrating Peppermint in this way, and then the fact that she literally made it to the top two, made a clear statement about how much everyone belongs here. I was so excited that she was there.

PEPPERMINT: I didn't know if they were going to think that I don't deserve to be here because people were saying, what's the challenge? If you're trans, you're a woman, and that's boring and you're not skilled at doing anything. You already had surgery, that's cheating. So I didn't even want to make that a factor. I thought there would be pushback and that the answer to that pushback would be to camp it up, show your drag, make it the best drag they've ever seen. But the opposite happened. Our cast was extremely progressive, liberal, gender variant, and comfortable with their gender variance. Half identified as nonbinary when we filmed it. Nonbinary people and gender nonconforming people have always been a part of drag but, in terms of *Drag Race*, the obsession was with this transformation from butch man to fem woman and so feminine that you can't even tell they're a man—that old-fashioned trope. That's not who was on Season 9. We were very queer, radical, let's fuck up the system, trans and nonbinary people who were doing drag. We were open about what everyone's experience was with their gender variance. And that felt good.

TRINITY THE TUCK: If anyone would have objected to that, there would have been a huge fight. So Peppermint is actually one of my favorite people out of all the Ru girls and one of the few that I am extremely close to.

AJA: I always looked at Peppermint as a legend. I always thought of her as someone very prestigious and aware. She was very powerful. She was one of the girls who had toured internationally, even before *Drag Race*. I really respect Peppermint.

VALENTINA: When she came out to us, I congratulated her and I thanked her. At the same time, I told her I am so excited and honored to be in this with you but at the same time I have never had a trans friend. So there's a lot of things that I'm gonna be learning and wanting to know and if ever I say something wrong or if I misgender you or something, please correct me. I want to learn so much through this experience and through you and I want to give you the respect and the verbiage you deserve. And my goodness do we have a kiki. We've gone on tour to all of Latin America. I've been to her place in New York and we are really good friends and connect on a lot of levels about a lot of things.

PEPPERMINT: When we were filming, we were sequestered. So I didn't know what was going on in the world. Come out of filming *Drag Race*, all of a sudden Hillary Clinton is behind in the polls. And so lots had changed. In the year that the show aired, there was pushback from people in the community, people who identify themselves as trans, people who identify themselves as drag entertainers, *RuPaul's Drag Race* queens alike, all who were saying, "Peppermint's not a good enough version of a trans woman." She's not passable; she's not "fish." We reject her. It was unfortunate but luckily I heard an anecdote from a very good friend of mine who was being misgendered as a man.

She realized she's a woman, and who she is isn't based on what anyone thinks she should be dressing or looking like. I needed to bring myself to that space because when you're a drag entertainer you go from being dressed to undressed and, somewhere in there, people would read me as male and I needed to be okay with that.

SHEA COULEÉ: I will never forget Peppermint's interview moment before the lip sync: "I'm scared, scared for Cynthia."

PEPPERMINT: I was nervous and unsure. But I knew I deserved it and it felt like something I finally have some control over. I'd rehearsed the hell out of that song and everything I was gonna do in my hotel room for two nights before. So I felt very prepared to give a good show.

AJA: I will never forget this lip sync because I was standing next to Shea and she goes, "You see this shit? If Peppermint goes home, this shit is rigged." And then when we saw the public assassination of Cynthia Lee Fontaine on *Drag Race*, I was like, whoa! That lip sync in person was fucking crazy. TV could not capture how well Peppermint did that fucking song. There were several points where I gagged.

SHEA COULEÉ: I love Madonna, don't get me wrong, but "Music" is one of my least favorite tracks of hers because it's hard to dance to. The beat is really all over the place. I remember thinking to myself I don't know how anyone is going to sell this on a lip sync. Not only did Peppermint sell it, but she pantomimed murdering Cynthia Lee Fontaine onstage. Wow! That was the shotgun heard 'round the world. We were like Cynthia is the sweetest person and you did not have to assassinate her like that.

FARRAH MOAN: That really changed my life. Peppermint really shook all of us. We knew she was already such a well-versed, versatile, talented, well-known iconic New York City nightlife performer. But when she assassinated Cynthia Lee Fontaine like that, I think that's when everyone started to see her as a real threat.

CYNTHIA LEE FONTAINE: There were two lip syncs. You have my lip sync that is the traditional one because I was impersonating Madonna. And then you have one of the funniest entertainers and personalities from New York City, Peppermint, in her accessories and her earrings and going crazy and doing Sebastian from *The Little Mermaid* movie everywhere across the stage. I'm like ayyyy no, what is happening? I did what I knew as an entertainer. You just perform what you feel from your heart and what you understand and execute the lyrics versus Peppermint going crazy onstage but at the same time being super, extremely funny. So she won the lip sync.

TRINITY THE TUCK: At that moment, I reflected and thought thank god Peppermint didn't get in the bottom two the episode that I lip synced because she is a strong lip syncer.

CYNTHIA LEE FONTAINE: I took this second opportunity seriously and with a blessing in my heart. For the very first time, the show aired in another network, VH1. It went from Logo TV for queers to the rest of the universe. It created a huge impact and the fandom grew. My fan base doubled in size. The love and support from everybody, even from Thailand, Germany, Spain, Philippines, Latin America, and so many places. I was part of this historic transition. I was living my dream in a historic moment for the TV show, with the Emmy nominations and airing on a network that everybody can watch more easily.

Eventually, the time came for Valentina to lip sync for her life. It didn't go well.

VALENTINA: Nina and I were really close during filming. I was friendless, kind of quiet, to myself, and so was Nina. Nina was herself and was never fake. She was always very honest and very creative and to herself and I really admired that about her. She was not fighting for camera time. She was not being shady. She was just doing her and minding her business and giving it her all and living her dream. And that's where we connected. She always thought something was going on behind her back. I tried to make jokes with her and was always there to give her emotional support because I always felt bad that she was on her own and had this chip on her shoulder.

TRINITY THE TUCK: Both Nina and Valentina landed in the bottom, rightfully so, and it gave us one of the most epic memories of *Drag Race* history, ever.

VALENTINA: My look was so damn iconic. I had the mask and I just created a look together in my mind that had never been done. To this day, I will get hundreds of kids tagging me that they dressed up as me for Halloween. You should have seen how many people dressed as me in that outfit for Halloween that year. I still have the mask. I still have all the stuff with me. The boots were rented from a friend of mine that's a costume designer. That look is gold to me.

SHEA COULEÉ: I remember the music starting, and about thirty seconds in, I felt like everyone started looking side to side at each other. Is she gonna leave that on? Or is she gonna take that off? And then I could see Michelle turning to Ru and I felt like I could see people in the crew looking at each other.

FARRAH MOAN: Nina was a tough cookie because you could tell that she'd probably been through so many different traumas in her life and she had a really hard time opening up to us or trusting any of us or really wanting to be friends with any of us. And I think she thought that we were all out to get her and get rid of her, which really wasn't the nature of Season 9 at all. But when people have grown up with certain experiences, sometimes they can get in their head. So it was super hard to get close to Nina. As the years have gone by and I've had my own fair share of the traumas and trusting people in this world, I feel like I totally understand where Nina was coming from now.

MICHELLE VISAGE: I'm sitting there going to Ru, "Uh, this is a lip sync, is she keeping that on? What's happening, Ru?" Ru is like, "I don't know." So there was some back-and-forth with Ru and me. I was like either this bitch doesn't know the words or she didn't have time to finish her makeup.

MICHELE "MEESH" MILLS: I think for the judges it definitely felt like an insult. For me, knowing the girls better, it was her delusional telenovela thing: I think I can sell this. I don't think I'm gonna be in the bottom so I'm not gonna learn the words, and then when I am, I think

I can sell this as a real shtick, like a thing. And I'm like, girl, you're being delusional, you cannot sell that.

RANDY BARBATO: It was a what-the-fuck moment. The producer in me was happy for it to play out a little but we're going to have to stop this and Ru is going to know how. It was bittersweet because we love Valentina. I thought it was a stunt. I thought something else was going to happen. But there were indications backstage that maybe she wasn't prepared. So at the beginning, there were moments that I was waiting for, I don't know, for butterflies to come out of her mouth or something.

TRINITY THE TUCK: We were all standing back there. We could tell she didn't take off her mask and we were thinking why is she not taking off her mask?

TOM CAMPBELL: Ru likes the music in the room really loud because he wants them to feel it. And Ru starts yelling, "Stop it! Stop everything!" We had never interrupted a lip sync before.

SHEA COULEÉ: It got to the first chorus, and the music stopped. I thought it was a technical difficulty because I had never seen them stop a lip sync. And then RuPaul goes, "Valentina, this is a lip sync, I need you to take that thing off your face." Valentina was clearly stunned and I just feel like it was an out-of-body experience. I don't feel like she even realized that she was saying it when she said, "I'd like to keep it on, please."

MICHELLE VISAGE: I was like oohhh no you don't! Girl, no!

ADORE DELANO: Ru looked like she wanted to snatch it off of her. That was some good TV!

CARSON KRESSLEY: You gotta give her credit. That do take nerve.

JOEY NOLFI: Pure. Cringe. Moment.

PEPPERMINT: I wasn't shocked because they basically communicated in one way or the other to Valentina that she could do anything she pleased. Obviously, Valentina was not quite prepared. I think her look was impeccable. And so I thought she was going to get by on her look. She had never been in the bottom. She knew what she was doing.

TRINITY THE TUCK: Well, what people didn't get to see is Ru had a moment that I had never seen before. She broke her character and she got really stern. I'm talkin' about really stern. Almost like the Tyra Banks "We were rooting for you, we were all rooting for you" moment. It was that intense. They edited a lot of that out. There was a long, awkward pause that they edited out.

SHEA COULEÉ: RuPaul literally was hands down on the desk, like, "So I stopped this lip sync for nothing?" And it was the longest pregnant pause that I had ever seen. She's looking at Valentina. Valentina is looking at RuPaul. Nobody is saying anything and RuPaul is like, "Hello, I am speaking to you!" I could tell Valentina was literally a pillar of salt. She just could not move.

PEPPERMINT: I was surprised to hear RuPaul challenge her or speak back to her because it felt like this was Valentina's house. But when Ru went in, she went in. She started banging the table. None of that's on the show. And I was like, ooof, they're gonna cancel this season.

VALENTINA: I remember RuPaul screaming at me. I remember being confused as to why the lip sync was stopped. Stop the music. Stop the music! I didn't understand why. I was having a mental breakdown and I was disassociated. That's kind of all I remember.

TRINITY THE TUCK: It was that intense. And we were all in the back, oh my god, oh my god! Where's the popcorn? It seemed like it dragged on for hours because it was so intense but in hindsight it probably was like a couple of seconds.

SASHA VELOUR: Ru could not believe that Valentina was not going to try. And I don't really think that was what it was for Valentina. She couldn't figure out how to click into gear. She wasn't a working drag artist before this so she didn't really quite know how to show up ready. She couldn't even deliver the barest minimum that was going to be more than enough, given how everything else had gone for her.

SHEA COULEÉ: And so RuPaul basically snapped her out of it and was like, you need to take that thing off your face.

VALENTINA: I do remember Nina actually looking over at me and being like it's okay, girl, it's okay, girl, just take the mask off, you're gonna be okay, you've got this, it's okay. I was just looking at her and I don't know if I was crying in between takes. I don't remember. It was a mess.

SASHA VELOUR: It felt completely in line with the many chances that I felt Valentina had been given. I was like, of course, she's getting a second chance at this lip sync even though she's messed it up the first time because everyone's always giving Valentina extra time and chances to do her work. But she couldn't even do it the second time. But to be given chances that no one else is given, and still mess up, that was a little bit disrespectful to the opportunity.

ADORE DELANO: I was at home, by myself, watching it, and I was like, what? First of all, how do you not know the lyrics? You can learn that song in three hours. What are you doing? On our season, we learned that shit within days. There was no excuse but I was still sad for her.

MICHELLE VISAGE: It turns out she didn't know the words. Listen, I get it. There's times when I'm performing that I forget the lyrics to my own fuckin' songs. It happens. But when that happened, I knew this moment was going to be iconic.

MICHELE "MEESH" MILLS: I had caught wind that she didn't seem to be practicing during *Untucked*. But sometimes that just means they know the song. But when she came out with the mask, I was hoping maybe she's gonna do this big reveal. She didn't. It was definitely a sort of live-tweeting kind of feeling where you're like wait, is this what's happening? Oh shit.

SHEA COULEÉ: Valentina was so shaken from the whole experience she could not bring herself back together. At the time I felt like she was giving up, too, like Charlie had. But I feel like there is a difference between giving up and feeling defeated and I felt like she just felt defeated. And that sucked. It sucked to watch her go out like that.

ADORE DELANO: I was actually heartbroken for her. A lot of the girls were like, that's what she gets. She should know the words, she was thinking she could get away with it because she's pretty. But I thought, that is humiliating. She didn't even have her makeup on from the mask down. I was like, ohhh girl, she doesn't even have the lips right now. I would be humiliated. So when she was crying, when she was going home, I was crying. I felt so bad for her because she was a top contender and I was a fan.

VALENTINA: I did not have time to learn it because we were preparing the things that we needed to prepare for the challenge. So we're doing that all day and filming all day. I went to my room that night and realized I didn't have the lyrics with me. I had lost the lyrics somewhere. So I had to stay up all night listening to the lyrics and writing them down, line by line. I practiced the song a couple times, to the point where I knew it enough and I had to go to sleep because I had to wake up at six.

TOM CAMPBELL: I am a huge Ariana Grande fan. I particularly loved the track "Greedy." It was never released as a single but it is everything a great lip sync song should be. And the song lyrics consist of like eleven words. I thought for sure the queens knew it, or could learn it during *Untucked*, which sometimes they do.

VALENTINA: When I perform, I do songs that I've been listening to for years and my body can interpret any little sound or any little flute or harp or break or whatever. I'm one with the music. When I'm in the bottom and all that stuff is happening, my mind is a blank. I'm having disassociation. I'm having some sort of mental breakdown where I'm disassociating.

RANDY BARBATO: She was a young queen without an enormous amount of performance experience and we knew that before she came in. We knew she was beautiful and we knew she was perfect and we wondered about her stage experience. There was always a feeling that we don't know how far she'll make it but we fell in love with her in casting and in every episode.

CARSON KRESSLEY: Who knew she'd be the bellwether and the fortune teller that we'd all be wearing masks two years later that were bedazzled? She was a trendsetter and we didn't even know it. She was a fashion Nostradamus.

JOHN POLLY: When we shot the finale in LA, so many fans showed up dressed as Valentina, both in her drag looks and out-of-drag look. The Latinx community just gravitated toward her, that magnetism that she has.

VANESSA VANJIE MATEO: She was so well received as a Latina diva. Before her, the fans didn't really feature the Latinx queens like that. But with Valentina, they were leaving hate for everybody. That was their queen.

VALENTINA: When I got eliminated, RuPaul told me I thought you had it in you to go all the way. I do remember that. I was hoping that RuPaul would tell me thank you so much, we loved you, you're really special. No, it was more like you really let me down. So I left with that energy, with that chip on my shoulder. I had lost so much weight coming back from the show. I lived in the dark for a month. I was really, really bad. It took a while for me to get speaking and talking and getting back in the groove, back to life. I felt like such a failure. I think the show has this ability to give you the opportunity to be big and great but it also has the ability to make you feel like you lost everything.

AJA: We had a group text. I left and then Farrah texted me when she got home and told me she was eliminated. Then the week after, nobody reached out. And we were like who got eliminated? The next person was Nina. When Nina responded in the group, she said Valentina went home last week and Nina told me the whole mask thing. I didn't see Valentina as perfect. I saw her as polarizing.

VALENTINA: When the show started airing, there were lines out the door to come see me perform in places, like in small towns that I never thought there was Latinos, there would be all these Latinos coming out to see me. Kentucky and all these random little places. I had blown up out of proportion. They would have to have security guards protecting me at the nightclubs because there was so many fans sneaking into the dressing rooms. I would perform and the fans would cry. It was really intense. And I got put on this pedestal so quickly, so fast, I was not prepared for it.

JOHN POLLY: We were shocked because I am pretty certain that we all imagined her in the top five or top four or whatever it was of the show because she was such a strong and magnetic personality. But there is no getting around that basic thing—you gotta know the song. This has been on for years. It was fully shocking for everyone involved.

VALENTINA: When I watched the episode, I had a show at Micky's that I was hosting so I was watching it in front of an audience watching me watch it. It was already rumored like crazy on Reddit that I was eliminated but people didn't want to believe it. The audience was so angry and they were angry at me but they loved me to death. It was so much attention happening at once that nobody prepared me for. I was truly broken inside but my career was going phenomenal. On paper, everything was great. In truth, it was a nightmare.

SHEA COULEÉ: The only reason that any tension developed between

Valentina and I was after the show had started airing and she had built this fan base that was unlike anything we had ever seen. She and I would talk on the phone after filming and I always remained neutral. But when her fandom really blew up, I wasn't really hearing from her as much. It sucked because her fans were being so nasty to me and I didn't even do anything to her. Things didn't even come to a head until our reunion when we had words. I still respected Valentina. I still thought that Valentina was really talented, but I felt like she was shutting down because everybody else was being cold to her. I felt like I got lumped in with everybody else.

VALENTINA: I think people forget that the queens were talking bad about me in interviews. They were all on tour together and on social media all the queens were speaking bad about me. I had never spoken badly against anyone online. Some of the backlash that the girls were getting was because they were going on the mic and talking about me at their performances and online.

SHEA COULEÉ: I saw her in Montreal and I saw her on her social media and we're all getting dragged and this girl is over here living for it. We are all getting dragged by our lace fronts and this girl just does not care. So much for sisterhood! At the time, we were like why don't you call off your fans? But now that I feel like we have all grown, there is nothing that she could have said that would have stopped them because if people want to be negative and nasty they will do that. They're just using Valentina as a scapegoat to be nasty.

VALENTINA: It was my fault for not acknowledging that kind of treatment from the queens and from my fans to the other queens. But at the time I was dealing with so much that I had to keep myself afloat. I didn't have the maturity to navigate how to process that back then, now I do. It takes experience and time to learn those things. And I have grown from that time and now I correct people and I hold people accountable, I hold myself accountable and I correct people.

VANESSA VANJIE MATEO: There was a lot of controversy with

Valentina. Did she do drag forever or just a few months? Was she congeniality or an evil bitch? Did she sew an outfit or use hot glue? It was
like a Mariah Carey situation where they are just in their fantasy. She
left an impression on the show and had the nerve to be like, bitch, I
ain't lip syncing. She was Covid before Covid. I think that's iconic.
Bitch, I live!

VALENTINA: I cannot regret having lived through the mask thing
because it's pretty much what people remember about me and some
people don't even have anything to be remembered for at all. It was a
pivotal moment in my life. You have highs and you have lows and that
was a low.

Sasha Velour and her bestie Shea Couleé, Peppermint, and Trinity the Tuck made it to the final four and expected for someone to
be eliminated before the finale. Instead producers introduced a new
lip-sync-battle format and one of the lip syncs became an instant
global sensation, sparking copycat performances in drag shows across
the world.

SHEA COULEÉ: They tricked us. They filmed everybody being eliminated. The last girl in line was Trinity. They asked us to come back
to the runway to refilm Trinity's. It had already been such a long day.
We were so tired. And RuPaul said there isn't a top three, there's a
top four. Bitch, what? RuPaul is sitting there all by herself at the table,
looking like God, so magical. The crew had cleared out and it just felt
so intimate. And RuPaul said he wanted to congratulate the four of us
for the work that we've done. All of the lights were turning off, and it
was such a magical end to such a wonderful experience because you
have someone that I've idolized since I was four years old looking at
me dead-ass and saying you're a star and I'm proud of you.

PEPPERMINT: I really had a hard time believing that I would get there
because my experience so far was just not a typical experience. My

trans-ness also positioned me differently. And so I had a lot of reasons to believe that they were gonna just take the opportunity to excuse me and they would be top three.

SASHA VELOUR: We've heard they've done this before and not done anything with it. So let's not get too excited but also, please.

TRINITY THE TUCK: This was new territory for the show. We didn't know what to expect so it was very nerve-racking leading up to the finale.

MICHELLE VISAGE: They all deserved to be there. In my opinion, it was anybody's game.

TOM CAMPBELL: As we were working on creative for the grand finale, Tim at VH1 asked, what if I can get you more money for lip syncs? Could you do something with lip syncs instead of original music? At first, I was hesitant, because I love our original songs. But we love to mix things up. Steven Corfe said we have four top queens this season, what if they did a lip-sync smackdown for the crown? Then we created the wheel. We were like, are we really gonna let the wheel decide who lip syncs against whom? We're like, yeah, we really are. It was this weird hand it over to the fates, like anyone can bring it and win.

RUPAUL: These are crafty kids. They are stunt queens. They know how to figure something out because they're smart so we have to keep them guessing. We have to keep them on their toes.

SHEA COULEÉ: We found out we were going to do lip-sync battles four days before the finale was filmed. Sasha and I were on tour together in London and Peppermint happened to be in London at the same time, so all three of us got together to have cocktails and were like so confused. Previously, they had written songs for girls around their personalities and conceptualized these numbers. But they sent the three of us the same four songs and we didn't get it. It wasn't until flying back from London that I found out it was going to be a battle situation. We had finished production nine months earlier.

TRINITY THE TUCK: I was not excited about this finale because I had made it to the end and in this new dynamic, what we did throughout the season doesn't matter. It's all up to a final lip sync. It crushed me as a competitor. I thought I did so well. I put in so much work. And now it has come down to two lip syncs. I didn't think it was fair. But it made for a hell of a finale.

SASHA VELOUR: I was excited. I was very happy. I felt like I was being thrown a bone honestly because I knew there was one special skill I had not shown anyone yet. I think I'm a good lip syncer and I was excited to do a real lip sync. In previous seasons, they had original song lip syncs. I wasn't that excited about that, to be honest. But the idea of getting to go all-out to a great Whitney Houston song or Britney or Christina, that was exciting.

SHEA COULEÉ: They encouraged us to think of clever things to do, like a reveal maybe. I remember being like I don't know what I would even do because I don't know what song I'm performing, I don't know what to prepare for. I had been confident because I'd won four challenges. But now we were going to be on an even playing field. So all I can do is try and outperform whoever I had to lip sync against. I've never been a reveal kind of person. That was never something that was part of my drag. If it was a reveal, it was only to take off a big, elaborate duster or coat to reveal a showgirl costume underneath.

MICHELLE VISAGE: We'd been doing the live finals for a while and of course in *Drag Race* fashion and in RuPaul fashion, they can't keep it the same. They always feel the need to up the ante and change it and do some fucked-up twist.

MICHELE "MEESH" MILLS: Jacqueline and I went to all the top four and we told them all the same speech, which was this lip sync is really important. Don't look at it like a regular lip sync. Sasha mentioned that he had some tricks.

SHEA COULEÉ: Rehearsal was basically for camera blocking, where we were going to walk and stand. It was mostly to learn our marks and where we needed to be for the camera angles and movement. But we didn't know who we were lip syncing against and we had to prepare all four songs.

PEPPERMINT: I made a pact with Trinity to break up Shea and Sasha. We couldn't allow Shea and Sasha to compete for the crown. One of them has to get eliminated. I don't know if there's [a] word for two ladies in a bromance, but the romance of the season was Shea and Sasha. That's the story that clearly was being written. And we were like, no, ma'am, we're gonna make them go against each other. And so we made a pact to pick each other if we got called.

SHEA COULEÉ: We did not know about these plans that were being conspired against us sisters. Trinity is a pageant girl. She knows how to play a game.

SASHA VELOUR: Peppermint and Trinity told me they thought the show would try to make Shea and me win our individual battles to put us up against each other. I think I was going to choose Peppermint, too. I thought that she was the most likely to go home fourth.

SHEA COULEÉ: I definitely wanted to perform "So Emotional." I love that song so much.

SASHA VELOUR: I didn't even have the rose petals until the day previous. It was so fast. I had the song list and then the song list changed and then I didn't have any ideas for the performances, I just had the costumes. And then it kind of all clicked together when they sent us "So Emotional" and the lyrics of the song clicked for me. It told the story of these increased emotions. And I brought my own personal emotions to it. I brought a little story about love that I imagined with someone giving someone a rose and how that gets twisted and changed and exaggerated. I was not going to do that exact performance if I had gotten "Stronger." I had different timing and I wasn't going to do all the reveals.

SHEA COULEÉ: I love me some Whitney Houston. I can go out there and I can serve Whitney and turn it and it'll be a fun, good kiki time.

SASHA VELOUR: I had everything planned out. I had a "Stronger" with rose petals, a "Stronger" without rose petals. I had a "So Emotional" with rose petals. But in a way I actually was hoping for "Stronger" because I felt like it was the more dramatic lip-sync song. But I think my performance for "So Emotional" was better so I feel like it was a blessing.

CYNTHIA LEE FONTAINE: The night of the filming of the finale, Sasha asked me to help with some packages that she had outside. I was all in makeup going into The Orpheum Theatre again in Los Angeles and I see these green containers with water and flowers and I said, "I'm not gonna ask but I am so proud of you." And she was like, "I love you and I know I can trust you so that's why I called you." I grabbed her hands and we prayed. It was a beautiful moment. I'm like, "I'm gonna let you go but I send you all of my positive energy and I love you so much."

TRINITY THE TUCK: I got to choose first and I picked Peppermint because I thought if I'm going to go home I want it to be against the lip-sync assassin of the season, which was Peppermint.

SHEA COULEÉ: In my interview, I made a joke about it because I literally did not think that that would happen. Lo and behold, Trinity picks Peppermint, forcing me to go against Sasha and I was like, oh that's not funny, though. That's not funny. I was joking. Now we gotta go against each other and this just sucks. This is my friend.

MICHELLE VISAGE: To me, that was Trinity's to lose and she did the reveal too quickly. She didn't make us wait for it and I was like what is going on? Peppermint was kinda slaying this. A lot of times anxiety, fear, endorphins, they all kick in and it's like shit, that's what happens.

CYNTHIA LEE FONTAINE: And then we have the first lip sync between Trinity and Peppermint. Peppermint had the double reveal with the wig and the dress. It was tough because...RuPaul said to the crowd, "Who should be the winner of this lip sync?" And people went crazy, like watching a Lady Gaga concert in a stadium. Everybody was saying both names at the same time, Peppermint and Trinity!

SHEA COULEÉ: I was shook, especially when it came to Trinity and Peppermint's lip sync. I felt in some ways that Trinity did outperform Peppermint, even though I love Peppermint and I think that she's sick'ning. We were watching from monitors. I did not know which way anything was going to go, so already going out there with Sasha I was trembling.

TOM CAMPBELL: Trinity the Tuck was considered to be a lip-sync assassin. Peppermint was great but we didn't think she was gonna win it. In the studio, it's always Ru's final decision. But when you're in front of a live audience it becomes a collective decision. Peppermint's timing and her reveals were like whoa! It was like this burst of applause and adulation washed over her. It was undeniable. Peppermint won. Right before he made the announcement, Ru came up to me and said, "Peppermint won, did you feel that?" and I said, "Yes, I did."

SASHA VELOUR: I thought Trinity did great. I was surprised that they chose Peppermint because I felt Trinity had done so well all season, so much better than Peppermint had, and it was a close lip sync. I also watched it on six different cameras. Now that I've seen it, I think Peppermint's full performance was better. I think Trinity was stronger at the beginning and then Peppermint was good the whole way.

TRINITY THE TUCK: I took the risk. I picked Peppermint, and she beat me. So I could leave the season knowing I did all I could do and I was beat fair and square.

SASHA VELOUR: When Ru declared Peppermint the winner, all bets were off for who the front-runners are. I think that affected Shea's and my dynamic going in 'cause it really felt like this is a complete open round. Now no one has an advantage.

PEPPERMINT: I heard the crowd go crazy. I think I knew she was doing rose petals because I saw her putting rose petals under her wig. I saw her over there at the mirror, and I was like, what's going on with her? I mean nobody's sticking things under their wig for no reason. It was epic. I heard about it before I saw it. When I saw it, it was beautiful and amazing.

MICHELE "MEESH" MILLS: When she came out, I thought, that's what she's wearing? We were all dying. We were rolling. It's like being in the audience at a bar, watching it, we were like, oh my god, oh my god! It was just so exciting to watch.

TRINITY THE TUCK: I was in the audience. They had me sit over right next to Valentina. The energy in the crowd when those rose petals came out of her wig I have witnessed in very few live performances. In that moment, you knew that bitch had won the season because she won that lip sync and there was no denying her. You could not crown anyone else. It was so incredible, unique, and innovative. It was ahead of its time.

SASHA VELOUR: Oh my god, I can remember every second of it. I can see the huge audience, Ru sitting completely still, so focused on us. And then the crowd's reaction, of course. I had really prepared a performance. I knew what I was going to do for every second and I just did it and tried to do my best. This is my favorite thing—to keep delivering the real emotion while touching my head and patting my stomach, or whatever I've decided to do for that number. That's my favorite thing about drag.

SHEA COULEÉ: When the petals came out of the gloves, I was like oh my god. You can't focus on them because you have to serve your own thing. But I kept wondering what the fuck does she keep throwing in the ground? I kept looking over my shoulder. As a performer, I was like fuck, because I knew those little shits looked slippery. And I like to boogie and dance and I'm screwed. At that point, I was dancing upstage and she was dancing downstage, closer to RuPaul, and I was like now that whole area is a danger zone at this point. I did not expect them out of the wig at all. No one did.

AJA: I honestly thought Shea was going to win. But I was curious to see what Sasha was going to bring. I had seen her perform but the people at home hadn't. I always knew Sasha to be very conceptual and very grand. When I saw Sasha's performance, I was drunk, but I was like, work bitch, this, this, this is drag. It was absolutely breathtaking. She deserved to win because that was iconic.

SHEA COULEÉ: What they did not show is that I slipped on the rose petals and I was like this is some *Showgirls*-ass sabotage. It was like a Marx Brothers sketch when someone slips on a banana peel and they're like, woo woo woo. From that point, I was so shook because everyone watched me just slip on these things and it took my confidence level even lower than it already was. It was in the basement at that point. Watching everyone cheer for the reveals, oh girl. It was my mom's birthday and she's sitting in the audience. I was thinking that this would be like past finales where they filmed multiple endings and my mom would at least get to sit there and watch me get crowned, even if it was just for TV. Instead, she was watching me getting my ass kicked by some white girl with rose petals to a Whitney Houston lip sync. It was not ideal. I feel like I'm really good at hiding those things while I perform but, on the inside, I was choking back tears. I was so upset.

FARRAH MOAN: I think we all had our opinions of who we felt deserved to win based on how they did while we were all there at *Drag Race*. But when it came to these new live lip-sync performances, Sasha

Velour just had done this monumental, historic performance that blew the entire world away. I remember seeing that first glove come off and seeing the roses fly in the air. To this day, I have traveled all over the world and seen drag queens do their own rendition of that performance. I mean it was the most talked-about thing that ever happened in *Drag Race* history.

CYNTHIA LEE FONTAINE: If you were at the theater, the energy was insane. People wouldn't stop screaming. People were crying.

MICHELLE VISAGE: It was epic. Holy shit. And the outfit she wore, all of it, amazing. Sasha is an artsy, smart queen.

CARSON KRESSLEY: The whole room was vibrating and there's five thousand people in there screaming and cheering and stamping their feet. And then the wig comes off and rose petals start fluttering out and the place went insane and the energy was off the charts. And we were just gagged beyond. That is the point where we're like okay, yeah, I think we know who won. We could feel the will to win in the room. It was all told in the intensity of her face and her body and then the rose petals coming out.

JOEY NOLFI: It's not like Sasha Velour was playing a character in that moment. She wasn't doing anything other than just being the artist that Sasha Velour is. Sasha's career after *Drag Race* is one of the most amazing things. There is nothing like a Sasha Velour show. It is conceptual art mixed with high art, mixed with drag and fashion and digital art. That lip sync is complete masterwork.

RUPAUL: She stayed true to her intellectual side because it was kinda meta. There was this certain other narrative that she was able to sell in the context of the song.

TOM CAMPBELL: During the grand finales, I am backstage. During commercials, I'll come out and brief Ru. Raven and I were in a curtained booth. The show is happening just feet away from you but we're watching on a small monitor. And it was just mind blowing. In Vegas odds, Shea Couleé, who is one of the best drag queens that God ever created, is gonna beat Sasha Velour, who is an amazing artiste and beautiful. We hadn't seen Sasha lip sync. Now we know that she brings her art perspective and her artistry to a lip sync. That is the most thrilling reveal lip sync.

FARRAH MOAN: Sasha Velour just really changed drag at that moment. I can't even believe I was in that audience. It was so monumental and iconic.

RANDY BARBATO: It was breathtaking! I remember the theater exploded. It was unbelievable. I ran out from the control room just to experience it because it was just so awesome and unbelievable. And, of course, it was also heartbreaking. It was so emotional. I get so emotional baby...every time...We all love Shea and then to see that happen and it was electric and unexpected and dynamic and stunt-y but stunt-y in an appropriate way. That was on point.

ADORE DELANO: I think I was on tour and someone sent me a video on my phone and I gay gasped. Ohhhh my god. I felt bad for Shea because she was killing it, too. But I was like, oh, it's over, girl, touchdown. It just shows you that you don't have to be the best dancer or do all these flips and kicks and shit. And Latrice points this out, too, although Latrice can kick, flip, and shit. Sasha deserved that win.

SASHA VELOUR: It was both a great memory for me but in that exact moment someone who I really cared about had had her dreams squashed. It actually was a very bittersweet performance. But I've gone on to perform it on my own and I try to have it be really great. People love to see it. I never would have come up with it without being forced to come up with something for "So Emotional." But I really enjoy performing it to this day.

SHEA COULEÉ: Sasha did such a beautiful job performing the song and it really was the reveal of the century. It just sucked because I felt like I was very unceremoniously dismissed and it felt like all of my accomplishments up until that point didn't really matter.

SASHA VELOUR: I had no idea what was happening. We were rushed backstage, changing costumes, I passed Peppermint, we hold hands and like swing around each other for a moment and then rush off to our mirrors and are touching up our lipstick. We had to walk underneath the whole theater 'cause they wanted us to enter from the audience. And I had this mask on so I couldn't see anything. It was definitely a case of both of us just diving into the deep of this wild experience and just going for it. I didn't have as much of a plan for the second lip sync other than to just deliver my best.

PEPPERMINT: Honestly, I was just exhausted. I can't even tell you how I felt in that moment. I knew that I wanted to give it my all. And honestly, my mind was with my mother because she was there and she wasn't in the best of health. I was just concerned for her and that was overwhelming at the time. I was not focused very much. I'm not making an excuse. Sasha did much better than I did.

TRINITY THE TUCK: Peppermint and Sasha's lip sync was just okay. I still think that Sasha beat her in that final lip sync. Neither of them lived up to that last moment. The petals won the season. That is probably one of the top three moments in *Drag Race* history.

SHEA COULEÉ: I had lost my dad and then a month later I lost my sister. I had thought that maybe all of that happened because I was meant to win *Drag Race* and experience the joy of this. And then this dream that I had had for so many years slipped through my fingers. And all of the people making fun of me, it was a lot to handle. Instead of using that moment to celebrate Sasha, the fandom weaponized it against me. It just brought out such nastiness in people and they used it as a means to bully me that it became hard to celebrate her achievement in doing something so wonderful because it always blew back on me in some way negatively. People would throw rose petals at me.

AJA: If somebody threw fucking rose petals at me, they would be getting these hands. I don't play that shit. I don't like that.

JOEY NOLFI: Something that you don't consider when watching Season 9 is that it was a traumatic thing for Shea because she put her heart and soul into the season and into that lip sync. To have it essentially rendered not good enough for her to continue because of this moment that so many other people are celebrating and heralding as one of the best things to ever happen on *Drag Race* could come at the expense of her emotions. I thought it was really brave of her to open up about that on *All Stars* 5.

SASHA VELOUR: It felt a little unprecedented because of the increased audience size from VH1. There were a lot of really hurtful, violent comments, scary comments. I got messages wishing happiness that my mother had died, wishing me death. I feel like the Black queens always have to bear so much more violent hate from the fans, though. But there was a lot of joy, too, because we were traveling the world and making money from it in a way we never thought was possible. To this day, I'll do a meet and greet for my show, *Smoke and Mirrors*, and someone will take their hat off and have rose petals inside. It's so cute. It all just worked in such a way to really make a huge impression in people's minds, I guess. And I love that. It's a moment of fantasy and fun, which is what drag is.

Chapter 10
SEASON 10

COMING OFF ITS BIGGEST SEASON, THANKS TO ITS NEW VH1 HOME, *RuPaul's Drag Race* kicked off in 2018 with a charismatic and dramatic cast that guided its tenth cycle toward introspection and reckoning. The season of sponges, pickles, and Tweety Bird couture had many highs and lows, as it crowned a young fashion icon and introduced a loud, cookie-loving queen who gave fans the ooh ah ah sensation with her spectacularly bizarre goodbye sashay. A decade in, the show was at a cultural crossroads.

Leading the charge into the werkroom, as promised, was Season 9 fan favorite Eureka and her high kicks; five New York queens, Monét X Change, Miz Cracker, Dusty Ray Bottoms, Yuhua Hamasaki, and Aquaria; Dallas pageant queen Asia O'Hara; The Vixen, who runs an all-Black show in Chicago called *Black Girl Magic*; lip-sync assassin Kameron Michaels; hilarious Kansas City queen Mo Heart; Indianapolis sweetie Blair St. Clair; Kalorie Karbdashian-Williams of New Mexico; LA super queen Mayhem Miller; and Vanessa Vanjie Mateo, drag daughter of Alexis Mateo.

The season kicked off with a fashion show attended by past contestants culminating in a ninety-nine-cent-store design challenge that Monét X Change has still not lived down. Along the way, the queens met Christina Aguilera and set off a pop-culture craze.

MONÉT X CHANGE: When Ru announced the drag on a dime challenge, I first went for the Barbie dolls that Vanessa used, but I realized there weren't a lot of them and couldn't conceptualize anything for that. So I saw an abundance of and a lot of different sponges. At first, my goal was to cover the entire dress in it but I was running out of material and time. So that's where it stops kind of abruptly and I just started putting them anywhere I could so that Michelle wouldn't tell me I was not embracing the materials enough. It was cute.

MICHELLE VISAGE: The sponge dress was hideous, let's be real. But that was also a drag on a dime challenge. She did what she gotta do. How she's making a thing out of it is beyond me, but god bless her.

ASIA O'HARA: It was terrible, absolutely terrible. Hearing her explanation of the idea that she thought she was conveying, I was like, you're not serious, you're not serious. Like that's supposed to be the dirt and that's supposed to be the sponge and this is supposed to be soap? You can't possibly think that that's reading. If the runway would have had a voice-over where she could have been explaining what was going on, then, yes, she could have made it work.

MIZ CRACKER: I love Monét, but Jesus. That thing was awful. But you know what? The world loved it. The world loved that thing. Her personality came through.

MO HEART: Trash. Just throw it in the trash, trash!

KAMERON MICHAELS: That was such an ugly dress. She cut up pieces of sponge and glued them. Innovative, yes. Ugly? Also yes. That's where I started loving Asia and why Asia and I get along so well because she was not going to let her live that down. She was not going to let her say that dress was cute. Shut up. Stop trying to convince us that that dress was cute. It's ugly. But then again, it becomes something funny and then it becomes something.

JOEY NOLFI: I hated it so much. I hated it so much. But I have since come to appreciate that it is in fact iconic because it is so bad and it's not meant to be loved, it is meant to be respected for being iconic and not good.

MONÉT X CHANGE: It did become its own thing. There are people who love to love it and people who love to hate it. It's a very polarizing look. Fans still wear sponge costumes to meet and greets or to the shows. For the past few years, people have been making these sponge cakes that look like yellow and green sponges and I get tagged in them literally dozens of times daily. I love it, I love it, I love it. I think it's fun. I think it's so funny that something I did in one episode of the show has lasted so long and become such a thing.

MAYHEM MILLER: I was originally working on an outfit that was made out of scouring pads. And as the day ended, I looked at it and I was like this is ugly. We all got in the van, I got in my room, and I just sobbed. I can't believe it took me all these seasons to get here and I'm going to be going home first. So I cried myself to sleep, woke up that next morning, and that was the day of the runway. I started thinking about my mom and what would she say to comfort me. She would lay her hands on me and pray with me and make sure that I was cool. The next day, I walked into the werkroom and we had an hour before we had to get ready to go out there. What's left in the fucking corner that no one wanted? An umbrella, some gardening gloves, and trash bags. I took all the gloves that were left in the corner and I shaped it out of that. When RuPaul said I won, I was a wreck.

MO HEART: I should have won. I had the card dressss. Iconic. They still talk about the card dress. Ain't nobody talking about Mayhem's trash bag dress, sis. They were like, oh it's fashion. No, bitch, I gave y'all hoes construction. I was so gagged. And then RuPaul goes, step your pussy up. Oh bitch, I was ready to throw my shoe then, girl, ugh.

MONÉT X CHANGE: The girls just didn't get it. And now looking back, it was a bit of a stretch. But I am grateful that it was good enough to keep me from the bottom two.

After RuPaul announced that Sponge Queen, Mo Heart, and a few other queens were safe, she told the cast she was adding another queen to the competition—Farrah Moan, Eureka's bestie from Season 9. "Wait a minute, Farrah Moan got some work done!" Mo observed from the back of the stage.

FARRAH MOAN: They flew me from New York DragCon straight to LA. I only had a day to think of what look I was going to wear. They didn't tell me what I was doing. They basically just told me that I was going to be meeting the celebrity guest judge and they had me in a dressing room for like four hours by myself, not knowing what's going on. I remember turning the corner and seeing this pink wig and I was like, who the fuck is this going to be? It was Christina Aguilera. When she said, hi, Farrah, I gasped for air so big that my blazer button popped and my jacket flew open and exposed my little boy nipples. So they made me go back and refilm my reaction to meeting her. I couldn't even breathe and I was supposed to walk in there like I didn't already just meet her. She laughed so hard when the thing popped open and she was like, could you imagine if that happened to me? It would be such a big problem. She said she saw my photos from my first DragCon that had gone viral.

KAMERON MICHAELS: I thought it was Farrah Moan the whole time. We're standing by [the] wall and this person walks out. I think I was deep in line so I wasn't even next to the runway when she walked out. I had no idea it wasn't Farrah Moan until she sang into the microphone. Christina was the first artist I ever performed in drag. She was the first song I ever did in drag. I got to sit in *Untucked* next to this celebrity star from my childhood and tell her that one of her songs was the first song that I ever performed in drag. So that was a monumental moment for me.

EUREKA: That was mind-blowing. I really thought it was Farrah because I didn't have my contacts in and I'm nearsighted, like the focus goes out. But I looked down at her feet and I was like that ain't Farrah Moan. She was not wearing Louboutins. Farrah has this little Barbie foot and thick legs, and I knew in that moment she'd be in Louboutins. I looked down at her feet and I said, that's not Farrah, y'all, I know it's not Farrah. I love Christina Aguilera. Every gay boy loves Christina, but she was not gonna top Gaga for me. I already was spoiled because I had my little Gaga moment.

MIZ CRACKER: I was slow on the uptake and I honestly thought it was just Farrah Moan. Even after they said it was Christina Aguilera, I still thought it was Farrah Moan. The first number that I ever did was Christina Aguilera.

FARRAH MOAN: That was one of the best days of my life. She gave me such an amazing pep talk, and from that point on, her team reached out to me on multiple occasions to do promotional stuff with her. I got to announce her onstage at LA Pride. I got to perform onstage with her at New York Fashion Week. I got to be on *Watch What Happens Live* with Andy Cohen with her. She sent me an exclusive Polaroid that she sent to ten of her fans. I got to perform onstage with her at Caesar's Palace in Las Vegas. I've gotten to take a shot of Patrón with her. Christina was everything and more than I ever could have hoped.

It didn't take long for two New York queens, Aquaria and Miz Cracker—friends or frenemies?—to go at it over their alleged similar looks, and for Chicago queen Vixen to call out Aquaria.

AQUARIA: We had done quite a few gigs together over the short time that I was working in New York and there was so many instances where I would do something and two weeks later a friend would send me a picture saying something like, didn't you just do this sliced neck thing last week but in blue and now she's sliced neck but in red?

Especially if other people are bringing it to your own attention, it's kind of odd.

MONÉT X CHANGE: Cracker and Aquaria had been known to wear similar things in New York but they were friends. What was confusing for me was seeing how it became such a negative thing because they both actively participated in painting like each other and wearing similar costumes and working together in New York. They have photo shoots together painted the same way, wearing the same hair, the same outfit. I was like I don't have time for this. I'm worried about these fucking sponges. I can't give y'all's drama energy when everyone knows this to be true.

MICHELE "MEESH" MILLS: It was a real thing that was going on social media before *Drag Race*. I know the whole story from both sides but both sides are a little different so you have to decide for yourself. Miz Cracker claims that her and Aquaria became friendly. Miz Cracker was more established at the time than Aquaria, but Aquaria had her whole little New York fashion tribe. They were friendly and Cracker would help her out with things. And then one day it was like that junior high thing where all of a sudden they're not your friend anymore. She felt very hurt by it. And then, according to her, she did some things that were kind of similar but she sugarcoats how that happened exactly. Aquaria's take is that they did know each other but weren't really friends. And that Cracker did do some looks that were very similar to hers but wasn't going to say anything about it.

KAMERON MICHAELS: I wasn't paying that much attention to whether they looked alike or not. I get maybe the eyebrows that day looked similar, but I don't know.

MO HEART: I was very confused. I didn't see it. I was very whaaaat? I didn't care. Let these little white hoes fight.

EUREKA: Cracker looked up to Aquaria a little bit for her talents and probably saw she was fierce and wanted to be fierce, too, and she might've done it subconsciously.

BLAIR ST. CLAIR: I stayed out of the drama. I don't want to go through this competition unhappy. I wanted to remain drama free.

MAYHEM MILLER: I think it's one of those things where queens do not like being compared. We hate that shit. I don't like when people do it with me with other people and I'm pretty sure the same is with other girls. Your art is your art, your person is your person, and it's an insult when someone says oh you're doing this because someone else did it or you're copying that person. It's an insult.

AQUARIA: On day one, one, it's pissing me off that everyone is coming after this story and demanding an answer. First of all, I think we can look around the room and know that I am going to be staying here for a little longer than day one, and especially, if this bitch looks like me I hope she's staying here a little longer than day one, too. It's the premiere episode. I think that obviously all just got blown out of proportion. Did I think she was doing the exact same makeup look I was doing? Meow.

EUREKA: When Cracker wasn't in there, Aquaria was talking about it with everybody, how she was annoyed that Cracker had the same makeup as her. And then when Cracker came in there, Vixen called it out and Aquaria didn't want to just call her on it in front of everybody. She didn't want to make it a thing. She was just venting. And then it just became a big thing.

MAYHEM MILLER: What had happened was I was sitting there with Vixen on one side of me and Aquaria on the other. I was always in the middle of all the fucking drama. The energy in that corner was strong. I just remember Aquaria mentioning how in New York people would compare them and say they look alike. Aquaria had said something about Cracker copies these things from her.

KAMERON MICHAELS: I didn't care. This is why I skated through the whole season with no drama. Every fight that happened that I wasn't involved in, I just wanted popcorn because I didn't care. It had nothing to do with me. It just didn't matter. But now I understand that I forgot I was on a television show. I just came to do drag. I forgot that it's not just drag. It's a TV show. This is why I did not succeed in the werkroom environment—because I didn't get that those interactions were important. I was like, who cares?

ASIA O'HARA: I didn't know how serious it was. I probably shouldn't get involved because I don't know their dynamic in New York. There were a lot of New York girls there, obviously. So I thought it'll be interesting to see how this plays out.

AQUARIA: I wasn't trying to beat around any sort of bush, necessarily. When I was without Miz Cracker and people were asking me questions, I'm like get off my back, here's your short answer. I'll worry about this on episode 3 because I'm not going anywhere. She's not going anywhere. Especially if y'all are starting a story, I'm here for a minute now unless I fuck up. It was definitely nothing personal. It is clearly some sort of elephant in the room. So it will be spoken about but I don't want to do it at the end of this long-ass day or while we're sitting here, having a good time. Let's worry about this when shit gets boring.

BLAIR ST. CLAIR: What I remember first and foremost is that I thought Vixen was super nice. To this day, still a very close friend of mine. She also knew that it was a TV show and was willing to put drama forward.

MAYHEM MILLER: I think Vixen was trying to have some fun because it gets boring in that room sometimes.

ASIA O'HARA: I understood where Aquaria was coming from and where The Vixen was coming from. The Vixen was trying to make everything completely transparent. And Aquaria said she didn't come here to talk about my feelings. So I understand where both of them were coming from. And when there's drama, so to speak, a lot of times you're just excited that it doesn't have anything to do with you.

MONÉT X CHANGE: Drag queens are already dramatic and narcissistic people. When you put that in the vacuum that is the show, emotions and feelings get heightened. So when someone says one thing, you don't have a normal reaction like you would in any other situation. Your emotions are on ten because you feel like everything that you do can be in danger of you going home and shattering your dreams of winning this show that you have too much stake in. We were talking about it in *Untucked*, so Vixen was just saying what she'd heard there. And to be fair, that's Aquaria's business if she was ready to talk about it but it's also The Vixen's business to say what she heard. So I don't think anyone was wrong. It was just a calamity of truths happening in that moment.

MIZ CRACKER: I don't recall. Whatever it says in the show is what happened.

Mama, the drama! Time for some laughs now. And some cookies.

VANESSA VANJIE MATEO: When I was in the bottom two, I didn't know what I was about to get into, especially being a super fan of the show. It happens so quick and it's just the craziest feeling. It's weird. I thought I knew Kalorie 'cause I'd seen her before, so I was thinking I could beat her or something. I don't know what I was thinking.

RUPAUL: Vanjie did that death drop and her shoe flew off and I thought, oh, I wanted to keep her just for that.

MIZ CRACKER: I felt so bad for Vanjie because backstage I told Vanjie I thought she might have won. This was the greatest outfit. This is so good. And then when she got out there and she just got reamed, I was like, I don't have any taste at all.

VANESSA VANJIE MATEO: The whole thing happened like a blur. When RuPaul says to sashay, I was thinking, is this for real? Or are they gonna say something else? I was waiting there. And then I thought let me just do what I'm supposed to do. At this moment, you do your exit.

EUREKA: I was really excited about Miss Vanjie because I just felt like I connected with her well. She was very supportive, she was like, girl, I understand you, I'm loud, too.

VANESSA VANJIE MATEO: I was just walking to the back and I'm like, well I know I'm supposed to say something or do something. So I turned around and started saying my name. I kept saying it because I was like, maybe they didn't hear me, let me make sure. I don't know what I was thinking. I just kept saying the name and doing like a little dance. "Miss Vanjie, Miss Vanjie," I don't even know. I was trying to make it cute but at the same time I was devastated. It was just the greatest fuckin' blur. It was just weird. Even watching it, I'm like what was goin' on?

MO HEART: By the time that last Miss Vaaanjie came out, I was confused to be perfectly honest.

KAMERON MICHAELS: It wasn't as iconic as it has become. It was fucking weird. We were like why is she awkwardly just repeating her name and walking backward chanting her own name as she's leaving? I don't get it.

BLAIR ST. CLAIR: Awkward! So awkward. Every single one of us looked at each other like, what the hell did she say? Because her name isn't really Vanjie. It's Vanessa Vanjie Mateo. Everyone has always called her Vanessa. No one ever called her Vanjie. She left saying Vanjie, Vanjie, we were all like, what is she saying?

ASIA O'HARA: I don't think any of us thought much of it. I mean, it was kind of weird, but it took some days for it to be funny to us because just randomly somebody would say it and then Ru would say it. At that moment, it wasn't like, oh my god, this is the funniest thing that ever happened in the history of television. It felt awkward. When you're filming something, you don't hear a laugh track or anything so you don't really know. And sometimes something is funny to you in your head but you don't know if it's funny to everybody else and you don't want to just laugh because it's like, what is she laughing about?

MONÉT X CHANGE: It didn't click in about how weird it was. It just felt sad. She's walking backward just saying her name, like she's so disoriented because she's going home. It's just sad.

MICHELLE VISAGE: It was so awkwardly uncomfortable. That why we started laughing. I've known Ru for nearly thirty years. We finish each other's sentences. We are in each other's brains. So when Vanjie went out dressed like that, walking backward, saying that stupid thing she said there or four times, Ru, being funny, she goes, "I'm not sure I got that, what did she say?" Because she repeated herself so many times. So I looked at Ru and said, "Oh Miss Vanjie, Vanjie," 'cause I knew she would crack up. And the rest is history.

MAYHEM MILLER: I remember thinking she was drunk. This drunk bitch don't know what she's doing, she's drunk. She's saying Miss Vanjie, just stumbling backward. She don't give no fucks at all. In my head, I was laughing, I was like, this bitch is so funny. Ru was laughing so hard. I was like, oh my god this is definitely going to be a moment because if she is laughing that hard and the rest of us are giggling this is going to be something that everyone's going to remember and sure enough everyone did. I didn't foresee it being that big, but as it was happening I was like, oh my god, what the fuck?

BLAIR ST. CLAIR: I don't think she was drunk at all.

MIZ CRACKER: It's all a blur for me but I just remember thinking, what the hell is going on? Is she going to leave or not? Nobody took much note of it in the moment.

BLAIR ST. CLAIR: As the days progressed and more people kept saying it, it became a running joke and that's when I thought, okay, the Miss Vanjie thing might catch on. But I never thought it would be the phenomenon that it was.

KAMERON MICHAELS: I think RuPaul's reaction is honestly what sold that into existence. Ru and Michelle kept making it a thing so we all just made it a thing. And because she was loud and she was boisterous, and fun, we all love Vanjie. We knew that you wanted to see more of her and we wanted her to stay longer because she is such a fun energy to have around. They knew exactly what they were doing making that a thing and then of course giving her redemption.

CARSON KRESSLEY: I wasn't there for that, but when I saw it, it did not strike me as anything. I know from watching the show and the clips and the memes that it tickled Ru to death and then that tickled Michelle. If I was there, I'd probably be over on the side going, what? What's so funny? I don't get it. But it became a cultural phenomenon and I still don't get it, but I'm glad it's fun and I'm glad everybody loves it.

AQUARIA: She was ridiculous since day one. I would venture to say even before we were supposed to meet people we could hear her screaming in our little quarantine rooms or whatever. Was that called quarantine? It may have been. She was so ridiculous on camera, off camera. Not that she deserved to stay, per se, but we were like this stupidity deserves a little more time on the TV so the more we can remind the world of it, the better.

MONÉT X CHANGE: We didn't really get to know Vanjie a whole lot but the little bit that we did get to experience her, we all did really like her. For obvious reasons, the whole world thinks it's funny. We thought it was funny to us because we were there and we experienced it in the moment. But the show did a good job of giving everyone that same feeling that we got being there in the room with her.

EUREKA: It was a cute moment. It was funny. But it was also kind of emotional. In person, it wasn't as comical because you could feel her heart. It became more of a viral thing on social media and stuff but in person it was actually kind of an emotional moment because you could tell she was very emotional and a little upset by going home first. That's a hard place to go home at.

She had such a lovable energy that even us queens were saying Miss Vanjie throughout the season. It was a thing very quickly. And we all missed her immediately because she just had this energetic, very genuine, and not giving a shit if anyone felt like she was loud. That's actually very genuine and very endearing to people too, especially in that kind of situation where everybody is sizing each other up and giving you the fake smiles and I love you.

AQUARIA: It's just as funny and silly as I think we all tried to share on the TV. Besides Shangela coming out of her box, this was the first time that that first out really made a name for themselves in such a monumental way. I don't think we were as gagged at her saying Miss Vanjie as Ru. But I couldn't wait to watch this episode and when I did, that dumb shit she was saying was funny. Let's say that shit.

MANDY SALANGSANG: There's something about Ru recognizing something in someone and laughing at things that maybe don't strike us right off the bat. I don't know that I recognized in the moment that that's what she'd become as she was exiting the stage on that night. But I knew she had that potential in all of our casting tapes and conversations and moments shared up to that point. I knew that she was somebody who would touch people. She's a character, she's got something special that just connects with people, and she is a riot.

TOM CAMPBELL: That is a moment that could have happened and ended. I almost forgot but it became an inside joke. I thought it was weird. We all kinda giggled. But I did not anticipate that it would be the meme of the year. Gavin Newsom came to the set when he was running for governor of California because Ru agreed to do a video with him. And we said at the very end, you should just say Vaaanjie. Miss Vanjie. And he's like, what is that? We explained it and he did it. I care about you, California, and you should vote for me. *Vaaanjie. Miss Vaaanjie.*

374 Maria Elena Fernandez

MAYHEM MILLER: I think it's a testament to the fact that when you are your authentic self, that's when magic happens, not when you make it happen. And I think a lot of people go into the show wanting to make themselves stand out and make moments and it's like magic moments just happen because it's magical and its organic.

MO HEART: She was crunchy when she came in, girl. I was like, ohh, Alexis Mateo let you wear this outside of the house day one? Ohhh girl. She was very much a truck driver in high heels that day, okay? But that voice, iconic. What's for you is for you. That girl went home and beat herself up. I went home first and I'm Alexis Mateo's daughter. And did not know God said I'm about to bless you, so I'm gonna set you up.

The show aired, episode 1, gold. Vanjie, Vanjie, Vanjie, Vanjie, Vanjie. Boom. Who knew? You're like, bitch.

EUREKA: I remember getting phone calls from her when we were still waiting for the season to get announced and she was really emotional and really beside herself because she felt like she let her family down and herself down. She was really in a negative space and really emotional about it and just hopeful that she would still get gigs and stuff. It couldn't have happened to a sweeter person. I don't blame her, she's like get these cookies.

MICHELE "MEESH" MILLS: When we got into post, we knew this had been a continued beat throughout the season, where Ru would bring up Miss Vanjie or Michelle would say it all the time. We thought it was amazing and fun.

LATRICE ROYALE: You get on *Drag Race* and you are a hint of likable and your life is gonna change. Look at Vanjie, you can go home first and still be the bitch they talk about the entire season. She was like a deer caught in the headlights. But I knew right away the kids are gonna eat this up. Right before the show went off, the memes were popping up all over the internet. "Miss Vaaanjie!"

MICHELLE VISAGE: The first person to go was the biggest star of the season, Miss Vanjie.

VANESSA VANJIE MATEO: At first, I was really kind of embarrassed. I hated watching the lip sync. I hated watching the whole thing. But with everyone being so nice and showing me so much love and making memes about it—the Simpsons and all that—I was just trying to make the most of it and reposting every meme. It kept going throughout the whole season and I was just embracing it.

MAYHEM MILLER: Maybe I should have went home first because that bitch went viral and fucking got a million followers in two weeks. So goddamn it! Shit! I should have worn the first outfit.

VANESSA VANJIE MATEO: I remember we did DragCon and RuPaul pulled me up onstage when he did his speech to close out DragCon. He was laughing and he wanted me to do it. And I was just like, bitch, I'm gonna walk backward everywhere. I will be backing up to every event. I'm gonna back up into the bank. I will back up to the gig, I will walk backward everywhere I go. I'll run into things but I'm gonna continue doing it. If this is what the ticket is, I'm gonna take it and run with it. I was a walking meme.

As the world rejoiced over new icon Miss Vanjie and her cookies, Aquaria and Vixen fought in the third episode over a wig. And more.

AQUARIA: There are obviously plenty of things happening beyond what we get to see on the TV. I definitely would not like to see the uncut version of *Untucked* but while The Vixen is trying to discuss this very important issue with me, we have Dusty over here looking like a cockatoo talking about oh, I skipped a gig with her to go shopping or some stupid shit. I don't know if that's in the episode or not. I was just feeling extremely weighed down and I'm seeing all the pieces falling together on top of each other over the past couple of episodes. Sigh. I know this is going to end up with all these people feeling hurt for some fuckin' reason.

EUREKA: The wig that The Vixen wore, I actually gave to Mo and Mo gave to The Vixen. Randomly. Aquaria was bitter because she felt like she should have won. That's the root of it.

BLAIR ST. CLAIR: The strategy in me was saying oh I'm so glad Aquaria is upset because she is good competition and if she gets knocked off her game that is really good for me. I viewed this whole thing as so ridiculous, so juvenile, just stupid. And I remember thinking, you guys can continue bickering while I'll continue to use this time to do my makeup and look beautiful.

MAYHEM MILLER: I was like, why is there drama? We are supposed to be here showing how fierce we are and why are we fighting? I was Oprah, all right, you guys, let's just smile and just have fun and enjoy this experience and everyone wanted to just argue and fight. These bitches are crazy.

KAMERON MICHAELS: I never wanted to have an opinion. I stayed out of it because it had nothing to do with me. And that's just me as a person. If the fight has nothing to do with me, I'm not throwing in my bet. I'm not jumping in the ring. I was an observer and I kept my opinions to myself.

ASIA O'HARA: I consider myself a good judge of character and when you're around The Vixen, you know that she's not a spiteful person. She's not a mean person. She's not there to pick fights. Vixen's one of the few people that is brave enough to talk about things that a lot of people are not comfortable talking about or bringing up situations or issues that a lot of people are not comfortable bringing up. But she's not a spiteful person. There's a method to her madness and there's a reason behind everything that she says and does. And I definitely think that The Vixen, Eureka, and Aquaria represent a group of people

AND DON'T F&%K IT UP   377

in our country. And those conversations are probably better had on

in our country. And those conversations are probably better had on television because everyone will hopefully see themselves in one of them but will also see the other side of the coin and maybe have a better understanding how the things that they say or do, or the things that they don't say or do, affect other people.

MIZ CRACKER: I still don't understand. I mean, I thought we were supposed share our resources when we were in the werkroom, we were supposed to help each other. And so I thought it was fine for her to have a borrowed wig.

AQUARIA: I think most people understand that I was not crying because I was trying to make someone feel bad for me. I want to be your friends and now I've got all y'all thinking I'm crazy.

ASIA O'HARA: At this point, I don't really know Vixen or Aquaria that much but I probably know The Vixen a little bit more. Generally speaking, if you're having a conversation and someone starts to cry, then you are the bad person. And sometimes that's accurate and a lot of times that's not accurate. But it's one of those things that definitely mirrors situations in our social society as a whole.

BLAIR ST. CLAIR: Aquaria was very intimidating. Very quiet. She wasn't really talking to anyone else. She kind of felt like it was the werkroom against her. And instead of using that to hurt her, she actually was able to use that energy to be like, well I'll show you guys. It actually helped her.

ASIA O'HARA: The Vixen's from the South Side of Chicago. She's had a very difficult journey in drag just in her city. And she is someone that has always had to work twice as hard in her city to get where she is in comparison to other people that are not queens of color. She's had a difficult journey in drag and probably in life as a whole. Eureka is from a small town in the South. She's always been a bigger person and so she has a large personality to match. And then Aquaria is young, she's talented, she's pretty, she lives in New York, she has nice clothes, she's from a good family. They represent a lot of people in this country between the three of them and so I think that those conversations are important to have because people will hopefully understand another piece of the puzzle or another side of the coin.

A week later, it was Eureka who jumped into the fray with The Vixen, while fan favorite Monét X Change landed in the bottom with her friend Dusty Ray Bottoms after a three-part ball. Monét's performance of Nicki Minaj's "Pound the Alarm" gagged the dragverse and took its rightful spot in the top lip syncs of the franchise.

EUREKA: We came into the werkroom, skipping together and shit. If you watch it back, we were arm in arm. She ended up wanting to be on my team for the challenge. But when I started doing well, it turned around.

ASIA O'HARA: We're all stuck here together, and they're not getting along and they're probably going to fight until the day one of them leaves. We're not all going to get along. We're not all going to be best friends. And it's another one of those moments when it's like this really doesn't have anything to do with me. But I'll let them duke it out.

MAYHEM MILLER: Once again, I'm sitting there like why? Why are these people crazy? Why are we doing this again? It sucked because I knew Eureka coming into it and we were cool and then I got to know The Vixen and we were cool. I am in the middle of this shit and I don't like being in the middle of it because I want everyone to get along. I want it to be a good time. I'm sure people at home love it because it's just some extra drama to watch. But you're like, what the fuck?

BLAIR ST. CLAIR: By that point in time, I had befriended both Eureka and The Vixen but I was closer to Vixen. And we had definitely created a friendship, a bond, and I felt really bad because I felt two friends of mine were at each other's throats and I didn't really know where I stood and I was just real uncomfortable with that. Because that was real drama, it wasn't just made for TV. They were actually really upset with each other.

MIZ CRACKER: I think that people were building a narrative. By today's standards, the way that Vixen expresses herself is not too loud. The issues that she was talking about then are the issues that we are struggling with today at top volume.

MONÉT X CHANGE: I was onstage 'cause I was in the bottom two. So when we came back, the girls didn't even allude to how dramatic it was. They just said, oh yeah, girl, they had an argument, girl, they're crazy. When I saw it on TV, that was the first time I genuinely got the gravity of it. I didn't even realize that they went at it like that. So watching it on TV was so crazy.

EUREKA: People ran with it and she ran with it, saying that like I went in and poked the bear to make her react that way. Girl, nobody can make you act any way. You have to be responsible for yourself. I had to be responsible for how I acted in that argument. I acted a damn fool. And I take full responsibility for that. I have apologized to her in the past and we have squashed it since. So this is definitely in the past.

MONÉT X CHANGE: I still don't believe mine was the worst garment. The Vixen had a way worse garment than mine but that is neither here nor there. We have moved on, most of us have. I was confused to be in the bottom but I thought this is my moment to make a statement. And it worked out for me. It is a super memorable lip sync. There are over a hundred lip syncs in the vault and to be one of the top ones that people talk about and remember and still tag me in to this day, I am happy that I was in the bottom to have that experience and that moment in *Drag Race* history.

MIZ CRACKER: That has to have been the most horrifying massacre, like just murder. Monét does Nicki Minaj as a staple of her work and Dusty does the Rolling Stones and Aerosmith and Queen. Before we went out onstage, she was just like, I can barely remember the words. We were like, you're going to do fine, you're going to do fine but we knew she was just going to get clobbered. She knew it, too. And she got clobbered.

KAMERON MICHAELS: Monét faked her split! When a girl does something like that, and then she gets to carry it with her to every fucking club after the show was off, it's so cool. The crowd lived. Like us. But Dusty's was good, too. She did the whole shaking thing and was cute and fun. That was a great lip sync.

RONAN FARROW: Monét's lip sync where she does the fake-out death drop is maybe my favorite individual lip sync on the show. I mean there is a lot of competition in that space but it's really memorable. She is so good.

MONÉT X CHANGE: Unless it involves a prop, anything I do in lip syncs is in the moment. It's how I feel in the song. There's only so many times you can do a split before it's boring. You have to push beyond that and tap into the true entertainer that you are to make these people want to come back and see the same show next week and not give them the same shit.

In one of the season's most poignant moments, Blair St. Clair revealed on the main stage she was raped in college and has never told her family about it. RuPaul advised her to consider it her declaration of independence before sending her home.

BLAIR ST. CLAIR: We were in *Untucked* and they showed my mom's video message to me. I was like, okay, I know I'm going home, I have accepted it. I knew if I was lip syncing against Miz Cracker or Vixen I wasn't going to be as strong as a lip syncer. The runway look was Hats Incredible and Ross was saying he didn't know enough about me and that I'm delicate. So I said there's a lot that's gone on in my past and I feel like the delicate things bring me joy and happiness because they make me feel safe and they make me feel like my youth has been rejuvenated. A lot of this had to be cut out to be able to get to the meat of it. I feel like my innocence and my youth was stolen from me and I'm trying to reclaim that in my drag today.

EUREKA: It was beautiful and it was emotional. I was really appreciative of her opening up like that. Because she saw herself going home, I think she really just wanted to take this last chance to open up about it because it was important for her to get it out. It was like watching a really beautiful, therapeutic moment for somebody. It was empowering to be honest. It really gave me a lot of strength just to watch her open up like that.

BLAIR ST. CLAIR: I think it was such an emotional release to actually talk about it for the first time. It had been this thing that had been building up and pressured within me for almost two years at that time. I had talked about it with two friends and even then I couldn't get all of it out. I feel like my heart knew when I was ready to talk before my brain did. After I was eliminated, I realized, holy shit, I just talked about that and that is going to be on television. And then I went through this whole spiral of depression and thinking everyone's going to know about my life, everyone's going to know all this stuff about me, my parents don't even know. It was a really emotional time.

ASIA O'HARA: I knew there were things with Blair that she was dealing with below the surface because we got in drag next to one another. But I didn't want to pry. It was sad to see Blair go because Blair was one of the people I just knew in my heart was going to make it all the way to the end. At this point, we consider each other family, we've been around each other all day every day. You never know what somebody is dealing with or what battles people are going through so it's just like a reminder that you don't know what's going on inside people's heads.

KAMERON MICHAELS: It's an emotional moment because it's so brave of her to share something like that not only with the people that are in the room but knowing that the whole world's going to see it. That is a big moment for her.

BLAIR ST. CLAIR: I, as a rape survivor at that point in time in my life, felt guilty for being raped because I thought that it was my fault because I put myself in danger by going to a college party, I was under the influence, and I had not gone through any therapy for it, whatsoever. I didn't understand that that moment was the beginning of my healing journey. Now I've been able to travel all over and talk with sexual assault survivors and thank everybody. The outpouring of love that came around it was pretty amazing.

MIZ CRACKER: It was a surprise and it was an honor to be there with her. It was really nice to be able to hold her hand and to be at her side for that. Blair and I would be there for each other like that for a long time after. When she went home, that was very sobering.

Catchphrase queen Mo Heart ended up on the bottom after playing Congresswoman Maxine Waters on Snatch Game. A fan favorite, Mo won the hearts of viewers when she opened up about her internal struggles as a Black gay man and disclosed that she was raised in a religious background where she was encouraged to "pray the gay away." After a disastrous lip sync against The Vixen—she forgot the words, took off her wig, and botched a cartwheel—Mo went home.

MO HEART: It should've been Vixen as Blue Ivy and Asia as Beyoncé. Mother-daughter battling it out. They were both the weakest links. But that was not my week. I had literally stayed up to three in the morning trying to sew that mermaid costume. I'm not gonna lie, my costume was weak. Very, very, very weak. I think that that's what landed me there. And I was so exhausted so I didn't learn my song. It just really hurts because I know I could've went further.

MONÉT X CHANGE: Mo can come out in a handkerchief and a baseball cap for her look and she doesn't think that she's in the bottom. She is always so sure that she's not in the bottom, which I think is why she didn't rehearse. She doesn't think that way. That is not a thing for her. That does not exist in her space/time continuum. The cartwheel, oh god, that was all very painful.

MIZ CRACKER: At the time, I heard the story of how hard Mo had had to work because she always told us that she didn't have any money before *Drag Race* and so she had to spend all of her time sewing and making things for the runway each day. As time goes on, I don't understand. Mo's wig won't stay on. There are just certain things that Mo doesn't want to show up for. I guess she just didn't feel like it.

KAMERON MICHAELS: If anybody ever tells you they didn't have enough time to learn a song, they're full of shit. There's plenty of time. Now, whether you're choosing to do other things in that time span is different. But I think in Mo's defense, she made her costume that day. And that's something that you have to give Mo credit for. Props to her for making her own stuff.

ASIA O'HARA: I felt the same way that everybody else felt. We had our iPods and we had the music and I don't feel like that was one of the more difficult songs. I would listen to the music because you never know who is going to be in the bottom or you never know what's going to happen. So I always wanted to be prepared and to know the music.

EUREKA: Poor Mo and that cartwheel. She didn't know none of the words, girl, she just went through it sadly. Bless her little heart. She went through it. I liked Mo. I think she had a really great personality. I think she's just such a hard worker.

KAMERON MICHAELS: This was hard. The girls knew that I knew every lip sync song, because I was in the werkroom with my headphones. This is also why I wasn't necessarily getting airtime because I was in the corner with my headphones in learning every lip-sync song, regardless of how well I did or not. That moment was very hard for me, especially because it was a fun song. It was Carly Rae Jepsen. It's very hard to watch someone fumble like that.

MONÉT X CHANGE: Cracker and I were already friends before the show, but I definitely bonded with Mo and Asia. As Black men, we came from similar experiences and we got a lot of the same jokes and we were able to play with each other like you play with your friends. It was really comforting to have that camaraderie backstage.

MO HEART: The world fell in love with me, yes, but I did not know what the impact would mean for Black queer people and even Black cis straight people. They tell me when I got up there and talked about what it is to be Black and gay, when I got up and talked about what it is to be Black, gay, and brought up in the church, this thing of struggling with faith and queerness, it is so identifiable. And you go, bitch, I thought y'all was just gonna read me about this damn wig being lopsided. We thank God that it did that.

The following week, it was The Vixen's turn to go home. But not before she and Asia O'Hara had a heart-to-heart about why the Chicago queen feels it's important to call out microaggressions and racism from other castmates.

ASIA O'HARA: I had planned on having that conversation with The Vixen. I didn't know if I was going to do it on or off camera. But I thought this might be my last day here so this might be my last chance to have this conversation with her. A lot of times, we don't sit down and try to understand one another. We don't have conversations with one another and actually listen to one another. And I felt like, as a friend, that was what I should be doing. The Vixen is not afraid to have conversations. The Vixen to me really is a fighter when it comes to queer artists of color. The Vixen has definitely proved that because she's not one of the most popular ones from that season. And it has nothing to do with her drag or her art. It's the fact that she challenges a whole thought process and she challenges people that other people love. So I have a lot of respect for that and I feel like it was necessary for her to know that I understood and respected her for that.

TOM CAMPBELL: I was really impressed with how Asia O'Hara was able to help Vixen and swoop in and create a sisterhood and share some wisdom. I can't begin to understand personally what it's like to be a Black person in America.

ASIA O' HARA: I think what I learned about The Vixen is the fact that listening to someone really does change everything. And The Vixen needed and deserved to be heard and, as I suspected, hearing her mattered to her.

TOM CAMPBELL: Because *Drag Race* is populated with queens from different parts of the social fabric, the show continues to change and grow as it reflects who they are…I love that Vixen was on and I love what Vixen had to say and how she challenged the show and challenged some of the queens. I think it was really wonderful. I don't know what her experience is with the show but I think it is so important to have all those different voices.

ASIA O'HARA: Once the music started, again, it was like walking into the werkroom. Okay, now I'm free to just do what I know how to do, which is perform. When you lip sync, you know you're sharing the stage with another person but it's a blur because you're focused on yourself. I felt confident in what I did but also I didn't know what else happened onstage and what The Vixen did.

I got another chance to get back on top. It's almost like the slate is wiped clean to start anew. We saw Vixen's mirror message—"Evil triumphs when good queens do nothing." I think maybe The Vixen was feeling like I know there are other people that feel the same way I do, but I can't do this by myself. If everybody else just stands around and watches and just looks, then nothing happens.

. . . .

For much of the season, Kameron Michaels lay low. In the werkroom, she did her makeup alone at the tables with her headphones on. In *Untucked*, she was quiet and reserved. The last half of the season revealed there had been a lip-sync assassin hiding inside her muscled physique. In the tenth episode, Kameron faced off with her only friend on the show, Eureka, who was also from Tennessee.

KAMERON MICHAELS: Being a performer and that being the favorite part of drag for a lot of us, when you go on the show, you don't get to do that. I missed performing and that was what I was best at. Let me perform, damn it.

EUREKA: Because before we did it, Kameron and I were talking outside and she was like, I'm just ready to go home. I'm probably gonna give up. And I was like, girl, you ain't lip syncing, we're not lip syncing. And we both were like, well if we ever had to lip sync against each other we would just give up, we're not gonna do that to each other.

As soon as we were called, I was like, oh god, what do I do? We're just both natural entertainers. We were like, oh no, ma'am, honey. When that music started, the more energy I gave, the more she gave, we went off.

KAMERON MICHAELS: "New Attitude" is nothing that I would ever perform in my normal drag. But a high-energy song regardless is something that I will do well at and make it fun. And the fact that we're two old ladies, you know, twirling around to this high-energy song, I think was what made that lip sync so iconic and fun. It's a drag queen thing—you know when the chorus is going to drop and you definitely do something fun, a cartwheel here, a split there, you got a couple choruses, throw your tricks, make the crowd go woooo. And it's like dance monkey. This is what we do. And it just so happens that we chose to do the same trick at the same time.

MIZ CRACKER: I thought they were hilarious, I thought they were both great, I thought they deserved to stay. You know, they gave it their all and they did simultaneous splits. It was everything, yeah.

KAMERON MICHAELS: Before she announced...the double save, I felt awful. To know that Eureka had been on Season 9, and now Season 10, and I was going to be the one who sent her home and she was my only friend, I was devastated. So of course I was super happy and emotional when she got to stay.

ASIA O'HARA: I think they both deserved to stay. I'm not a let's-get-all-the-queens-out-so-I-can-win kind of girl. I'm all about good drag and if both of them stay, great.

EUREKA: Ru said Kameron, shantay you stay. I just knew I was going home, girl, and I was emotional. And then when she said I got to stay, too, bitch, I collapsed to the floor. I didn't come here to go home like this. I'm a fighter, I'm gonna keep fighting. I got up and I was like, Miss Thing! I just about had a heart attack! I was like, you got me, bitch. Even when I went all the way to the back, I was still screaming at her. I was like, ohhh, Miss Thing, you got me, girl! You got me, Miss Thing.

Time to grab your box of sponges to dry your tears. Monét X Change exited the building, after battling with Kameron Michaels over Lizzo's "Good as Hell."

MONÉT X CHANGE: When the makeover challenge came around, I was a little nervous but I still think that Aquaria made her person look crazy and I didn't deserve to be there. I am pretty forthcoming. When I do bad, I can admit it. But ya know, it is what it is. I wasn't nervous about Kameron's lip syncing. I think Kameron is a good lip syncer. We just have two different styles and the judges were more into Kameron's style of lip that day.

388 Maria Elena Fernandez

ASIA O' HARA: We all know Kameron's a force to be reckoned with when it comes to the lip syncing so you're worried for anybody that has to go up against Kameron. But I definitely remember that lip sync. I felt bad because I felt like everybody did a pretty good job on the makeover. Cracker definitely won that one, but it just felt like it was splitting hairs with who's in the bottom so you feel bad for whoever's in the bottom. Monét wasn't terrible. Somebody's got to be in the bottom.

KAMERON MICHAELS: I tend to stay away from certain songs in drag that I don't know if I'm allowed to do. And I think "Good as Hell" is one of those that I don't know if that would be welcome for me to do that type of song. But again, I didn't pick these songs. I'm going to perform it to the best of my ability. I do love songs like that. You can clearly see that I have fun doing it. But it was another unhappy day for me. I knew that would be the beginning of my demise. That's when I would start getting in trouble with the fans. I put a lot of personality into that number, I knew every word. I gave them a good show. I think I clearly won the lip sync. But I wasn't necessarily a fan favorite compared to Monét. So I knew that there would be some backlash for sure.

EUREKA: I was sad to see Monét go, it broke my heart, to be honest. It sucked to see her go.

MIZ CRACKER: Monét's wiping tears with a sponge. He's a ridiculous, absurd person who continues to be absurd.

MONÉT X CHANGE: I can't really describe how upsetting it is to go home on *Drag Race*. A lot of girls now, from the beginning think if I don't get this, at least I can get on *All Stars*. It just didn't seem like something that a lot of girls would get a chance to do. So I felt my dreams of getting on the show are ruined. My dreams of winning *Drag Race* are ruined. No one is gonna wanna book me, I suck. Lucky for me, my personality rang true for a lot of people. And again, I'm so grateful for having someone like Jacqueline Wilson, my story producer, who helped me tell my story. People adore Monét X Change because of what Jacqueline helped pull out of me in all of my interviews.

For the third week in a row, Kameron Michaels had to lip sync for her life. This time, she sent home Miz Cracker, who had never been in the bottom and detested the song "Nasty Girl."

KAMERON MICHAELS: I knew that I was a force to be reckoned with and that any girl on that season would have a fight on their hands if I was lip syncing. So I wasn't nervous about Cracker. The only reason I was nervous was because it was my third time and you have an expiration date.

MIZ CRACKER: I fucking hated that song. I hate that song now. I hated it when I first heard it, which by the way was on Season 10. And I spent the entire season listening to it in my headphones saying I hope I don't ever have to lip sync to this thing because this is awful. I cursed myself into lip syncing to it and I hated it. I hated practicing it, I hated doing it, I hate hearing it in the bars now.

KAMERON MICHAELS: I wouldn't say I hated it. But again, I wouldn't have chosen it. That's the thing about *Drag Race*. We're so harsh when we're judging these lip syncs of these girls and a lot of us are doing songs that we would never normally perform. It was kind of hard to learn from what I remember. I struggled with that one with the lyrics. It definitely wasn't my favorite thing.

MIZ CRACKER: I knew that it was not going to happen for me because I had only won one challenge and the other girls kept saying, if anyone should go home, it should be me. The writing was on the wall at that point. I knew what was happening.

KAMERON MICHAELS: I was floored and didn't even realize until I got offstage after all that, after Cracker was sent home, I was standing back behind the curtain, and I realized that I was top four. That didn't hit me until I got backstage. I had to sit down. I almost passed out. It was a good moment and a bad moment for me because I knew that Cracker was going to be a fan favorite. She's funny. She's quirky. She's weird. She was Miss Pickles and it was her first time in the bottom. It's completely validated that the fans would hate me because I was in the bottom so many times and that was Cracker's first time.

With Miz Cracker's exit, Kameron Michaels joined Eureka, Asia O'Hara, and Aquaria in the top four.

KAMERON MICHAELS: At that point I was just kind of skating on a high. The fight isn't over but you made it farther than you ever thought you'd make it. You're going to get to watch Ru hold up your picture. So at that point, I was just happy and I was just there to keep doing the best that I could do.

EUREKA: I was elated, ecstatic, beside myself. It was just such a relief. I was so exhausted at that point but I didn't even care, it was worth the pain. Girl, I was so happy to be there. My biggest dream was to have that moment where I got to talk to my baby picture and get to live those moments.

ASIA O'HARA: I was excited, but I also still was just in the place of being excited I made it this far. This is a success. I'm hoping I make it all the way to the end. I'm hoping that I win but anything past this point is a success for me.

AQUARIA: I knew that I came in prepared with an excellent package of visual moments. I had really put a lot of fucking time and thought and effort and devotion—blood, sweat, and tears—into. But I purposefully tried to pretend like I had the thing in the bag because I'm someone who clearly has these imposter issues. You just have to convince yourself sometimes, and that's what I did.

MANILA LUZON: Fuck, Aquaria was just everything. She had a twist on her looks that's something that I enjoy with my looks. She didn't just do a look, there was always two elements or themes that were combined, like the rabbit with the hat on the ear or the mermaid that was covered in an oil slick. I thought that was such creativity. And the fact that she was so young and that she had started because she had been watching *Drag Race*, I loved that. Season 10 was one of the best seasons ever.

With the success of the previous season's finale and Sasha Velour's meteoric rise in drag culture, producers opted to stick with their lip-sync-battle format. The episode proved just as memorable, but for the wrong reasons.

ASIA O'HARA: We learned that the finale would be a battle like Season 9 a couple weeks before filming it. I really was hoping for a finale like Season 7 where they all did a performance with dancers. I just felt like that was more my speed. It was brought up by a lot of people close to me that Aquaria is a trained dancer, Kameron can do flips and splits, Eureka can high kick and split, and I can't do any of that. So I was kind of hoping that it would be something a little bit more controlled because I felt like I would have had a better chance.

KAMERON MICHAELS: I kind of hoped it wouldn't be a lip sync for the crown. I kind of hoped they would do something different. But I think they realized with the ratings that this is gold, we have to do this again. So we were pretty sure that we were going to have to do that.

EUREKA: I think it was probably the fairest way since we were such a high-performance top four. I think it was a really good way to end the season. All four of us are great entertainers.

ASIA O'HARA: None of us really discussed it at all. We all were very separate at that point. I don't think us four really got close until after the finale. So yeah, we were all kind of just doing our own thing. I had been happy to be that successful thus far, but at that point, I was like I've come this close, I may actually be able to win.

EUREKA: Kameron and I got ready together in the same dressing room and Asia and Aquaria got ready in the same dressing room. Kameron and I had made a pact that if it landed on either of us we would pick each other so that at least one of the Tennessee girls would make the top two.

KAMERON MICHAELS: I just knew that it would be a good TV moment to see Eureka and I lip sync again. I knew the other three girls deserved to be there more than I had because they all won more challenges and I knew that the fans would be tired of seeing me lip sync at that point and skating by with my performance skills. So my theory was I'll pick Eureka. We'll get another dual lip sync, I'll go home, and my friend will get to make it to the final. That was my original thought. I told them I was going to do that because I knew if I kept going, the fans would hate me because I already sent two fan favorites home, Monét and Cracker. The top four was good enough for me.

AQUARIA: I actually hoped that I didn't get to choose because I'd been letting nature take its course. I don't know who I would have chosen.

ASIA O' HARA: I had already told myself, whoever picks whoever, it's just it is what it is. There's only four of us so there's not that many matchups. You know, I do think that Kameron probably knew that of the three of us, I would be the easiest to beat. She hadn't seen Aquaria lip sync but we all knew that Aquaria was a trained dancer and we saw her do those pirouettes in the heels in "American."

KAMERON MICHAELS: The decision landed on me. We have conspiracy theories about whether the wheel was weighted or not. We spun it in rehearsals and it landed on somebody different every time, but we were convinced that I lip synced so many times in a row and then this would be me lip syncing again and choosing the pairs. I totally chose opposite of what I told production that I would choose. So they may have been sitting behind their screens saying what the fuck is she doing? I said I would pick Eureka and I ended up picking Asia.

EUREKA: When it landed on her and she picked Asia, I was shocked.

KAMERON MICHAELS: I think we knew Aquaria was going to win because she had done so well the entire season. She'd never been on the bottom. The other three of us had hit the bottom. We'd had weak moments. I'd already lip synced against Eureka. And for some reason, I just said Asia because I hadn't lip synced against her. I don't know why I picked her. It goes completely against my plan to not make myself look bad by sending somebody else home. But it just came out of my mouth.

ASIA O'HARA: Kameron didn't stand out to me at first. But after a couple competitions, the way that Kameron works in the dressing room, I knew that she was competition. And even though she's quiet, it's something about the way that people get in drag and the way that they do their makeup, you can just tell that they're very serious about their craft. And Kameron is one of those people.

KAMERON MICHAELS: I don't have a lot of friends, I'm not good at connecting with people, which is weird because I'm really good at connecting with my fans. I guess we have something to talk about and something in common. But with strangers and people that I don't know, it's hard for me to connect with. Eureka, with us being from Tennessee, we connect in that aspect. I knew I needed to make a friend and so that was like my one friend. I don't know that I really developed relationships with the other girls until after the show.

The first matchup was Janet Jackson's "Nasty" between Kameron Michaels and Asia O'Hara.

ASIA O'HARA: I had gone to an event and they did this butterfly release. I was wondering if I could do that out of a costume. So I contacted this company in Florida, the actual company that did the butterfly release for this event. So I talked to them, like, is this possible? They sent the butterflies for me to do a rehearsal in Texas. The butterflies come dormant in a cold pack. You have to let them rise to room temperature in order for them to be awake to fly. I rehearsed it in Dallas, and I was like, oh my god, this is great, this is perfect. This is going to be the best thing ever. I wrote down everything I did.

JOHN POLLY: There was another producer working on it specifically dealing with the queens about their plans for their performances. Apparently Aquaria had said she was going to have confetti. She popped a can or something for the final number, "Bang Bang." She cleared it like they're supposed to do. But Asia never hinted at anything.

ASIA O'HARA: For the finale, I took one packet of them up to the roof of the hotel just to check to make sure that everything was still a go. I let them rise to room temperature in my hotel room, then went upstairs when there was nobody else on the roof at this little rooftop bar, I did the whole release thing and I was like, okay, this is great.

So my dressing room is cold and my assistant is telling me, what can we do because it's super cold in here? And so he was trying to use a blow dryer. Everything is very rushed; you don't have a lot of time to get everything situated. And so, get upstairs, and we're holding to go onto the stage and feel my hands and my hands are ice-cold. I don't know if it's the adrenaline, or is it too cold in here? So I opened one of the ones on my breast and tried to peek in it and they seem to be fine.

KAMERON MICHAELS: I was not excited about any of the songs. None of these songs are songs that I would choose to perform myself. Janet Jackson is an amazing artist, iconic, but not part of my drag aesthetic. But I wasn't even nervous. I was just happy to be there.

VANESSA VANJIE MATEO: When I saw Asia come out to do the lip sync, I was like what is she doing? She doesn't look like she's gonna dance a lot because her shoe was a stiletto. She was in an outfit, the hair didn't look like she was gonna move much. And the song was Janet so I was just wondering what is she gonna do?

JOHN POLLY: The lip sync begins and I'm behind the curtains. I can't see out there, so I'm backstage looking at the monitors with Raven, who is Ru's makeup person, and maybe Randy was there. We're all just watching and we're like, what? What?

ASIA O'HARA: I had planned four releases. In the moment, you're just like, get through it, just get through the performance. I did the first one and I thought maybe that's just a fluke. The ones on my body that are closer to my chest will be warmer and it will be fine. But no. I kept thinking the next one is going to work. It's all a flash. In the blink of an eye, it's over with. I was trying to stay optimistic. Well, obviously, as we saw, it was not fine. It was too cold. They were all still dormant and so it was a complete disaster.

KAMERON MICHAELS: When I'm performing, I'm not paying attention to the other person. I'm worried about connecting with my audience and putting on a show. And I don't care what the other person is doing, nor am I looking in their direction. And I had no clue what happened, no idea at all. There was a meme of me that was going around after the finale where I'm holding my arm and looking down at the ground. I saw a butterfly on the ground at that point. In my mind, I said, this bitch really had mechanical butterflies in her costume that flew out of her. I thought I'm definitely going home. She had some fun reveal that I missed somehow in my performance. This was her Sasha Velour moment. She had a cool reveal and I had a tearaway.

RANDY BARBATO: We didn't know she was planning on doing that. And I wish we had in a way. She wasn't intentionally misleading anyone. I think it was her intent to do a surprise that backfired. Nobody expected it. When we were in the control room, we didn't even understand what was going on. I'm like, what is that? We couldn't figure it out and then it was, oh my god, there are butterflies on the floor.

TOM CAMPBELL: Oh my god, what's happening? The look on her face and knowing that it didn't happen, it was shocking and heartbreaking. I give Asia so much credit for walking through that, living through that, and coming out of the other end of it.

MICHELLE VISAGE: When we were there, I knew exactly what they were. I knew what she was trying to do. I told Ross and Carson. I had those butterfly kits at home where you grew them and let them go. I did that with my kids. When I saw the things on the wrist, I was like, guys, she's got live butterflies in there and I'm telling you right now it's really hot in here and they've been in there for hours. This is not going to be good. She started opening them and I almost feel like I manifested it. I'm sorry to those butterflies, I'm sorry, Asia. I can't tell you how much I love Asia. But I knew it was happening when I saw it.

RONAN FARROW: The reaction shot of Mo Heart and Vanjie in the audience, gasping, is one of the great reality TV reaction shots ever. It is a train going slowly off the tracks and you feel for Asia so much. She worked so hard, she prepared such an elaborate thing, and it is so awful. I was shook. It took me a while to recover from it. It is one of the most riveting pieces of television I have ever seen.

VANESSA VANJIE MATEO: I don't know what the hell I was thinking. It was so quick. I was standing up outta my seat and people were saying, "Sit down!" I'm looking, squinting, and I saw butterflies on the floor. I was thinking, okay, are these real or is it like papier-mâché, is it origami? It was right after Season 9 when Sasha Velour did her gag so I knew these bitches gonna come out here and try to do the pyrotechnics, bubble machines, they're gonna try to top it. I couldn't tell what the hell was going on. But everyone was starting to say oh my gosh, those are butterflies! I was like, bitch, I can't see no butterflies so the gag is not a gag. It was horrible but now it's one of the most iconic things that ever happened.

BLAIR ST. CLAIR: I was really rooting for Asia and I was really, really bummed when the butterflies didn't work. It was like a Vanjie moment. We were just sitting there like, what is happening? We couldn't really tell they were butterflies. I actually thought they were confetti butterflies, like, fake. I was really, really rooting for her. I knew that Aquaria had a really strong chance of winning.

ADORE DELANO: If you see my apartment, I have butterflies everywhere. I am so obsessed with butterflies. I felt so bad. I was like who in your god-loving team said that this was going to work? What are you doing? You suffocated them with your chi-chis. How long were they in there, girl? They only have so long to live.

I love butterflies so it broke my heart. They're all on the floor and they're dancing. You can see them flapping on the floor.

CARSON KRESSLEY: She is so sweet and so kind, and she is one of the most lovable, warmest, most wonderful queens we have ever had on the show. So to see what seemed like a good idea go south essentially on live TV, it was heartbreaking. I was literally thinking oh my gosh, is she gonna get in trouble? It wound up being iconic for all the wrong reasons. But trauma builds character, they say, and she has gone on to slay many other days.

JOHN POLLY: I guess the idea sounds fun, but they're probably not gonna show up on TV and the margin of error just seemed so great. Just thinking how that must have felt. You're in the moment, you're doing that, and then you've got to keep going and you've got to keep performing and smiling or whatever. Everyone in the audience was aghast. It's that shot you saw of Vanjie and Mo in the audience when it pans to them up the aisle.

MICHELE "MEESH" MILLS: You could see Asia realizing that it was all over, the look on her face. And then Kameron was trying to still dance but not knowing what to do.

AQUARIA: Eureka, Sasha, and me were sitting backstage watching the monitor because Asia and Kameron went on first. Let's go see these girls turn it. I think they showed different camera shots but we were confused probably as long as the audience was. Nothing made sense. We had shared a dressing room that day and she was in the refrigerator and I asked what that's for and she said she had real flowers for her headpiece. And I was thinking she's doing the most, just take the crown, girl. Had I known that she was lying about real flowers but was not lying about the real garden of it all, I would have known that was not going to go over well and that live animals were not gonna fly. Oops. Nope, that was not gonna fly.

KAMERON MICHAELS: I did not know they were live butterflies until later in the day. I don't think I even knew when I got downstairs because once I won, I was to go downstairs and I had fifteen minutes to change. I had no time. I had to change wigs and change my outfit and be back up for the finale. So I don't think I knew until later that day.

EUREKA: Kameron is a really good performer, honestly. I wasn't shocked when she would win the lip syncs. If nothing else, she was gonna save her ass if she ever ended up in the bottom.

STEVEN CORFE: We would not have allowed this because we don't believe you should use live animals in entertainment acts.

VANESSA VANJIE MATEO: There were butterflies flying! But it was too late. The damn thing was done.

ADORE DELANO: They're probably still there, girl, like the little birds in the airports every now and then.

JOHN POLLY: It was certainly iconic and just strange and kind of heartbreaking.

AQUARIA: To see one of your good friends flop beyond flopping, especially for someone so incredible as Asia, that was definitely extremely disappointing for me. And then I was like, oh shit, the pressure is on, now that she can't win I've got to do my thing. It was upsetting.

ASIA O' HARA: I went outside and was by myself until they got me to change to come back on for the filming of the actual crowning. I didn't watch the lip sync between Eureka and Aquaria or the lip sync between all three of them.

JOHN POLLY: It's such a strange thing to navigate. It was a landmark strange moment.

RANDY BARBATO: Asia in so many ways was the mama heart and soul of that season, and was surprising in her ability to navigate incredibly challenging conversations with a level of wisdom that left me in awe. She is a true pageant girl and perfectionist. So that was so devastating to her and to everyone.

ASIA O'HARA: It was a very difficult six months for me, probably. I had nobody to blame but myself. Everybody wants to win but I was just more excited to have this cool moment, regardless of the outcome. And I remember thinking to myself even with this, if it works, great, I still may or may not beat Kameron or whoever I ended up lip syncing against. Remember, this is coming right off of two weeks prior me saying something ugly about Cracker and I was in the top four with three fan favorites. So there wasn't a lot of sympathy, it was honestly just a lot of nothingness.

With butterflies still fluttering in the theater, Aquaria and Eureka faced off to Janet Jackson's "If." This number didn't go as planned, either.

AQUARIA: This is a big-ass bitch—tall, wide, big in character, big in costume and just persona, and she would agree. This is David and Goliath and I know how that one turned out in the end. I could literally grow wings out of my back and fly on this stage and it still might not draw anyone's eye to me because she just has so much visual weight. Not to sell myself short, but who would you want to see compared to you and Eureka? I'd be like, bitch, I wanna see Eureka turn the damn party. I was stressed out from the first second.

KAMERON MICHAELS: I was downstairs getting ready for the second performance and the wheels started clicking in my head. Wait a minute, there are three artists in "Bang, Bang." I see what we're doing here. Watch, they are going to do a final three lip sync.

AQUARIA: That first lip sync was so disappointing to me. We are on about five minutes after. I had just sprayed my hair with oil sheen because I had all these spikes and stones on my outfit and I guess I was just trying to check all my boxes. I had no issues downstairs and I had no issues backstage. But the second that the fucking track starts, I realized the bottom of my shoes must have picked up some of the spray from my hair that naturally lands on the linoleum floor. If anyone knows me, I always have a no-skid bottom on my shoe. I'm fuckin' prepared. Y'all saw what I did on *Drag Race*! I'm very prepared. So I was like, ohhh my fuckin' god. There were so many thoughts going through my head.

EUREKA: She just was really nervous, you could tell. She did an okay job and she knew the choreo for the Janet part and stuff so it looked great in the edit but she had some trouble.

AQUARIA: My shoes are somehow fuckin' slick and I end up slipping on the floor. I had taught myself the majority of the iconic choreography and I knew RuPaul loves Janet Jackson, but now I was setting up myself to ca-ca-ca-ca-coowww fall on the floor. It was a lot of emotions at once. To not even be able to feel like I could give Eureka a decent fight made me feel very defeated. I don't particularly gag over super-traditional drag reveals like that but when I'm not able to be giving it my all, all I hear is this hubbub for her. And she's big and loud in the colors and loud in the fabrics and the textures and I felt like I couldn't give it my all and there was nothing I could do.

EUREKA: It was cute. She was all over the place that first lip sync, though. She slipped and fell a few times. She was kind of sloppy. She slipped and fell. She dropped the fan.

AQUARIA: I think I fell twice, if I remember correctly. When I was originally watching it, I wanted that to be seen because obviously I knew that I had made it past that and I thought that that would give a little bit of context as to why it just was a level of sloppy and desperate that I wished I wasn't. I felt like I was the ugly girl in the design challenge who's wearing some fucked-up ugly thing and has to convince everyone that this is their drag and let me lip sync for my life while you look like a fuckin' foot. I felt like the biggest fucking loser and floppianna for that.

BLAIR ST. CLAIR: She did fall and they played it off. The whole crowd was chanting "Eureka" because she was actually a stronger lip syncer in that moment. It probably should have been Eureka and Kameron in the final lip sync.

EUREKA: When it was a double shantay, I was surprised because the whole crowd was chanting my name at the finale during that lip sync. I was like, girl, whatever, but in that moment I knew she was gonna win, to be honest. So by the time I got to the next lip sync my energy was drained, I was already down about it. So I kinda got in my own head for the last lip sync.

AQUARIA: I did my best for as shook as I was throughout the rest of the number. From my perspective, I really made some massive fumbles on this. The good part was I knew that I did deserve a second chance because I had been exceptional for the past thirteen episodes.

RuPaul opted to make the last contest a triple lip sync to "Bang Bang" by Jessie J, Ariana Grande, and Nicki Minaj.

KAMERON MICHAELS: It was a hot shit show, an absolute hot shit show mess. Three people on that stage, which was a decent size, is not enough space. We were trying to navigate around each other and hold the attention of the crowd and those two were fighting for the center stage. And you can see me doing laps around them. It was an absolute mess. We knew who the winner was. We knew who had performed the best and who the fans loved the most and who had the best track record the whole season. That's something that Eureka may have not realized until the final three, but that's something that I had accepted long before the finale started.

EUREKA: I did well but I didn't do my best because I was in my head and I felt that. I was exhausted, my energy was drained, and then my emotional energy was drained when we were both saved for that lip sync after the whole crowd was chanting my name. It just kind of put me in this headspace of it doesn't matter if I pull fireworks out of my ass, I'm not gonna win this.

AQUARIA: It was actually quite funny that we were doing "Bang Bang." That is a song that feels like it has followed me all through my drag career. Once I knew that I'd made it that far it was like, Aquaria, shake off what just happened. And more importantly, shake off how emotionally fucked I was with what Asia had done. I don't think I had ever been so fucking silent in my life.

I need to do this and do it well for Eureka and Kameron to give them a fair fight. I'm still anxious as fuck performing it but I was aware it was a song I knew like the back of my hand and just a bit of commitment and choice and direction would be a way to forget about what had happened before and focus on going out with a bang, bitch.

KAMERON MICHAELS: That all happened within a three-week period—the episodes where I sent Cracker and Monét home aired, then filming the finale and the reunion, and airing the finale. At that point, I'd had a really tumultuous relationship with fans because they were attacking me online. They were sending me death threats. I got a call from production asking me if I need to address the death threats, if I was okay. I had to turn off comments on my posts. They attacked me for a few weeks. So I was terrified that day sitting in the room watching the finale. I didn't think I won but I was terrified of that feeling that if they said my name, the fans would riot. It was not a fun day until she won.

BLAIR ST. CLAIR: I remember there had been a lot of things circulating with the fandom at the point in time that the finale was airing on TV and they were kind of anti-Eureka at that time.

MAYHEM MILLER: Aquaria worked her ass off and she fuckin' shined. The rest of the girls were great, too. Asia and Kameron and Eureka were great, but I remember when I left the show I was rooting for Aquaria because I had followed her before getting there. I knew that she was a star. Maybe she is the future of drag. So it was a deserved win.

ASIA O'HARA: The right person won. I think when we look at the season as a whole, Aquaria is to me the clear winner. As far as greatness is concerned, she had the most consistency, and I definitely think she was the clear winner.

MIZ CRACKER: I thought it was a great finale. It will go down in history forever because of the butterflies. And Asia has made it a joke of her own since then. It was a beautiful finale because we got to get together with girls from the first ten seasons and showed the whole history of ten years. So I thought it was great. My mom and my sister got to come.

JOHN POLLY: So the next day Asia has to sit there at the reunion and be optimistic about her chances of winning and talk about her season and, of course, she breaks up during the reunion on behalf of The Vixen. But also she's just working through everything that she has gone through, which is a lot.

BLAIR ST. CLAIR: I can't imagine being eliminated and waking up the next day, having to put on a fresh face of makeup, a happy smile, and pretending like the finale hasn't happened yet. She was mortified, I'm sure.

JOHN POLLY: And in the meantime, the next day you're seeing an occasional butterfly fly through the theater. Maybe for the next month there were a few butterflies every so often flying through that theater.

BLAIR ST. CLAIR: I thought it could be between Eureka or Aquaria. Now, Aquaria did perform the best out of the season out of the three and she did perform very well in the ending. But I also knew too that it could've been an amazing thing for the *RuPaul's Drag Race* franchise with Eureka winning to show after hurting herself the season before, being the first plus-size winner, which would've been amazing for a huge audience of people to identify with her. But when Aquaria won, I wasn't surprised.

AQUARIA: It's so inspiring to have that under my belt at such a young age and to be able to use that as leverage to make sure that shit is correct and other queens aren't fucked with the wrong way. I have this weird-level confidence that I don't think I would have in the past to continue to try to make things better for other queer performers and try to do more in the world.

The finale had drama, and the reunion had more. Although it aired first, it was filmed the morning after the finale in the same theater in Los Angeles, with occasional butterflies fluttering by the queens and RuPaul. Confronted again with the suggestion that she's an angry Black woman picking fights, The Vixen opted to walk out of the taping.

MONÉT X CHANGE: The reunion was super interesting. The more and more heated Ru got, I understood exactly what Ru was saying. Ru is someone who has built his entire career and he had to pull himself up by his bootstraps and make it happen. Obviously, I admire that type of tenacity. Not a lot of people can do that. But I think Asia was saying Vixen isn't someone that can do it like you. And perhaps there's something that could help her if we get her back in this room. It is a tricky thing to navigate. It was so shocking but it was such an interesting moment.

ASIA O'HARA: A lot of times *Drag Race* in general is *I like her better than her.* For the specific challenges and runways, that's great. But, as a whole, I feel like a lot of times, we lack exactly what we need at the core of the LGBTQ community—togetherness. Drag queens or gay people as a whole, a lot of times we walk around preaching that we want to be treated as equals and we want the same rights as everyone else. And in a sense, a lot of times, we turn right around and create division within ourselves. And so I was just fed up with it. It was June. It was Pride Month. And I felt like we were just sitting there dividing ourselves more and more and that is just counterproductive to what the counterculture of drag is supposed to be for me. Even if you're on opposite ends the spectrum of the topic, I think it's important to talk and speak their mind and hear and listen and understand other people's point of view.

MAYHEM MILLER: For me, it was shocking to see Ru get emotional and yell. I've never seen that before so I was just like oh shit. But I understood where The Vixen was coming from because it is frustrating to be misunderstood and the things that you're saying are valid and real and still be glanced over. I totally felt for her. The best part about that whole situation was years later for people to finally say she was right.

RUPAUL: I've always felt like an outsider. I felt like the little boy who fell to earth. Even when I was thirteen or fourteen, I made a pact with myself to never join into the matrix. I never wanted to fill into any type of box. The ego likes to put other people down to make itself feel better. Racism is an extension of that. I've been discriminated against by white folks for being Black, by gay people for being femme, and by women for being too damn pretty. I put it all together and none of those are different. It's all the ego—let them children be. It's okay.

KAMERON MICHAELS: Our season started the conversation of something we know very much to be true: that the fandom does have a tendency to be a little racist. Looking back at that moment, it was very important that that happened because it started this change of all of us expecting and asking more from the fans.

ASIA O'HARA: Drag is like ice skating was in the '80s. If you're an ice princess, people are going to love you, you're going to score well. If you're the Tonya Harding, if you're from a rough neighborhood and you're not aesthetically what people relate to, it doesn't matter how good you skate, you're never going to be a Nancy Kerrigan. The fact is we are biochemically engineered to gravitate toward things that look like us, that are familiar to us. But we have to consciously try and move forward from that and try and be accepting of all people's art. No matter how good my drag is or isn't, I will never be as popular as Aquaria or Miz Cracker.

RONAN FARROW: Ru is right that at a certain point you can't help people if they're not going to help themselves and Asia is also right that compassion is important when someone is struggling and lashing out. It's one of these rare moments in reality TV where everyone involved is being completely real. It felt unusual and I guess that's at the heart of the show's power. It has been a platform for discourse about the LGBT community and how best we support ourselves amongst ourselves and the role we play in the world.

VANESSA VANJIE MATEO: I was definitely inspired by Asia. At the time of filming, it was Gay Pride and seeing somebody crying and basically feeling alone and having to walk off set because they couldn't take it, it was hard. And I'm friends with both of them, Eureka and Vixen. I did feel like things were being said that needed to be said and Asia is one of the people that I do look up to. She is a voice of reason. I was trying to take it all in. I felt like this was a good conversation that needed to be had and Asia was saying what she needed to say to RuPaul. I was gagged the way the girls were not holding back.

ASIA O'HARA: It's kind of like Vixen's lipstick message. Competition is in a sense designed to drive us away from one another. And there's not a lot that we do or not a lot that happens that brings us back together as a group or encourages us to be on the same accord with one another. At that point, I was maybe just a little fed up with it.

I think the show has a responsibility and the show is doing its part. It's hosted by a person of color. There have been plenty of persons of color that won. The judges' panel always has diversity. There's always diversity in the contestants. But the fans will always pick the winner. At the end, Ru is going to decide who gets a crown and a scepter and $100,000, but the fans will always pick the winner, meaning the fans will pick who is popular, who gets endorsements, who they're excited to see, who they're going to buy tickets to see. And the fans will always gravitate toward people that look like them.

MIZ CRACKER: Ru got very upset. And I think Ru was frustrated because what she wanted was for Vixen to see past the things that made her angry. And I can see both sides of the argument. Vixen wanted to speak about the challenges she faced. And Ru wanted her to see past them. You can see it either way.

MAYHEM MILLER: I died. I was like, oh, she's done. And when we had our break, they were trying to get her to come back and she was like, no, bitch, I said what I said and I'm done. I wish she had come back and continued to have the conversation because it was such an important conversation to have. But I understand that I'm not her and the way that she felt is the way that she felt. And if she felt she had to remove herself from the situation, all power to her. I'm all about self-help and keeping your mental fucking health in check and everything's good. So if that's what she needed to do, that's what she needed to do.

MICHELLE VISAGE: Everybody's got their own path in life. I'm not gonna sit here and go that was a mistake or whatever. That's her journey. You have to do what you need to do to protect your own self mentally, emotionally, physically, whatever you need to do. So that was her thing.

BLAIR ST. CLAIR: It's hard to remember that RuPaul is a human because he has done so many things and he has been such an icon to so many. In that moment, I saw him emotionally involved in the conversation. It was another clicking point of like, oh, he really cares.

KAMERON MICHAELS: I think it's hard for me, especially as a non-confrontational person and somebody that's introverted, to watch someone approach confrontation with confidence because that's something The Vixen does. Being confident and reacting to confrontation is not a bad quality, especially if it's something you had to fight for your entire life, which is something that I, as a privileged white person, cannot relate to at that level. Growing up in Chicago like the Vixen did, where she had to fight to get where she is, I don't know what that's like. I did not come from that.

MONÉT X CHANGE: I think The Vixen was super valid in everything that she did and said. For example, I am watching old episodes of *Survivor*, and every time a person of color says something, they are pegged. Everyone gets on them—you're being really aggressive, you're being really mean. No! No, they're not. They're saying exactly what everyone else is saying but because they are women of color you are automatically pegging them as these mean, vicious, evil people. And that is exactly what Vixen was pointing out in our season. By her saying whatever she's saying, by her going back and forth with Aquaria when they are both engaging in the same behavior, by Aquaria flipping that and crying, automatically everyone else who's looking at it is going to point The Vixen out as the aggressor, even though they were playing and volleying and reading and whatever with each other, you know? The Vixen brought up excellent points that we can all still learn from today.

AQUARIA: The fucking butterflies are still flying around when we are doing this. I was traumatized by everything that was going on. I was incredibly emotional and I was extremely hurt by how everything was going. I didn't have many talking points because I had made peace with the things that I've needed to make peace with. Even before Vixen left the show, she understood that I was not meaning to be a bad guy and I understood that she was not meaning to be a bad guy and we had at least squashed it in terms of animosity and tension between us.

EUREKA: It was a lot of growth even for me in the public light, how to address stuff like that versus being defensive. There were a lot of moments where I was very defensive and just came off at the mouth, pissed off, saying shit that got twisted, you know. It's social media and fame. It's how it works sometimes. I just had to educate myself more on that whole topic and conversation, to be honest. You learn from every situation and I learned a lot and I'm very honored to have, to be honest. It actually was a very beneficial educational time because I was able to navigate the Black Lives Matter movement as an ally, so it really helped me a lot weirdly. A lot of light came from such a dark time in my life.

RANDY BARBATO: I think the awareness of that, the shocking reality of the racial intolerance of some of the people who claim to be fans of this show, makes no sense. How can you be a fan of this show and display any of that kind of behavior? How can you be fans of this show and be ignorant, actually? It is important to talk about that stuff and the awareness that came through during the pandemic has been amazing because when you look at the queens of color of this show, it's like they are the engine of *RuPaul's Drag Race*. RuPaul is a queen of color.

LATRICE ROYALE: You have a new generation of millennial girls who are not having it. It should have happened sooner but everyone's experience and struggle is not the same. I have been called everything you can imagine under the sun. Most of the time my size keeps people at bay. They don't want to cross me. But in someone like Vixen's case, where they feel like they can say whatever they want and there would be no repercussions, it's a lot harder. She is the one that has been the most vocal in the franchise as a whole about the racial and social injustices within the *Drag Race* community and fandom. I'm glad it's been brought to the forefront. As you can see, we now have a situation where our nation is seeing full-on, on a major and broader scale, the craziness that we've been enduring for centuries.

DIDA RITZ: After the show, I still had to really work and hustle and grind to get to where I really am now. I think people have started to come around and really respect me and respect my drag and defend me and really have my back. It wasn't like that for a really long time.

JOEY NOLFI: It felt uncomfortable. I'm not saying it's not important, but it felt uncomfortable and surprising and jarring for a lot of people. I think The Vixen deserves all the credit in the world for saying what she [said] and knowing very well that she was risking a lot in saying what she said. But The Vixen believes in what she believes in and I respect the hell out of her for it. I think she has a lot of courage and a lot of strength and she used her voice, I think, at the expense of her own career in many ways, and I think that is the ultimate sign of a genuine person.

TOM CAMPBELL: Our show is not about race but inevitably it has to be about it at times. They are uncomfortable conversations but they are worth having. We all learn at different times in our lives, too. We can always be better.

LATRICE ROYALE: The conversation was necessary because I don't think the fans even know that they're being racist when they're being racist. They have a trend of liking white, skinny, pretty bitches. They don't follow us. So it's been an uphill climb.

VANESSA VANJIE MATEO: It was definitely something I felt like was going to create a shift and start to open the eyes for the girls to check the fans and have to say something when things are happening. If one of our sisters reaches out about the fans bullying, we need to use our platform and say something. I feel like it did help put the spotlight on the fact that the fans can be toxic and these things are happening and the queens of color do not get the same respect.

MICHELLE VISAGE: I love that The Vixen does what she does for Black queens and queens of color. She is very young to be so socially conscious and I love that.

RANDY BARBATO: It is hard to take a deep dive into this show and to look at who has been on it and what has happened on it and to not come away from it knowing that its mission has always been a progressive one and one that is always hell-bent on not just providing a platform to the world for these beautiful artists but to provoke people to think about what we all have in common, because that's the surprise. That's the secret sauce of *Drag Race*—you come for the drag show, you stay for the family of it.

Chapter 11
ALL STARS AND BEYOND

FROM NICHE BASIC CABLE SHOW TO GLOBAL CULTURAL JUGGERNAUT, *RuPaul's Drag Race* has morphed into an epic triumph that crowned its first Queen of All Queens last year in the seventh cycle of *All Stars*. Fifth-season champion Jinkx Monsoon took home the extra-special crown in the only-winners competition. By then, the franchise had been doling out second chances to fan favorites for a decade.

RANDY BARBATO: If any brand on TV, if any show on television should have an *All Stars* spin-off, it should be *Drag Race*, because there are so many stars that come out of *Drag Race* and there's just not enough drag real estate on TV. So it was a no-brainer that there should be a *Drag Race All Stars*. But then the challenge became what should it be, how should we do it, how do we pay tribute and respect to the queens because we are their number one fans. How do we do that and also deliver something different than regular *Drag Race*, keeping a bit of drama and excitement?

TOM CAMPBELL: I feel like *Drag Race* is a fabulous but much more traditional talent show where people come, they show their talents, there are eliminations, there's a winner. When people show up on *Drag Race*, it's early. They don't know how to be on TV, they don't know that there are cameras there and they should play. They learn it all very quickly. On *All Stars*, they come back with that skill set, plus they have had some life experience. They've seen themselves on television, which I think must be one of the most enlightening things one can do for one oneself.

RANDY BARBATO: Every season, girls go home in the first and the second and the third episode and you barely get to know them. And there are so many amazing drag queens now, brilliant queens. When did Vanjie go home? What episode? Hello!

TOM CAMPBELL: In the pageant system, which has existed for decades and decades, queens are on the same circuit. Think of sports or the Olympics. People come back. There's fresh ones but people do come back and could always be your competition.

CARSON KRESSLEY: There is a sisterhood between the contestants and it's a little less cutthroat. People have already been out there. They've been successful, they're working, and they've toured together. There's a little bit more camaraderie.

RANDY BARBATO: You should always be surprised who has been cast on *All Stars* and what the show is. That's what *All Stars* will always deliver.

TOM CAMPBELL: Thairin Smothers is the one who interfaces with the queens once they leave the show. He knows everybody and has a beat on everyone. The queens have to be in the right place. They have to feel like they have something they want to show. Sometimes they're so busy working that the idea of prepping for *Drag Race* is out of the question. Or they're booked in Europe or they've put down drag for a little bit.

MANDY SALANGSANG: Thairin will give us a group of twenty people who might be interested and we, with RuPaul and the other producers, will start to see who in the group would make a good ensemble. We are looking for compelling story lines—who went home too soon and have voiced they have more to prove? Who has had a glow up since their season? There are so many variables.

CARSON KRESSLEY: *All Stars* is my favorite of the franchise because often queens come on the show and they're not quite ready for all that it entails. They get to go out in the real world, they get to be part of the tour, they get to work in the clubs, which I think is so important, and they get to really learn the art of drag. And then they come back with all of this knowledge and polish. So to see people really hone their craft and polish their art and come back and slay is very gratifying for all of us involved with the show.

ALEXIS MATEO: We were touring and I got the call to go back to *All Stars*. I got such great feedback that I was like, oh yeah, people want to see more of me, so let's go. It was intimidating to walk into the werkroom and see every fan favorite, girl, from the first four seasons of *Drag Race* in there. It was scary as hell.

MORGAN MCMICHAELS: I felt like this time around was going to be very good for me because during Season 2 I was impersonating so many other people that I didn't really have an identity of my own. It had been ten years when I got on *All Stars*. I knew who I was and I knew what I was doing.

TAMMIE BROWN: After Season 1, I don't even think I made $1,000. I was a sitting duck. Misunderstood. I was not given the respect and the appreciation for who I was. I struggled. After *All Stars*, I was no longer an underdog anymore. I'm really grateful to have been able to be on *All Stars*.

VALENTINA: My elimination definitely made me want to go on *All Stars*. I was immature on Season 9. I was hyperfocused and not making friends or having fun. I was tense and eager to win so I wanted to come back and let people have fun with me and show my heart and my humor. The way that it ended for me is not how I wanted to be remembered.

TATIANNA: I got to introduce myself to a whole entire new generation of fans of the show. I got to reestablish who Tatianna is, what she does.

RONAN FARROW: Even though I was bowled over by the professionalism the show has acquired after those earlier, scrappier seasons, I also was less surprised by that than I was that it still maintains a bit of the scrappy heart. I don't think it has lost its identity for all the ways it has changed. When I first showed up on set, the producers were briefing me and were describing how the camera blocking works, and what the process is going to be, and the lighting. And then they said that the queens may be a little horny, so watch out! And I'm like, wait, wait, hold on a second, the queens may be horny? And of course everyone was extremely professional, though appropriately for the medium, because it's part of the DNA, also a little horny, which I thought was really funny. I should only be so lucky!

Although the fan-favorite format is a reality television staple, it almost didn't work on *Drag Race*. Created as a team sport featuring pairs of favorite queens from the first four seasons who had the ability to stop each other mid–lip sync by pressing a shemergency button, the first *All Stars* didn't goop anyone, although the cast did. The teams were Raven and Jujubee, Nina Flowers and Tammie Brown, Latrice Royale and Manila Luzon, Chad Michaels and Shannel, Alexis Mateo and Yara Sofia, and Pandora Boxx and Mimi Imfurst.

TOM CAMPBELL: Because Logo had a small budget, they offered us six episodes for the first *All Stars*. That's not enough. So from the goodness of our hearts but not from the brains of our producers, we decided to have them compete as teams. That was my bad idea. My desire was to get as many drag queens on the show as possible.

ALEXIS MATEO: I hate *All Stars* 1.

JOHN POLLY: I believe I suggested this line: "This season is about charisma, uniqueness, nerve, talent, and synergy." The S fits into CUNTS because of having to come together. I will take credit for that.

TOM CAMPBELL: This was my butterflies, okay? We were thinking it would be like *The Amazing Race*. But we learned a couple of things—it's hard enough to see an All Star go away, eliminated, period. To see two of them felt like the massacre at Moldavia. As we were doing it, we were like, ohhhh no. It was brutal and we felt bad about it.

JUJUBEE: I thought the idea was incredibly strange but I immediately wondered if we get to pick teams because I knew who I would pick and who would pick me. Raven and I loved each other and needed each other in the competition.

ALEXIS MATEO: Ohhh my god, the teams news was probably the worst news we had ever heard in *Drag Race* history. Nobody wants to carry someone around. But I was very happy to be paired with Yara Sofia. At least we had a connection.

YARA SOFIA: I was so excited to do *All Stars* because I had money. I know the system better. If we had time to get ready for it, we can bring stuff that matches and turn the party. To be in teams you have to be cohesive or you have to be opposite, so everything changed when we heard this. It was the worst.

NINA FLOWERS: We were all like, what the fuck? Competing with someone in teams, that's the hardest shit ever. You can't really do your thing. You have to think about your partnership.

LATRICE ROYALE: Horrible. Horr-i-ble. How dare you make me come here for this? I was so mad.

CHAD MICHAELS: I think we all wanted to compete as solo entertainers but everybody knew each other, and everyone had a special relationship there with somebody. It was not an ideal situation but it worked out.

MANILA LUZON: The best part about *All Stars* 1 for me was the fact that I got to become partners with Latrice Royale and, bitch, now we are the best of friends.

LATRICE ROYALE: The best part about it was my friendship and relationship with Manila. So if nothing else, that was well worth the aggravation, disappointment, and humiliation.

Teamwork wasn't the only aspect of the season that backfired. Producers gave the queens a 911 button to press if their teammate needed a lip-sync rescue, but only one queen took advantage of it.

JOHN POLLY: It's not genius but the shemergency button that they were supposed to press, that was me.

TOM CAMPBELL: They say if you introduce a gun in a play the gun has to go off at some point. We have introduced a button so that you can both lip sync, but only one person used it and at the end of the song. Push the button! Make something with the button. I'm angry about the button.

JUJUBEE: I thought that that was crazy and I was never going to press the button because I trust my teammate.

CHAD MICHAELS: It's a team thing so I think that made it fair for the other team member if they were feeling threatened that at least they had an option to do something, so I was totally okay with it. That made it a little bit more fair.

YARA SOFIA: You know why nobody would press the button? Because nobody has the nerve to say, "Hey, you're fucking it up." We gotta press it! It's fun.

ALEXIS MATEO: I started the performance, and not even thirty-five seconds later, Yara pressed that button. She should have told me that from the beginning. I would have let her lip sync.

YARA SOFIA: We planned it! I said to Alexis that she was gonna start the song and I'm gonna finish it. She knew I was pressing the button. We were saying it in the werkroom. We didn't even know how it sounds. It would be fun.

ALEXIS MATEO: I was so upset with Yara. That was like a slap in the face. We never got over this, girl. We grew apart after *All Stars* 1.

TOM CAMPBELL: I thought it was a great way to get them both onstage but I guess we didn't communicate that well. So my bad. I take full responsibility. I'm glad I still have my job after *All Stars* 1.

NINA FLOWERS: They never did it again. That should tell you everything.

It would be four years before producers dared to make another season of *All Stars*. When it returned in 2016, the rules had changed: Each week, the top two queens would battle in a lip sync to win cash and the right to send one of the queens in the bottom home. The cast was lit, with Season 5 girls and other favorite faves, like Adore Delano, who crushed the fandom when she quit after the first episode. The format stuck around until Season 5, much to BenDeLaCreme's disappointment in the third cycle.

TOM CAMPBELL: What we have learned along the way, we've done little twists and turns since then, but any group of queens make great *Drag Race* television.

DETOX: All of us were fuckin' gagged, gooped, and bewildered. It was an interesting twist but also we probably should have expected that coming.

ALASKA: For a harmonious few hours, we legitimately thought RuPaul's not sending anyone home. We're all gonna stay the whole time. Then the other shoe dropped. It becomes a disadvantage when the hard choices have to be made and you have to start choosing who gets sent home. That would be easier if you didn't really know people 'cause you'd just be like, yeah, you can get the fuck out of here, I don't know who the fuck you are.

BENDELACREME: When I watched *All Stars* 2 and they created the new rules of the queens sending other queens home, it was hard for me as a viewer and a friend because I cared so much about those queens. I had worked with most of them and formed really strong friendships with a lot of them. I didn't want to see queens hurting each other unnecessarily, so I just had difficulty with the format.

TOM CAMPBELL: When BenDeLaCreme left, my initial reaction in the moment was it is unfathomable. She could have won. The next week she was gone.

BENDELACREME: It started to occur to me that I don't feel like I have a lot left to prove. I remembered that Thorgy had been painting her fingernails with Wite-Out and I asked her if she still had it so I could write my name. I just knew I needed to work as fast as possible so that nobody has time to stop me because, of course, there's people watching. I was so nervous and I didn't know what anybody was going to think and I didn't know if anybody was going to stop me. The cameraman Sarge, who is everybody's favorite cameraman on set, mouthed to me *You're a rock star.* In that moment, I knew I had done the right thing. It felt really right.

THORGY THOR: I didn't have any white nail polish so I had painted my nails with Wite-Out right before one of the challenges because I wanted white nails. So Ben goes, "Do you still have that Wite-Out that you have for your nails?" I gave it to her, apparently she went in the back, did that, and then gave it back to me, and I was like, thanks girl, and I put it back in my bag and that was that. When she pulled it out, I was like ohhh shit.

BENDELACREME: It was a really powerful feeling and it felt very linked to how Ru made me feel when I was young, which is that the rules of the world around me didn't work for me and they didn't work for Ru and so she broke all those rules. I had been so conflicted all along and it felt like this is the best way to honor this art form that I love.

TRIXIE MATTEL: Iconic, defining moment and 100 percent shocking.

AJA: Is this bitch serious? This is corny as fuck. Girl, I was like, whatever, Ben pulling the shenanigan.

JOEY NOLFI: I believe that DeLa maybe was anticipating backlash from other queens for sending certain people home because she was tasked with sending very popular people home.

KENNEDY DAVENPORT: I truly believe that Ben was keeping her integrity intact. She didn't want to be put in that type of position anymore.

RONAN FARROW: I thought it was really unsportsmanlike and just overplaying his hand. I think that she got caught up in the self-mythologizing of, like, oh I have this winning streak. It felt disrespectful to me.

TRIXIE MATTEL: On television, it appeared that the decision was entirely in goodwill. But in real life there's a lot of aspects of *Drag Race* that Ben doesn't appreciate. Ben could feel the season shaping in her favor and Ben thought what if I fuck this whole thing up? I really think a part of Ben was *I'm gonna teach everyone here a lesson.*

TOM CAMPBELL: We are trying to find ways to give the queens the responsibility of the elimination, so we created a jury of queers. But

422 Maria Elena Fernandez

it didn't turn out the way people wanted. It's hard to dispute Trixie Mattel because she is an amazing queen. But we're not going to repeat that. It was an interesting experiment.

BENDELACREME: I just solved the Matrix and then there I was sitting around in my big, red hat in the jury. That was a doozie. I did not enjoy that at all. I don't know if that made any sense.

TRIXIE MATTEL: I couldn't believe they chose me. It was crazy. Shangela is crouching and fake crying. You notice there's no tears. Kennedy runs backstage like she's not the father. And I'm just stunned. But I'm not going to convince the person who's won five challenges to stay. I felt like a one-legged horse and Seabiscuit just left the race. I was like, yes!

RONAN FARROW: It was sad because Shangela was someone who had a real arc that was very fulfilling—had been small and bitchy in those earlier appearances on the show and then had really grown to be this kind of elder stateswoman and is terrific on that season.

TRIXIE MATTEL: I love *Drag Race*. I love the drama, I love the pettiness, I love the competition, the greatness, I love all of it. I am proud to wear a crown that represents everything it stands for. Ben, as a competitor who is not about the drama, realized she wasn't gonna be proud to win that title. It's not even personal. She didn't want the crown because it's a reality show.

The fourth season of *All Stars* would also make *Drag Race* herstory—this time, it was RuPaul who surprised everyone.

TOM CAMPBELL: We have always thought about doing a tie and Monét and Trinity were both really good. It was hard to pick. It was Ru's decision.

MONÉT X CHANGE: My honest reaction was I would've much rather

Trinity get it and then me get a chance to come back sometime later. And she felt the same way about me. So in that moment we were like, girl, come on. But now in retrospect, we both got the money. We both got the crown and we both worked really hard for it. It's also the only tie I think that will probably ever happen in *Drag Race* history so we are cemented in *Drag Race* forever in that way. I'm not mad at that.

TRINITY THE TUCK: Now that I have had time to digest it, I wouldn't change it. I feel like it's not even really about winning. It's about the fact that we got representation—not just one gay man on TV, we got two gay men winning together in equality—[it's] such a statement. I'm getting chills right now. To me, that is more important than me having my own moment. I feel like we made a statement and will always be forever remembered that way. I call her my twinner.

To become a Ru girl means an induction to the world's most colorful and self-possessed sorority. These days, drag and *Drag Race* are big business. The show has spawned an entire economy, a slate of powerhouse stars, and a dominant presence in mass culture. No longer relegated to special queer corners of the arts, Ru girls have taken over fashion, entertainment, and music. They tour the world, star in spin-offs, create their own podcasts and shows, and sell lots of merchandise. They push the boundaries of fashion, sashaying onto the runways of Paris, London, and Milan and starring in high-profile campaigns for Prada, Moschino, and others. They top the Billboard charts and star in commercials and movies. Some, like Shangela, who glammed it up for McDonald's and Lady Gaga on *A Star Is Born*, have done both. Every year, blockbuster DragCons worldwide draw tens of thousands of guests of all shapes, colors, and sizes.

FENTON BAILEY: DragCon came out of the desire to expand the show beyond TV and our screens. *Drag Race* became this event at the gay bars, which wasn't something that we anticipated because everyone was hooking up online and people just weren't going to gay bars anymore. But *Drag Race* brought people back into the bars and we were thinking about that. We had never run a convention but we just scratched together all the money we could and booked the convention hall.

RANDY BARBATO: It felt like it was time to bring the tribe together. RuPaul also pushed us to do DragCon.

TOM CAMPBELL: Based on the ratings on Logo, we were the lowest-rated show in the country every week and yet we knew people were watching it and fans were responding. It's one of the reasons that Fenton and Randy took the risk on DragCon.

RUPAUL: It is the most beautiful thing in the world. It's every flower in every bloom. We're talking straight, gay, black, white. We're talking eight-year-old kids and seventy-five-year-old women. We're talking everybody. A utopia.

TOM CAMPBELL: It was moms and daughters and dads and gay people and old gay people and young gay people and people in drag and people dressed as lobsters and people in leather and people in street clothes.

RANDY BARBATO: I remember standing at the first DragCon and we were all looking at all the people in line to get in and it was like oh my god. We knew we were selling tickets. But just seeing how many people and seeing what kind of people were showing up. That was when it became clear that *Drag Race* was touching people the way it was touching us.

FENTON BAILEY: It's great for us to see the audience of the show because the research says our demographic is young, male, and gay. But it really isn't. It's more female than male and it's not particularly gay. And one of the great things to see is that it's so multi-generational. What DragCon showed us is that drag is a universally relatable thing. It's not very niche like some network executives thought it was.

BENDELACREME: I was at DragCon and there were people coming through my booth and I had it closed off with curtains so that it would be more intimate when people were in there and we could really share a moment. But it has to move quickly because there's a lot of people. And this kid came in with his mom and Gus, my partner, was there with me, and we both just had the breath sucked out of our bodies. I saw him look at me and I instantly knew that he registered exactly what I was registering—which is that this kid looked exactly like me as a child. I mean, the spitting image. It was wild. At his age, my mom was my support, too. I got to sit down with him and we probably talked for fifteen minutes and told him everything I wish I could've been told. I told him he was valuable and that there were people out there who loved him and would love him and that there was a future for him and that I believed in him and it was maybe the most cathartic moment of my life. Those are the kinds of things that *Drag Race* has allowed that I think shift our culture and are changing our culture for the better, and I'm really grateful for that.

TOM CAMPBELL: Where other people might see them as freaks, we see them as heroes and we celebrate them. If you have a lisp, we love that. All the things that were knocked away because you're queer or you're feminine-acting or this or that, we celebrate that because you are expressing who you want to be and isn't that the most powerful thing? And to have that out in the universe and for people to see it and then to go to DragCon and see little kids there with their parents, you know people are watching and getting it.

JOHN POLLY: As it moved to VH1 and became more visible for people, the way it took off makes sense, but it's still crazily unexpected. But seeing queens talk about what they have been through and being hell-bent on being themselves, no matter what, and being the star of their own show, people relate to it. People aspire to it, I think. At DragCon the first time, we saw people celebrating dressing up. They were celebrating the courage to be whoever the hell you want to be, and it's moms with their kids who are so appreciative of seeing these bright, powerful, colorful people.

TOM CAMPBELL: It's not lost on us that we've had this second bite at fame once Chris McCarthy put us on VH1 and that it look a long time. Long ago, we had been told by an executive that *Drag Race* is a filler show until you find a branded show that defines your network. So we were fun for now but we weren't a definitional show. Look at us now, heeeeyyy.

VICTORIA "PORKCHOP" PARKER: Before *RuPaul's Drag Race*, the highest honor that you could have in the world of drag or female impersonation was to win a national pageant. If you wanted to make top dollar, if you wanted to be a huge success, that's what you did. And RuPaul turned it around for us. If you can get cast on the show, you can still get paid top dollar never having done drag. The pageant owners and the pageants have lost contestants. There used to be forty to fifty contestants in a national competition. Now they're lucky if they have twenty or thirty because people see that RuPaul has given them an opportunity to not have to spend every dime they have to satisfy a judges' panel that may turn their nose up at them. If I get cast on the show, and get the national exposure, that puts me further from the pageant field.

BENDELACREME: I think sometimes about that thirteen-year-old lost, sad kid who thought maybe there was no future for him. And I think about the idea of being able to travel back in time and say not only are you gonna be okay, but this is what your life is going to look like. *Drag Race* has shifted our culture for the better.

CHAD MICHAELS: Before *Drag Race*, I was traveling nationally, sometimes a little bit internationally. Cher took me a lot of places. I wasn't just Chad who does drag from San Diego. I was Chad who does Cher. So I got to do things. But *Drag Race* really blew it out. I got to really travel and meet people and really enjoy the fruits of what I'd accomplished on the show. There's also DragCon and this whole merchandising thing, which if you're smart and have a good team, you can do really well and have a good time at the same time.

PANDORA BOXX: It's opened the doors for so many people that aren't even on *Drag Race*. It's created this whole world and subculture. There are places to get all this jewelry. There's places to get costumes designed, there's so many places to get wigs and wigs styled. There are makeup lines made by drag queens for drag queens. It's this whole world that *Drag Race* has helped create.

RANDY BARBATO: I love that there is a drag economy that exists. The thing that excites me the most about the drag economy are the actual drag queens and hoping that they are putting money in their pockets, paying taxes and investing in an IRA. It's exciting to see that.

SASHA VELOUR: I learned from Ru and from *Drag Race* about how there are certain things that just work, that hook people, that get them excited, that get them paying attention. And the first step is getting people to listen before you start sharing your crazy, or more challenging thoughts. I learned how to capture people's excitement and attention through *Drag Race*, which has done that around the whole world to great success. I learned where to invest my time and my money into my drag to make it really pay off. There's no rules really for drag, but it's become much more serious business in the last couple years.

KATYA: A rich drag queen is a very new concept. Even queens who were nationally or internationally known, before *Drag Race*, whether they were in the comedy circuit or the pageant scene or had somehow managed to get cameos in film or television, they still didn't have any money. None of them. Maybe they were able to do drag as a full-time job and make ends meet, but nobody was ever rich. To see drag queens on TV in the *All Stars* seasons, where they're coming in with a $50,000 wardrobe, is bizarre and new viewers are getting to know that as their first experience of drag. And I'm like oh, no, no, no, no, no, no, no. We were haggling for $3.99 fabric a yard! I had never, ever owned a costume that cost more than $100, $200.

RANDY BARBATO: It's hard work to be a drag queen. And to be able to help some of them actually be able to work and make a living and buy a home and be respected like any other entertainer is a great thing.

And I really believe that long after *Drag Race*, drag queens and drag as a form of entertainment will be a legitimate form of entertainment. It won't be just our show. It will be legitimate everywhere. There is this whole group of artists that have existed since the beginning of humanity but have been so marginalized. And *Drag Race* has helped open people's eyes to hiring them for other jobs. It's our gift to the entertainment industry.

ADORE DELANO: It changed my life tremendously. I got to do and I'm still doing music. I have a number three album. This type of stuff would've never happened if I wouldn't have gotten on the show. That's why I'm forever grateful. My dream was to chart on the Billboard charts and the show catapulted me to do that and make dozens and dozens of music videos. After *Idol*, I traveled to Pittsburgh one time and then I went to Vegas and slept with a promoter. But nothing like this. I am traveling almost every week somewhere different. I've gotten to see an entire world, almost, and vibe with people from everywhere and hear their stories. You can't ask for more. You can't buy that type of education.

MORGAN MCMICHAELS: Because of *Drag Race* I got to be in Lady Gaga's video and Rihanna's video and Lizzo's video. I was featured on so many different television shows and I'm grateful. Drag was always work and then *Drag Race* made it a career. Girls have traveled the world because of *RuPaul's Drag Race*.

THORGY THOR: When I'm interviewing Adam Rippon, the Olympic skater, for Vice, that's a great opportunity and that's mainstream. Everyone finally has caught up to how smart and eloquent and dirty we are. I just love that we can do whatever we want as artistic people. But it has become so mainstream now that we have to be role models for eleven-year-old little girls. We have to do family shows that are sold out. Everywhere I look, it's somebody in makeup and a wig. Pretty soon I think we're gonna go all right, we're bored with drag, what's next?

ALEXIS MATEO: Being on *Drag Race* gave me the opportunity to save my mom from cancer. Not only can I afford my life but I can literally afford her life. It was a gift. Even though I grew up in a Latin culture where everything that you do that is not by a gender identification as a male is considered a sin, I got to watch her and spend more time with her and know that she is okay. And I get to inspire little kids to grow up and not go through the things that I have gone through. I have inspired the Latin community to know that we are not just a language or a place out there around the world. We are human beings and I think we are being respected everywhere. I understand the impact that it's having right now in the world because I know how big the impact is in my life. I finally found what I was born to do. And it was a beautiful, beautiful moment in my life.

MARIAH PARIS BALENCIAGA: I'm a professional drag queen now. I was a hairstylist by trade and I've gotten opportunities to travel to places doing drag that I never heard of. I'm a drag queen, a gay man from Gainesville, Georgia, and I went to fucking Croatia. I've done drag in Vienna. It's crazy some of the places that I've been to that I would've never have dreamt to have been able to afford to visit, let alone do drag there. It's a very privileged life I have.

MANILA LUZON: I never expected to be working ten years later. I thought that after the show I would go back to my job, maybe do a gig in Florida or Illinois on weekends, and I would come back and do my job. But it hasn't slowed down. It keeps getting bigger and bigger and bigger and more people are interested in it every year.

BLAIR ST. CLAIR: I own two businesses from the name I have built with the exposure of *RuPaul's Drag Race*. I would not have been able to do that at the accelerated rate that I have been able to do it. In 2020, the year of Covid, I didn't have any income from performance but because of those businesses, I was able to survive.

DIDA RITZ: It helps being a Ru girl in the industry of drag. I think there is a sense of respect and responsibility that comes with that because you are representing RuPaul and you are representing World of

Wonder and you're representing *RuPaul's Drag Race* and Logo or now VH1. You're representing so much for your community. That is the cool part. It really warms my heart that I have been blessed to be able to make people happy.

ALYSSA EDWARDS: A highlight of it all is me goin' to the MTV Movie Awards with RuPaul right after Season 5. I was his plus-one. I thought that was the win. You didn't get the crown, here I am, sittin' in a car with him, we pull up to those awards, I got a picture of that that I still look at. I giggle sometimes 'cause things happen the way they're supposed to happen. I didn't win the crown but I won the hearts of the people all around the world. That's a bigger win. And, honey, she got the spin-off. Okay?

MONÉT X CHANGE: Without *RuPaul's Drag Race*, I might still be trying to make it and still trying to audition for Broadway shows and movies and probably never finding my way. But because of *Drag Race*, I have now developed this global platform and the opportunities have been bountiful and endless. RuPaul is an icon and a trailblazer and I am forever eternally grateful for what he has done for me and how he has afforded me the chances and the opportunities to take care of my family and to take care of my friends, by just allowing me to do a fake split on his international TV show.

COCO MONTRESE: Companies are comfortable now to hire us to entertain people. The experience of being at the MTV Awards and walking the red carpet and the likes of Rihanna and all these people knowing us by name, just like we know them by name. It's surreal. If the show had never happened, I don't think that this is where drag would be in the world at all.

FENTON BAILEY: Being British and knowing what amazing drag we have in the UK, I incorrectly assumed a UK version would quickly follow the US version. Instead it took five years of pitching all the networks and re-pitching them until they were sick of the sight of me. But it couldn't have worked out better because the BBC is the ideal home for the show in the UK. The BBC is a non-commercial channel created to provide a public service—which is exactly what *Drag Race* does. The only downside is that we aren't allowed to provide a cash prize to the winner.

MICHELLE VISAGE: One of the reasons I fought so hard to get *Drag Race UK* done was because I saw the impact *Drag Race* was having on queer culture and drag culture in the United Kingdom. That's why I did *Big Brother*, to bring eyes on *RuPaul's Drag Race*. It took five years but ultimately we got it done on the biggest network in the UK.

But we had taken it around for years and nobody wanted it. Around the world, I've seen it go from me just doing gay bars to me touring. I got to play Wembley Arena with drag queens. We sold out Wembley. The best thing in the world has been seeing the progression in all these countries.

RUPAUL: We've created a platform for these fabulous performers to launch a career that spans the globe. They're out there working right now, and they're making really, really big bucks doing it. They literally are getting rich and I fucking love that.

With twenty-six Emmy wins, *Drag Race* is the most awarded reality competition show in television history. For seven consecutive years, RuPaul also has won the Emmy for outstanding reality host, a job with several roles that he plays in and out of drag: tough taskmaster, therapist, runway slayer, and judge. Nowhere else in the TV universe is there a reality host doling out wisdom and messages of acceptance and tough love like on *Drag Race*. But now with twelve total Emmys under his purse, RuPaul stands as the most decorated Black artist in Emmys herstory.

FENTON BAILEY: When I think about America, I think about Andy Warhol or Liberace or Walt Disney. These are all people who invented themselves, who to differing degrees of seriousness didn't take themselves too seriously, and who completely shaped what we understand America to be. I see drag as fitting right in there and I think that people have responded to *Drag Race* because they recognize that, yes, that's what America is, that's what's making America great.

RANDY BARBATO: *Drag Race* has always offered hope about the human race in general. It's this show that people go to and it inspires people. During these dark times, it's not only inspiring that die-hard fan base, but I think it has also inspired the industry a little bit. I think that's why we've been invited to the big kids' table at the Emmys.

TOM CAMPBELL: We lived eight seasons without ever being considered for an award. We didn't do this thinking let's make award-winning programming. It was quite the opposite.

RANDY BARBATO: It was such a slow-burning thing. It was very gradual.

JOEY NOLFI: When have you ever heard of another show not getting any sort of attention, scripted or otherwise, and then nine seasons in, it starts becoming a damn Emmys juggernaut? It defies all statistics. And now here we are talking about RuPaul being the most decorated Black artist in Emmys history. It blows my mind. I hate to put so much stock into conforming or being accepted by the mainstream, by the machine, but you can't deny it. It's not like they are just throwing a bone to someone. There is a reason why this is the show that was able to do it. Did it ever cross my mind that it could have gotten to this level? Absolutely not. I never thought that that community could be accepted in that way because that is not what my experience was. It's a really significant thing to see that it has transcended that.

THAIRIN SMOTHERS: Walking down the red carpet for the Emmys the first time, talk about your body overheating to a point where you can't even control your own emotions because your childhood dreams are coming true. And to hear RuPaul's name, that first time he won host, I can tell you it was probably the only time I have had an out-of-body experience without drugs or alcohol.

TOM CAMPBELL: *Drag Race* is like the tree that grew from the crack in the sidewalk. It was not properly nurtured, it was not planted. And it has blossomed into this beautiful thing which is now being rewarded and recognized in the second part of its life. I don't take for granted that it's going to last forever. There's so much good work that's done out there, but it is so amazing to have an industry and Academy members come back and say good job. We get to work really hard on a show that spreads love and self-expression and tolerance and a lot of dirty puns into the world.

FENTON BAILEY: It's like those posters he was sticking up in Atlanta in the early '80s—it was true then and it's true now—RUPAUL IS EVERYTHING. But in addition, one of the things about the show is that the format of the show is actually inspired by and attributed to a drag queen. The show itself is a drag queen. The show takes bits and pieces from all different other shows, from popular culture, mixes it all up, celebrates it, and makes fun of it. And as all drag queens know, you can't wear the same outfit twice. You have to keep changing it up and reinventing it and a wig on a wig on a wig and a twist on a twist on a twist. What hopefully will keep the Emmys coming, 'cause you can never have too many, is the fact that the show keeps on reinventing itself.

RANDY BARBATO: The secret sauce of *Drag Race* is the heart, the soul, the humanity. And it becomes about the connection we have, what we have in common with these queens. You come for the spectacle, you leave feeling connected deeply. That is the contribution not just to the queer community but to the world at large because I do think it's about reminding everyone how much we all have in common.

FENTON BAILEY: One of the most moving things, and I get a little teary actually, is seeing queens on the show who remember watching the show before they knew what they wanted to do with their creativity and it inspired them to do drag. That is so moving because gay people struggle to find their place in the world and it isn't easy to be your authentic self. I think that the very idea that people could watch this show or see this show and then identify for themselves a career and a vocation and succeed at it and do well at it is better than any Emmy.

Chapter 12

THE LEGACY

A MONTH BEFORE THE FIRST SEASON OF *RuPaul's Drag Race* PRE-miered on then five-year-old gay niche cable network Logo, RuPaul and three of the first season's contestants appeared at a press junket in Los Angeles to promote the new show. When asked about the reality competition's inspiration, RuPaul let loose: "The universe called and we answered that call! This was a show that had to be made. Whether it came up at a toilet stall at Illusions on Santa Monica Boulevard, I mean, really, it doesn't matter. The fact is that we have this show that is going to turn TV upside down."

At the time, it just seemed like typical hyperbolic claims from an enthusiastic TV producer and star. But fourteen years and a global empire later, the tea had been served.

BOB THE DRAG QUEEN: Let's face it, there's a whole lot of fucking drag queens. I think that the overt queerness, the overt fem-ness and faggy-ness that *RuPaul's Drag Race* uplifts has really allowed a lot of people to be so much more themselves. When I was a kid, if me and all the other gays at school had *Drag Race* to fawn over, we would have found each other. Instead, we had to hide around *The Sound of Music* in the theater department.

NINA FLOWERS: Everybody wants to be a drag queen these days, *everybody*. Do you remember the movie *The Gremlins*? They were wet and reproduced. That's what happened with queens after *RuPaul's Drag Race*, honey. *RuPaul's Drag Race* wet all of us and we all reproduced. There's so many legendary children now. That's the truth. People are taking drag more seriously, and they see the art behind all the hard work. I think it's fucking awesome.

LAGANJA ESTRANJA: Drag *is* the culture, honey! We are the culture, honey. The only reason to go to bars, at least when I was out, on Monday nights was because of *RuPaul's Drag Race*. We became the new norm. We are what queer people look up to. Now there are plenty of queer people who don't watch *RuPaul's Drag Race*, and specifically maybe in the lesbian category, because my sister and her wife, *girl, please*. They watched it for me and that was it. It has influenced everything. It has influenced beauty and makeup, it has influenced the way we use social media because the queens are so savvy. It has influenced vocabulary. It has influenced acceptance.

RONAN FARROW: I have to stop myself all the time from saying condragulations in a non–*Drag Race* context. I love that. I have the full lexicon at my disposal now. I do find myself saying that I'm gooped a lot to people's confusion because that one still hasn't made it out of the *Drag Race* culture and into the mainstream as much.

TOM CAMPBELL: When Michelle Obama was sitting next to the Bushes at an inaugural event in 2017, there was an article that said she threw shade. We're not the only people that say "throw shade" but I kept wondering, are they using drag terms to report about the First Lady of the United States?

RAVEN: Drag now has so many different fan groups in social media. It's not just *RuPaul's Drag Race*, but fans of drag. And there are people now who understand it's not this creepy weird thing that guys do for sexual pleasure. So everyone wants to do drag and then there's queens who think, because they're in drag, they have to get onstage but it's boring because they have no stage presence. But you don't have to get in drag and be onstage. You can get in drag and go try and make money at being a model, you can be someone who is a host at a party, or run the bingo or something else. It's an art form now with a lot of possibilities.

RANDY BARBATO: We have lived through the development of the relationship between social media and television and its impact on a show like *RuPaul's Drag Race*. As the show was growing, it made some girls a little more reserved because of the anxiety of how they would be received by social media, because the fans are so intense. But I think we survived that because the sisterhood of the queens is so strong that they can have an argument, they can have a fight, but they have each other's backs. The last three or four seasons we've come through the fire of social media and I believe we're headed to the other side.

CARSON KRESSLEY: As a lover of drag and the artistry of drag and someone who saw it growing up in the nightclubs of New York, you think that everybody knows who Lady Bunny is and RuPaul and Varla Jean Merman and Miss Richfield 1981. And then you get out into the world and people are like, *who*? With the exception of Ru. But the show has allowed this cloistered artwork to be seen by millions and millions of people around the world that would have never seen it because in the past, unless you were going to a gay club or Wigstock or maybe a Pride parade, you weren't going to be exposed to drag artistry.

BEBE ZAHARA BENET: There is this fusion now between pop culture and drag where a lot of pop culture is taking a lot from the drag art form and the drag art form is taking stuff from pop culture. We get the opportunity now to bring up many different interpretations of drag. Even cis women now want to do drag. They are so inspired. That's why I say don't say "drag queen" because I feel like that term has evolved and people are becoming drag artists. People are using this heightened version of whatever that is to create and to celebrate and to elevate. And I think that a lot of it has to do with the fact that they can watch *Drag Race*. They don't have to go to the clubs. They can just turn on the television and they can get to see entertainers do all these different things. It's so beautiful to see how *Drag Race* has also really helped drag have a stamp on pop culture.

ASIA O'HARA: Prior to *Drag Race*, drag would have to find inspiration in mainstream culture and mainstream music and fashion. And now, thanks to *Drag Race*, pop stars and designers can look at drag and be inspired by that to make mainstream art.

RONAN FARROW: For so many LGBT people growing up, it introduced their community to people around them. They know a lot more about gay people and gay culture because of it. And as the show has gone on, there's now great trans representation and other denominations of LGBT. For those young people watching the show growing up, and for me individually, as an adult watching the show, it has played an indispensable role in pushing back against the devaluing of femininity in our culture. At a time when toxic masculinity is entwined with so many cultural problems and political problems we face, and there is a segment of the population, gay and straight, that is hurting and struggling and feels adrift because of a broken relationship with their femininity, that role that the show plays in elevating the feminine and tearing down walls in what it means to be a man or be someone of any gender or no gender, wearing feminine clothes, that is of a value that can't be overstated.

TOM CAMPBELL: Being gay, historically, is a lot about trauma and self-loathing. I have it. The *Drag Race* queens have it. RuPaul has it. The queer folk at World of Wonder have it. But instead of being defined by that, somewhere along the way, we decided to rise above the pain and revel in the fact that we see the truth through a different lens—and that is and has always been incredibly important. When you find your tribe, it's truly fantastic. A lot of the things that we celebrate on *Drag Race*—bright colors and dirty jokes and laughter and tears and Britney Spears and jockstraps—come from our common language of love, survival, and joy.

JINKX MONSOON: Before *Drag Race* existed, you got into drag because there was something dark you needed to overcome. You didn't get into drag because you loved makeup. That might be an aspect of it. You didn't get into drag because you wanted to be famous. Certainly not, because we were all treated like shit in our own community. We were stigmatized and discriminated against and people treated us like freaks. You didn't get into drag because it was fun and everyone was going to celebrate you. You got into drag as a suit of armor to protect you from something dark. And that has decreased and I think that's a good thing. I think it's good that people are getting into drag as a way to celebrate themselves and a way to celebrate drag as an art form.

FENTON BAILEY: Without being overtly political, I do think drag and *Drag Race* is going to be identified as the essence of the opposition. *Drag Race* is about, yes, we are all snowflakes and that is fucking fabulous. We are all unique creations. Let's celebrate that. I think drag is about opening your heart and welcoming in other people. For many, many years with gay rights, people have talked about tolerance, about being tolerated. Well, honestly, who wants to be tolerated? You tolerate a bad smell or you tolerate an uncomfortable seat. No, we don't want to be tolerated, we want to be embraced and loved. And *Drag Race*, as a show, is about embracing and loving people, not just loving our own kind but loving everybody. It's not about building walls, it's actually about tearing them down. It's not about being violent and hostile, it's actually about being vulnerable and open. So in every respect I think the values of *Drag Race* are the exact opposite of what Trump and the Republicans have tried to sell people for the last several years.

JUJUBEE: There's so much more respect for drag now. Before, the only people who did drag were people who couldn't get a job, people who couldn't cut it as a man, people who didn't have any aspirations, and they assumed that we were just dirt. And now the aspiration is to be this great queen. I think that people felt uncomfortable with drag because of the idea that we empower femininity when society has told us for centuries that femininity is weak. As queens, we've done a great fucking job showing that femininity is power. And drag is this form that's showing the world that femininity and queenliness is available to everybody.

SASHA VELOUR: It refocused what pride around being queer was all about for me and celebrated gender play and imagination and queer gender expressions as part of what it means to be part of this community and protect in our community. *Drag Race* and the messages and the people and the stories that have been shared for the past fourteen years have taught people around the world about the kind of fluidity that exists within them. And I think it's opened up new conversations about gender, not just in terms of who's represented but what all kinds of people might experience in their lives and be able to tap into and play with.

ADORE DELANO: It has changed the queer community in terms of identity. It's not just black and white. There's nonbinary folk, there's trans people. *RuPaul's Drag Race* helps you understand a human and get to see their personality. We're not sexual beings. We're actually people with stories and families and backgrounds and lovers. But it's in pop culture in general. Like, yes girl, mama, okrrrrrr, it's everywhere.

DETOX: It's made queer culture a huge part of pop culture where people are looking at queer people a lot differently and more celebratory, which is amazing. You see drag popping up in all kinds of things, you see queer culture popping up in all kinds of things, whether it's a Pepsi commercial or television programs or movies. I think that it's done really amazing things to get our message out there as a queer community that we should be celebrated, that we have creativity, that we have value, that we belong in a mainstream society. To be a part of that history has been really an amazing and rewarding opportunity.

BLAIR ST. CLAIR: It has just meant the world to me to be a part of a social movement of gender equality and gender identity and also sexual orientation which is now publicized all over the world. I feel I have such an important job to do in the world, to help keep pushing us for more social change.

VICTORIA "PORKCHOP" PARKER: All those kids, who were nine or ten when I was on the show in 2009, have grown up watching *RuPaul's Drag Race*. Whether they are gay, straight, lesbian, whatever they are, they have an understanding and they have an appreciation of everyone and they are not shocked or appalled or taken aback by someone who dresses as a woman to be an entertainer or someone who is a trans or someone who is gay because they have learned and had that experience from the time they were a small child to be accepting of everyone because everyone has a destiny that they have to follow. They have learned to appreciate people. And RuPaul is a large part of that.

RUPAUL: Young people know it's a safe place to go. They know it's a place where they can learn a vernacular that will help them get through their lives. The survivors on our show—the people who have been thrown out of their families, who are excommunicated from their churches and their communities—have survived and found a family outside of their birth family. Young people know the show is a place to get these survival tools and a vernacular that will make them sound cool and look cool and also pick up a few style tips while they're at it.

TOM CAMPBELL: In the broadest sense, it's about representation. I can just contrast it to my childhood a thousand years ago when the closest thing to gay people on television was Uncle Arthur from *Bewitched* or Charles Nelson Reilly on a game show, *Match Game*. All these coded ideas of homosexuals. When I was in college, I could be gay because no one knew what gay was. I just was the guy that loved Diana Ross and seemed a little light in the loafers and dated lots of virgins. Since then, there's been a lot of queer representation on television. But oftentimes, there's been a sprinkling of gay characters or a quota. We have a stage that is filled with queer people, different backgrounds, different socioeconomic backgrounds. While they're all drag queens, they have very different stories.

LATRICE ROYALE: It has brought families together. You have had questions about your kids and you don't know why they act a certain way and then you sit down and you watch an episode of *Drag Race* and, all the sudden, the lightbulb comes on and now you're bonding over something and you have a newfound love. It's been remarkable as far as families ties. I really appreciate it because I wish I had something like that when I was young, something I can look on TV and say okay, my people. I think we need more of it.

RUPAUL: I grew up in San Diego watching *Monty Python* on PBS and it was the first time I thought, okay, my tribe exists out there. It was such a lifeline for me. I knew my tribe was out there; all I had to do was go find them. So I think about the young people out there in Saudi Arabia and Asia and South America and Wyoming, who have watched the show and have found refuge here with our girls and our vernacular and our outlook on life. I feel that the legacy of our show, *Drag Race*, is in those young people, and they will carry that legacy with them for the rest of their lives.

JINKX MONSOON: *Drag Race* has always brought up the issues that are prevalent in the LGBTQ community and in the drag community. It has never shied away from talking about substance abuse, mental health. I think the critics of the show want it to go further. And yes, *Drag Race* could go further in what it does, but *Drag Race* is a show about drag queens competing for a crown that chooses to also tackle a lot of difficult issues. We cannot put all of our expectations on one show. We cannot ask one group of people to be a voice for the entire community because our community is too diverse and has too much nuance in it to ask drag queens and a TV show about drag to be the voice for everyone. I think the fact that they're willing to go to those hard places is commendable for the biggest TV show that's for queer people and by queer people. [It] needs to just be more commonplace to have television that tells our stories from firsthand accounts. And it can't all be on the shoulders of a TV show that's about drag competition.

MICHELLE VISAGE: When they talk in the werkroom about their experiences, whether it's being HIV-positive or trans or conversion therapy or homelessness or addiction, I think that is so real and so raw and people relate to that. As the show grew, I think it became more and more popular with hetero kids that were ten, eleven, twelve, thirteen years old, because these are the ages where we don't fit in. These are the ages where we feel awkward and we might not necessarily identify as queer but we certainly identify as not normal by normal standards. I was a bullied kid. I never felt like I fit in. If I had something like *RuPaul's Drag Race* maybe I wouldn't have inflicted the self-harm that I inflicted upon myself because I would have known I wasn't alone.

MANILA LUZON: When we had *Drag U*, we realized that women were the ones tuning into the show. The show was made by drag queens for drag queens in a way, and now people are tuning in and really enjoying it. Some frumpy girl sitting at home sees this big old dude put on all this makeup and cinched and turn into the most glamorous thing in the world. It's inspiring for a young woman to realize she has the ability to create herself in whatever image she wants to.

DARIENNE LAKE: The hugeness of the show changed my life completely. But the greatest thing that I got from it was definitely the change in my parents and their relationship with me. I feel that was really the turning point for them to really start caring about who I was as a person.

BENDELACREME: *Drag Race* has created an international community. Drag has always been a sistership, long before it was popular. There has always been a sistership to this common experience but now that sistership has connected all over the world. I have been able to make connections with queens everywhere and with fans of drag, everywhere.

SHANNEL: When you receive emails from kids and they're eleven years old and they say I feel like I'm gay and I watched *RuPaul's Drag Race* and you make me feel comfortable in my skin, that's amazing. Our generation didn't have that. There were no social media platforms that would allow people to understand who you are. So aside from the monetary gain of being able to go out and make more money, it allowed me to have a voice in places with people that I probably would not have been able to.

COCO MONTRESE: I have been allowed to not only grow in my art but I've been allowed to travel the world and take care of my family, take care of my husband, and build my own empire and become this person. All the pictures on my wall are *Drag Race* girls. Alyssa's up there in that corner. Chad is right there, Yara Sofia. These are people that mean the world to me and it's just been the ride of my life.

ALEXIS MATEO: We have been inspiring people everywhere. We got to open doors and visit people everywhere in the world and inspire them. I think people are changing the way that they see themselves through the art of drag. Gender is not even followed any longer. We got to open that barrier and allow people to be free in their sexual expressions and their gender identification and their human rights. We have been shifting the way that people look at the world, period.

AJA: I think *Drag Race* is very influential and it created a lot of safe areas for queer communities. I've been to a lot of countries, like the Philippines or places in South America, where there is high crime on trans and LGBT communities. For them to have a safe space to gather together because of *Drag Race*, because of their love for drag or because they want to congregate and celebrate it, *Drag Race* has impacted that and forced that to happen quicker.

ALYSSA EDWARDS: This changed so much of my life because I feel like I'm more open. I feel like that fear of what people would think in Mesquite of how I lived my life, that judgment, it's all gone. It was so interesting because everybody embraced me. If I wouldn't have been on this show, I don't think I would have had the life experiences that I've had. I've traveled the world, I've met so many people. I've learned so much about drag. I've learned so much about myself. Talk about self-discovery, I didn't even know I had some of these magical powers inside of me.

MAYHEM MILLER: For the longest time, I was very upset and down because I was constantly compared to my peers and my hard work for so long was being overlooked. And when I finally got my validation and got on the show, lots of doors opened up, and I got to see more of the world that I had never seen before. I had a fan base that grew substantially. So even though the bad seeds in the fan base have made it not easy, the good fans have made it amazing. And *Drag Race* has truly just really been a great thing for me.

JUJUBEE: Back in Season 2, I knew that it was magic, but I am still mesmerized by the fact that people are accepting drag as an art. And they see what we're doing is something that we love and that we're passionate about and that we study this. A lot of us come from a place where we're broken and we're just looking for a space where we feel that we're part of a family.

ACID BETTY: Fifteen years ago, people were throwing shit at me and trying to hurt me on the street and calling me names and now they see me and they're like, "Art!" I've gotten better visually but I have always looked like a freak. I have not really changed the way I look, it's just that people's attitudes have changed.

MANILA LUZON: The biggest thing that I noticed after Season 3 aired was getting clocked out of drag. I would be on 125th Street at the Popeyes and I would get tapped on the shoulder and this lady and her boyfriend would be like, "Ain't you from the RuPaul?" It was something that I had never really experienced before because when I did drag, my audience doesn't know what I look like out of drag. They just see the drag queen. I show up that way. I didn't even know what the drag queens looked like out of drag until *RuPaul's Drag Race* and then people started to be able to relate to us more.

MARIAH PARIS BALENCIAGA: Now people realize we are not two-dimensional characters. We are multifaceted, we have depth, we have opinions, we have creativity, we have hearts, we have real relationships, we desire the same thing that most people want, which is just happiness and being able to live. I think the show has helped humanize what other people see or are taught to see as alien. It gives people a visual tool to be able to relate and to articulate things that they might not have the vocabulary to describe or to relate to family members.

JOSLYN FOX: This experience has made me feel worthy and that is really important to me. I've had people tell me that they decided not to kill themselves because of my story. Nothing can top the platform that I am blessed to have.

DIDA RITZ: It makes me more proud to be part of the earlier seasons because I am a part of the start. I'm looked at as the OG. At that time in my career, I needed that in order to go to the next level and to be able to be respected, where people were like oh she's good enough, she got on *RuPaul's Drag Race*. Now there's a formula and I think some of the girls in the drag industry know the formula and they have used it to get on the show. But back then, we didn't know the formula, we didn't know what they were looking for.

RAVEN: Back when I first started, you put on your drag, you hid, you ran, you did your gig, you took it off, and there were no remnants of it anywhere else. You had a lot of the straight community who looked at you like you were weird but you also had a lot of the gay community who looked at you like you were weird. A lot of guys would say if I wanted to date a girl, I'd date a girl. They didn't see it as art.

ADORE DELANO: In the queer community, it's hot to date a drag queen now. They think it's cool because it's so commercialized. It's so accepted the way we're in mainstream media in your parents' living room TV now. A lot of the people that are in their early to mid-twenties grew up watching us. I didn't get to have that in middle school. So I think that is changing the generation behind us more than anything and making everybody all the way around just more accepting.

MANILA LUZON: Drag used to be the lowest denominator when you would go to the gay club if you were looking to hook up with anyone. You'd go to the gay club and you'd see all the gay boys and they're like hey, I'm attracted to men so I'm going to go for the men. No one ever looked at the drag queens. And then we started seeing the people that would never have done drag, who always thought it was too flamboyant or feminine to do drag, getting more comfortable talking about drag and experimenting in drag. You could be a muscle queen. You could be a big, butch top and have the confidence to give it a try and to see how gorgeous you can be. It's actually really funny how many people ask me to put them in drag, these super-hot muscle daddies. I'll paint you, baby! Heck yeah! I'll paint you, I'll get up real close to your face. I'm gonna touch your lips, babe.

LAGANJA ESTRANJA: Drag was an underground art form and now it is totally mainstream. I know RuPaul says it's not but I have to disagree with Mother and say when you've got queens selling for Starbucks, we are internationally known. Its influence is astounding and I think that is why it continues to stay a staple in our community and will for pretty much as long as RuPaul keeps it going.

PANDORA BOXX: The more mainstream it is, I will get more jobs and I will make good money and so I like that part of it. When it becomes something people take and don't know where it comes from, that's a problem. But I think we are becoming a world where cultures are combining and where we can appreciate other cultures and acknowledge it. If more people were able to freely express themselves, it would be a happier world to be in.

BIANCA DEL RIO: Everybody wants to go on *Drag Race* now and they assume they're going to have fame and travel the world. That might happen but you have to hustle. Drag is overexposed, so the opportunities don't always exist for everyone. I wonder where things will be five years from now.

RAJA: I did drag when I started because I wanted to fucking look gorgeous, drinking to all hours of the morning, making out with men, looking stunning, lights onstage. The behind-the-scenes of it: the dressing room, the gossip, the glamour, the danger of it. That part is missing from drag for me now. And it's hard. There's a part of me that loves how everyone has access to it now. But part of me misses what drag meant to me when I was a kid. It was something you had to research. You had to be smart and charming and interesting and gorgeous and everything was word of mouth. I miss that. I sound like the old fogey talking about it, but I remember it in a different way.

THORGY THOR: I really, really, really do miss and believe that drag is an underground, two in the morning on a Monday night in a dark club kind of thing. I love that. I was that night creature for years and years and years and I like that. If somebody wanted to come see my drag show where I could curse and talk about pornography and do whatever I wanted to, I could do that and you had to come out on a Monday at one in the morning to see it. Now it has become so mainstream, that has washed away some of the grit that I fell in love with. I have to use different words, clean things up, and I feel like I have to act a certain way a lot of the time or I don't get booked.

JINKX MONSOON: I think that the double-edged sword of drag becoming mainstream and *Drag Race* becoming as popular as it is, is that it's a good thing that more people are accessing it. And it's a good thing that more people are exploring deconstructing gender in this way and more people are exploring makeup as an art form and self-expression as an art form. More people are finding confidence in themselves through drag. More people are benefiting from drag being mainstream. But it is also taking away drag as a means of survival. For me, it felt like to make it through this world and to make it through my life, I needed drag. It was not easy to do, it was not celebrated. I chose to do it because I needed it to survive. Now you see young people doing drag because it's fun. So they're never going to have the experience I had of crawling on my hands and knees in an industry that didn't pay you for your work in a community that didn't celebrate you for what you were doing. They're not going to get to experience drag the way that I experienced it. And that's not a bad thing. It's just something we have to acknowledge.

SHEA COULEÉ: I love having the opportunity to have a platform to share my story and my art and myself with people and to see people respond in such positive and supportive ways—people that I have been fans of since I was young, people whose pictures I had on my walls, seeing them comment on something on Instagram or see that they see you. It's just so wild. Every day I wake up feeling so blessed to be living my dreams.

VALENTINA: I am always going to be grateful and humbled to know that RuPaul paved the way and created this show and became a drag queen superstar so that people like me and us can be respected and be in an industry and have a career and have this platform. I will always know where I come from and I am so grateful to know that it's *Drag Race*, one of my favorite shows and that I got to be a part of, that catapulted me to be the star that I have always dreamt of being. I'm so honored to be a part of the golden era of drag.

MICHELLE VISAGE: I always knew how incredible drag queens were from the very beginning of my life when I would see them perform. But people in my circle, even gay people, were like, why are you so obsessed? I'd be like, why are you not? It was always such an incredible art form to me and I never understood why it was not looked at as this incredible valuable source of art. So the bigger this show got, the more appreciated drag became and still is becoming, and that's what matters most to me—that these kids are being validated as artists.

CARSON KRESSLEY: For a show to have started nearly fifteen years ago, essentially putting a spotlight on drag queens, a marginalized community that people didn't understand—a subset of the LGBTQ world—giving them a stage and a platform to be exposed and visible but also to be celebrated and uplifted, was very, very powerful. And little kids all over the world now, thanks to streaming, can see people that maybe they identify with or people that are not what they are used to seeing being celebrated and lifted up. That's very, very powerful because those same kids can say I can be whatever I want to be and whatever I'm supposed to be and however I feel like I want to be. And that's really impactful and powerful and that can change the world.

BOB THE DRAG QUEEN: It is this thing where you walk in and you uplift this counterculture inside of a culture that may not accept it or quiets it or doesn't even know it exists. So when you get to acknowledge each other, you're like, wow, look at us.

IVY WINTERS: Drag is not one thing. It is many things. It's talent, it's beauty, it's art, it's gender, it's confusion. There's so many levels that it touches upon that I feel like straight men, straight women, gay men, whatever, they can find a part of it and relate to or enjoy. The reality TV show and the drama is enjoyable to watch and it's addicting. But besides the drama, it really shows so much more than that. It touches everyone. Even though I'm not even doing drag anymore, I'm still thrilled and brag about what an amazing journey that was and what an amazing journey it still is for society these days. What the world needs now more than ever is just happiness and creativity and art and love. And I feel like *Drag Race* has really put a big splash in that market.

RONAN FARROW: In my own life, like many people, I have had to go on a journey to embrace that side of me. And the show is really helpful for that. The show makes one understand the power of not just your masculine side. And that has many, many ramifications. That's good for women, that's good for trans people, that's good for gay people, and honestly I think a really valuable lesson for straight guys, too, who are probably the last refuge in terms of audiences, less at the heart of the *Drag Race* viewing community. But I hope that young, straight boys are able to be exposed to *Drag Race* because a generation of straight guys that are more embracing of their femininity would be a really wonderful thing for a lot of the world's problems.

ALASKA: We are still in the midst of this phenomenon and we won't really know the impact that it has had for years to come, but it's immense. For myself, the world of drag has changed. [In the past] if you decided to do drag, you were throwing away any chance at having a normal life or happiness or anything. It was like you were giving up everything. Now everybody wants to be a drag queen, everybody. It's a viable career choice suddenly, and that's because of *RuPaul's Drag*

Race. It has shined a light on this culture that runs so deep and has been around for so long. It's an important art form. It's celebrating feminine energy, which is what the world needs. The planet needs that and that's why drag is such a huge thing right now, because I think it's correcting an imbalance in the world.

PANDORA BOXX: I had always wanted to be an entertainer full-time and *Drag Race* has allowed me to do that. It's crazy to me that Season 2 was thirteen years ago and I'm still working and people still talk about this show still make me say "raspberries." I would've tried to think of better taglines! It's very rare for a show to get more popular as it goes on. That's just crazy that it's become this global phenomenon. I'm excited that I'm a part of it. No matter what, I'll always be a Ru girl.

TRINITY THE TUCK: This show will be just like *The Golden Girls* and *Friends*, where it's on reruns for decades. So, long after this show is no longer being filmed, I am going to be part of that. To be one of the torch holders that forwards on Ru's legacy is amazing.

RONAN FARROW: It's given a platform to people who might not otherwise have it over and over again. I know there are obviously drag queens that came before and there is a rich history. But *Drag Race* has diversified drag and created more spaces for the Jinkxes of the world, who are more complicated and nuanced. It's astonishing and it really makes you reflect on what a futurist RuPaul was.

ALYSSA EDWARDS: I think that people all around the world now are just celebrating the art form known as drag and there are no rules, there's no rhyme or reason. When I started doin' drag, we had so many rules in pageants. And then you go on *Drag Race* and it was just like Ru just loved the art. And it gave me confidence. It showed up at the right time in my life. I don't know if I'd be really who I am today without it. So for that I say: To *RuPaul's Drag Race*, thank you for everything! Alyssa Edwards.

BOB THE DRAG QUEEN: When you win, you are kind of the gay president for a little bit, the drag queen president. That's what it felt like to win *Drag Race* except that your term limit is one year. I took it really seriously. In the moment, it was validation, and after that, it became a representation of a thing. I decided to double down on my advocacy and really speak out about things and realize that what BeBe Zahara Benet was to me, I can be that to someone else. I saw BeBe on *Drag Race* and I said, if she can win *Drag Race*, I can. And then I did. I saw someone doing something, being Black and great, and I realize how much impact that had on my life. Maybe I am that to someone.

RUPAUL: I know that inside of every human being there's a child that loves colors and sparkly things and things that are exciting. What's brilliant about drag is that it is actually the truth of who we all are. We are all shape shifters. We change. For that to be mainstream, everybody would have to be open to being a shape shifter and accept who you really, really are. For everybody to be able to get that would take a lot but what's so brilliant about drag is you can be whatever you wanna be. Lift up your skirt and fly.

ACKNOWLEDGMENTS

World of Wonder

Thank you to Ru, to all the queens, judges, crew, and viewers who have made *Drag Race* possible around the world.

Maria Elena Fernandez

To World of Wonder, thank you from the bottom of my drag heart for trusting and believing in me. To RuPaul, thank you for lighting the way.

Thank you to all the beautiful drag artists who took this journey with me. Talking with you during the dark days of the pandemic touched me, lifted me, and inspired me in so many ways. You are a testament that art is a healer and a uniter. Oh, and you absolutely gagged me, too.

Thank you very much to my partners in crime, Kelly Dirck, Edward Bochniak, and Marin, who juggled schedules, sat through interviews, and motivated me; and to transcriptionist Abigail Royle for being a consummate professional.

Thank you to PJ Mark, who made this all happen with unrelenting kindness and support, and to my hilarious editor, Maddie Caldwell, who gives some of the best pep talks I've ever heard.

Special shout-outs: To my little dog Pancho Samuel Lopez, who stuck by me (literally) during the massive rewatch, interviews, and writing process. And to his little brother, Pepper, I love you, too! To my loving parents, José Antonio and Norma Fernández, and mi familia, who always encouraged a little girl to lift up her skirt and fly. And to my husband, José Angel Castro, the best partner a queen could ask for.

BIBLIOGRAPHY

P. 11: "I told myself I'm done with my black hooker *Soul Train* dancer look." —RuPaul speech 2017 at Los Angeles Public Library

P. 27: "The show's mission statement was to celebrate the art of drag." —Vulture, Aug. 22, 2017

P. 30: "All of us are in drag in some form or fashion." —Vulture, Aug. 22, 2017

P. 118: "I remember coming in the room and they had that box for me backstage, and I got in it but they hadn't put any breathing holes in the box." —Entertainment Weekly's *Binge* podcast, episode 3

P. 118: "When I gave it back to her, she sent me this text saying, 'How do you return the wig all ratty into a knot?'" —Entertainment Weekly's *Binge* podcast, episode 3

P. 119: "The only thing on my mind was that this [is] the first time..." —Entertainment Weekly's *Binge* podcast, episode 3

P. 123: "I wasn't familiar with the movie *Heathers*. Even to this day, I've never seen it." —Entertainment Weekly's *Binge* podcast, episode 3

P. 125: "By today's standards, we were all very irresponsible with some of the things that we said about each other." —Entertainment Weekly's *Binge* podcast, episode 3

P. 424: "It is the most beautiful thing in the world." —*New York* magazine, June 23, 2019

P. 431: "We've created a platform for these fabulous performers to launch a career that spans the globe." —*New York* magazine, June 23, 2019

ABOUT THE AUTHOR

Maria Elena Fernandez is an award-winning journalist, who covered *RuPaul's Drag Race* before the world was introduced to the term "halleloo." Fernandez was the first mainstream journalist to be allowed on set to write about the show for the *Los Angeles Times* after being dazzled by RuPaul and the first-season queens at a promotional event before the show's launch. Fernandez covered entertainment for the *Los Angeles Times*, Vulture, the Daily Beast, *Newsweek*, and NBC News for fifteen years.